JANE
FEARNLEY-WHITTINGSTALL'S

GARDENING MADE EASY

JANE FEARNLEY-WHITTINGSTALL'S

GARDENING MADE EASY

A STEP-BY-STEP GUIDE TO PLANNING, PREPARING, PLANTING, MAINTAINING AND ENJOYING YOUR GARDEN

PHOENIX ILLUSTRATED

CONTENTS

PART 2
LOOKING AFTER YOUR GARDEN

PART 3
BECOMING A SPECIALIST

for Rob

First published in 1995
by George Weidenfeld & Nicolson Ltd

This paperback edition first published in 1997 by Phoenix Illustrated
The Orion Publishing Group, Orion House
5 Upper St Martin's Lane
London WC2H 9EA

ISBN 1-85799-933-9

A CIP catalogue record for this book is available from the British Library.

Designed and produced by Blackjacks
Edited by Richard Atkinson
Styled by Harry Green
Illustrations by Ian Sidaway
Colour reproduction by Scanners
Printed and bound in Italy

Jacket photographs by Clive Boursnell, Andrew Lawson, The Garden Picture Library, Harry Smith Horticultural Photographic Collection

Acknowledgements
I would like to thank everyone involved in the production of this book, specially Jonathan Baker at Blackjacks, for working so hard against the clock to achieve such a brilliant marriage of text and illustrations; Richard Atkinson at Weidenfeld & Nicolson, for his editing skill and for having the patience of a saint; Lin Hawthorne, for her expertise and meticulous editing; Ian Sidaway, for his splendidly clear and confidence-inspiring drawings; Dilly Williams, for her garden plans; and Andrew Lawson, for supplying so many of the photographs.

I also owe thanks to Bill Heritage, from whom I learnt about water gardens; David Austin and John Scarman, who first taught me about roses; Lynne Woods, for her invaluable help in our own garden; and the many people who trusted me to make gardens for them on chalk, limestone, clay and sand.

INTRODUCTION

What matters is not what we do to our gardens, but what our gardens do to us...
We are its servants and not its masters, and that I think is an extremely good feeling...
It is the watching of growth that matters.

Clare Leighton, *The Philosophy of Gardening*

The purpose of this book is to help you enjoy gardening. Although we talk about 'working in the garden', gardening should be more like play than work. If you get no pleasure from it you might as well lay the whole garden down to concrete and go out and play football or golf; or go indoors and make macramé, or watch televison.

In the garden the difference between pleasure and pain is, to a great extent, knowledge. Without it, gardening can be a laborious and frustrating struggle punctuated by disasters. All too often, experience is gained by a bitter process of trial and error. This is expensive in time and money, and for many people, instead of being a delight, gardening becomes a dreary chore. I believe that we have an inborn instinct to nurture plants, but we cannot know by instinct what type of soil a camellia needs, how to prune a rose, or how deep to plant a tulip. Success is based on knowledge of basic principles and techniques, and with success comes fulfilment.

This book takes the gardener through those techniques step by step, explaining why, how, where and when they should be used and what the best tools for the job are. None of the techniques is difficult to master, and knowledge of them saves time and effort. Getting things right first time is far more rewarding than learning by your mistakes, and understanding the reasons for processes like pruning or mulching makes carrying them out more interesting and satisfying as well as easier. Where there are short cuts to good results, I have explained them, and I have described traditional 'green' methods alongside modern methods using chemicals. When chemicals are the most effective way to solve a problem, I have recommended the safest products available.

Learner-gardeners can, by following the course chapter by chapter, gain the knowledge and experience that they need to become skilled and, much more importantly, to enjoy their gardens. More experienced gardeners can use the book as a refresher course and a quick reference guide to specific techniques and specialist subjects.

The purpose of the course is, above all, to enable its users to get maximum enjoyment from their gardens. Gardening has always been one of man's most creative and satisfying activities. Fortunately gardening is also an occupation that anyone can enjoy, regardless of age and physical strength, provided they have access to a small plot of ground, and it's never too late to start.

The work of making, developing and maintaining a garden is itself a pleasure, but the ultimate delight of gardening lies in contemplating the results: the form, scent, texture and colour of plants; their leaves, flowers and seedheads; the taste of fruit and vegetables. There is excitement in watching plants develop under your care from tiny seedlings to maturity; in planning and bringing to fruition pleasing groups of harmonizing or contrasting colour, shape and texture. In the garden you are in tune with (and sometimes at war with) animals, birds and insects. You share in the rhythm of changing seasons and the passage of years is compensated for by the increasing beauty of trees and shrubs as they develop.

Jane Fearnley-Whittingstall
Gloucestershire, 1995

Gardener's Calendar

You can use this book as a gardening course, starting at any time of year. Chapters 1 and 2 deal with designing and planning your garden. They explain how to assess your garden's potential and how to plan it for your maximum satisfaction and pleasure.

Chapters 3, 4 and 5 are about understanding and choosing plants, from trees and shrubs to herbaceous perennials, bulbs and bedding plants.

Chapter 6 gives advice on how to equip yourself as a gardener. It will be helpful to read these chapters before you pick up a spade or buy any plants.

The rest of the book describes specific gardening techniques. Many of them are seasonal and this calendar tells you what you should be doing when, and refers you to appropriate chapters to explain where, and how, and with what tools.

The changing of the seasons varies from year to year: spring can come early or late and in some years summer and autumn last longer than in others. Therefore the calendar need not be adhered to too rigidly. Don't panic if you miss the 'correct' time for a particular gardening job. Most jobs can be done a few weeks before or after the recommended season. Moreover, rather than putting something off for a year it is often better to do it when you feel like it even if it is the 'wrong' time. Daffodils, for example, are supposed to be planted in September, but sometimes I have had to put off planting them until February and they have still flowered in April at the normal time and with no ill effects.

The calendar is only an approximate guide, not a rigid timetable. It is there to help you get maximum enjoyment from your garden.

There is a convention that the gardening year, like the school year, starts in autumn. Many autumn jobs can also be done during mild winter weather, or in spring. But you will find that spring is a hectic time, so it pays to get as far ahead in autumn as the weather allows.

Early autumn

WHEN LEAVES ARE CHANGING COLOUR

- PLANT or move evergreen trees and shrubs.
See: PLANT SELECTION *chapters 4, 5*
TECHNIQUE *chapter 8*
- PLANT daffodils and other spring-flowering bulbs, except tulips, outdoors and in pots for the house. Plant lilies.
See: PLANT SELECTION *chapters 4, 5*
TECHNIQUE *chapter 8*
- PLANT biennials (wallflowers, foxgloves, forget-me-nots etc).
See: PLANT SELECTION *chapters 4, 5*
TECHNIQUE *chapter 8*
- SOW new lawns and bare patches on existing ones – last chance until next spring.
See: TECHNIQUE *chapter 9*
- PRUNE rambler roses.
See: TECHNIQUE *chapter 19*
- PROPAGATE BY DIVISION: summer-flowering herbaceous perennials.
See: TECHNIQUE *chapter 15*

Late autumn

WHEN LEAVES FALL

- PREPARE ground for new beds, borders, lawns and vegetable plot for spring planting, specially on clay soil.
See: ASSESS NEEDS *chapters 1, 2, 3*
TECHNIQUE *chapter 7*
- SWEEP UP leaves, make leaf mould.
See: TOOLS *chapter 6*
TECHNIQUE *chapter 13*
- PLANT deciduous trees, shrubs, climbers.
See: PLANT SELECTION *chapters 4, 5*
TECHNIQUE *chapter 8*
- PLANT herbaceous perennials on light soil only.
See: PLANT SELECTION *chapters 4, 5*
TECHNIQUE *chapter 8*
- PLANT spring bulbs, including tulips, from November on.
See: PLANT SELECTION *chapters 4, 5*
TECHNIQUE *chapter 8*
- SPIKE and scarify lawns in need of renovation or moss-infested.
See: TECHNIQUE *chapter 9*
- PRUNE roses to reduce wind-rock.
See: TECHNIQUE *chapter 19*
- PROPAGATE trees and shrubs from hardwood cuttings.
See: TECHNIQUE *chapter 15*

Winter

- PREPARE ground for new beds and lawns. Dig vegetable plot.
See: ASSESS NEEDS *chapters 1, 2, 3*
TECHNIQUE *chapters 7, 16*
- PLANT trees and shrubs, if weather is suitable.
See: PLANT SELECTION *chapters 4, 5*
TECHNIQUE *chapter 8*
- PRUNE deciduous trees and shrubs to improve their shape.
See: TECHNIQUE *chapter 10*
- INDOORS in bad weather tidy greenhouse and toolshed. Oil tools. Service machinery.
See: TECHNIQUE *chapter 6*
- MAKE PLANS for next season.
See: *chapters 1, 4, 5*
- ORDER plants and seeds.
See: *chapters 4, 5, 15*

Late winter/early spring

WHEN SNOWDROPS AND EARLIEST CROCUS FLOWER

- PREPARE new beds, lawns, vegetable plot in suitable weather, if not done earlier.
See: ASSESS NEEDS *chapters 1, 2, 3*
TECHNIQUE *chapter 7*
- PLANT trees and shrubs, if weather is suitable.
See: PLANT SELECTION *chapters 4, 5*
TECHNIQUE *chapter 8*
- PLANT autumn-flowering herbaceous perennials and summer-flowering on heavy soils, and on light soils, if not done earlier.
See: PLANT SELECTION *chapters 4, 5*
TECHNIQUE *chapter 8*
- PRUNE clematis, except early-flowering kinds.
See: TECHNIQUE *chapter 10*
- PRUNE wisteria.
See: TECHNIQUE *chapter 10*

PROPAGATE shrubs and climbers by layering.
See: TECHNIQUE *chapter 15*

PROPAGATE annuals and bedding plants by sowing seeds.
See: TECHNIQUE *chapter 15*

PROPAGATE herbaceous perennials by division.
See: TECHNIQUE *chapter 15*

Spring

WHEN DAFFODILS AND OTHER BULBS, MAGNOLIAS AND CHERRIES FLOWER

PREPARE new beds, lawns, vegetable plot in suitable weather, if not done earlier.
See: ASSESS NEEDS *chapters 1, 2, 3*
TECHNIQUE *chapters 7, 16*

PLANT trees, shrubs and climbers, if weather is suitable and provided they have not yet come into leaf (last chance except for plants in containers).
See: PLANT SELECTION *chapters 4, 5*
TECHNIQUE *chapter 8*

PLANT conifers and other evergreens.
See: PLANT SELECTION *chapters 4, 5*
TECHNIQUE *chapter 8*

PLANT autumn-flowering and summer-flowering herbaceous perennials, if not done earlier.
See: PLANT SELECTION *chapters 4, 5*
TECHNIQUE *chapter 8*

PRUNE late-flowering shrubs (e.g. buddleja, caryopteris), shrubs with ornamental stems (dogwood, willow), shrubs with ever-grey leaves (lavender, santolina) and roses, if not done earlier.
See: TECHNIQUE *chapters 10, 19*

DEADHEAD daffodils, hyacinths, tulips as they fade. Weed, feed and mulch established and newly planted plants.
See: TECHNIQUE *chapters 10, 11, 13*

SPRAY roses and any other vulnerable plants against pests and diseases.
See: TECHNIQUE *chapter 14*

TIE in new shoots on climbing plants as they develop.
See: TECHNIQUE *chapter 8*

STAKE herbaceous plants if needed.
See: TECHNIQUE *chapter 8*

WATER newly planted trees, shrubs and herbaceous perennials during dry spells, and seeds indoors.
See: TECHNIQUE *chapter 12*

PROPAGATE annuals by seed, climbers and shrubs by layering and herbaceous perennials by division.
See: TECHNIQUE *chapter 15*

PRICK OUT annuals and bedding plants sown earlier.
See: TECHNIQUE *chapter 15*

PLANT water plants in ponds.
See: TECHNIQUE *chapter 17*

SOW new lawns and bare patches on existing lawns when soil has warmed up.
See: TECHNIQUE *chapter 9*

TREAT established lawns with feed-and-weed and mow as necessary.
See: TECHNIQUE *chapter 9*

FEED and repot container plants if necessary.
See: TECHNIQUE *chapter 18*

Early to midsummer

THE TIME OF FLOWERING SHRUBS INCLUDING ROSES

WEED, feed and mulch newly planted and established plants if not yet done.
See: TECHNIQUE *chapters 11, 13*

WATER newly planted trees, shrubs and herbaceous perennials during dry spells and water seeds growing indoors.
See: TECHNIQUE *chapter 12*

SPRAY roses and any other vulnerable plants against pests and diseases.
See: TECHNIQUE *chapter 14*

PRUNE shrubs after they have flowered.
See: TECHNIQUE *chapter 10*

DEADHEAD roses and other flowering plants.
See: TECHNIQUE *chapters 10, 19*

TIE IN new shoots on climbing plants as they develop.
See: TECHNIQUE *chapter 8*

PROPAGATE annuals outdoors from seed (last chance), biennials and perennials outdoors from seed and shrubs from softwood cuttings.
See: TECHNIQUE *chapter 15*

HARDEN OFF and plant out annuals and bedding plants sown earlier.
See: TECHNIQUE *chapters 8, 15*

PLANT OUT bought bedding plants.
See: PLANT SELECTION *chapters 4, 5*
TECHNIQUE *chapter 8*

PLANT UP containers/hanging baskets.
See: TECHNIQUE *chapter 18*

FEED AND WATER plants in containers and hanging baskets regularly.
See: TECHNIQUE *chapter 18*

Mid- to late summer

MANY HERBACEOUS PERENNIALS IN FULL FLOWER, BUDDLEJAS, HYDRANGEAS

WEED wherever necessary.
See: TECHNIQUE *chapter 11*

FEED roses after their first flush of flowers, feed regularly containers, hanging baskets, tomatoes.
See: TECHNIQUE *chapters 13, 18, 19*

WATER newly planted trees and shrubs, and other plants showing stress in drought periods.
See: TECHNIQUE *chapter 12*

SPRAY roses and any other vulnerable plants against pests and diseases.
See: TECHNIQUE *chapter 14*

PRUNE hedges, wisteria, shrubs after flowering.
See: TECHNIQUE *chapter 10*

DEADHEAD roses, herbaceous perennials, biennials.
See: TECHNIQUE *chapters 10, 19*

PROPAGATE shrubs by semi-hardwood cuttings and irises and other herbaceous plants that have finished flowering by division.
See: TECHNIQUE *chapter 15*

THIN OUT or prick out biennial and herbaceous seedlings.
See: TECHNIQUE *chapter 15*

TIE IN new shoots on climbing plants as they develop.
See: TECHNIQUE *chapter 8*

PLANT spring- and summer-flowering perennials.
See: PLANT SELECTION *chapters 4, 5*
TECHNIQUE *chapter 8*

SOW new lawns.
See: TECHNIQUE *chapter 9*

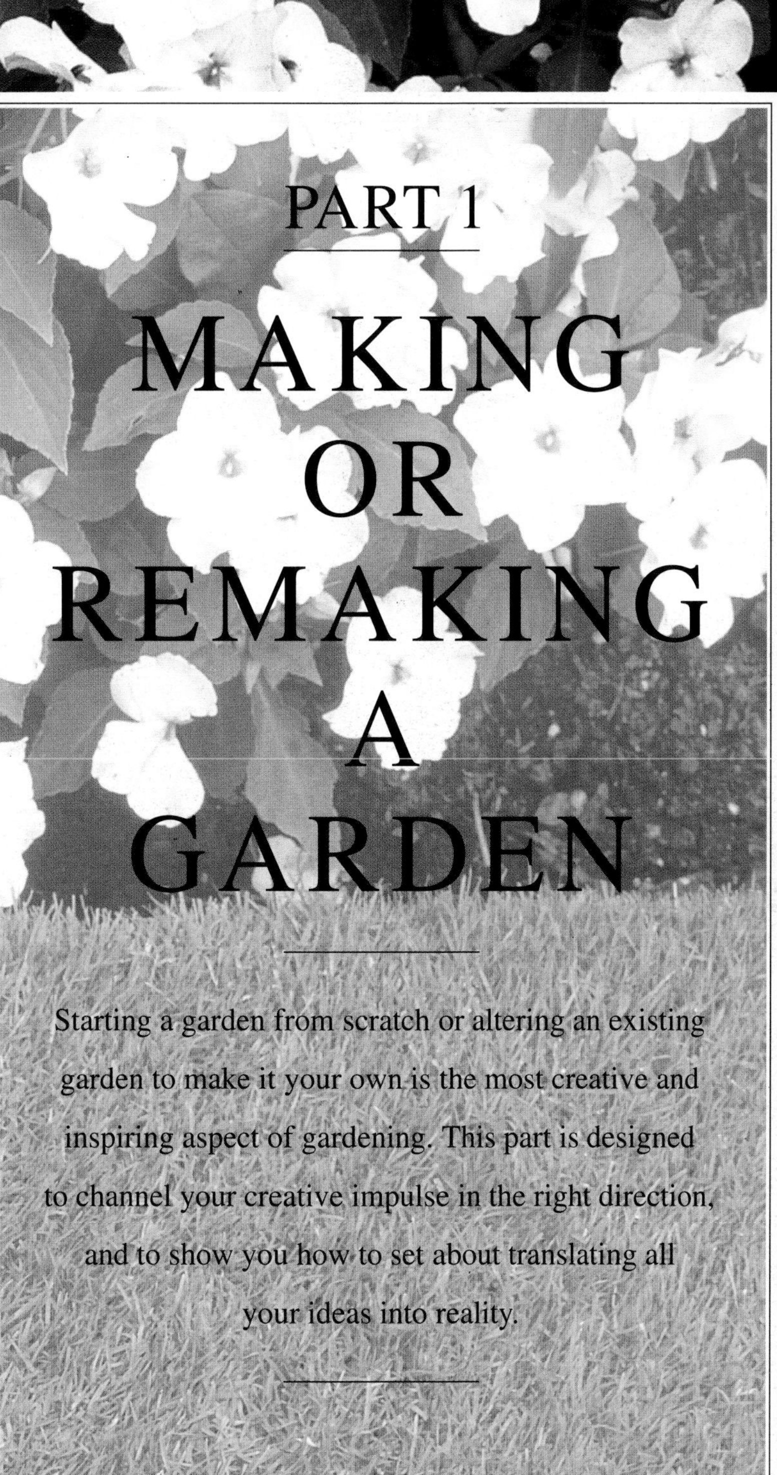

PART 1

MAKING OR REMAKING A GARDEN

Starting a garden from scratch or altering an existing garden to make it your own is the most creative and inspiring aspect of gardening. This part is designed to channel your creative impulse in the right direction, and to show you how to set about translating all your ideas into reality.

Planning Your Needs

Starting a garden from scratch or altering an existing garden to make it your own is the most creative and inspiring aspect of gardening.

You may have moved to a house with a neglected garden, or one laid out and planted in a style you do not care for. Or you may have lived with your garden for so long that your earlier plantings are past maturity, and the whole thing needs rethinking. Or perhaps yours is a newly built house where the garden is just a heap of builders' rubbish.

Whatever your reasons for designing or redesigning your garden, the secret of success lies in practical planning at the outset. You do not need to be 'artistic' to design a successful garden; you need sound common sense. If you start out with a clear understanding of the site, the demands of your family and the requirements of your plants, you will have the reward of a garden created in your own unique style.

There is far more to good design than an attractive appearance; a garden that functions well gives an added dimension of pleasure. Garden design is more about solving practical problems, such as where to put the dustbins, or how to avoid carrying the mowing machine up steps, than about making pretty drawings. The garden should be as easy to work in as a well-planned kitchen and as comfortable to relax in as a well-designed chair. So, before you pick up a spade, rush out to hire a strimmer, or load your trolley at the garden centre, take a careful look at your plot and think about what you (and other members of the household) want from it.

Personal requirements

The checklist that follows relates to the way you want to use your garden, and will help you decide what space to allocate to which activities.

Eating and drinking

A paved area is ideal for meals and drinks outdoors. Tables and chairs can be moved around easily on a hard surface whereas the legs of furniture will sink into a lawn. Decide first what furniture you will use: what size table? How many chairs? Make the paved area wide enough to push chairs back from the table and to walk behind them. Where space is limited, low walls can be used as seats. One's sense of scale is different outdoors from inside, and an area adequate in a kitchen or dining room will seem cramped on a patio.

Shade at midday, however welcome the sun may be, is advisable if butter and ice-cream (and perhaps your lunch-time guests as well) are not to melt. If shade from buildings or trees is not available, strategically placed garden umbrellas can provide it.

A barbecue, whether portable or built in, should be positioned so that the prevailing wind (usually from the southwest in Britain in the summer) blows smoke away from where you sit without blowing it onto the neighbours' patio. Flagstones under and around a barbecue will quickly become stained by spluttering fat; gravel laid on a firm base is more practical.

Easy access from the kitchen to the sitting area is important: if possible avoid having to carry trays up and down steps.

Above A built-in barbecue is safer and more stable than a portable one, and can be planned to include a work surface and storage.

Sports and games

If your garden is large enough you may want to consider a tennis court, a croquet lawn or a swimming pool, or perhaps all three. Even if there is no question of installing them immediately, if you are likely to do so in the future, it is as well to earmark the site from the beginning.

The best orientation for a tennis court is NNW-SSE, or failing that, North-South, and it should measure 34.75x17.07m (114x56ft).

A championship croquet pitch measures 35x 28yds (32x25.6m), but the hoops layout can be adapted for any reasonably sized lawn.

An outdoor swimming pool can be almost any size or shape; remember to allow space for a sheltered sunbathing area.

Below If wildlife is your priority, plan the planting to include shrubs like *Buddleja davidii*, easy to grow and attractive to butterflies.

Above This sitting area is sheltered from the wind by tall shrubs. The tree provides shade from the sun at midday and the paved ground surface makes it easy to move furniture about.

Children's play

Even if your child is still in a pram, it is worth considering any future requirements. Sandpit, climbing frame, paddling pool and other play equipment are best positioned where you can see them from the part of the house where you spend most time – probably the kitchen. The ground underneath a climbing frame should be soft to fall on: grass, sand or bark chippings.

Cats tend to use sandpits as latrines, so a cover should be fitted, and used. Plan the sandpit so that, when the children grow too old to use it, it can be adapted to make a pond.

A sandpit or paddling pool should ideally be surrounded by a hard surface, so that sand can be swept up and spills from a pool do not create a muddy mess where there was once a lawn.

Football, hide and seek and other children's pursuits are incompatible with serious plantsmanship, but gardeners should keep a sense of proportion and be patient. The children are more important than the garden, and they grow up and leave home all too soon. If necessary, precious plants can be protected by planting dense, prickly shrubs around them, to deter children and pets.

TIP

Raised flower beds make gardening easier for the elderly and/or disabled.

The elderly

If elderly people are part of your household or frequent visitors, you will want to make access to the garden easy, avoiding changes of level or providing ramps instead of, or as well as, steps.

Pets

Cats and dogs make bad gardeners; if you love your animals it is no good fretting about broken shrubs and buried bones. Dogs can be trained not to make their messes in the garden but it is difficult to prevent them urinating on the same spot again and again. Rabbits, guinea pigs and other caged creatures need shade; but there is no reason why hutches should not look decorative.

Wildlife

The garden can be planned to attract birds, bees, butterflies and water creatures by providing food plants and shrubs as well as climbers for shelter and nesting sites.

Contemplation

A secluded corner where you can sit and read or look at the view should be sheltered from the wind and surrounded with scented plants.

Practical considerations

A garden has practical requirements if it is to function efficiently. They dictate the layout of the garden and, unless they are planned for and sited with care, gardening will be a frustrating chore instead of a delight.

Essential

SOMEWHERE TO STORE TOOLS The more space you can allow, the better, as clutter soon builds up. A mundane off-the-shelf garden shed can be embellished with a range of attractive wood stains or trellis, plywood turrets or other architectural fantasy to transform it into an ornamental folly. In town gardens with limited space, the store may have to be indoors, perhaps in a large broom cupboard or under the stairs. Ideally tools should be stored near an outdoor water point, so that they can be rinsed before putting them away.

SPACE FOR HOUSEHOLD DUSTBINS Near the kitchen door. A standard dustbin is 60cm (2ft) in diameter. Unless dustbins can be tucked away out of sight, you may want to construct a wooden bin box with a hinged lid or door, or a trellised enclosure to hide them. An area measuring a minimum of 75x140cm (30x54in) will hold two bins.

RUBBISH HEAP OR BIN FOR GARDEN REFUSE Not near the house because of flies and smells.

Above Plan a site for your greenhouse at the start – even if you have to wait to buy.

Desirable

The list which follows is to remind you of other items which may be useful. You may not want or need them all, and you may not have space for them all, but the list should help you to decide your priorities.

WASHING LINE OR CAROUSEL Out of sight of your windows, the garden sitting area and, if you are a good neighbour, next door's as well.

Below Clematis montana draped over trellis to disguise a compost heap.

Right An underplanting of herbs makes it a pleasure to hang out the washing.

Combine the useful with the beautiful by underplanting a carousel with aromatic herbs such as thyme and camomile, which release their scent when trodden on.

BONFIRE SITE OR INCINERATOR Keep these well away from the house and away from overhanging trees or wooden fences which might catch fire. It should be sited so that the prevailing winds do not blow smoke and ash towards your own or your neighbours' windows and washing lines.

COMPOST HEAP To make full use of organic refuse from garden and house, best placed with easy access from the kitchen but not so close that flies and smells will be a nuisance.

GREENHOUSE If you plan to raise your own plants from seeds and cuttings, or overwinter semi-tender plants in pots. A greenhouse must be in sunlight for at least part of the day.

Right Trelliswork can make an attractive dividing feature, or a screen for dustbins or compost heap.

Defining Your Personal and Practical Needs

- Who will use the garden? Adults, children, people with restricted mobility, dogs, cats and other pets, wildlife?
- How will it be used? Sitting, eating, drinking, sleeping? For hobbies, games, children's play?
- How much time can you spend on your garden? Weekends, evenings, daytime, your holidays? Winter as well as spring, summer and autumn?
- How much time do you want to spend? Do you enjoy growing plants, operating machines such as mowers and hedge trimmers, producing your own food?
- How much money can you spend? On the layout, on equipment, on plants? You may want to phase your investment in the garden over several seasons in which case you will need to decide on priorities.

Design considerations

You have been through the checklists and decided what you want to incorporate into your garden. You can probably add more ideas to form a picture, however blurred, of your ideal garden. How do you set about creating it?

To achieve the best possible result, it helps to be aware of some design concepts. Different designers emphasize different concepts, but if you take balance as the overriding consideration, the rest fall into place more easily. Balance does not necessarily mean symmetry, and symmetrically laid out gardens do not always achieve a good balance.

Movement is another principle to bear in mind. The way the garden is laid out can lead the eye through the garden, inviting exploration. Focal points at the end of vistas or at other strategic points bring the eye to rest, but too many focal points will bounce the attention to and fro with the opposite effect, and create a feeling of restlessness instead of tranquillity.

Scale is important if the right atmosphere is to be created.

Balance, movement and scale are aesthetic concepts to carry in the back of your mind when planning your garden. It helps to get into the habit of applying them critically to other gardens, until they have become part of your subconscious design equipment.

Plants

The space given over to growing plants depends on how much space is used for the other activities listed above, on your enthusiasm and on the time you will have available. As a rough guide, well-planned mixed borders of shrubs and herbaceous plants should take about six hours per 10 sq m (108 sq ft) per year to look after, roughly equivalent to a border 2x5m (7x17ft).

If plants are your first priority, you may need to reduce the number of other facilities in your garden. Plan the practical and structural requirements to enhance your well-chosen groups of plants, providing the background setting, viewing positions and access to them. Plan for as many different plant habitats as the site will allow: sun, shade, dappled shade, dry and damp areas each support a different range of plants (see Chapter 5, Plants to Learn With).

Lawns

A well-kept lawn is the perfect background to flowering plants and trees. It is restful to the eye and a pleasant contrast to paved surfaces under foot. However, if your garden is small or too densely shaded for grass to thrive, think seriously about whether you really want a lawn. It may not be worth investing in a lawn mower and finding the space to store it, and there are delightful alternatives to grass. Lawns need to be mown at least once a week from spring until autumn. It will take approximately twenty-two hours of your time each year to mow 100 sq m (1100 sq ft) of lawn. See Chapter 9, Lawns.

Above A restful garden. The ratio of plants to lawn is well balanced. The lawn curving away beyond the tree gives a sense of movement.

Below Paving is a more practical surface than grass in a seating area, and adds interest to the design.

Defining Your Garden Style

Personal style Do you prefer tidiness and formality or informality and luxuriance; does this conflict with your partner's style?
Architectural style What is the style and period of your house? Traditional or modern? Tudor, Georgian, Victorian, Edwardian, Pre-war, Post-war?
Building materials Stone, red brick, yellow brick, rendered (what colour?), timber?
Colour What colours best express your personality, for instance what colours do you like to wear? What colours blend with the architecture of your house? With the colour schemes indoors?
Nostalgia Do you have happy memories of gardens and plants of your childhood, or of those you have known at other times? Do you want to echo them in your own garden?

TIP

In large gardens, reduce the workload by having areas of longer grass planted with bulbs and wild flowers. For maintenance regimes, see Chapter 22, Growing Wild Flowers.

Golden Rules of Garden Design

The practical rules that follow are not sacrosanct and breaking them will not necessarily ruin your garden. However, following them will help you to achieve a successful design.

- Respect the architecture of your house and the landscape it is set in: choose paving and walling materials that are appropriate.
- A path should take the shortest route between two points. Paths which twist and wind without reason are irritating and even if you don't take shortcuts across the curves, other people will, creating bald patches on turf or crushed plants and flattened edges on borders.
- Paths should lead somewhere. Place a seat, urn, statue or other ornamental feature at the end of a vista to draw the eye and invite exploration.
- Check your garden layout from the windows of the house: because of the climate in Britain, more time is spent looking at the garden from indoors than being outside in it.
- Think big. Paved areas should be generous, beds and borders wide. Outdoor steps should be broad and shallow with treads at least 30cm (1ft) wide and risers no steeper than 15cm (6in). Wherever possible, steps, paths and arches should be wide enough for two people to walk abreast: 1.5m (5ft) for steps and paths, 2m (7ft) for arches.
- Plan the planting vertically as well as horizontally, using house walls, garden boundaries and divisions, arches and pergolas for climbing plants. Use plants of varied height in beds and borders.
- Keep the centre empty, whether it is lawn, paving or water. Concentrate the planting and other features at the boundaries, giving a sense of privacy and enclosure. This is especially important in small gardens.
- Don't try to make every area colourful all the year round; it is impossible. It is more realistic to aim at having one area at its best in spring, another in summer, and so on.
- Extend the seasons of interest by planting in layers: spring bulbs can be tucked in among herbaceous plants; shrubs that are bare in winter can be underplanted with evergreen ground cover plants, winter flowering pansies, snowdrops, aconites and early crocuses.
- Be ruthless. Do not be sentimental about consigning to the bonfire plants you have inherited from the previous owner. If they are sickly or mis-shapen, or if you simply don't like them, grub them up and get rid of them. If you hate the colour or shape of your predecessor's paving slabs, get rid of them too. It is your garden and you must not be inhibited by what you inherit. Getting rid of unwanted gifts from friends and relations is not always so easy: a matter for each gardener's own conscience.
- Use natural materials for buildings, paving and furniture. They are often expensive, but it is worth waiting until you can afford them. Timber, brick and natural or reconstituted stone will all weather to give a mellow, settled appearance. Metal can be painted in subtle colours to blend with your plants, or bold colours to make a focal point. Concrete is also an 'honest' material, provided it is not dyed pink, green or yellow. Avoid plastic; it almost always strikes a false note. If necessary, phase the project to suit your budget.

Above The circular shape and still water create a tranquil atmosphere. Plants soften the hard edge.

Far right Moving water charms the ear as well as the eye.

Right A pool overgrown with plants to attract and protect wildlife.

Water

For many people water is an essential part of their garden, completing with stone, soil and plants the natural elements with which the creative gardener works. But think twice about ponds and pools, whether formal or informal, if you have small children (see Chapter 17, Water Gardening).

Choosing a garden style

The layout and planting plan for your garden will be influenced by the style you prefer. Your personal style will emerge naturally during the planning and making of the garden but it helps to be aware of various recognized styles and their components. You can then decide whether the style that you like is in harmony with the architecture of your house, the surrounding landscape and your way of life. Most gardens fall into one of the following categories, or a combination of them.

The formal garden

Straight paths, symmetrical borders and flower beds laid out in geometric shapes give an air of formality, often enhanced by patterns of paving in brick or stone. Such formal layouts are often found inside rectangular walled gardens or in spaces enclosed by neatly clipped hedges of yew, beech, lonicera or privet. Sometimes the formality is further emphasized by edgings to beds and borders of low hedges of box, lavender or other tidy evergreen plants. The knot garden with its geometric pattern of contrasting foliage plants is the ultimate in formality.

Many of the most loved British gardens of the twentieth century, such as Sissinghurst and Hidcote, have a strong formal layout as a contrasting framework to informally arranged, luxuriantly billowing plants. The architectural framework is used to form enclosures with different themes without making a 'fussy' garden. Such gardens are living proof that a formal approach need not be rigid and inflexible. Formal layouts are well suited to symmetrical architecture, but they can also make an interesting contrast to rambling houses of mixed periods and styles. A formal design is specially appropriate for the rectangular gardens of terraced town houses.

The cottage garden

A style of gardening which was once the norm in every village is now mostly found in romantic idealizations of a vanished rural past. Paths are narrow and patches of lawn or paving are small, every possible inch of space being given to a haphazard and colourful mixture of ornamental and useful plants: herbs, fruit, vegetables and favourite old-fashioned flowers like pinks, lavender, wallflowers, polyanthus, campanulas, foxgloves and marigolds. The result is the traditional, uncontrived 'riot of colour'.

Much-loved cottage garden plants can also be woven into more sophisticated schemes in the enduringly popular style of planting practised earlier this century by Gertrude Jekyll, Vita Sackville-West and Margery Fish. These great gardeners used familiar plants in new, carefully planned ways. The more haphazard traditional

Above The traditional knot garden with precise geometric symmetry. High maintenance, but appropriate for confined space and modern courtyard gardens.

Below The classic English cottage garden with riotous colours and exuberant planting spilling over to soften the edges of the path.

cottage style is best suited to traditional cottages, but is also popular as a setting for more modern village houses.

The country house garden

Garden styles for country houses are many and varied, but the archetypal style is a marriage of the eighteenth-century landscape garden of trees and sweeping lawns with the later flower gardens of shrubberies and roses. A typical example has a broad, paved terrace in front of a house partly concealed by climbing plants. Beyond the terrace a lawn carries the eye across a ha-ha into the farming landscape. There are one or more specimen trees on the lawn, a majestic Cedar of Lebanon or a group of limes, and the view is framed by broad belts of flowering shrubs interplanted with herbaceous plants. At the garden boundaries, belts of trees are underplanted with snowdrops, aconites, daffodils, fritillaries and scillas growing out of the grass.

If you like this style but your garden is too small to emulate it, follow the general principles on a smaller scale using, for example, a crab apple tree instead of a cedar.

Right Seasonal planting; in the late summer border, warm, vibrant colours of golds, orange and a range of rich reds predominate.

Below The shelter of the woodland garden provides a naturalistic setting for plants that need moist, leafy soils and thrive in dappled shade.

The woodland garden

The shelter and shade of woodland glades often combine with acid or neutral soil to provide ideal conditions for rhododendrons and azaleas. Other calcifuge (lime-hating) shrubs, trees and herbaceous perennials extend the season. Woodland gardens are in essence informal and are designed as idealized natural landscapes, with winding paths and streams that meander over pebbles and cascade from rocks.

The wildlife garden

Like the woodland garden, the wildlife garden idealizes nature but gives first place to animals, birds and insects, and their requirements for food and shelter. The plants that they need, and one or more pools to supply them with water and to support aquatic creatures, can be arranged to make an attractive, informal garden with mysterious hidden corners where seats can be placed from which to observe the wildlife.

Below The flowery meadow and slow-moving stream provide ideal conditions for beneficial insects and amphibians.

Food plants will include many trees and shrubs with berries or other fruits that are edible to birds and small mammals, so that such a garden is likely to be at its best in spring, when these plants blossom, and again in autumn, when they are decorated with colourful ripe fruits. Wildlife gardens are especially refreshing to the spirit in dingy industrial areas where green leaves are at a premium. They can form important linking elements in urban 'corridors' for wildlife and provide havens for beneficial insects, making organic gardening possible.

The seasonal garden

The character of a garden can be defined by concentrating on a particular season. In winter, the leaves of evergreen plants with yellow, cream and white variegations can be planned to contrast with plain greens, yellows and greys. Deciduous trees with beautiful bark like the Sheraton cherry (*Prunus serrula*) can be appreciated in winter, and colour is added by the scarlet stems of the dogwood, *Cornus alba* 'Sibirica' ('Westonbirt'), or the yellow-stemmed willow *Salix alba vitellina*. The winter garden will have occasional flower colour in spring and summer, and some bright autumn leaves, but the overall impression will be of cool foliage.

A spring garden is all blossom and bulbs, giving that surge of optimism that comes with the start of a new flowering season. In summer there are endless choices. The garden's style could be dictated by concentrating on one or two species: roses, perhaps, for high summer; hydrangeas and fuchsias for a later flowering. The use of a restricted colour scheme is another way of giving a summer garden its own character. The autumn garden will be full of plants with colourful fruits and blazing red and golden leaves.

The challenge of the seasonal garden lies in finding plants which add to the beauty of the garden at other seasons besides the chosen one.

Planning the layout

When you have decided on all your requirements, you may find that you are trying to fit a quart into a pint pot. To see how everything can be fitted in, the usual advice is to draw a plan of your garden to scale on graph paper. The process is described on p.44. This is how most professional garden designers work things out, and it is fine if you find it easy to visualize how the plan will look when it is transferred from paper to the ground.

But it is not the only way. Many people find it easier to experiment on the actual site with canes, tape and lengths of hosepipe which are useful for marking out curved beds and borders. With tape stretched between canes stuck in the ground, you can judge heights as well as flat space. It also helps when planning the position of plants to use cut branches of greenery of different heights and widths.

The layout of the garden will develop and alter over the years, as your way of life and your requirements change. And it is the essence of gardening that the plants will change. But careful planning at the start will provide a firm structure within which you can continue to enrich your private landscape over the years.

Permanent structures

Whether you are planning on paper or on the ground, start with the permanent, long-term elements – paths, steps, paved areas, and walls or fences. These are expensive to install and therefore important to get right first time.

Services

LIGHTING If you need to find your way safely at night from house to garage, or if you plan to eat out of doors on fine evenings, lighting is important. Carefully placed lighting will also enable you to see and enjoy the garden from the house windows at night.

ELECTRICITY Light in a potting shed or greenhouse extends the gardener's day in winter. In a pool an electric pump is useful to circulate the water and essential if there is to be a fountain or waterfall. If you are going to use an electric lawn mower or hedge trimmer, an outdoor power point in the right position is invaluable.

WARNING Electric plugs and tools must be fitted with safety cut-out devices: statistics for garden accidents are alarming.

WATER At least one strategically placed standpipe in the garden will make watering your plants at times of drought easier. It may be used just to fill a watering can or as the starting point for a sophisticated, electronically controlled irrigation system. Ponds and other water features need a source of water for topping them up. Water pipes, together with electric cables, should be buried 60cm (2ft) deep before beds are planted or lawns seeded. It is only too easy to forget where pipes and cables run, so keep a diagram of their location for your own reference and, if you ever sell the house, for the new owners.

Above Railway sleepers make an unusual, natural looking path.

Soil and climate

The layout and planting of your garden will of course be influenced by the local climate and soil type. An assessment (dealt with later in Chapter 2, Understanding Your Garden) will help you site:

- Barriers to provide shelter from the wind (hedges, walls, fences, shrub belts).
- Sitting areas to provide shade at midday and to take advantage of the evening sun. A sitting area should be sheltered from the wind and will depend on whether you prefer to be in sun or shade. For most people the ideal position is a spot sheltered from the sun at midday, perhaps by the dappled shade of a tree, but catching the evening sun.
- Planting sites for sun- and shade-loving plants and plants with different soil and moisture requirements.

Below Shade and shelter are important if you eat in the garden.

The lie of the land

Is your garden flat or sloping? This crucial factor influences the earliest decisions. If the garden slopes steeply, one option is to terrace it. Terracing has several advantages:

- Two or more level areas are more versatile than a continuous slope.

TIP

Earmark the best soil for the vegetable plot or, if you do not plan to have one, for the choicest plants.

TIPS

- A gravel path on a slope steeper than 1 in 20 will cause problems, as loose gravel will gradually be washed downhill.
- Where there is no natural change of level, you may wish to introduce one by digging out one area and building up another, or by creating a sunken garden.

Terracing will retain soil which otherwise might be washed down by heavy rainfall.

Even quite small changes of level, one or two 15cm (6in) steps up or down, can make a garden more interesting and varied.

Mowing grass and tending flower beds will be easier.

WARNING Make sure terraces laid to lawn can be mown without having to move a mower up and down steps. Otherwise lay paving or gravel instead of grass.

It is essential to decide at the outset whether to terrace the garden. If you decide to do it several years after planting, the job will involve moving established plants; it is a difficult operation and some may not survive. In a small garden, digging out and levelling can be done by hand, but in a larger garden terracing is a job for a JCB, and although a skilled operator can work wonders with the minimum disruption, in an established garden access is often impossible for a large machine without knocking down walls or removing yards of hedge.

Even if the garden does not slope steeply, look carefully at the levels at the planning stage. Often what appears to be a flat surface has a considerable fall on it, which, although not a problem if it is grassed over or planted up, will be awkward and slippery if paved.

Electric and telephone cables and gas, water and sewage pipes are sometimes so near the surface of the ground that they will prevent you from digging out foundations for walls and other structures, specially if you are planning to change levels. If you are having work done on the house, your builder will know where cables and drains are buried.

Common problems

Before you make your final plan it helps to be aware of some of the problems which you may encounter. If you can solve them at the outset it will save trouble later on.

ACCESS TO THE GARDEN In terraced houses there is often no access to the garden except through the house. Most people, when they move house, think about the garden last of all, when the house is newly decorated. But if walls are to be built in the garden, paving laid, or topsoil brought in, the garden should come first, so that materials can be brought through the house without damage to new carpets and paintwork.

CARS Many gardens are laid out with a parking area outside the front door. All too often this means that the view from the living room windows has a foreground of cars. It may be possible to reorganize the entrance so that cars can be parked out of sight of the main windows.

Below Raised flower beds add interest to the design and make weeding and planting easier. The path of flagstones set in turf saves the lawn from wear and tear.

NEIGHBOURS Gardeners can be on good terms with their neighbours, swapping cuttings and commiserating over late frosts. Or they can be at loggerheads, resenting bonfire smoke, weeds creeping across the boundary and shade cast by each other's trees. In the latter case, legally it is within your rights to remove encroaching branches provided you return the timber to its rightful owner. Don't be tempted to hack off the offending limbs and lob them over the fence. The civilized approach is to ask your neighbour round for a drink, explain the problem and suggest you share the cost of a professional tree surgeon who can prune the tree without spoiling its shape. Making a neighbour's life a misery is a game that two can play, so tact and charm are always the best policy.

PERMANENT PLANTING Large plants need siting with care. When you plant a tree it will not be much more than 2.5m (8ft) high, with a crown of 90 or 120cm (3 or 4ft) diameter, casting little shade. But it will outlive you and it will probably also outlive the built structure of the garden. Don't count on leaving the problem for posterity to deal with: an unwisely placed tree may be knocking on your windows after ten years or less. As well as the space occupied by the tree, think about the shade it will cast, as this will restrict the plants that can be grown near it. Trees take nourishment from the soil, leaving smaller plants unable to compete. The roots of most trees spread as wide as the canopy and can destabilize walls and paving and undermine house foundations.

CHOOSING TREES

Before you choose a tree, it is important to know how big it will grow. Trees are difficult to move once established, and some, specially willows and poplars, can damage drains and foundations. The dimensions given here are only a rough guide. The final height and spread, vary according to the fertility of the soil, and the climate. Trees planted as large specimens take several years to re-establish. Many forest trees grow slowly for the first ten or fifteen years, then increase at 60-100cm (2-3ft) per year. Others reach their final height in a relatively short time, thereafter increasing only their girth and spread.

1 Like most crab apples, *Malus floribunda* is ideal for small gardens. It bears masses of pink flowers in spring, followed by tiny, red and yellow crab apples in autumn. Size at maturity 5x5m (16x16ft).

2 The genus *Sorbus* includes many trees suitable for smaller gardens. *S. vilmorinii* is one of the most elegant, with fern-like foliage that colours beautifully in autumn, and clusters of long-lasting white berries flushed with rose-pink. 8x8m (25x25ft).

3 The Japanese cherries are among the loveliest of spring-flowering trees. *Prunus* 'Tai-haku', the Great White Cherry, is one of the finest. At maturity, it is usually broader than it is tall. 10x12m (33x40ft).

4 The weeping willow, *Salix* 'Chrysocoma', grows at an alarming rate. After ten years, it can reach 10m (33ft), and will still be growing apace. Best planted beside water, where its reflection doubles its beauty. 20x20m (66x66ft).

5 With dark, blue-tinted leaves and a beautiful tiered shape, the cedar of Lebanon is seductive. Do not be tempted unless you have lots of space. 40x25m (130x80ft).

Planning the planting

When you are clear in your mind what you intend to achieve, and have marked out the layout on paper or on the ground, your next thoughts will be about plants. Some are probably already in the garden. You will have ideas about others that you want from visiting other gardens and from looking at catalogues and books. A list of what you want will probably be long enough to fill Kew Gardens and will have to be whittled down.

It is not necessarily 'correct' to make a detailed planting plan for your garden. Some of the most beautiful gardens have been allowed to develop in an organic way over the years. Their owners have put plants in as they acquired them, and moved them around from season to season until they found the perfect place. You may prefer to go about planting your garden in this way rather than working to an overall plan. After all, it is as well to remember that a garden is never finished. There is never a moment when you can sit back and say that it is perfect. Part of the endless fascination of gardening lies in adapting to the changes brought about by growth and decay, not just from season to season but from year to year and decade to decade.

On the other hand, drawing up a plan can be a truly fascinating occupation. Working out each plant's particular virtues and seeing how it will complement its neighbours is one of the easiest ways to get to know plants: their forms, their textures, ranges of colour, preferred conditions and seasons of interest.

Chapter 3, Understanding Plants, will help you to understand how plants behave and which

Above This bold, sophisticated planting contrasts foliage shape, size, colour and texture, throwing the bright colours of the well placed flowers into high relief.

Far left, above *Phygelius aequalis* 'Yellow Trumpet', variegated *Hosta, Salvia azurea* and chives make a bold composition of complementary colours and contrasting forms.

Far left, below A complex border, crowded with different species linked by their colours: crimson, pink and purple.

Left Dahlias are invaluable for cutting in autumn but their bright colours make them difficult to place in the border. An overall colour theme helps.

kinds are most suitable for your soil and climate, and Chapter 4, Choosing the Plants, will help you select the best plants for your garden.

Do not be ashamed of making mistakes. The experts do, it's a good way of learning, and most mistakes can be easily corrected.

Common mistakes

NARROW BEDS AND BORDERS In many gardens the borders are so narrow that there is only room for a single row of plants, which makes it difficult to create contrasts and harmonies of shapes, textures and colours. If space permits, shrub borders should be at least 1.8m (6ft) wide, and preferably 2.5m (9ft).

OVERCROWDED PLANTS It is tempting but wasteful to plant shrubs and other plants too close together in order to get a quick result. Check the mature height and width of shrubs in a reliable book or catalogue and allow them space to develop fully. Some shrubs take seven years to reach their mature size: the space around them can be filled temporarily with shorter-lived herbaceous plants, biennials and annuals. Herbaceous plants, bulbs, biennials and annuals also need enough space to develop their full potential. If planted too close together they have to compete for food, moisture and light, and will be poor, straggly specimens.

SPOTTY PLANTING Unless you are aiming at the multicoloured, spangled effect that is sometimes seen in old cottage gardens or in wild flower meadows, it is more effective to plant smaller shrubs in groups of three or five, and herbaceous plants in groups of anything from five to nine of the same kind and colour. Odd numbers always give a more natural effect.

Far right, above A mixed summer border in cottage garden style, where roses and delphiniums complement each other in a naturalistic and informal manner.

Far right, below The cool associations of creams, whites and yellows create the elegant effects that were first made famous by Vita Sackville-West at Sissinghurst, Kent.

Right A blue and yellow colour theme, understandably a favourite of Gertrude Jekyll.

Four garden designs

The four designs illustrated here are for the same plot: the typical back garden of a semi-detached house. The different priorities of the owners have resulted in the creation of four gardens very different in style and character.

The family garden

The activities of a family with young children dictate the practical layout. As the children grow up and their requirements change, the borders can be widened to increase the variety of plants. The sandpit can be lined to make a small pond, perhaps with a fountain, a water lily, some irises and a few fish. The informal area at the bottom of the garden will cease to be an adventure jungle and become a haven for all manner of wild creatures.

The low maintenance garden

The garden here has been designed for people who are far too busy to do much mowing, weeding, watering and pruning. They want to enjoy their precious leisure time in a tranquil environment. Much of the garden is taken up by the pool: far less labour-intensive than a lawn, and restful to watch. The timber decking, unlike paving, provides no niches for weed seedlings. The plants have been chosen for their efficient weed-smothering qualities, with the emphasis placed on attractive foliage rather than flowers.

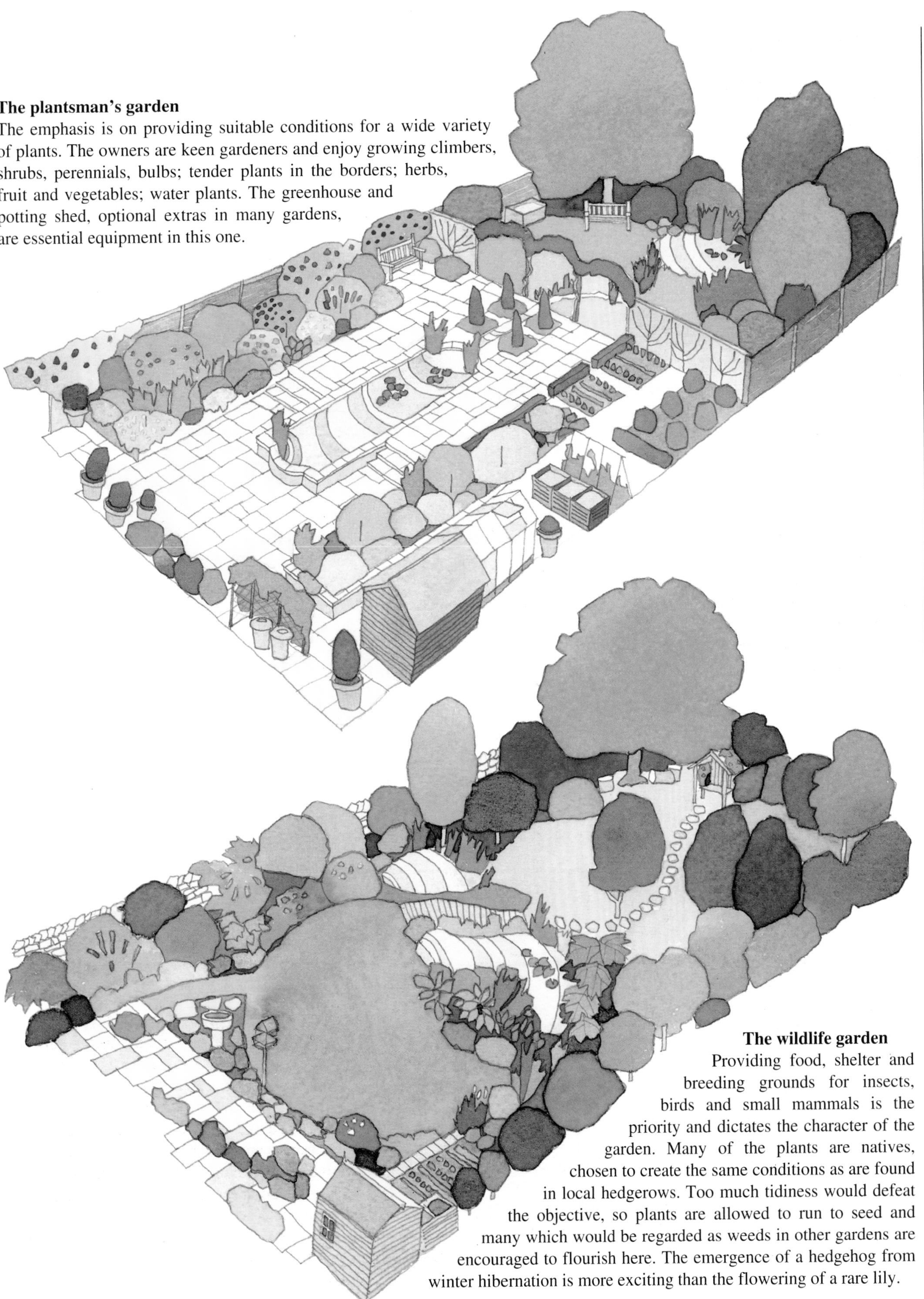

The plantsman's garden

The emphasis is on providing suitable conditions for a wide variety of plants. The owners are keen gardeners and enjoy growing climbers, shrubs, perennials, bulbs; tender plants in the borders; herbs, fruit and vegetables; water plants. The greenhouse and potting shed, optional extras in many gardens, are essential equipment in this one.

The wildlife garden

Providing food, shelter and breeding grounds for insects, birds and small mammals is the priority and dictates the character of the garden. Many of the plants are natives, chosen to create the same conditions as are found in local hedgerows. Too much tidiness would defeat the objective, so plants are allowed to run to seed and many which would be regarded as weeds in other gardens are encouraged to flourish here. The emergence of a hedgehog from winter hibernation is more exciting than the flowering of a rare lily.

Understanding Your Garden

The secret of successful gardening is to make creative use of the site's potential. This may seem well nigh impossible when you confront your patch of mud and builder's rubble, or your acre of brambles and nettles, but you must not despair. Every plot, however unpromising, has unique possibilities as well as limitations, and by understanding and taking advantage of them, you can create a unique garden.

Fulfilment for gardeners comes from working with nature rather than fighting a losing battle against it. Different plant types enjoy different conditions, so understanding the soil and local climate will help you to plan your garden for the best possible results.

The soil

Soil provides anchorage for plant roots and holds the water and nutrients that are necessary for maintaining life. It is made up of the following elements:

ROCK PARTICLES All soils except peat are mineral soils formed from rock particles. They have been ground out of the rocks on the planet's surface by the relentless action of rain, wind and frost, and by the ceaseless rhythm of the oceans' tides.

The size and shape of the particles vary according to the parent rock and the weather action, so that different types of soil are formed: clay, silt, sand or chalk. Each type of soil has different qualities of aeration, drainage and nutrient holding capacity.

HUMUS The product of decayed and decaying plants and animals, humus or 'organic matter' is the magic ingredient which gives fertility to the soil. Humus improves the structure of the soil, making it dark brown and crumbly. It holds moisture without impeding drainage and is home to a wide range of bacteria and other micro-organisms that help the gardener by breaking down organic matter to release plant nutrients. Earthworms thrive in humus-rich soils, and their movement through the soil aids drainage and aeration.

The proportion of humus to mineral particles varies in different soils. It can be added to poor soil in the form of well-rotted manure, compost or leaf-mould.

WATER Entering the soil by precipitation (rain and snowfall), by absorption upwards from the water table underground and by seepage from rivers, lakes and ponds, water is lost from the soil through natural drainage, through evaporation and through plants taking it up through their roots. Plants need access to water for the food-making process of photosynthesis (see Chapter 3, Understanding Plants).

AIR Plants breathe through their roots, using the air trapped between the particles of rock and humus. Without air soil becomes waterlogged, suffocating plant roots. The living organisms in the soil, on which plants depend, also need air.

Acid and alkaline soil

Soil with a high lime or chalk content is alkaline. When lime is not present it is neutral or acid. Peat is acid, as are most clay soils. Acidity and alkalinity is measured in terms of the soil's pH level.

Neutral or nearly neutral (5.5–7.5) soils are ideal for most plants. At this pH level nutrients are readily available. Some plants prefer alkaline soil and a few will only thrive in acid soils.

Ways of altering the pH level of the soil are discussed in greater detail in Chapter 7, Preparing the Ground.

Above A limestone dry wall smothered in plants which enjoy the alkaline, free-draining conditions provided by the site.

Below, left to right
Clay soil: very small particles forming a sticky, pliable mass.
Sandy soil: like sand on the beach mixed with soil. Particles can be fine or coarse, and will not stick together when handled.
Chalk soil: contains lumps of whitish chalk, will not stick together when handled.

TYPICAL SOIL PROFILES

1 Clay soil. At the top there is a layer of humus-rich topsoil of varying depth. Beneath it is quite recognizable clay of varying intensity. The colour may be reddish brown or yellow. If the clay is grey the soil is anaerobic (devoid of air) and will not support plant or animal life. Depending on the depth of the clay subsoil, you may reach down to the parent rock when you dig. Docks, thistles, plantains and creeping buttercups are weed plants which thrive on clay soil. Wild flowers may include bluebells, cowslips, primroses, ragged robin, white campion and wood anemones.

2 Peaty soil. Peat is found in areas of high rainfall and is often so wet that you can squeeze water out of it like a sponge. Peat is dark brown to black, and fibrous with identifiable bits of twig, leaf and other decaying plant material. In peaty soils the water table is often near the surface, so the inspection pit may fill up with water. Plants on peat may include tussocks of reedy grasses, a wide variety of mosses, bladderwort, fragrant orchid, ragged robin, red campion, and water violet.

3 Sandy soil. The depth of topsoil and the sand content of the topsoil depend on how much organic material has been added over the years. The colour of the sandy subsoil varies from orange-yellow to light grey-buff. If it is dry the sandy granules will be loose and it will be difficult to dig a straight-sided pit. Gorse and broom thrive on sandy soil, together with heather, common cudweed and heath violet.

4 Limestone soil. The topsoil may be quite deep in gardens that have been cultivated for many years, but it is likely to be full of stones of varying sizes. The deeper you dig the less soil and the more stones you will find. In extreme cases stone in various stages of disintegration is just below the surface. Limestone and chalk, the two markedly alkaline soils, support a wide range of wild species including cowslip, primrose, heartsease (wild pansy), knapweed, lesser butterfly orchid, scabious, wild strawberry, wild thyme, violet. Grassland on chalk or limestone usually has a high proportion of clover, daisies and bird's foot trefoil.

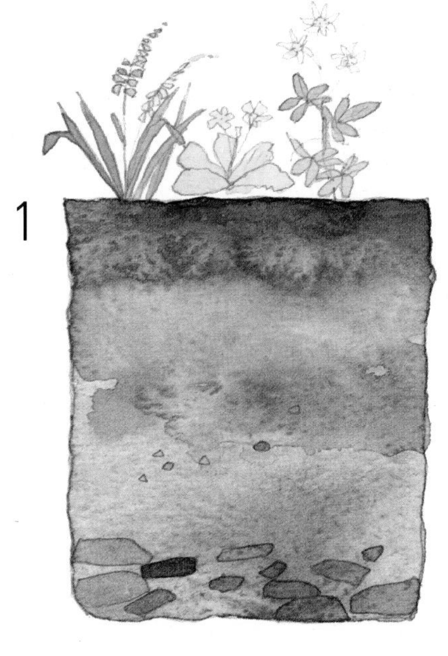

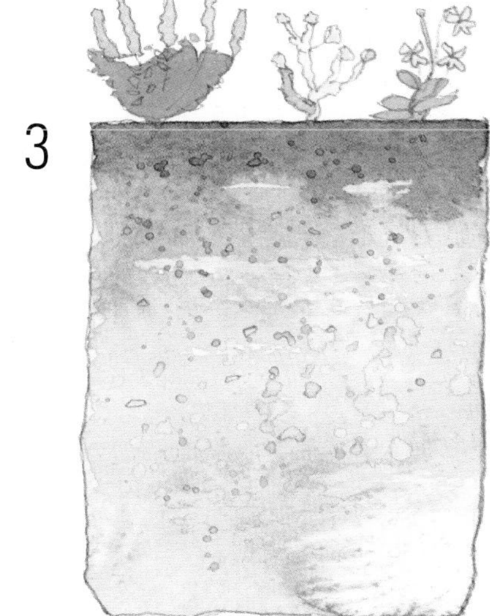

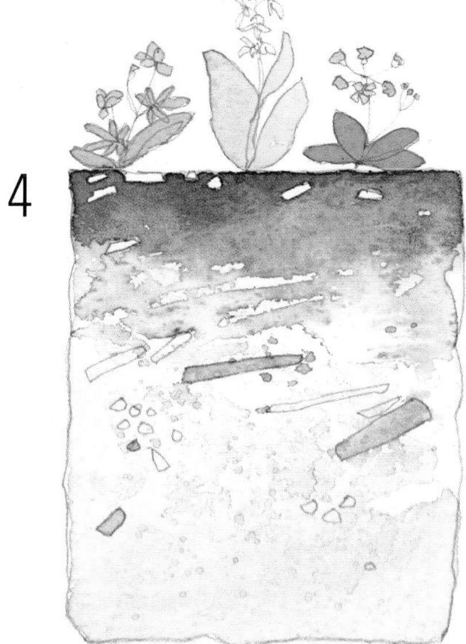

Types of soil

CLAY SOIL Slow to dry out after rain. Clings to your boots when damp. A lump squeezed in the hand feels dense, sticky and pliable like the clay used for pottery.

Clay soils are known as 'heavy' soils. They are cold, and also difficult to dig when wet. When dry they bake to an impenetrable crust, shrinking and cracking. On the plus side, clay is rich in nutrients and can be improved by the addition of organic matter. Clay can be acid, neutral or alkaline.

SANDY SOIL Dries out quickly. Does not cling when damp. Light colour. Loose granular texture with fine or coarse particles. Disintegrates when handled.

Sandy soils are 'light'. Water runs through quickly, washing away nutrients – they need regular feeding with organic matter. Lime is also washed away, so sandy soils tend to be acid.

PEATY SOIL Holds water like a sponge. Dark brown to black in colour. Coarse textured with partly decayed plant remains visible. Usually acid and not very fertile.

CHALKY SOIL Contains smooth white lumps like blackboard chalk. Drains rapidly washing nutrients away. Very alkaline; the parent rock is often close to the surface.

LIMESTONE SOIL Numerous stones are present, from tiny ones to large rocks. Disintegrates when handled. Drains rapidly. Alkaline but less so than chalk.

Perfect garden soil

The best all-purpose soil is known as loam. It is a balanced mixture of clay and sand with plenty of humus and is neither acid nor alkaline. Soils are usually described in terms of their relationship to this ideal, for instance sandy loam, clay loam, silty loam.

Finding out about your soil

To get good results in your garden you need to know whether the soil is predominantly clay, chalk, sand or peat, whether it is acid or alkaline and whether the drainage is good or poor.

Some gardens have areas of different soil types and different levels of acidity/alkalinity (pH levels) within them. Problem areas can be improved but will still retain their basic characteristics, so it is important to understand which category your garden soil falls into.

Local clues

BUILDINGS AND FIELD WALLS Before the construction of canals and railways made it possible to move loads of brick and stone from one part of the country to another, houses and boundary walls were built using materials local to the area.

Many limestones break easily on the horizontal plane to provide ideal material for building drystone walls. In the Cotswolds, grey and golden buildings and field boundaries are built of local limestone. In such places the layer of topsoil above the rock is often thin and full of stones, providing rapid drainage.

In other areas the older buildings are constructed in brick made from local clay. They vary in colour from the yellow-grey of London brick to the mellow red found in parts of East Anglia. The basic soil will be of the same clay as the bricks, but it may have been improved by centuries of cultivation.

The use of flintstones for building or the presence of lumps of chalk in cultivated fields indicates chalky soil.

WEEDS The weeds in your or nearby gardens are good indicators of fertility and drainage. Docks, thistles, plantains and creeping buttercups indicate acid or clay soil; clover indicates alkaline soil; and moss indicates poor drainage.

NEIGHBOURING GARDENS Talk to neighbours about their gardening successes and failures, or look at their gardens to see if lime-hating plants grow there.

Rhododendrons, azaleas, camellias, blue-flowered hydrangeas and most heathers will only grow in acid soil, so their presence in neighbouring gardens indicates acidity.

Testing your soil

Soil-testing kits can be bought to measure the pH, or a sample can be sent for testing to an agricultural or horticultural laboratory.

Neutral soil is the best from the gardener's point of view, as it suits the widest possible range of plants.

Above Stinging nettles *(Urtica dioica)* indicate fertile soil. Other weeds that indicate fertility are sow-thistle, fat-hen, chickweed and groundsel.

INSPECTING THE SOIL PROFILE To find out more about the soil, dig a straight-sided pit 60cm (2ft) square by 60cm (2ft) deep. The exposed vertical sides show the soil 'profile'. Before rain, the soil profile will also show the level of the water table.

In the soil profile there may be a layer of dark material forming a hard pan which water and roots cannot penetrate. This may be due to compaction by heavy vehicles or to a layer of iron or aluminium particles leached through the soil. Break it up before planting.

FRIENDLY WORMS If there are plenty of earthworms in the soil, that is a good sign. They help to break down the soil into a good, crumbly texture, to aerate it and to distribute the humus.

Drainage

Plants need plenty of water, especially in windy or sunny positions where they lose moisture through evaporation. But they also need air circulating in the soil so that roots can function properly, and water trapped in the soil excludes air. Only a few kinds of plant are adapted to thrive with waterlogged roots, so poor drainage is a serious problem. Fortunately it can usually be rectified. Signs of bad drainage include:

- Water lying on the surface after rain.
- Soil below the surface (usually clay) that is

TIP

If you have neighbours who are keen gardeners, they may be able to save you the trouble of testing the soil.

grey rather than brown when you turn it up with a spade or fork. Sometimes it also has an unpleasant, rotten smell. This shows that the soil is lacking in air (anaerobic).

The handling test

For a more detailed diagnosis of soil, the following is a simple method taught in colleges of horticulture and agriculture. You shouldn't be squeamish about handling soil: it is not dirt, but the source of life.

- If it feels heavy and forms a smooth lump that can be moulded without breaking, it has a high clay content (if you have ever done pottery, the feel of it will be familiar).
- If the soil will not form a lump, or the lump breaks easily, rub a little between finger and thumb: if it feels gritty, it is sandy soil. If it feels silky, it is silty soil.
- If the soil holds water like a sponge and is made up mainly of particles of organic material (derived from decomposed mosses), it is peaty.

Once you have understood the nature of your soil, you will be able to set about improving it to its maximum potential. This is dealt with in Chapter 7, Preparing the Ground.

Right Blue hydrangeas show that the soil is acid. On alkaline soil their colour turns to dingy pink.

Below Azaleas must have acid soil to thrive.

The climate

Climate is the single most important factor in determining what will grow in your garden. If the soil is hopeless you can import good topsoil from elsewhere, but the ways in which the climate can be improved are limited.

What is climate?

The way plants grow is affected by sun, rain, wind and temperature. The weather throughout an average year is also influenced by distance from the equator, altitude and distance from the sea, and all these factors together make the climate.

TEMPERATE CLIMATE In Britain and much of Northern Europe the climate is temperate; there are no violent extremes of temperature, although there are frost and snow in winter. Rainfall is moderate and occurs throughout the year.

TROPICAL CLIMATE Within, or close to, the tropics of Cancer and Capricorn on either side of the equator, temperatures are high throughout the year and rainfall is often violent and seasonal, with 'the rains' or 'the Monsoon' occurring either once or twice a year.

SUBTROPICAL CLIMATE In the Mediterranean and parts of Asia, North and South America and Australia the climate is a pleasant compromise between tropical and temperate. In subtropical areas the main problem for the gardener is summer drought.

Local climate

Even in an area as small as the British Isles, local climates vary enormously.

Coastal areas are warmer in winter and cooler in summer than inland areas, and the west coasts of the British Isles have mild winters because of the warm Gulf Stream. The most damaging frosts occur in the northeast of Scotland and in the Midlands.

Up north temperatures are lower, especially so in the winter; the growing season is shorter and in mountainous areas the wind is more damaging.

Rainfall

In Britain most of the weather comes from the west. Rain clouds from the Atlantic break on the hills of Ireland, Scotland and Wales and on the Pennines. They are often spent before they reach the Midlands and east coast. As a result, the average annual rainfall in the Welsh and Scottish mountains is 445cm (175in) whereas to the east of London it is only 50cm (20in). These figures can be compared with an average of 104cm (41in) for the British Isles.

Too much rain can cause problems by washing topsoil away on steep slopes or by causing permanently waterlogged conditions in hollows. It can also prevent the gardener from working in or enjoying his garden.

Lack of rain makes plants vulnerable, specially trees which need many gallons of water on a regular basis. In Britain this was painfully demonstrated in the drought years of the 1980s, and it is possible that global warming may bring such conditions more frequently in the future. Techniques for irrigation and for the conservation of moisture are described in Chapter 12, Watering, and drought-resistant plants are listed on p.143.

Snow can provide a welcome insulating layer on beds and borders, but its weight on evergreen plants can break branches, so be prepared to brush snow off vulnerable plants, even if this does mean sacrificing part of the picturesque winter scene.

Wind

Apart from causing broken branches, torn leaves and flowers and, in extreme gales, uprooted plants, wind also harms plants by drying out the leaves, causing stress to the whole plant. In

HARDINESS ZONES

The zone maps are based on average annual winter minimum temperatures, split into bands with 5°C difference between each band. They give a general guide to the average minimum temperatures you can expect, but do not take account of local variations. For example, if your garden is in a frost pocket, its temperature will be lower than average. But a south-facing site with well-drained soil and shelter from winds and frost may upgrade your garden to a higher zone.

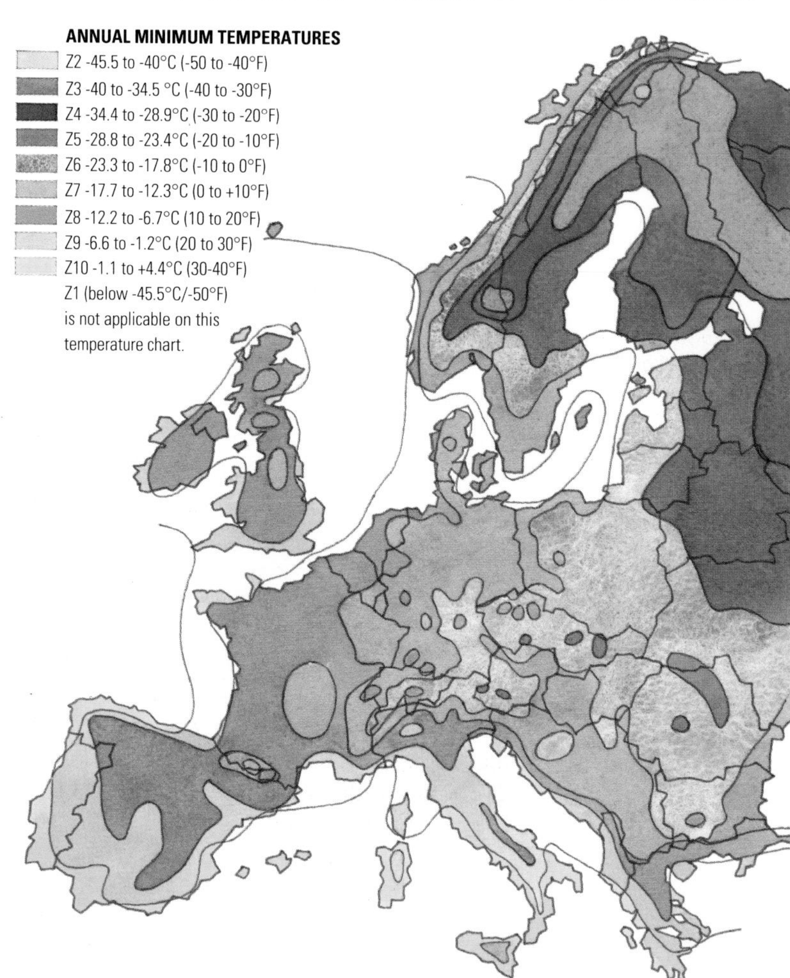

TIPS

- One of the secrets of successful gardening is to choose plants whose native climate is similar to that of your garden.
- To protect plants vulnerable to frost, cover them with a layer of bracken or leaf mould, or wrap them in sacking, horticultural fleece or other insulating material.

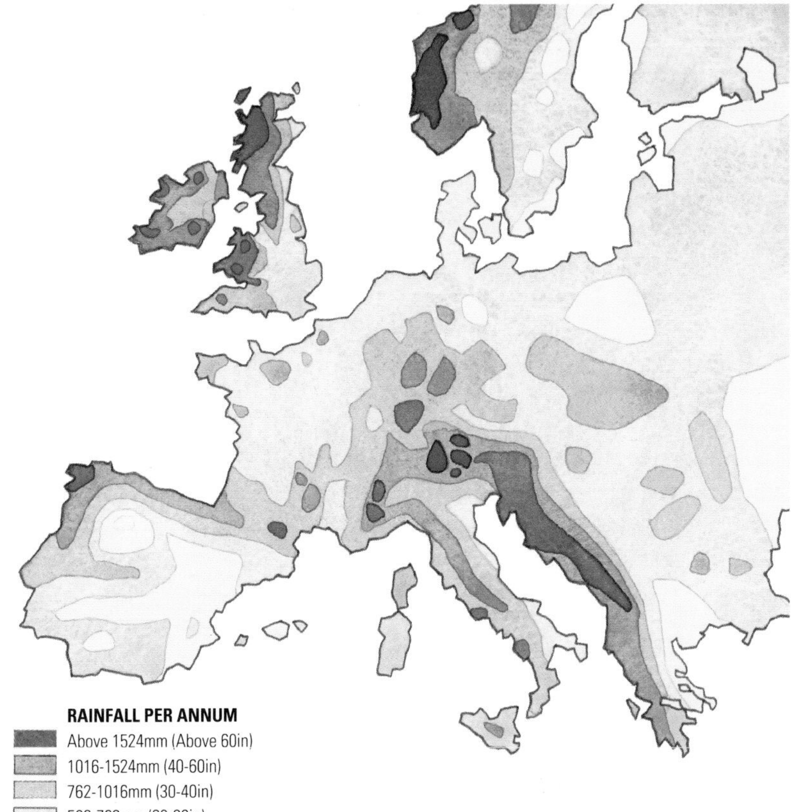

areas exposed to persistent winds, the growth of trees and shrubs is stunted on the windward side, making them lopsided. Wind also affects the amount of rain that reaches plants, leading to dry conditions on the sheltered side of walls, fences, trees and hedges: a rain shadow.

Ways of creating a more sheltered climate within your garden are discussed in Chapter 3, Understanding Plants. When you assess how much your garden is exposed to wind, remember that the effects of wind vary according to its direction and the time of year. In most parts of Britain the prevailing wind blows from the southwest for most of the year. It can be a nuisance, particularly in coastal areas, where it carries damaging salt with it. But far more damaging are the winter winds from the north and east which are cold and desiccating, and especially to evergreen plants.

Right In temperate climates, snow provides an insulating layer in winter. The weight of snow on evergreen shrubs and trees can break the branches, so brush it off.

Far right A dry, subtropical garden with appropriate plants.

Temperature

Plants start into growth each spring when the temperature of the soil reaches 6°C (43°F). They need to complete their cycle of growth before it falls again below that level. There is therefore a longer growing season in the south where the temperature remains higher for longer, than in the north. The temperature is also affected by altitude: it drops by an average of 0.5°C (1°F) for every 76m (250ft) of height.

Rainfall plays an indirect part in determining the temperature, as areas that are under cloud cover for long periods will get less warmth from the sun. The growing season will also be shorter in areas that are in shade for a large part of the day, whether from trees and buildings or because they are on a north-facing slope which the sun reaches only obliquely. The temperature of the soil is affected by the soil type. Clay soils are slow to warm up but retain heat for longer than light, sandy soils, which warm quickly but also lose heat quickly and are therefore more susceptible to frosts.

Frost

When the temperature drops below 0°C (32°F) frost occurs. Plants that can tolerate frost are known as 'frost-hardy', those that cannot are 'tender' plants.

Late spring frosts can ruin fruit crops or ornamental blossoming trees and shrubs by nipping them in the bud, and susceptible plants should be positioned where they are least at risk.

Just as hot air rises, cold air sinks, and the coldest parts of the garden will be those where a solid barrier such as a wall, fence or dense hedge prevents the progress of frosty air down a slope. Where such barriers are needed to keep animals out of the garden, or as part of the design of the garden, keep them open enough to allow the air to flow through. Pockets of frost also form in hollows from which the cold air cannot escape.

Microclimates

The climate of a town garden can be very different from one in the country. The heat given off by buildings is absorbed and retained in the soil, giving higher temperatures in winter and summer, and reducing the risk of frost in winter. On the other hand, the polluted atmosphere in some cities can reduce the amount of light available to plants.

The walls of buildings provide shelter from the wind in many urban situations, but in others they create wind tunnels, increasing the speed and strength of the wind, which can put plants at risk. Shade cast by buildings can also limit town gardening: many gardens in built-up areas only see the sun for a short time each day in the summer, and in the winter not at all.

Changing the microclimate

You cannot do much to alter the local temperature, rainfall or prevailing winds, but you can modify their effect on your garden to create different plant habitats within the garden.

Creating shelter from the wind is a requirement in most gardens. It can be achieved by building walls or fences and by planting trees and hedges along the garden's boundaries or within the garden to make separate enclosures. When planning beds and borders, aim to create south-facing niches between shrubs for smaller, vulnerable plants.

A wall has the advantage of providing a solid vertical surface on which to train climbing plants and, if built of brick, it will retain warmth from the sun and confer up to 5°C (41°F) of frost protection. This can make all the difference between success and failure with plants of doubtful hardiness. The wall's warmth also helps to ripen the wood on young shoots, making them more cold resistant. In old kitchen gardens even stone walls were often lined with brick so that wall-trained fruit would ripen early.

DESIGN TIP

Where space is limited, a narrow screen for shelter can be made by training ivies on a fence of chainlink or chicken wire. Once the ivies are established, the wire will be invisible and the fence can be clipped over once a year to keep it tidy.

Below Carefully chosen plants can give a climatic illusion, as these tropical-looking kniphofias and 'hot' colours do.

Right Walled enclosures make gardens-within-a-garden, each with a sheltered microclimate.

Below right A hedge slows wind by filtering it, but a wall redirects it, sometimes causing turbulence on the leeward side.

However, a wall is not a good windbreak as a solid barrier causes turbulence on the leeward side. A semi-open fence, a hedge or an informal belt of tall shrubs is more effective: it can provide effective wind reduction over a distance equal to five times its height.

A small group of trees, or even a single tree in the right place, will create an environment where woodland plants will thrive. A heap of stones picked out of carefully cultivated parts of the garden and covered with a thin layer of soil will provide a site for plants from the Mediterranean and other arid parts of the world. The main requirement of such plants is very well-drained soil, and in a relatively dry site they can survive surprising extremes of cold. It is cold, wet soil that kills them.

If there are barriers in the garden running more or less east to west they will have a south-facing side where you can grow sun-loving plants sheltered from the cold winter wind and a north-facing side where you can grow shade-loving plants. Hedges or groups of plants as low as 60cm (2ft) will provide ample shelter for small plants.

The creation of habitats that will suit plants from different climates is one of the pleasures of gardening. The ideal conditions for water plants, roses, alpines, herbs and wild flowers are described in Part 3.

Understanding Plants

Whether you are planting a forest or a row of beans, understanding how they develop adds to the pleasure of gardening and increases your chances of success. You don't have to be a biologist or a botanist to understand how plants grow. You just need to be interested.

Knowledge of how different plants behave will help you to choose the right plants for the soil and climate in your garden. For example, taprooted plants (those with a single, long, downward-growing main root) like oriental poppies, carrots and parsnips need deep, well-cultivated soil. In stony soil their roots will contort when they encounter obstacles and you will get forked carrots or corkscrew parsnips.

Reproduction

The purpose of all living things is to reproduce themselves. Nearly all plants do this from seeds, but many have supplementary ways of creating the next generation: bulbs multiply by dividing (daffodils, lilies and tulips); strawberries send out stems known as runners (stolons) above the ground, from which new plantlets form and root down; other plants have underground roots (rhizomes) which travel horizontally and produce new shoots at varying distances from the parent plant (three of the worst weeds in the garden, ground elder, couch grass and bindweed, belong to this category).

Pollination

If growing conditions are right, and the plant is healthy it will in due course produce flowers. Some plants, such as ten-week stocks, flower just a few months after germination. But a tree can take twelve or more years to flower. The majority of garden plants have showy, colourful flowers, but some, including many trees, have flowers that are scarcely noticeable.

Before a flower can fulfil its purpose of producing seeds, fertilization must take place. This is done by transferring the pollen from the stamen (the male element) to the stigma (the female element). This often takes place on the same plant (either because the flowers are male and female or because the plant bears male and female flowers), but some species carry male and female parts on different individual plants.

Either way, this is where the birds, bees, butterflies and other insects come in. Each plant has evolved the flower best designed to attract the right bird or insect to perform the task of transferring pollen from one flower to another, hence the rich diversity of flower shape, colour and scent.

Plant breeders carry out the process artificially, often using a paint brush for the delicate operation. Some plants are pollinated by the wind. For this to succeed, they produce large quantities of very fine pollen, and this is what causes problems for hay fever sufferers.

Seed production and distribution

Once fertilized, the flower sheds its petals. They have served their purpose, and the efforts of the plant are now concentrated on producing and distributing the seeds of the next generation.

The need for efficient distribution has led to great diversity among seeds, whether they are carried in fruits, berries or pods: a mistletoe seed is encased in a sticky berry so that the missel thrush will plant it when she cleans her beak on the bark of a tree. Many fruits provide food for

Above Dandelions make use of the wind to distribute their seeds.

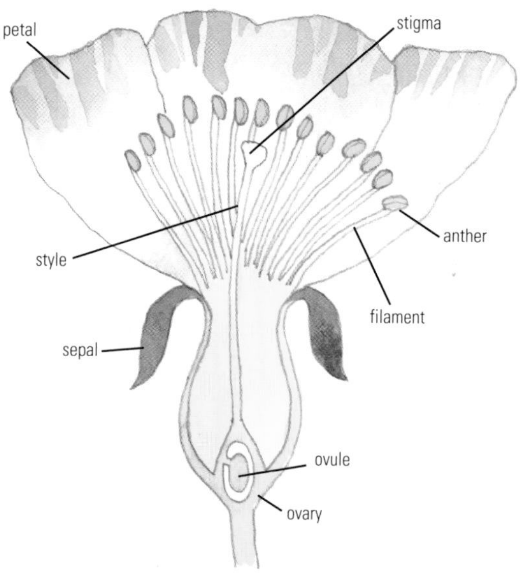

POLLINATION

The male part of the cherry blossom is the *stamen*, which consists of a *filament*, and *anthers* that carry pollen. The female parts are the *stigma* and *ovary*. When pollen lands on the stigma, fertilization of the *ovule* takes place, and the embryo develops into a seed. The cherry seed is enclosed in a woody shell, which, in turn, is enclosed in the fleshy fruit. Most flowers have mechanisms to prevent self-fertilization ensuring greater variety and usually, more seed. Sometimes the pollen and stigma ripen at different times, some plants carry both male and female flowers on the same plant, and in others, male and female flowers are carried on different plants.

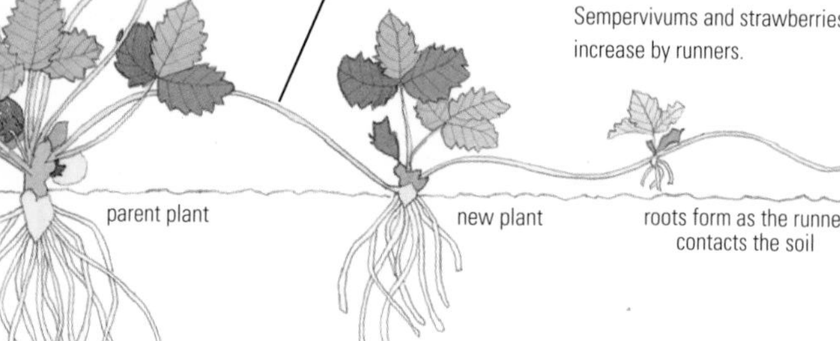

RUNNERS

A *runner* is a horizontal, above-ground stem. Where the runner's nodes touch the ground, a new plant with an independent root system is formed. Once established, it can be lifted and re-planted. New plants, in turn, throw out runners, and in this way spread can be indefinite. Sempervivums and strawberries increase by runners.

DESIGN TIP

Include some plants with berries in your garden for autumn colour and to encourage birds.

GERMINATION

1 Protected by the *seed coat*, the *cotyledons* provide a food store to ensure survival until the true leaves form. The water needed for germination is absorbed through a tiny hole called the *micropyle*. The *radicle* is a rudimentary root, the *hypocotyl* a primitive stem, and the *plumule* will emerge to bear the first leaves.

2 As the seed absorbs water, it swells and weakens the seed coat. The radicle emerges to form the root system. The plumule begins its upward journey to the light. The root branches, and develops hairs which absorb water. The stem pushes the cotyledons above soil level. As the stem reaches the light, new leaves, characteristic of the plant unfurl.

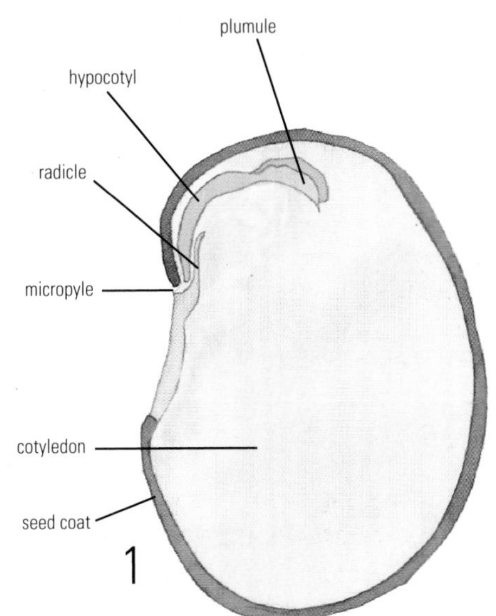

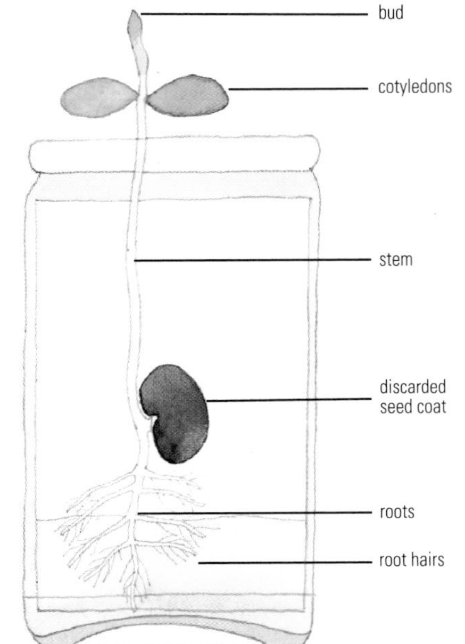

birds and mammals who will discard or evacuate the stone or pips in a position where they can germinate.

Plants use a number of mechanisms to distribute their seeds. In late summer the dried pods on broom plants can be heard exploding like little guns to eject their seeds. Dandelion clocks, thistledown and the winged propellers of ash and sycamore trees all make use of the wind. Others, like goose grass and burdock, produce seeds with tiny hooks which cling to the fur of passing animals. Most weeds have very efficient distribution systems: that is what makes them such a nuisance.

Germination

Seeds need water and a suitable temperature (which varies with different plants) to start into growth, and this beginning of growth is known as germination.

Each seed contains leaves with food for the plant in its early stages. These leaves are called cotyledons. Moisture causes them to swell and break the shell of the seed. The root emerges downwards, branching as it develops; from the cotyledons the stem and leaves characteristic of the new plant begin to grow.

Plant growth

The roots will continue to grow below the ground, providing a wind-firm anchor and taking up water and nutrients from the soil to supply the top growth with some of the raw ingredients with which they make food.

Above ground, the leaves absorb carbon dioxide from the air and trap the energy from sunlight by means of chlorophyll, the green pigment which gives leaves their colour. Using complex chemical processes, this energy combines carbon dioxide and water to produce sugars and carbohydrates, the food that plants need for growth. Oxygen is also produced and released into the atmosphere. This process is known as photosynthesis.

The process whereby all living things derive energy from food for growth is known as respiration – the breakdown of carbohydrates to release energy, producing carbon dioxide and water as waste products. Superficially, the two processes appear to be the reverse of each other, but in reality they occur at different places in the plant cells and by different chemical pathways.

BULBS

Bulbs are modified stems containing condensed flowers, buds and leaves. They have plump *scales* which store food as starch or sugar. In some, the outer scales dry out forming a papery tunic, which protects the bulb against drying. The main growing point rises from the centre of the bulb, producing leaves and flowers. The leaves make food to swell the following year's bulb – so do not cut them off until they wither. Bulbs divide, producing new bulbs which may take two years or more to flower. Hyacinth, tulips and snowdrops are bulbous plants.

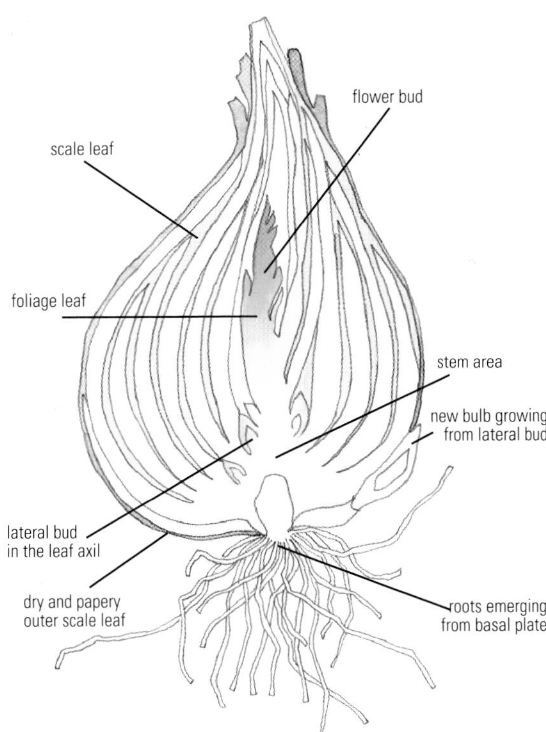

Plant names

The naming of plants is internationally standardized, using Latin, although many familiar and much-loved plants have names in other languages and some have several names – historic, regional or descriptive. The English dandelion is the French pis-en-lit. Cow parsley is also known as Queen Anne's lace, and lords and ladies as cuckoo pint.

The Latin naming system can seem daunting but it is logical and universal. Mastering it will make identifying plants from labels in garden centres, from lists in books and from catalogues much easier. Each plant is described by two and sometimes three names, all of which give different information about it. There is also a botanical family name describing the group to which each plant belongs; for instance the hawthorn and the rose both belong to the family Rosaceae.

The family name is used less often by gardeners than by botanists, plants usually being referred to by genus, species and variety (or cultivar, a cultivated variety), and in that order.

Left *Pyracantha coccinea* 'Lalandei', named to describe its scarlet berries.

Right The waterlily, *Nymphaea* 'Marliacea Carnea', named 'Carnea' for its flesh-pink flowers.

Plant names and their meanings

Colours
alba white
argentea silver
aurantiacus orange
aurea gold
caerulea blue
carnea flesh
cinerea ash grey
coccinea scarlet
ferrugineum rusty
flava pale yellow
glauca blue-green
lactea milk white
lutea yellow
nigra black
punicea crimson
rubra red
sanguineum blood red
tricolor three-coloured
viride green

Describing flowers (*flora* means 'flower')
campanulata bell-shaped
floribunda free-flowering
grandiflora large-flowered
macropetala large-petalled
nudiflora flowering on bare branches
nutans nodding
paniculata in panicles
parviflora small-flowered
pauciflora few-flowered
polyantha many-flowered
praecox early
racemosa in racemes
spicata on spikes
stellata star-shaped
umbellata in umbels

Describing leaves (*folia* and *phylla* both mean 'leaf')
angustifolia narrow
arguta sharp
crassifolia thick
glabra hairless
hirsuta hairy
incana with grey down
integrifolia without teeth
latifolia, platyphylla broad
macrophylla large
microphylla, parvifolia small
mollis soft
nitida, splendens shining
sempervirens evergreen
tomentosa downy
velutina velvety

Geographical names
atlantica from the Atlas Mountains (N. Africa)
australis southern
borealis northern
californica from California
capensis from the Cape (S. Africa)
europaea from Europe
hispanica from Spain
japonica, nipponica from Japan
occidentalis western
orientalis eastern
sinensis from China

Habitats
alpina from the Alps or similar region
aquatica of water
arvensis of fields
campestris of plains
littoralis of the sea shore
maritima by the sea
montana of mountains
palustris of marshes
rivularis of streams
rupestre of rocks
sylvatica of woods

Habit of growth
arborea tree-like
fastigiata with erect branches
fruticosa shrubby
horizontalis spreading horizontally
humilis low-growing
pendula weeping
procera very tall
procumbens, prostratus ground-hugging
repens creeping and rooting as it goes

Scents
citriodora lemon-scented
foetida unpleasant smell
fragrans, fragrantissima fragrant, very fragrant
graveolens strong-smelling
odorata, odoratissima sweet, very sweet
moschata musk-scented
suaveolens sweet-smelling

Seasons
vernalis spring
aestivum summer
autumnalis autumn
hiemalis winter

Other descriptive names
edulis edible
officinalis of the shop (usually herbal)
sativa cultivated (as a crop)
vulgare common (often wild)

Above Trollius europeaus, the European globeflower.

Above right Wisteria sinensis. The familiar and beautiful climber, shown here grown as a standard shrub, comes from China.

Below Seasonal names: *Leucojum aestivum* 'Gravetye' is summer-flowering.

Right The name *Caragana arborescens* describes this shrub's tree-like habit of growth.

Below Saponaria officinalis (soapwort) was commercially available in the past *('officinalis')*.

An example of this is *Betula pendula* 'Youngii' (Young's silver birch).

The first two names are written in italics, the first name starting with a capital letter and the second with a small letter. They tell you about plants which occur in the wild. The first name tells you the genus: *Betula* or birch in the example above: *pendula* tells you what species (what type) of birch it is: *Betula pendula* is the silver birch which grows wild in Europe and Asia Minor. The species name is descriptive of its pendulous branches. The third name is not in italics but is in quotation marks and starts with a capital letter. It gives information about a garden variety of the plant so different from the wild species that it merits a name of its own. A new variety may occur in a garden by accident as a seedling or 'sport', or by design as a result of the efforts of a plant breeder. A sport is an uncharacteristic shoot which appears on a plant for no apparent reason, such as one with variegated leaves on a plant with otherwise plain leaves. A hybrid plant is indicated by the multiplication sign 'x', for example *Malus* x *robusta*, a crab-apple produced by crossing *M. baccata* with *M. prunifolia.*

Varieties are sometimes named in honour of a person, as for example *Betula pendula* 'Youngii' (Mr Young), and sometimes descriptively or with reference to the garden where they first occurred. Some names are doubly informative, as with the oriental poppy, *Papaver orientale* 'Perry's White'. *Papaver* means 'poppy', *orientale* distinguishes the oriental poppy from the opium poppy (*Papaver somniferum*, sleep-inducing poppy) and others, and the variety's name tells you that Mr Perry bred the poppy and that it has white flowers.

In books, nurserymen's catalogues and in garden centres, this standard naming system is generally used, although the English names are sometimes given as well.

It can be a great help to know the meanings of some of the Latin descriptive words. Such knowledge makes plant names easier to remember and can tell you useful things about the plant: if a plant comes from China (*sinensis*, as in *Wisteria sinensis*), it is quite likely to be hardy in all but the harshest climates. A plant from California (*californica* as in *Fremontodendron californicum*) is more likely to need some degree of winter protection. Names that describe the plant's habitat (see table opposite) give valuable clues as to whether it will thrive in the conditions in your garden.

Plant categories

Plant lists in catalogues and books are usually arranged in the categories listed below.

Trees

Trees are the largest and longest-living of all plants, and the oxygen which they contribute to the atmosphere is of immense importance to the planet's ecology. They develop a single, woody stem or trunk, and can take from twenty to over one hundred years to reach their full height and spread. Trees can be evergreen, retaining their leaves all the year round, or deciduous, losing their leaves in autumn.

Conifers, including the familiar fir and pine families, are primitive trees which bear their seeds in cones and have distinctive needle-like leaves. Most conifers are evergreen but there are exceptions, like the larch native to Britain and other parts of Europe, *Larix decidua*.

Trees come in all sizes from the stately lime (*Tilia*) at 35m (100ft) to the laburnum at 6m (20ft). They reproduce themselves from seeds and many have highly ornamental flowers, leaves and fruit. Seed receptacles include fleshy fruits like apples, pears and plums; the protective prickly coats of chestnuts; the hard shells of walnuts, hazel and beech; the bright berries of holly and hawthorn; the winged propellers of maple and ash; and the giant pods of *Catalpa bignonioïdes*, the Indian bean tree.

Provided they are chosen and sited with care, trees are practically maintenance-free and give pleasure at all seasons. Space can be found for at least one tree in even the smallest garden.

Shrubs

A shrub is a deciduous or evergreen bush with several woody stems. Shrubs vary in size from a few inches to several metres high and wide, and include plants to suit every garden situation and purpose. The borderline between small trees and large shrubs is blurred. If catalogues do not list the plant you want under 'trees', look under 'shrubs' and vice versa.

Roses and soft fruit such as gooseberries and currants are shrubs. Other familiar ornamental shrubs include lilac (*Syringa*), hydrangea and *Buddleja davidii*, the butterfly bush.

Herbaceous perennials

'Perennial' means continuing from year to year. 'Herbaceous' plants have non-woody stems which die down in winter but produce new shoots the following spring. Some perennials continue to grow and flower for many years, whilst others are relatively short lived. Herbaceous borders filled with such favourites as delphiniums, lupins, Michaelmas daisies and Japanese anemones were fashionable at the beginning of this century, but they are labour-intensive as the dead stems have to be cut down each year and most herbaceous plants form clumps that need to be split up and replanted every few years.

In spite of the work involved, herbaceous plants are good value, many of them bearing

Above Shrubs: *Rosa* 'Cécile Brünner'. Like other plants with woody stems, roses fall into the category of shrubs.

DESIGN TIPS

- Use trees to provide shade, to form screens and barriers, and to add height in plant groupings.
- Use herbaceous plants to fill gaps between newly planted shrubs until the shrubs reach their mature size.
- Annuals and biennials can be used for informal as well as formal schemes. Plant or sow them in bold drifts in places where they can be left to seed themselves.
- For a continuous display plant bulbs in layers: late-flowering tulips deepest with narcissus above them and snowdrops or scillas on top.

Far left Trees: *Robinia pseudoacacia* 'Frisia', a medium-sized tree with attractive yellow-green leaves, suitable for small gardens.

Left Herbaceous perennials can live for many years: *Geranium psilostemon*, a hardy perennial, should not be confused with the tender *Pelargonium*.

Above Biennials: hollyhocks *(Alcea rosea)* and other biennials develop roots and leaves in their first year and flower the following year.

spectacular flowers for many weeks. They are frequently used as one of the components in mixed borders, together with shrubs, bulbs and ground cover plants.

Biennials

Plants which are grown from seed one year to flower the following year, but do not survive for a third season, are known as biennials. Many biennials and annuals (see below) are known as bedding plants because they are grown in the greenhouse or in nursery beds outside and are then moved and set out as young plants in the flower beds. Biennials include wallflowers, sweet williams, forget-me-nots, hollyhocks and foxgloves.

Annuals

As their name implies, annuals are sown, flower and die all in the space of one year. Some, like love-in-a-mist (*Nigella damascena*) and Shirley poppy (*Papaver rhoeas*), are hardy and can be sown outdoors. If the seedheads are left to ripen, these and many other annuals will sow themselves and thus you will always have some in the garden. This is known as 'self-seeding'. Half-hardy annuals, for example snapdragons (*Antirrhinum*) and tobacco plant (*Nicotiana*), are susceptible to frost, so they are grown under glass in a greenhouse or on a windowsill and planted out in early summer when all risk of frost is past.

Annuals are often planted in containers or in formal beds to follow spring flowering biennials, and displays of *Antirrhinum,* busy lizzies (*Impatiens*), lobelias, nasturtiums, *Nicotiana,* verbena or any other annuals, separately or combined, will last from midsummer until the autumn's first frost.

Although annuals and biennials can be raised from seed, many are available as young plants from nurseries and garden centres at the appropriate time of year. Both biennials and annuals provide colourful flowers over a long period and are invaluable for tubs, pots and window boxes, and for filling spring and summer gaps between other, more long-term plants.

Bulbs

The bulbs of daffodils, hyacinths and tulips are familiar to most people. If you cut one in half you will see that it consists of close layers of fleshy leaves like an onion (which is also a bulb). The food for the plant is stored in the bulb. When water and a suitable temperature is provided, roots grow from the hard callous at the base of the bulb, and leaves and flowers from the pointed tip. Because the bulb contains nourishment for the plant, leafy shoots will often appear even without water, whilst the bulbs are in store. In time, small bulbils develop round the parent bulb and split away to form a new plant.

Many bulbs will grow in grass and in light shade underneath trees, including *Scilla* (this genus includes bluebells), daffodils (*Narcissus*) and snowdrops (*Galanthus nivalis*). These and other spring-flowering bulbs are invaluable for planting among shrubs and herbaceous plants to extend the garden's season. By the time the other plants come into leaf and flower, the bulbs' flowers will be fading and their leaves will soon die down and disappear until next spring.

Examples of summer-flowering bulbs include alliums and lilies.

Right Annuals: trailing lobelias are in flower from early summer till the first frost. Annuals die after just one season.

Far right Bulbs: as well as the familiar spring bulbs, some, like *Allium flavum,* flower in summer, and others in the autumn.

Corms, rhizomes and tubers

Like bulbous plants, these carry their food store underground. Corms look similar to bulbs, consisting of a thickened underground stem base. Roots and leaves both grow from a single bud on the corm. In rhizomes and tubers the store is a thickened root or underground stem. Crocuses are corms, irises have rhizomes, and dahlias and potatoes are both tuberous plants.

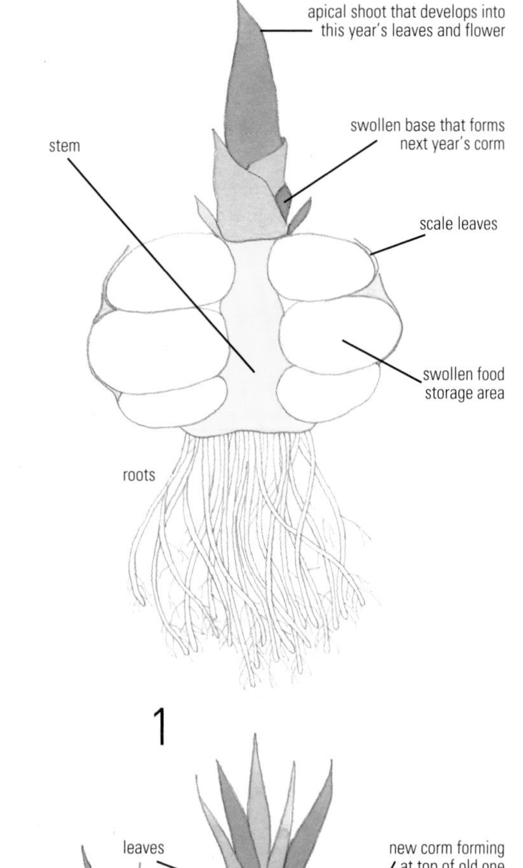

Hardy, half-hardy and tender plants

Plant hardiness is the plant's ability to grow in the environment provided for it. It depends on temperature, rainfall and the degree of shelter from the wind. Another crucial factor is light: growth is influenced by sun and shade, by the length of days, the angle of the sun and the length of the growing season. A hardy plant is one that will survive in a given environment. Plants that tolerate frost are sometimes referred to as frost-hardy. Plants that will not survive outdoors in a local climate are described as tender, and those that are doubtful as half-hardy.

Ground cover

This general term is used to describe plants which are so dense and leafy that, if planted closely on weed-free soil, they will cover the ground well enough to prevent weed seeds from growing. They are very useful labour-saving plants, and many that are decorative as well as

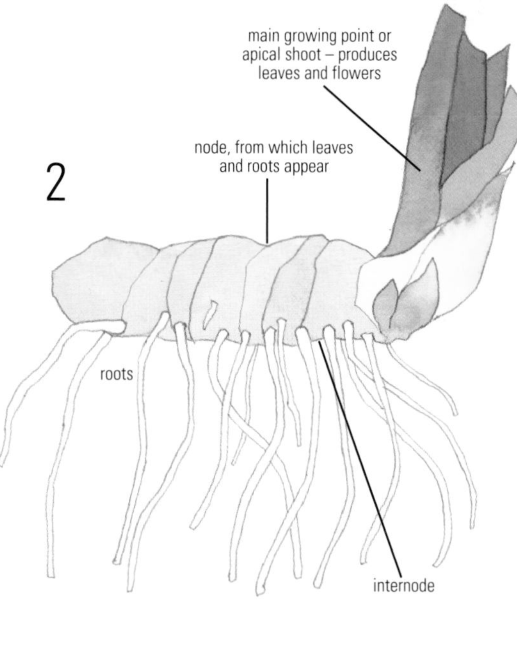

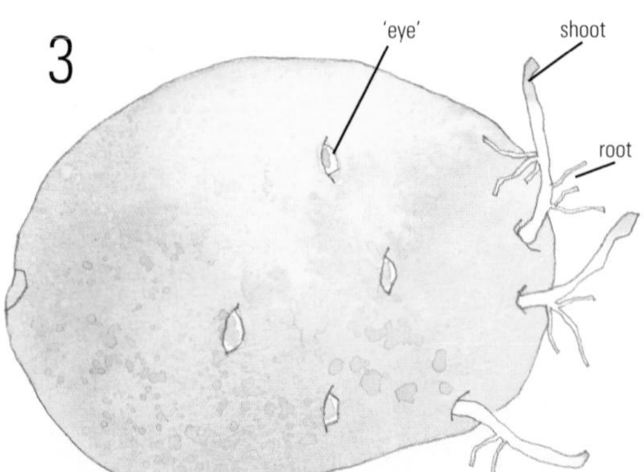

DESIGN TIPS

- In dense shade where grass will only grow sparsely, plant ivies, hardy cyclamen or other shade-tolerant ground cover instead of struggling to establish a lawn.
- Some climbing plants also make good ground cover: ivies, clematis and some of the rambler roses, for example.
- Use prostrate alpines to soften the margins of gravel paths or patios.

CORMS, RHIZOMES AND TUBERS

1 *Corms* are formed from the base of a solid stem, which has swollen food storage organs arising from it. The scale leaves become membrane-like, enclosing and protecting the corm from damage and drying. New corms are formed at the base of each flowering stem, and the old corm eventually withers away.

2 *Rhizomes* are modified stems that grow horizontally at or below ground level. They often store food. The main growing point produces leaves and flowers, and roots grow mainly at the nodes. Each *node* usually has buds that can produce leaves and flowers, so if rhizomes are cut into sections, provided it has a growth bud, each section will grow into a new plant. Many common garden plants are rhizomatous, and some, like mint and lily of the valley, are invasive.

3 A potato *tuber* is a stem, modified to store food as starch. From the potato 'eye' (a cluster of buds above a leaf scar) a shoot and root will develop. Each eye is capable of forming a new plant. The new shoots and roots use the food store of the 'seed potato'. New tubers form during the growing season, converting the sugars formed by the leafy top growth into the starch that makes the potato such a valuable food source.

functional can be found among both shrubs and herbaceous perennials.

Climbers

In the wild, climbing plants cling to tree trunks or twine into trees and shrubs supporting themselves in several different ways. Vines (*Vitis*) and clematis are among those plants which cling by means of twisting tendrils. Wisteria and convolvulus climb by twining; ivies and the climbing hydrangea (*Hydrangea petiolaris*) have aerial rootlets along their stems which grip the support. Boston ivy (*Parthenocissus tricuspidata*) climbs by means of tiny adhesive pads. On climbing roses in the wild, the thorns anchor the branches, but in garden situations they need tying. Climbers make beautiful covering for walls and fences, and are indispensable for hiding eyesores and decorating features of vertical interest, such as arches and pergolas.

Above Ground cover: primroses will grow in the shade under shrubs, forming a weed-smothering carpet.

Right Climbers: *Parthenocissus tricuspidata* (Boston ivy) is self-clinging and will cover a very large wall, or make extensive ground cover on a bank.

Alpines

Plants which come from mountainous regions such as the Alps are classified as 'alpines'. Some will only grow in very specialized conditions, and enthusiasts rear them on rock gardens and in special glass alpine houses. Others, like aubretia and *Helianthemum* (rock rose), are easy to grow. They make ideal plants for rock gardens, drystone walls, the margins of gravel paths and the crevices between paving stones. They need good drainage. See Chapter 21, Growing Alpines.

Aquatics

These plants grow under water or in water with their leaves floating on the surface. The classic example is the water lily, *Nymphaea*. Plants which thrive in the permanently wet conditions at the edge of water, as do astilbes and many kinds of primula, are called marginal plants. An area designed for such plants can be called a bog garden. See Chapter 17, Water Gardening.

Vegetables

Plants that are grown for food are traditionally grown in a separate area, the vegetable garden or kitchen garden. However, many vegetables, such as red-stemmed beet and climbing beans, are decorative enough to be included in the ornamental garden. In the large, walled kitchen gardens of country houses, flowers to cut for the house used to be grown alongside the vegetables and fruit. A vegetable garden laid out symmetrically so that it is attractive as well as useful is known by the French word, *potager*.

The edible part of a vegetable plant may be the root or tuber (carrots, parsnips, potatoes), the stem (asparagus, celery), the leaves (cabbage, lettuce, spinach) or the fruit and seed (peas, beans, tomatoes). See Chapter 16, The Kitchen Garden.

Herbs

The plants which we know as herbs are historically among the earliest garden plants. They were grown for their useful qualities in medicine, in cooking (as flavouring), as cosmetics and for general domestic use to keep rooms and clothes smelling sweet. Many of the most beautiful plants, like lavender and irises, were first introduced to gardens as useful plants. You don't need a separate herb garden to grow kitchen herbs; plant rosemary, sage, chives and parsley among other ornamental plants. See Chapter 21, Growing Herbs.

Choosing the Plants

There is no shopping addict like a keen gardener. A mud-spattered, handwritten sign by the roadside announcing 'plants for sale' will have the plant hunter slamming on the car's brakes and charging down the narrowest country lane in pursuit of the quarry – some little treasure that is to be had for neither love nor money from any garden centre in the land. But will the new plant survive in the addict's garden? Will it take to the soil? Will the addict kill it with kindness by overwatering? Or kill it with neglect by leaving it to fend for itself during a rainless week? And if the little treasure thrives, will it have smuggled a pernicious weed into your garden in its pot?

The first rule when choosing plants is to check whether they will thrive in the soil and climate of your garden, so it helps if you go shopping for plants armed with a 'wish list' of suitable candidates.

However, impulse buys are part of the fun of gardening, and you are bound to be tempted by plants that are not on your list. If they don't die on you or turn out to be bullies that take over the whole garden, they will give you nothing but pleasure. So, the advice which follows is not intended to take away the fun, merely to reduce the element of risk.

Lists of reliable and beautiful plants to suit various types of garden are given in Chapter 5, Plants to Learn With.

Making a planting plan

Plants are expensive, and it may not be possible to stock your garden completely at the outset. But it helps to have a clear idea of what you want so that you can decide what the priorities are, which plants you can raise yourself from seeds or cuttings and what to ask for if friends offer plants as housewarming presents or for Christmas, birthdays and anniversaries.

HOW? To put your ideas about planting into focus, start by drawing a plan of the garden. You do not necessarily have to design the garden on paper. You may prefer to mark the layout on the ground, using bamboo canes, tape and, for curves, heavy rope or hosepipe, as suggested in Chapter 1, Planning Your Needs. By this method you can make on-the-spot adjustments until you have got the plan right. But it is still worth taking the trouble to transfer it to paper as a permanent record.

You may have already sketched out a plan for the layout of the garden, but a planting plan

Above The astilbes and irises in the foreground are moisture-loving plants. The bold foliage of the hostas at the end of the path draws the eye and emphasizes the curve of the path.

TIP

Have a bird's-eye view of the garden beside you: a photograph taken from a top floor window if possible, or a series of photographs taped together.

Below left Planting Plan: Stage 1, Survey Plan of existing features.

Below Stage 2, Layout Sketch Plan.

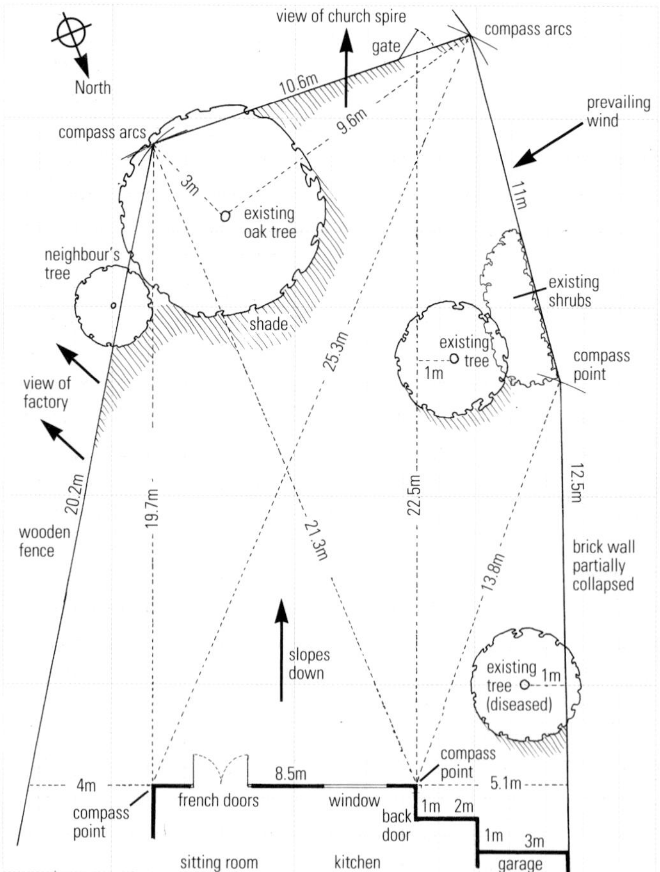

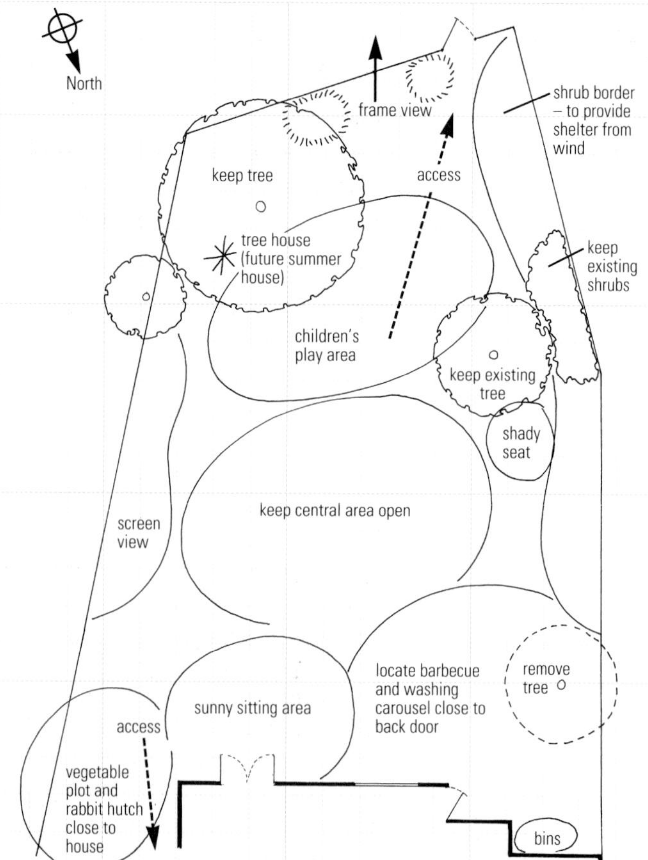

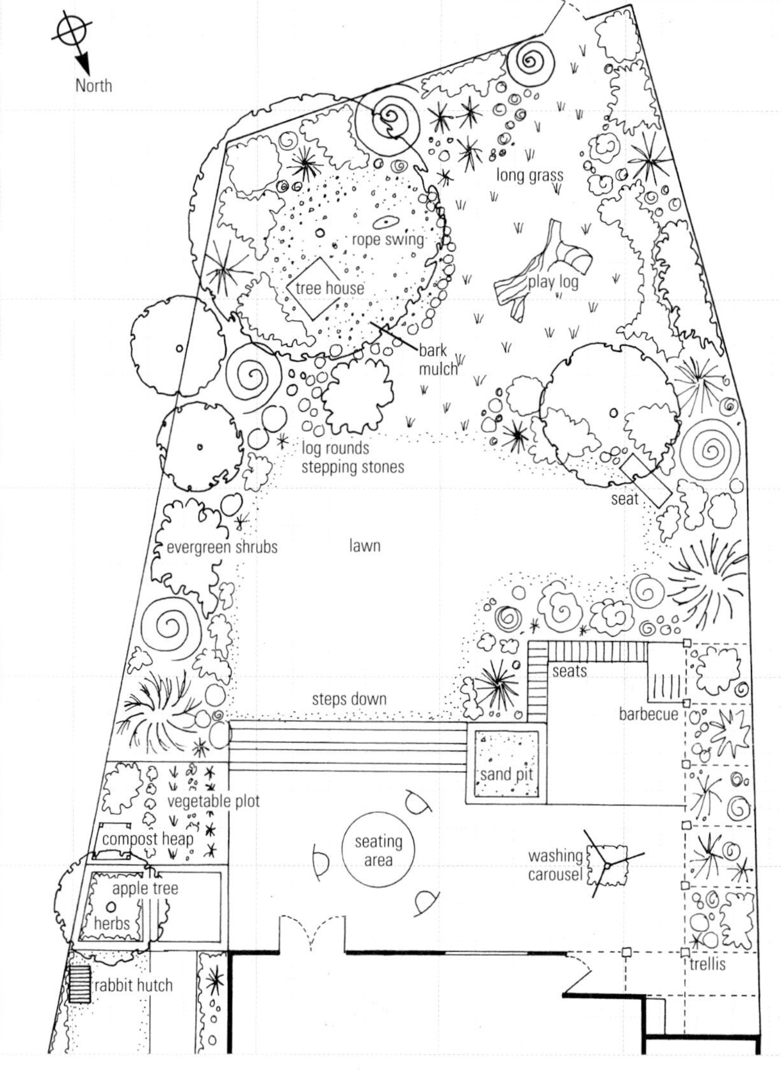

Above Stage 3, Sketch Planting Plan.

needs to be drawn in more detail, and you may need to draw all or part of the plan to a larger scale. A plan of your garden drawn roughly to scale is an invaluable record to keep, refer to and update over the years. Making such a plan does not require artistry: it doesn't matter if you can't draw, it is a common-sense operation.

Drawing a plan to scale

What size paper you choose and the scale you decide to work to depend on the size of your garden. Paper larger than A2 (59x42cm, 23½x 16½in) is difficult to manage unless you have a drawing board.

A good scale at which to show planting details is 1:50 (2cm = 1m). Using graph paper with the right grid will save a lot of measuring, and a scale ruler is useful. A circle template is also worth acquiring, to mark the positions of trees and shrubs of different sizes.

If your garden is too large to fit onto one sheet of paper at a scale of 1:50, draw it at 1:100 (1cm = 1m); it is still possible to show clearly the positions of trees and the shapes of shrub groups, beds and borders. You can then draw separate planting plans for each area at the larger scale of 1:50.

Below Rounded shrubs give structure to this border. The paved strip between bed and lawn makes mowing easier.

Before you draw to scale, make a rough diagram of the garden. If you have an estate agent's plan of the property showing its boundaries, it is helpful to sketch an enlarged version of that. Show the house, the boundaries, paved areas, paths, buildings and structures, trees and any other features you intend to keep. Use a soft pencil so that you can rub out mistakes.

Take the diagram into the garden, take the measurements you need (a two-person job, one to hold the tape, one to read it off at the other end) and note them down on the sketch diagram. Check all angles carefully: very often what appear to be right angles at boundaries are in fact quite a lot more acute or obtuse than 90°.

Then, transfer the information on to graph paper, drawing it on at the chosen scale. You should include paving, paths, garden shed, steps, walls or hedges, trees and large shrubs or groups of shrubs that you intend to keep. If you have not yet planned the layout, look at the checklists in Chapter 1.

Mark the north point on the plan. This will help you see which areas are in sun and which in shade. It helps to hatch in permanent shade cast by trees and buildings.

Draw arrows to show the direction of the prevailing wind. This will show you where you need plants that give shelter.

Do you want to divide the garden up further, and if so will you use hedges as barriers, or more expensive walls or fences? You may not want to enclose areas with tall hedges, but even a short hedge of lavender or box will make a visual barrier and provide shelter for smaller plants. Mark these subdivisions on the plan.

Next, mark on the diagram the positions of your main structural plants: trees and large shrubs which form the living architectural framework for more detailed planting or provide strong focal points. This is where the circle template is useful to draw in the mature spread of the plants. Don't get bogged down in detail at this stage. Just identify where you need trees or large shrubs to give height, to screen unwelcome views or to frame attractive views.

Identify and draw in general areas for shrubs, roses and/or perennials, vegetables if you are going to grow them, bulbs and bedding plants.

At this stage, rather than choosing actual plants for each position, just note the space that needs to be filled and the height you want the plant groups to be, adding, perhaps, such notes as 'evergreen' or 'silver foliage?' and colour themes to help your ideas to crystallize.

Making a plant list

At this stage you are planning the bones of the garden. Before you move on to make a detailed planting plan, it pays to build up a list of plants that you want to grow. Keep a notebook that goes with you everywhere, to jot down plants seen, where and when. It is especially helpful to note combinations or groups of plants that please you.

However little you think you know about plants, as soon as you start a list, you will find plenty come to mind. You may not be familiar with their Latin names, or even their English names. But someone in the family will be able to identify 'that shrub with the scented white flowers that Granny had by the back door'.

If you can bear to wait before planting up your garden, spend a season from spring through autumn visiting gardens with your notebook. Many private gardens are open under the National Gardens Scheme once or twice a year when they are at their best. They vary enormously in size and style and are a fertile source of ideas. Make a special effort to visit those with similar soils and climate to your own, and look with a critical eye: occasionally a garden will demonstrate what not to do.

These gardens are listed in the Yellow Book, which is published each year, and you will see yellow posters advertising them in country towns and villages on Saturdays and Sundays.

Above and opposite above The same garden photographed in early summer and late autumn. When planning what to plant, remember that areas that are sunny at midsummer may be in shade for most of the year.

DESIGN TIP

For year-round interest aim at about one-third evergreen shrubs to two-thirds deciduous.

Far left A garden planted to have maximum impact in the spring.

Left A strong colour statement for late summer. Purple background foliage tones down the hot reds of the dahlias in the foreground.

Most garden owners are very friendly and happy to chat about the merits and preferences of their plants. If you live near a botanical garden, visit often to see plants at different seasons. Most have collections that are impeccably labelled, which is immensely helpful in identification.

If you are longing to get started, it is still worth doing a little research. Go to a garden centre and have a look at the plants on display. Don't buy anything yet. See whether the plants on your list are available (and how much they cost) and add to your list any others that appeal to you. Most garden centres use labels which give information about size, colour and cultural requirements of each plant and often a colour picture too. There should also be a member of staff who can advise you about whether the plants you like will grow in your garden.

You can also do your research from books and catalogues, selecting suitable plants for the conditions in your garden. But avoid following a ready-made planting scheme; it is your garden and you will get the greatest satisfaction from choosing your own plants.

The list of reliable plants in Chapter 5, Plants to Learn With, can be used for guidance in working out your own ideas.

TIP

Cut out coloured paper discs scaled to the size of your chosen trees and shrubs. On each disc write the name of the plant and draw a diagram of its shape. Shuffle the discs around on the diagram until the effect pleases you.

The next step is to make a firm shopping list. By now you will have quite a long list of 'wants'. Divide it up into separate lists for sun, shade and semi-shade, if all these situations occur in your garden. List trees, shrubs and herbaceous plants separately in descending order of height and note their eventual spread (width). A note or simple diagram of the shape is also useful. Mark evergreens with a star. You will probably find that there is not enough space for all the plants on your list. Be selective, choosing those with the longest season of interest.

Choosing a garden theme

Selection is easier, and the resulting garden will have greater unity, if you decide on an overall theme. With a theme you can then eliminate from your list any plants that do not contribute to it.

SEASONAL Put the main emphasis on plants which flower in spring, or on those which have berries or coloured leaves in autumn.

PRACTICAL A fruit and vegetable garden, or a garden planned to provide food and shelter for wildlife, can be decorative as well as practical.

COLOUR SCHEMES You might choose to work to specific colour schemes in different parts of the garden.

SCENT By restricting your plants to those with scented flowers or foliage you will give your garden a special character.

HISTORY The period of your house might inspire your theme.

Drawing a planting plan

Use your layout plan if it is at a scale of 1:50, or draw the various beds and borders at this scale. Overlay this base plan with tracing paper for the planting plan. Equip yourself with plenty of tracing paper. It will save rubbing out your mistakes and enable you to compare alternative schemes.

Referring to your plant list, position structural plants first: trees, large shrubs and groups of shrubs, then fill in with smaller plants to suit your theme or colour scheme.

Try to make pleasing groups of different shaped plants: upright, spikey shapes contrasting with low domes. Contrasts in the colour, size and texture of the leaves are important as well as the flowers.

Planning *in situ*

If planning on paper is not your style, stick canes in the ground to see how your chosen plants will fit into the available space. Mark the circle each plant will occupy at maturity with sand (relatively easy to 'rub out' mistakes).

Grouping the plants

You may not be able to afford to fill your garden at first, so make the structural plants (trees and large shrubs for key positions) your priority. Unless yours is a large garden you are only likely to need one of each variety.

Hedges

A single row is sufficient, with the plants spaced at the distances apart given below:

MEDIUM TO TALL HEDGES

45cm (18in) – beech, blackthorn (sloe), box, *Euonymus japonicus*, holly, hornbeam, field maple, *Symphoricarpos* x *doorenbosii* 'White Hedge'.

50-60cm (20-24in) – *Berberis*, *Prunus cerasifera* 'Nigra', Portugal laurel, *Pyracantha*, *Viburnum tinus*, Leyland cypress, *Thuja*, yew.

30cm (1ft) – hawthorn (quickthorn), *Lonicera nitida*, Myrobalan plum, privet.

LOW HEDGES

60cm (2ft) – Rosemary.

45cm (18in) – *Lavandula angustifolia* (Old English lavender), *Santolina virens*.

Left Box *(Buxus* 'Suffruticosa'*)* makes neat and compact low hedging or edging; used here to confine the border plants which makes mowing easier.

35cm (15in) – Munstead lavender, Dutch lavender.

30cm (1ft) – Hidcote lavender.

20cm (9in) – Hyssop, santolina, wall germander.

10-15cm (4-6in) – Box edging.

Shrubs

Smaller shrubs with an eventual spread of less than 80cm (30in), particularly roses, usually look far better grouped three or five together. A few bold groups look more satisfying than a lot of single plants which can give a rather spotty effect.

DESIGN TIP

Crocuses and daffodils look best in drifts of one kind or colour, rather than mixed.

Below A colour coordinated, late summer border in the Jekyll style. Although often associated with soft, pastel colour schemes, she was also very skilled in (and not afraid of) the use of strong, hot colours. Success depends on using large groups of each plant.

Right *Euonymus japonicus*, a hardy, salt-resistant evergreen for hedges in coastal areas. Plant 45cm (18in) apart.

Far right Plant tulips in groups of seven or more to give late spring colour in borders.

Herbaceous perennials, biennials and annuals

Make groups as big as space permits, with five, seven or nine plants to a group, interlocking one group with the next. Clever gardeners interplant early flowering species with late ones to follow them. There are a few exceptions to this rule, however.

Some specimen plants are big and bold enough to stand alone, such as *Crambe cordifolia, Cynara cardunculus* and *Onopordum acanthium.*

If you are deliberately aiming at a spotty effect (a very cottagey garden or a Botticelli *millefiori* tapestry), you will also only want one of each plant.

Bulbs

In grass under trees, the more the better; buy them by the hundred if you can.

In beds and borders daffodils are a nuisance; their dying foliage spoils the effect of later displays. As most daffodil varieties will grow happily in grass it makes sense to reserve the border for other things, and especially for tulips, which can be planted between shrubs or among herbaceous plants which will grow up as the tulips fade. Seven is the minimum number for a group of tulips to make an impact.

Below *Lonicera nitida* withstands close clipping and makes excellent, evergreen hedging. The form shown here, *L. nitida* 'Baggesen's Gold' has bright yellow leaves. As a single specimen it adds year-round colour to the border.

Below right Lavender makes a beautiful and aromatic low hedge, but is equally at home in the border. Its nectar-rich flowers are very attractive to bees and other beneficial insects.

Buying plants

Selecting trees, shrubs and herbaceous plants
When you are looking at plants in containers, there are a few indicators of a strong and healthy specimen to look for. Whether it is a shrub, a tree or a herbaceous plant, its stems and branches should be stout and strong rather than thin and spindly and the whole plant should be shapely and fairly symmetrical. Leaf buds and flower buds should look fat and full. Leaves and flowers should show no signs of wilting or disease or insect activity.

The most important part of the plant is the part that you cannot see – the root system. The advice usually given is to lift the plant out of its pot to inspect it. There is no need to be furtive about it. If the plant comes out spilling a shower of compost, it is the supplier, not you, who should feel embarrassed: he is trying to sell you a 9cm plant in a 1- or 2-litre (2- or 3½-pint) pot.

- Look for a rootball which fills the pot but has not reached the stage of spiralling round in the cramped space.
- Avoid plants with roots coming out of the holes at the base of the pot. Also avoid any plants growing in compost that is either dry or sodden.
- Weeds growing in the pot don't necessarily mean that the plant is a poor specimen, but it does mean that the plant has had to compete for water and food and that plant care in that nursery or garden centre is uneven at best. You don't want to take weeds home with you; you probably have enough already.
- Acclimatize plants that have been reared under protection by leaving them in their pots in a sheltered place until there is a spell of milder weather.
- If, although you planted and looked after them correctly, plants die, take them back to where you bought them. However, if you choose strong, healthy plants from the list in Chapter 5, Plants to Learn With, you will not have many casualties. They are surprisingly difficult to kill.

Selecting bulbs
When selecting bulbs, look for plump, firm specimens which have their papery overcoat intact (except for bluebells, scillas and grape hyacinths, which do not have overcoats).

- Avoid damaged, soft or shrivelled bulbs and any with mould on them.
- Avoid bulbs with roots or shoots already growing, except for lilies, which are alright with roots in growth. Small shoots on crocuses and tulips are acceptable. Also, avoid daffodil and narcissus bulbs with several 'babies' attached.
- Snowdrops (*Galanthus*), snowflake (*Leucojum*) and hardy cyclamen are best bought and planted 'in the green', that is to say whilst they are growing. Once they have been allowed to dry out they do not always grow again.
- Winter aconites (*Eranthis*) are tubers and anemones are corms. Both look dry and shrivelled: it does not mean there is anything wrong with them, but *Eranthis*, too, are easier to establish in the green.

Buying from garden centres
Plants do not necessarily cost more from a garden centre than from other sources. Like supermarkets, large garden centres have such a volume of trade that they are often able to sell at competitive prices.

Contrary to the belief of gardeners who specialize in one or another particular type of plant, many garden centres stock a very wide range, including house plants and plants for the conservatory. Expert advice should be available at garden centres, though this is by no means always so.

Many garden centre plants have been imported from countries with milder climates than ours, or grown in this country in protected conditions. Such plants often have succulent-looking green stems and very lush leaves. If you move a plant from a warm and windproof polytunnel into a draughty, chilly spot in the garden, it will suffer a shock to its system and, at worst, you may lose it.

From nurseries
Some growers are wholesale traders only, but many others will sell direct to the public.

Above Choose tulip bulbs with the crisp, papery outer skin intact.

CHOOSING PLANTS

1 The shrub here is a good specimen with strong, bushy branches and healthy leaves. The root ball just fills the pot.

2 By comparison, this shrub is sickly. Its roots have outgrown the pot and are spiralling in search of food and anchorage.

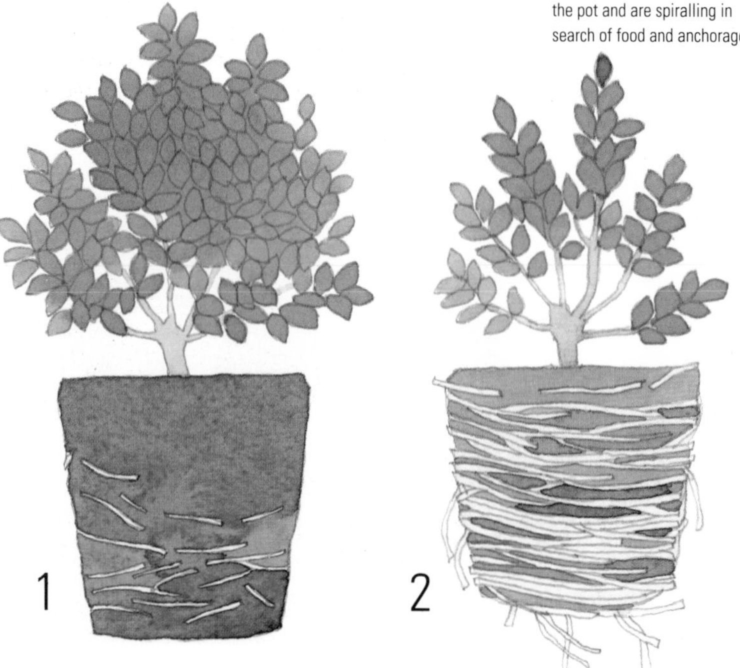

TIPS

- Buy plants that are in bud rather than in flower. Open flowers will probably have fallen by the time you get home.
- Mail order bulb suppliers deal with orders in rotation, so the earlier you can get your order in, the sooner the bulbs will arrive. It is frustrating to have to wait, and planting is less arduous on a sunny September day than in chill November.

Above Plump, healthy bulbs produce good, strong plants.

Many nurseries specialize in one type of plant such as conifers, herbs, alpines or bedding plants, and their plants are often relatively cheap. Small nurseries can be fascinating places to browse in for unusual or rare plants.

A local nursery is a good source for hardy plants as they will probably have been grown in a soil and climate similar to those found in your garden.

From garden societies

Garden societies usually have a 'for sale' or 'swap' table of rare and unusual plants from members' gardens at their meetings. You do not have to be an expert gardener to belong to the Hardy Plant Society, the Cottage Garden Society or the National Council for the Conservation of Plants and Gardens. Many areas have thriving local horticultural societies where you can exchange ideas – most gardeners are generous with their knowledge, advice and even with cuttings and surplus plants – and benefit from bulk buying of fertilizers and composts.

By mail order

Ordering your plants by mail can give you the pleasure of armchair gardening at times when the weather makes gardening impossible and, later on, the excitement of the arrival of a parcel, when you have long ago given up anticipating it.

If you are ordering from an untried source it is wise to place a small order initially as a test of quality. The quality of the plants sent out by mail order companies can vary enormously.

Be ruthless about returning substandard plants and asking for your money back. However, many strong and healthy plants look unpromising in the dormant state in which suppliers send them out. Tell-tale signs to look for are dry and shrivelled roots, soft and rotting stems, and very sparse root systems. Don't plant the poor specimens and wait to see how they do; return them as soon as possible.

The veracity of catalogue descriptions can vary, and caution is needed in interpreting them. This goes for illustrations as well as verbal descriptions: it is notoriously difficult to get accurate flower colour reproduction by cheap printing processes, and the size and density of flowers on a stem is sometimes shown in a misleading fashion. You should always check out the plants that attract you in an impartial plant encyclopaedia before you order.

From other sources

Small local shops sometimes sell a few plants; in our village the greengrocer, the flower shop and the hardware shop all sell plants at lower prices than the nearest big garden centre.

Many of the private gardens which open under the National Gardens Scheme have a plant sales stall and owners are often at hand to give you some tips about the conditions their plants enjoy. The plants, when established in your own garden, will serve as a memento of the visit.

Producing your own plants

The cheapest way to get plants is to grow them yourself, from seeds or cuttings. It takes more years than most people would willingly wait to produce a tree or shrub of any reasonable size from a seed, but for herbaceous plants you need only wait one year, and in some cases plants sown in spring will flower the same summer.

Herbaceous plants can also be increased by division. Large herbaceous plants bought in 2-litre (3½-pint) pots rather than small ones in 9cm (3½in) pots are worth the extra cost as the large plant will split into five or six lesser ones.

For methods of producing plants from seeds and cuttings see Chapter 15, Increase and Multiply.

Right Snowdrops establish best if bought 'in the green', whilst growing, rather than as dry bulbs.

Misleading plant descriptions

Catalogue descriptions are often over-optimistic about the length of flowering season, the rate of growth and the hardiness of the plants listed. It's also as well to be aware of some frequently encountered euphemisms:

- 'Repays careful cultivation' may mean 'weak and disease prone'.
- 'Good rockery plant' may mean 'difficult to keep alive except in the Alps'.
- 'Prefers a warm, dry site' may mean 'will not survive an average winter'.
- 'Easy ground-cover plant' may mean 'aggressive and invasive'.

The plants listed below should come with a warning, but usually don't.

Climbers

The following need more space than is usually recommended. They reach a minimum of 5m (17ft) height and spread. If you plant them on an arch, pergola or porch, they will need annual pruning so severe that it amounts to mutilation.

Actinidia chinensis (Chinese gooseberry, Kiwi fruit) Leaves the size of dinner plates; likes a semi-shaded position.

Clematis montana Spring-flowering, vanilla-scented. Spectacular growing up a large yew tree. On a wall or fence of at least 1.8m (6ft) high it can be trained sideways to hang down from the top like a curtain. *Clematis flammula, C. armandii,* and *C. cirrhosa* var. *balearica* are just as vigorous as *C. montana.*

Jasminum officinale The scented white jasmine will make a tangled mess if not trained as it grows.

Parthenocissus henryana and *P. tricuspidata veitchii* (Virginia creeper) Magnificent scarlet autumn leaves. If you don't have the wall space grow it on a sombre yew, holly or Leyland cypress, or as ground cover tumbling down a bank.

Passiflora caerulea (passion flower) Can be controlled by pruning but looks spectacular if allowed enough space to spread to its full size.

Polygonum baldschuanicum (Russian vine) Sometimes recommended for hiding an unsightly garden shed, it is an aggressively rampant twiner, and will dismantle the average timber shed in a few years.

Vitis Both the fruiting and the ornamental vines need space.

Wisteria A wisteria covering the entire front of a large house is a wonderful sight, and it does need a large house. An additional caution: eventually the trunk will become so thick and stout that it can damage masonry if planted too close to a wall. Plant it at least 60cm (2ft) out from the wall and lean the young stem towards the wire or trellis that will support it.

Some climbers are simply too vigorous for the average small garden, and will soon grow too large: *(above) Jasminum officinale, (below) Actinidia deliciosa* syn. *A. chinensis*, and *(bottom) Passiflora caerulea.*

Shrubs

Some shrubs recommended as 'easy' or as ground cover spread only too rapidly by suckers or shoots above ground, which root as they grow. Less robust neighbouring plants are put at risk. Some of the worst offenders are:

Hypericum calycinum (Rose of Sharon) A good weed-smothering plant for really terrible sites, for example on stony soil in quite dense shade. It has therefore been much used in municipal landscaping. It needs keeping an eye on and digging out if it travels too far.

Kerria japonica Easy and will tolerate shade, which makes it useful. Chop out unwanted suckers.

Rubus tricolor This low-growing decorative bramble gallops along, sending out long, stout prostrate shoots, each of which puts down roots at intervals to make several new plants. Once the roots have taken hold, they are not easy to dig out. Only plant this if you have a really large area to cover. In its favour, it has handsome glossy leaves, smothers weeds and will grow almost anywhere.

Symphoricarpos The snowberry has white or pink berries in winter. Invaluable for poor soil in sun or deep shade, the wild kind spreads far and wide by suckers and is difficult to eliminate. Look for varieties which do not have the suckering habit: *S.* x *doorenbosii* 'Magic Berry', 'Mother of Pearl' and 'White Hedge'.

Plants which spread aggressively and may be a threat to their neighbours: *(above) Symphoricarpos* x *chenaultii* 'Hancock', *(below) Euphorbia amygdaloïdes* var. *robbiae* and *(below right) Lamium galeobdolon* 'Variegatum'.

Herbaceous

Perennial plants which spread by suckers and runners are a problem because, once their roots tangle with those of their neighbours, it is almost impossible to remove them without damaging the neighbour. Others seed themselves rather too generously and the seedlings can be difficult to extract from where they are not wanted. Avoid planting the following invasive plants near more precious ones:

Alchemilla mollis Lady's mantle is so attractive that it seems churlish to include it among the gangsters. But it seeds itself too freely. Don't let it establish itself in paving cracks, as fully grown plants are difficult to remove.

Euphorbia amygdaloïdes var. *robbiae* The euphorbias have flowers of a unique lime-yellow, valuable in *E. a. robbiae* because it thrives in shade and the flowers bring light to gloomy corners. But it will bully other plants, creeping along by underground roots and disturbing their more delicate root systems.

Euphorbia cyparissias This euphorbia is small and delicate in appearance but has a tenacious root system, travelling fast and wide. It is strong enough to dislodge paving slabs.

Lamium galeobdolon 'Variegatum' (*Galeobdolon argentatum*) Yellow, deadnettle flowers above silvery variegated leaves making excellent cover in dry shade under trees, but it should be prevented from spreading too far.

Lysimachia punctata (yellow loosestrife) A cheerful, strong, spreading plant for wilder parts of the garden, especially beside water, but don't let it into beds and borders.

Saponaria officinalis (soapwort) An extract from the leaves is still used for washing delicate fabrics. It has pretty, pale pink flowers and spreads by underground roots, almost impossible to eliminate among other plants. Grow it in its own bed.

Plants to Learn With

Some of the most beautiful garden plants are also the easiest to grow. If you start with a limited range of trustworthy, foolproof plants, you will soon become familiar with the way plants grow and their individual needs.

Choose your 'starter' plants from this chapter. They are easy to grow in average garden soil and many of them are suitable for practising pruning and propagation methods. I have also suggested some easy plants for difficult sites. All the plants listed give good value in the garden, either flowering over a long period or providing a bonus of fruit, autumn colour or evergreen foliage.

In a new garden it is important to establish a long-term framework of trees and shrubs. These bigger, slower-growing plants give a garden its overall structure, provide shelter for other plants, create the frame for a view out of, or a vista within, the garden, and provide the all-important vertical dimension.

Left Amelanchier larmarckii, the snowy mespilus or Canadian shad bush, can be grown as a small tree or large shrub. It has white blossom in spring and brilliant autumn colour.

Below Cotoneaster 'Cornubia', an elegant, spreading small tree with clusters of cream-white flowers in summer and long-lasting red berries in winter.

Trees

If I was only allowed one plant in my garden, it would be a carefully chosen and positioned tree: as it changes through the seasons, a tree encapsulates all the garden's pleasures. It is always interesting to watch, from when the buds unfurl in spring to the winter tracery of twigs against the sky. A newly planted tree changes the character of the garden as it develops over the years.

Siting your tree

Choose a position where the tree has enough space to develop to maturity. Plant books and catalogues often give the height and spread of the trees they list. This can be misleading as it refers to the size after just ten years. The sizes given below are approximate sizes at maturity, but bear in mind that it is difficult to be accurate about the eventual size of a plant: its development depends so much on local soil and climate.

If possible, plant your tree where it can be seen from the house windows, but make sure it will not rob the windows of too much light. Avoid planting a tree too close to your boundary. Your neighbours are legally entitled to remove any branches that overhang their garden, and if they choose to do so it will ruin the shape of your tree.

If you need a shady place to sit in summer, a tree can provide it in due course: work out where the tree's shadow will fall. But if your garden is shaded by buildings or other trees and you value your small patch of sunlight, plant your tree on the north side to minimize the shade it casts.

Choosing a tree

It is worth taking trouble over the choice of trees. Majestic forest trees like beech, oak, ash or lime are not suitable for the average garden. Their roots rob other plants of nourishment, their canopies cast too much shade, and eventually you will probably need to call in the tree surgeon with his chain saw.

Those suggested below are small trees suitable for the garden of an average terraced house and medium-sized trees for medium gardens. They are easy to grow in ordinary soil in a position that is in sun for at least part of the day. Trees for difficult conditions are listed separately. My criteria for trees that give good value are that they should have a graceful or interesting shape and at least two of the following attributes: blossom, fruit or berries, autumn colour and coloured bark or twigs. Where there

TIP

Use a small group of trees to shelter other plants from the wind: the northeast winter wind does most damage, but on exposed sites the prevailing wind is often from the southwest and can also be damaging.

is a choice between similar varieties, I have favoured those with scented flowers. Of course, apple, pear and plum trees are just as ornamental in blossom and fruit as many less useful trees can be; for further listings, see Chapter 16, The Kitchen Garden.

Small trees

Below 8m (25ft) high. The sizes given refer to height x spread:

Amelanchier lamarckii 7x6m (23x20ft) Snowy mespilus or Canadian shadbush. Smothered all over in April with starry white flowers, edible berries ripen from crimson to black in June. Orange and red autumn leaves. Sun or part shade.

Cotoneaster frigidus 'Cornubia' 4x4m (13x13ft) Semi-evergreen, somewhere between a shrub and a tree: spreading and arching branches bear clusters of cream flowers in June and are weighed down in autumn by long-lasting bunches of red berries. Sun or part shade.

Cotoneaster salicifolius 'Rothschildianus' 5x5m (17x17ft) Like *C. frigidus* 'Cornubia' but with creamy-yellow berries. Sun or part shade.

Crataegus laevigata 'Plena' 6x5m (20x16ft) Double-flowered hawthorn. Clusters of scented white flowers in May, small crimson berries (haws). There are also pink ('Rosea Flore Pleno') and red ('Paul's Scarlet') forms. Sun or part shade.

Right *Crataegus monogyna*, the English hawthorn, has white flowers.

Below The pink-flowered form, *Crataegus monogyna* 'Pendula Rosea'.

Crataegus x *lavallei* 7x10m (23x30ft) Glossy leaves held until December, sparse thorns, orange berries throughout winter. Sun or light shade.

Malus I rate crab apples highest of all for small gardens. Traditional cottage garden plants, they are effective in shrub borders, on lawns or at the margin of woodland. Blossom in spring and colourful fruit in autumn. Although sour, the fruit makes good jelly. Sun or part shade.

Malus 'Evereste' 4x4m (13x13ft) Suitable for the smallest garden, can be kept even smaller if the roots are restrained in a tub or large pot. White flowers, orange-red apples.

Malus toringo ssp. *sargentii* 4x4m (13x13ft) Small enough for a balcony. White flowers, flesh-coloured in bud. Fruit like red currants.

Mespilus germanica 6x7m (20x23ft) Medlars form broad umbrellas. White blossom, orange-brown autumn leaves, fruit eaten when rotten.

Pyrus salicifolia 'Pendula' 7x6m (23x20ft) The weeping silver pear. Elegant if the branches are thinned out occasionally. Sun or part shade.

Salix purpurea 'Pendula' 4x3m (13x10ft) A willow with sinuous purplish stems which weep to the ground. Unless you have space, resist the temptation to plant a weeping willow (*Salix* x *sepulcralis chrysocoma* or *S. babylonica*). The graceful little thing will grow (and quickly too) to 12x12m (39x39ft) and more.

WARNING *Willows* (Salix) *and poplars* (Populus) *have invasive roots which travel with great persistence in search of moisture. Avoid planting them near house or boundary walls or close to where drains run underground.*

Sorbus aucuparia The rowan or mountain ash. Robust yet graceful small- to medium-sized trees. Leaves like those of the ash but much smaller. Tiny cream-white flowers in large, flat clusters developing into colourful berries. Sun or part shade.

Sorbus 'Ghose' 5x3m (16x10ft) One of the most compact varieties. Bright red berries remain on the branches till late autumn. Sun or part shade.

Sorbus x *hostii* 3.5x2.5m (11x8ft) Miniature whitebeam. Serrated leaves with grey undersides, pink flower clusters and orange berries. Sun or part shade.

Sorbus sargentiana 6x6m (20x20ft) Red-brown sticky buds all winter on stout stems. Large heads of orange berries, flaming autumn leaves. Sun or part shade.

Sorbus vilmorinii 5x4m (16x13ft) Branches of feathery leaves and pink berries arch elegantly. Sun or part shade.

Medium-sized trees
8-12m (26-40ft):

Acer rufinerve 10x7m (30x23ft) One of the snake-bark maples, grey-green bark with pinkish-white stripes, leaves red and orange in autumn. Sun or light shade.

Aesculus indica 12x10m (40x30ft) A horse-chestnut of manageable size with pinkish flowers in early summer, smooth 'conkers' and red or yellow leaves in autumn. Sun or light shade.

Betula utilis var. *jacquemontii* 12x6m (40x20ft) A tall, graceful Himalayan birch with dazzling white bark and yellow autumn colour. Stunning in winter specially if planted where the sun catches the white trunk. Sun or shade.

Crataegus crus-galli 8x10m (26x30ft) Cockspur thorn, a tree of character, broad and flat-topped, comparatively large white flowers, scarlet autumn leaves, red haws lasting into the new year. Vicious thorns. Sun or part shade.

Laburnum x *watereri* 'Vossii' 10x8m (30x25ft) Dense clusters up to 30cm (1ft) long of slightly scented, yellow pea flowers hang in profusion from the branches from late May to early June.The gracefully arching branches give the tree a Japanese look. No wonder it is in every suburban garden since it is beautiful (provided the usual combination with mauve-red lilac is avoided) and easy to grow. Laburnum's flexible branches respond to training over arches and tunnels. Makes an attractive small avenue for formal gardens. Sun or part shade.

WARNING The pollen-pods of laburnum are poisonous, so do not plant it where children will play.

Malus coronaria 'Charlottae' 9x9m (30x30ft) Large, scented, semi-double shell-pink flowers on a broad head. The round, green-yellow fruit is not particularly attractive but the leaves turn orange and yellow in autumn.

Malus x *zumi* 'Golden Hornet' 8x7m (26x23ft) White flowers. Its heavy crop of golden-yellow apples stay on the tree until December.

Malus 'John Downie' 8x6m (26x20ft) White flowers, pink in bud on a tree which arches gracefully when mature, especially when weighted down with golden apples flushed with red. They are the prettiest of all crab apples and make the best jelly.

Malus x *moerlandsii* 'Liset' 8x7m (26x23ft) Deep crimson flowers, small ox-blood red apples, purplish leaves. Similar to 'Profusion' but more resistant to the disease of scab.

Malus x *robusta* 'Red Sentinel' 12x10m (40x30ft) One of the best. The heavy crop of glossy bright red fruit remains on the tree until March, causing the branches to arch gracefully. White flowers.

Prunus avium 'Plena' 12x12m (40x40ft) Double form of the native Gean, or wild cherry. Almost too big to include, but lovely for a wild garden. Clouds of pendulous white blossoms in April, reddish leaves in autumn. Sun.

Prunus 'Pandora' 8x7m (26x23ft) Shell-pink cherry blossom covers the branches in March. The new leaves are bronze in spring and purple-red in autumn. Sun.

Prunus sargentii 10x15m (30x45ft) Bronze-red young leaves open as the clear pink flowers fade. Brightest and earliest flame-coloured autumn colour. Sun.

Prunus x *yedoensis* 9x10m (30x30ft) Profuse, scented, single blush-white flowers on gracefully arching branches. The leaves sometimes colour well in autumn. Sun.

Pyrus communis 'Beech Hill' 10x7m (30x22ft) Pear blossom in spring, orange and red leaves in autumn, small brown fruit. Sun.

Below left *Prunus avium* 'Plena', the double-flowered Gean, or wild cherry, is one of the loveliest of spring-flowering trees.

Below centre *Prunus sargentii* has a long season of interest and colours beautifully in autumn.

Below *Prunus* 'Pandora', an early-flowering hybrid cherry with strongly ascending branches.

Above *Malus* 'John Downie', one of the best fruiting crab apples, bears large, bright orange-red fruits in autumn.

Above right *Malus* x *zumi* 'Golden Hornet' produces yellow fruits that often persist into winter.

Salix daphnoïdes 8x7m (25x22ft) A willow with violet-purple stems covered in white bloom and catkins in early spring. Fast-growing, it can be allowed to grow naturally as a tree or stooled to produce stems for winter effect. Like all willows it looks good beside water. Sun.

Sorbus aria 'Lutescens' 12x8m (40x25ft) Whitebeam with large, downy leaves, silvery-white when young. Opening leaf buds look like magnolia flowers. Whitish flower clusters, orange-red berries. Sun or part shade.

Sorbus cashmiriana 9 x 9m (30 x 30ft) Fern-like leaves turn red in autumn. Pale pink flowers, white or pale pink, long-lasting berries. Sun or part shade.

Sorbus commixta 'Embley' 12x9m (40x30ft) Red berries, vivid autumn colour. Sun or part shade.

Sorbus hupehensis 12x8m (40x25ft) Soft blue-green leaves turn red or orange in autumn. White flowers and berries. Sun or part shade.

Sorbus 'Joseph Rock' 8x6m (25x20ft) In autumn creamy-yellow berries contrast with orange-red leaves. Sun or part shade.

Trees for difficult sites

CHALKY SOIL *Amelanchier*, *Caragana*, *Crataegus laevigata (oxyacantha)*, *Laburnum*, *Malus*, *Pyrus*, *Sorbus aria*.

HEAVY CLAY *Crataegus*, *Laburnum*, *Malus*, *Prunus*, *Pyrus*, *Sorbus*.

SANDY, DRY SOIL *Betula* (birch), *Caragana*, *Robinia*, *Salix daphnoïdes* (violet willow).

COLD, EXPOSED SITES *Crataegus*, *Laburnum*, *Sorbus*.

SHADE *Caragana*, *Crataegus*, *Sorbus*.

SEASIDE (SALT RESISTANT) *Crataegus*, *Salix*, *Sorbus aria*.

SOIL CONSOLIDATED BY BUILDERS' ACTIVITIES (conditions often to be found in the gardens of newly built or recently renovated houses) *Crataegus*, *Prunus avium*, *Salix*, *Sorbus*.

Below *Sorbus commixta* 'Embley' colours reliably in autumn and bears a profusion of small, orange-red fruits.

Below right *Sorbus* 'Joseph Rock' is noted for its autumn colour and creamy yellow fruits that turn golden-amber when ripe.

Shrubs

Evergreen shrubs

When you are planning a garden it is tempting to think only in terms of flowers and colourful foliage. But a proportion of shrubs chosen for their evergreen leaves adds to the interest of the garden in winter, permanently hides unsightly features and provides a sober background for more colourful plants. Many of the following selection, listed alphabetically, have the bonus of flowers and/or fruit.

Left Holly *(Ilex aquifolium)*, an easy evergreen for sun or shade, grows slowly and eventually forms a tall tree.

FOR SUNNY SITES

Berberis x *stenophylla* 2.5x2m (8x7ft) There are lots of berberis varieties to choose from, evergreen and deciduous, easy to please. They are all very prickly. For a stock-proof and vandal-proof hedge, *Berberis* x *stenophylla* quickly forms an impenetrable thorny thicket. The branches arch elegantly at the tips and in spring are wreathed with countless golden-yellow, scented flowers.

Brachyglottis Dunedin Hybrids Group 'Sunshine' (*Senecio* 'Sunshine') 1x1.5m (3x5ft) Large, rounded silver-grey leaves make a good textural contrast with lavender and santolina, and it likes similar conditions.

Buxus sempervirens Various sizes. Box grows wild throughout Europe. Dense shoots of fresh-looking small green leaves. Excellent growing naturally, edging beds and knot gardens, or clipped into balls, pyramids or peacocks.

Choisya ternata 2x2m (7x7ft) Mexican orange blossom. White scented flowers appear in April and May and continue spasmodically until winter. The leaves, aromatic when crushed, retain a glossy freshness all the year round. Choisyas develop slowly into dense, rounded shrubs. They need shelter from winter winds to avoid frost damage to the leaves. The golden-leaved form looks sickly.

Cistus x *corbariensis* 1x1.5m (3x5ft) Like most plants from the Mediterranean area, cistuses grow in the poorest soil, but must have good drainage and plenty of sun. The flowers last only a day but come thick and fast in June and July, with occasional blooms later. A spreading, rounded bush. Matt-textured, dark green leaves on red stems. Smothered in May and June with red-tinged buds opening into single, white, tissue-paper flowers with a yellow blotch at the base of each petal.

Cistus laurifolius 1.5x1m (5x3ft) is one of the hardiest, forming an open bush. Large, leathery leaves, white flowers about 5cm (2in) wide with prominent yellow stamens.

Cotoneaster congestus 15x120cm (6x48in) One of the prettiest of the prostrate cotoneasters. It creeps along the ground and over rocks making a dense carpet of tiny, glossy leaves. Small pale pink flowers in June, small red berries. As with most cotoneasters, the flowers are much visited by bees.

Cotoneaster lacteus 3x2.5m (10x8ft) Dense. Pendulous twigs, oval dark green leaves with grey undersides. Clusters of creamy flowers in summer, plentiful red berries lasting well into the winter.

Elaeagnus x *ebbingei* 4x2.5m (13x8ft) Fast-growing, well known to landscapers but not much used in gardens. Smooth-edged leaves grey-green above and silvery below, giving overall, soft, grey-green effect. The white flowers are hardly noticeable but in October and November they scent the air with vanilla.

Elaeagnus pungens 'Maculata' 3x2m (10x7ft) Slowly reaches 3m (10ft). Allow at least 2m (7ft) diameter for spreading. The best evergreen with yellow variegation, the centre of each leaf brushed with soft, buttery yellow. From afar it gives a sunlit effect on dull winter days.

Euonymus fortunei Emerald Gaiety 25x80cm (9x30in) Weed-smothering ground cover and cheerful winter colour, this and *E. f.* Emerald 'n' Gold are invaluable. Broad, creamy-white leaf margins, they appear prettily tinged with pink in frosty weather.

Ilex aquifolium Holly grows into a tree 20m (70ft) tall, but very slowly. As shrubs, the green kinds are slightly faster and easier to grow than those with variegated leaves, reaching 2.5-3m (8-10 ft) in about ten years. Any soil except very wet or very dry sites. Grow holly as a stock- and vandal-proof hedge, clip it into formal architectural shapes and, if the birds don't get all the berries first, deck the halls at Christmas. The varieties 'J.C. Van Tol' and 'Pyramidalis' produce berries when planted alone but others,

TIP

Some grey-leaved shrubs *(Senecio, Santolina)* have rather brassy yellow flowers. Clip over with shears to remove the buds before they flower, and to keep the plants compact.

Right Elaeagnus pungens 'Maculata', a large, variegated evergreen shrub with soft yellow colouring. Easy and deservedly popular.

Right Pyracantha 'Soleil d'Or'. Pyracanthas have white flowers in summer and spectacular berries in autumn.

Below Choisya ternata, a dense and shapely evergreen shrub with glossy, aromatic leaves and white flowers over a long period.

including common holly, should have one male tree planted with one or more female to ensure a good crop.

Juniperus x *media* 'Pfitzeriana' 1x2.5m (3x8ft) Very tough conifer. Wide-spreading branches, pendulous young shoots. A graceful, sculptural plant of soft grey-green texture. The yellowish form, 'Pfitzeriana Aurea', is slower growing.

Lavandula angustifolia 1x1m (3x3ft) Old English lavender. Hummocks of silver-grey narrow leaves, spikes of blue-mauve flowers. Both flowers and leaves are scented. Must have sun. Clip over yearly after flowering to keep it from sprawling (see Chapter 10, Pruning). 'Hidcote' is compact with rich purple-blue flowers. Pink- and white-flowered varieties are less hardy.

Pyracantha 3x2.5m (10x8ft) Firethorn. Red, orange or yellow berries make a fine autumn show against glossy dark green leaves. Often trained against house walls, pyracanthas also grow as freestanding shrubs. All varieties have creamy-white, hawthorn-like clusters of flowers in June. 'Alexander Pendula' has weeping branches and coral-red berries, *P. rogersiana* bright red berries, *P. rogersiana* f. *flava* yellow berries.

Rhamnus alaternus 'Argenteovariegatus' 2.5x1.8m (8x6ft) Small grey-green leaves are edged with white; a pretty contrast among plain evergreens.

Rosmarinus officinalis 1.5x1.5m (5x5ft), taller if grown against a wall. One of the best-loved garden plants and one of the most useful kitchen herbs. Dense, spreading bush, upward-pointing, grey-green, spikey leaves all along the stems, aromatic when crushed. Pale mauve flowers in March or April. 'Miss Jessopp's Upright' is a tidy, erect variety.

Santolina pinnata ssp. *neapolitana* 60x120cm (2x4ft) Needs full sun and good drainage but is not fussy about soil. Very fine cut and feathery, whitish-silver foliage. The variety 'Sulphurea' has pale yellow flowers. *Santolina chamaecyparissus* 50x80cm (20x40in) is tighter and more compact.

Viburnum x *burkwoodii* 3x4m (10x13ft) Wonderfully sweet-scented, white flowers from pink buds from March to May (from January in mild winters) in large ball-shaped clusters on an openly branched shrub, with glossy, dark green leaves. Avoid very dry positions and poor soils.

Viburnum tinus 'Eve Price' 2.5x2m (8x7ft) One of the most useful evergreen shrubs. Dark green leaves, dense enough for an informal hedge or screen. Clusters of pink and white flowers from November to March or April.

FOR SHADY SITES

All those listed above, except *Cistus*, *Lavandula*, *Rosmarinus* and *Santolina*, will thrive in light shade under trees with fairly open canopies or in the shade cast by trees or buildings, provided they are in sun for part of the day. The following also thrive in those conditions:

Mahonia x *media* 'Charity' 1.8x1.5m (6x5ft) and *Mahonia japonica*. Scented yellow flowers in winter, in spectacular long, arching spikes. Handsome, upright plants, dramatically large deeply cut leaves. *M.* x *wagneri* 'Undulata' (1.8x1.2m) is more bushy with yellow flowers in spring.

Osmanthus x *burkwoodii* 2x2m (7x7ft) Small, smooth, pointed leaves. Slow growing. Plant it for its compact shape and elegant little tubular white flowers, in April and May, deliciously scented.

Prunus laurocerasus Various sizes. Laurels, depressing components of dripping, overgrown driveways, are useful where little else will survive. Exceptional variety: 'Zabeliana' 1.2x3m (4x10ft). Low, spreading shrub, narrow glossy leaves, numerous bottle-brush spikes of white flowers in April and May. Excellent weed-smotherer.

Skimmia japonica 1x1m (3x3ft) Tidy mounds of shiny green leaves, clusters of small scented flowers in spring. In its female form, 'Veitchii' ('Foremanii'), the cream-white flowers develop into brilliant red berries retained all winter. To ensure fruit, plant one male, 'Rubella', to pollinate up to three females. 'Rubella' has crimson flower buds in winter.

In complete shade, the following evergreen shrubs (described above) will succeed: *Buxus sempervirens*, *Elaeagnus* x *ebbingei*, *Euonymus fortunei*, *Ilex aquifolium*, *Prunus laurocerasus*, *Skimmia*.

Evergreen shrubs for difficult sites

CHALKY SOIL *Berberis*, *Choisya*, *Cistus*, *Elaeagnus*, *Escallonia*, *Euonymus*, *Ilex*, *Osmanthus*, *Prunus laurocerasus*, *Pyracantha*, *Rosmarinus*, *Santolina*, *Senecio*, *Viburnum*.

HEAVY CLAY SOIL *Berberis*, *Choisya*, *Cotoneaster*, *Osmanthus*, *Prunus laurocerasus*, *Pyracantha*, *Viburnum*.

SANDY SOIL *Berberis*, *Cistus*, *Cotoneaster*, *Elaeagnus*, *Lavandula*, *Rosmarinus*, *Senecio*.

COLD, EXPOSED SITES *Berberis*, *Cotoneaster*, *Elaeagnus*, *Euonymus*.

SEASIDE *Choisya*, *Cotoneaster*, *Elaeagnus* x *ebbingei*, *Escallonia*, *Pyracantha*, *Rosmarinus*, *Senecio*, *Viburnum tinus*.

CONSOLIDATED SOIL *Cotoneaster*, *Prunus laurocerasus*.

Above Skimmia japonica 'Rubella', male, in the foreground; *Skimmia japonica* 'Veitchii' ('Foremanii'), female.

Deciduous shrubs

Flowering shrubs give the best value of all garden plants. Roses, the best loved of all shrubs, are listed separately in Chapter 19, Growing Roses. Shrubs with edible fruit include currants and gooseberries; they are listed in Chapter 16, The Kitchen Garden. The following are reliable shrubs, flowering either early, before the main flowering period of herbaceous plants and roses, or late in the season. I have chosen shrubs with a bonus, such as scent or autumn colour in addition to flowers.

EARLY FLOWERING SHRUBS

Chaenomeles japonica Flowering quince. 1x2m (3x6ft). Flowers like large apple blossoms in a colour range from white to orange-red, March or earlier, lasting till May. Golden edible quinces, sour but good for jelly.

Spiraea thunbergii 90x120cm (3x4ft) *Spiraea* 'Arguta' (bridal wreath) is grown more often, but *S. thunbergii* is more compact and flowers earlier. Slender, arching branches smothered in small white flowers, March to April. Delicate pale green leaves appear as early as February and stay till late autumn. Needs sun.

Viburnum x *bodnantense* 'Deben' 3x2m (10x7ft) Quick-growing. Fragrant, frost-resistant white flowers from pink buds November to April. Kept smaller by pruning.

LATE SPRING FLOWERING SHRUBS

Cytisus x *praecox* 1.2x1.5m (4x5ft) Warminster broom, spectacular in May with green

Above Syringa 'Souvenir de Louis Spaeth' has well-scented, dark red-purple flowers in long slender panicles; justifiably popular, not least because it is so reliable in flowering.

branches arched with the weight of profuse cream flowers. 'Albus' has white flowers, 'Allgold' bright yellow. Must have sun.

Syringa 3x3m (10x10ft) Lilac, often confused with *Philadelphus* (mock orange). Most lilacs only flower for three weeks in May or early June but are much loved for the scent of their showy pyramids of bloom. Not all are scented; choose from these scented, free-flowering varieties: 'Firmament', mauve-blue, early May; 'Katherine Havemeyer', purple-mauve, mid-May; 'Congo', dark red-pink, mid-May; 'Madame Lemoine', white, late May.

Viburnum plicatum 'Mariesii' 1.8x2m (6x7ft) In May, broad, flat heads of white flowers cover horizontally tiered branches. In autumn the leaves turn reddish purple. Not for very dry soil.

LATE SUMMER/AUTUMN FLOWERING SHRUBS

Buddleja davidii 3x3m (10x10ft) Fast-growing, open and arching scented shrub loved by butterflies. Flowers in long, tapering plumes from July to October. Choose from deep violet 'Black Knight', violet-blue 'Empire Blue', 'Royal Red' and 'White Profusion'.

Colutea arborescens 2.5x2m (8x7ft) Bladder senna. Light green pinnate leaves always look fresh. Yellow pea-flowers, June to September. The bladder senna has dramatic inflated seed pods. Children love to pop them.

Hypericum 'Hidcote' 1.5x1.5m (5x5ft) A dome of almost evergreen leaves smothered from June to October in golden-yellow, saucer-shaped flowers. Sun.

Spartium junceum 3x2m (10x7ft) Spanish broom. The flowers, which appear from June till August, smell of honey. Sun.

Deciduous shrubs for difficult sites

CHALKY SOIL *Berberis, Buddleja, Colutea, Cotoneaster, Hypericum, Philadelphus, Potentilla, Spartium, Spiraea, Syringa, Viburnum.*

HEAVY CLAY SOIL *Berberis, Chaenomeles, Cornus, Cotoneaster, Hypericum, Philadelphus, Potentilla, Salix, Spiraea, Syringa, Viburnum.*

SANDY SOIL *Berberis, Cotoneaster, Cytisus, Genista, Hypericum, Potentilla, Spartium.*

COLD, EXPOSED SITES *Berberis, Buddleja, Chaenomeles, Cornus, Cotoneaster, Philadelphus, Potentilla, Salix, Spiraea, Viburnum.*

SEASIDE *Berberis, Buddleja, Colutea, Fuchsia, Hypericum, Salix, Spartium.*

CONSOLIDATED SOIL *Buddleja, Colutea, Cornus, Cotoneaster, Hypericum, Philadelphus, Potentilla, Salix, Spiraea, Viburnum.*

Right Prunus laurocerasus 'Otto Luyken', an invaluable plant for ground cover under trees.

Far right Viburnum plicatum 'Mariesii' has an elegantly tiered habit of growth.

If you are new to gardening, you will be hoping for quick results: get them by starting with annuals and perennials which give a fine display of flower and foliage in the first season.

Buy perennials in large sizes and split them up to make several plants.

Perennials for sunny sites

WINTER FLOWERING

Aubrieta 15x50cm (6x18in) Cottage garden favourite. Grows anywhere given sun and good drainage, even in the crevices of walls. Dense cushion of neat little grey-green leaves. Flowers from March until June in shades from blue-mauve to red-purple.

Bergenia x *schmidtii* 30x60cm (1x2ft) Weed-smothering foliage plants for sun or partial shade in almost any soil. Evergreen, elephant's ear leaves, some colouring purple or crimson in winter. *B.* x *schmidtii* flowers from February, others bloom in April. The flowers have a tropical, waxy look and are held in sprays on stout fleshy stems. *B.* x *schmidtii*'s flowers are clear pink, the leaves a fresh green. *B.* 'Abendglut' ('evening glow') is also early, with deep magenta-crimson flowers and leaves that are maroon in winter.

Iris unguicularis (formerly called *I. stylosa*) Height 20cm (8in). Scented mauve flowers October to March. Plant in clumps in poor, dry soil at the foot of a sunny wall. They may not flower for the first year or two, but don't give up on them.

SPRING FLOWERING

Aubrieta See above.

Bergenia See above.

Doronicum plantagineum 'Excelsum' 90x60cm (3x2ft). Bright yellow daisies held elegantly above bright green, heart-shaped leaves. 'Miss Mason' is shorter at 45cm (18in). Doronicums grow in shade or sun.

Euphorbia polychroma 50x50cm (20x20in). A rounded dome of glowing lime-yellow bracts for several weeks.

Left *Euphorbia polychroma*, a spring-flowering perennial giving colour for many weeks. A good colour contrast to forget-me-nots.

Above Perennials with contrasting colour and form for midsummer: blue *Campanula lactiflora* and the yellow daisy, *Anthemis tinctoria* 'E.C. Buxton'.

Iberis sempervirens 25x50cm (9x20in) Candytuft. A dense mat of narrow, dark, evergreen leaves covered in April and May with flat heads of chalk-white flowers. Happy in poor, stony soil.

Pulsatilla vulgaris 30x30cm (1x1ft). The pasque flower, one of the loveliest British natives. Anemone flowers of soft mauve-purple above clumps of fine-cut ferny leaves. The buds are surrounded with silky filaments, the seedheads are fluffy, feathery, pale grey. There are also pink and red forms.

EARLY TO MIDSUMMER FLOWERING

Achillea 'Moonshine' 60x45cm (24x18in). Flat heads of bright yellow flowers above evergreen, silvery-green, feathery leaves. *A.* 'Taygetea' has flowers of softer, sulphur yellow, and less silvery leaves.

Aquilegia 60-90x45cm (24-36x18in) Columbine, granny's bonnet. Shade or sun. The long-spurred flowers of the McKana Hybrids and the tightly fluted Granny's bonnets of *A. vulgaris* are both fascinating and beautiful. Sea-green leaves, elegantly rounded and divided. The usual colour range is violet, pink and plum. Long-spurred hybrids are often bi-coloured with yellow, red and white added. All-white aquilegias are worth seeking out.

Campanula lactiflora 'Prichard's Variety' 120x60cm (4x2ft). Dense heads of mauve-blue bell-shaped flowers at the top of leafy upright stems over a long period. 'Loddon Anna' is wishy-washy pink. 'Pouffe' is low-growing (45x45cm, 18x18in), pale blue. Good companions for old roses. *C. persicifolia*

Above Aubrieta. The aubretias are usually sold as named cultivars, and are available in single or double-flowered forms, with a colour range from white through many shades of pink to deep purple. All are easy to grow.

Above centre Coreopsis verticillata provides colour in a sunny border from midsummer to early autumn.

Above right Rock roses *(Helianthemum)* are available in huge variety; most are hybrids with grey or grey-green leaves, with colours ranging from white through to dark red.

90x30cm (3x1ft) has rosettes of slender leaves and wiry stems from which blue or white bell-flowers hang.

Coreopsis verticillata 50x30cm (20x12in). Masses of golden yellow daisies from June till September. Finely divided leaves. *C. v.* 'Moonbeam' is shorter (45cm/18in) with creamy-yellow flowers.

Dianthus From 30x40cm (12x15in) to almost prostrate. Much-loved cottage garden plants, pinks make dense mats of evergreen spikey blue-grey foliage. Reliable scented varieties include 'Doris' (30cm/1ft, shrimp pink with a red eye), 'White Ladies' (30cm/1ft, double white) and 'Musgrave's White' (15cm/6in, single white). Highland Hybrids 25x30cm (9x12in) are covered with smaller, single flowers in shades from deep pink to white, with dark red centres.

Geranium Hardy geraniums, not to be confused with the red, pink or white geraniums used in summer bedding schemes, tubs and window-boxes – those are pelargoniums. True geraniums (cranesbills) are invaluable ground cover for sun or partial shade. *G. endressii* 45x60cm (18x24in) has fresh green leaves with bright pink flowers all summer. *G.* 'Johnson's Blue' 45x45cm (18x18in) has large flowers of soft but glowing mauve-blue, and *G. renardii* 30x30cm (1x1ft) has quiet mauve-white flowers on a low dome of beautiful deep-veined sage-green leaves. Others worth growing include varieties of *G. sanguinem*, the bloody cranesbill, and *G. pratense*, the meadow cranesbill. Good companions for roses, and long-flowering.

Helianthemum (rock rose) 15x30cm (6x12in) Shrubby carpeting plants to grow among rocks, in paving cracks, on walls and as edging. The small narrow leaves vary from dark green to silver-grey, and the flowers come in sunset shades from pale yellows and pinks to brick and crimson.

Iris germanica There are hundreds of varieties of bearded iris in almost any colour you can think of. From 25cm to 1.5m (9in to 5ft), the taller kinds flower later than the short ones. Where there is space, plant them in a separate iris border.

Nepeta x *faassenii* 45x45cm (18x18in). Catmint's bushy, soft-textured grey leaves and sprays of lavender flowers are a wonderful foil to other plants of almost any colouring. It flowers throughout June and later. If cut back by half when the first flowers fade, it will go on until September. *Nepeta* 'Six Hills Giant' 90x90cm (3x3ft) is twice as big in all its parts.

Salvia x *sylvestris* 'Mainacht' ('May Night') 90x45cm (36x18in) Spikes of intense violet-blue-hooded, lipped flowers over clumps of crepe-textured sage-like foliage.

Stachys byzantina (*S. lanata*, *S. olympica*) 30x60cm (1x2ft). Bunnies' ears or lambs' tongues make dense mats of evergreen woolly grey leaves, an excellent foil to other plants, for edging beds and for ground cover between shrubs. Small mauve flowers are borne on woolly white spikes. 'Silver Carpet' 15x60cm (6x24in) is a tidy, non-flowering variety.

Thymus Thyme, the familiar tiny-leaved aromatic herb with white, mauve-pink or crimson flowers, is as versatile in the garden as it is in the kitchen, provided it has good drainage. Planted in the cracks between paving stones it will soften the hard lines of a patio. The lowest-growing kinds are *T. serpyllum albus* (2.5cm/1in, white), *coccineus* (2.5cm/1in, crimson) and *T. pseudolanuginosus* (5cm/2in, grey-green woolly leaves). Planted 10-15cm (4-6in) apart, thymes will knit together to form a carpet that can be walked on, or a scented bank on which to recline.

Veronica austriaca ssp. *teucrium* 'Royal Blue', 'Crater Lake Blue' 45x30cm (18x12in). One of the few true blue flowers without a hint of mauve. Individually tiny, they clothe the upright stems densely, giving an impression of pure, strong colour.

TIPS

- A dome of chicken wire placed over catmint will prevent cats from rolling in the plant, and will be invisible when the foliage grows through.
- Columbines seed themselves freely, so if you are not too thorough with the weeding, you can increase your stock with no effort. They can be naturalized in grass under trees.

LATE SUMMER TO EARLY AUTUMN FLOWERING

Aster x *frikartii* 'Mönch' 75x45cm (30x18in) Many Michaelmas daisies need spraying against mildew but this one is healthy and long in flower. Clear lavender-blue daisy-flowers with yellow centres on strong stems. Similar but shorter is *Aster thomsonii* 'Nanus' 45x20cm (18x8in). *Aster turbinellus* 120x60cm (4x2ft) is also disease-resistant, and has violet-blue flowers on airy stems.

Eryngium alpinum 75x45cm (30x18in). Sea holly. Thistly cone-shaped flowers surrounded by fine-cut spikey collars. *E. alpinum*'s and *E.* x *oliverianum*'s flowers and bracts are metallic purplish-blue. *E.* x *tripartitum* has numerous, small, darker blue flower-heads.

Geranium x *riversleainum* 'Russell Prichard' 25x90cm (9x36in). Weed-smotherer with long flowering season. Clear pink flowers on a mat of greyish green leaves.

Geranium wallichianum 'Buxton's Variety' 30x90cm (1x3ft). Another that keeps on flowering. Clear blue flowers with broad white centres, dark stamens.

Hemerocallis (day lily) 45-90cm (18-36in) Plant 45cm (18in) apart. Strap-shaped, arching light green leaves, handsome from spring onwards. Trumpet-shaped flowers ranging from yellow and pale apricot to dark brick-red and maroon.

Scabiosa caucasica 60x60cm (2x2ft). 'Clive Greaves' is mauvish-blue, 'Miss Willmott' creamy white. Lightly frilled scabious flowers with pin-cushion centres on long bare stems. Exceptionally long flowering season.

Sedum spectabile 'Brilliant' 45x45cm (18x18in). Fleshy grey-green leaves, handsome in their own right. Flat heads of fluffy dark pink flowers. *Sedum* 'Vera Jameson' 25x25cm (9x9in) has purple leaves with a grape-like bloom and dusky pink flowers.

Perennials for shady sites

Of the plants listed above, the following will grow in partly shaded positions: *Bergenia*, *Campanula*, *Doronicum*, *Geranium*, *Hemerocallis*, *Salvia*, *Sedum*, *Veronica*. Those listed below tolerate full shade.

WINTER FLOWERING

Helleborus niger, 30x30cm (1x1ft). The white Christmas rose is first to flower, from December to March. Then the Lenten rose *H. orientalis* 45x45cm (18x18in), in January or February, with shades from white to plum purple. Next is pale green *H. foetidus* (stinking hellebore) 45x45cm (18x18in), then *H. corsicus* 60x90cm (2x3ft), with green flowers and handsome grey-green leaves.

SPRING FLOWERING

Lamium maculatum 15x30cm (6x12in). Compact creeping dead-nettles with a central silver stripe on each leaf. *L. m. album* has white flowers, *L. m. roseum* pale pink flowers. On 'White Nancy' and 'Beacon Silver', the leaves are silvered up to the margins.

Polygonatum x *hybridum* (*P. multiflorum*) 90x30cm (3x1ft). Solomon's seal has graceful arching stems of glossy, ribbed leaves. In late spring green-tinged tubular white flowers hang down all along each stem.

Below *Scabiosa caucasica* flowers all summer and autumn.

Below centre *Hemerocallis* 'Linda', one of the many day lilies available.

Primula vulgaris 15x15cm (6x6in). The delicate wild primrose is hard to beat for informal planting under shrubs.

Pulmonaria 20-30x30cm (8-12x12in) Lungwort. Dense clumps of lance-like leaves make invaluable ground cover. *P. saccharata* has broad leaves blotched with creamy white; the flowers turn from pink to blue as they age. *P. officinalis* 'Sissinghurst White' has leaves spotted with pale green and white flowers.

Above *Sedum spectabile*, attractive to butterflies.

EARLY TO MIDSUMMER FLOWERING

Ajuga Semi-evergreen ground cover, spreading by runners. Upright spikes of blue bugle

Above Helleborus niger, the Christmas rose.

flowers. *A. pyramidalis* 'Metallica Crispa' 15x45cm (6x18in) has crimped, metallic bronzed leaves. *A. reptans* 'Atropurpurea' 15x45cm (6x18in) has rosettes of shiny dark purple leaves. 'Jungle Beauty' has taller (25cm/10in) spikes of intense blue flowers.

Alchemilla mollis 15x60cm (6x24in) Lady's mantle. A beautiful plant that will grow almost anywhere. Rounded, velvety pale green leaves and a foam of tiny lime-yellow flowers. Seeds itself freely, so remove the stems before they set seed where they are not wanted.

Below Primula vulgaris, primrose.

Brunnera macrophylla 45x60cm (18x24in) After the sprays of bright blue forget-me-not flowers are over the matt heart-shaped leaves grow big and make good ground cover. The variegated forms, 'Variegata' and 'Hadspen Cream' need shelter and moist soil.

Geranium macrorrhizum 'Ingwersen's Variety' 30x60cm (1x2ft) A trusty weed smotherer, soft pink flowers, semi-evergreen, rounded light green leaves which turn bronze and scarlet in autumn. *G. m.* 'Album' has blush-white flowers.

Saxifraga x *urbium* 30cm (1ft), with indefinite spread. London pride's evergreen rosettes make imperturbable ground cover. In May and June they are covered in a mist of tiny star-shaped, pink-white flowers.

Tiarella cordifolia 15x30cm (6x12in) Evergreen ground cover for moist shade, spreading by runners. Handsome pale green maple-shaped leaves, in early summer the plants foam with numerous spikes of little white flowers. In winter the leaf veins turn red-bronze.

LATE SUMMER TO EARLY AUTUMN FLOWERING

Anemone x *hybrida* 150x60cm (5x2ft) Japanese anemones. Handsome in leaf, beautiful in flower and trouble-free. Can be slow to get started. 'Honorine Jobert' has white flowers, and *A. hupehensis* 'September Charm' pink.

Hosta Handsome leaves, ribbed, twisted or undulating, grey, green or variegated with yellow, cream or white. Spikes of white or pale mauve flowers. *H. sieboldiana* var. 'Elegans' 80x90cm (32x36in) has huge ribbed blue-grey leaves and pale lilac-coloured flowers. The leaves of *H. fortunei* var. *albopicta* 45x60cm (18x24in) are butter-yellow, edged with green in spring. *H.* 'Royal Standard' has plain green leaves and scented white flowers. Hostas must have moist soil. Protect from slugs.

Perennials for difficult sites

CHALKY SOIL *Achillea*, *Bergenia*, *Doronicum*, irises, *Salvia* x *sylvestris*, *Scabiosa caucasica*, *Veronica spicata*.

SANDY SOIL *Acanthus spinosus*, *Centranthus ruber*, *Eryngium*, *Foeniculum vulgare* 'Purpureum', *Nepeta* x *faassenii*, *Origanum vulgare* 'Aureum', *Papaver orientale*.

HEAVY CLAY *Aruncus dioicus*, *Filipendula ulmaria*, *Iris laevigata*, *Lythrum*, *Primula florindae*, *Primula japonica*, *Trollius*.

SEASIDE *Anaphalis margaritacea*, *Artemisia*, *Eryngium*, *Geranium sanguinem*, irises, lupins, *Phormium tenax*.

Annuals and biennials

Annuals flower and then die in the same year that the seeds are sown, biennials in the following year. They are often referred to as bedding plants and can be bought in trays or as individual plants at garden centres or local flower shops and greengrocers. But it is cheaper and more fun to raise your own, and if your crop fails, there is still time to go out and buy plants. F1 hybrid seeds, specially bred for uniformity and vigour, are the most reliable.

If you can find them, buy packets of single colours rather than mixed and plant them out in bold groups. Those listed here are easy to grow: follow the instructions on the seed packet. Many annuals and biennials have familiar English names: an indication of their popularity over the centuries.

Peas, beans and many other vegetables are annuals or biennials and can be grown either in a separate vegetable plot, in mixed beds and borders, or in containers; see Chapter 16, The Kitchen Garden.

Annuals for sunny sites

Alyssum maritimum (correct name *Lobularia maritima*) 8-15x20-30cm (3-6x8-12in) Alyssum makes a carpet smothered in honey-scented white, pink or red-purple flowers from June to September. It will grow in walls and paving and among rocks. Once in your garden, it keeps going from year to year by self-sowing.

Antirrhinum majus ssp. *linkianum* Approx. 45x45cm (18x18in) Snapdragon. A perennial treated as an annual, cottage garden plant and childhood favourite. 'Black Prince', velvety blood-red flowers, leaves suffused with dark crimson; 'Yellow Monarch', bright clear yellow; the flowers of 'White Wonder' have a touch of yellow at the throat. Different suppliers have different named varieties in these colours and red, pink and lavender-pink. Also multi-coloured kinds, from tall to dwarf.

Borago officinalis 90x30cm (3x1ft). Borage, a hairy plant with sprays of blue flowers. The leaves taste like cucumber. Add them with the flowers to long summer drinks, particularly Pimm's No. 1.

Calendula officinalis 60x30cm (2x1ft). Double and multicoloured orange, cream and yellow varieties are available, none with the charm of the traditional pot marigold: large daisy flowers of pure, clear orange. The petals can be added to salads.

Centaurea cyanus 30-90x30cm (1-3x1ft) Cornflower. Now very rare in the wild. Intense blue double flowers on long stems above grey-green leaves. They last well as cut flowers.

Lavatera trimestris 60x45cm (24x15in) Annual mallow. Plenty of large funnel-shaped flowers on upright bushy plants. 'Mont Blanc' is pure white, 'Silver Cup' sugar-pink and 'Pink Beauty' a softer shade of pale pink with darker veining.

Limnanthes douglasii 15x10cm (6x4in) Masses of saucer-shaped white flowers with yolk-yellow centres, hence 'poached egg flower'. Attractive light green ferny leaves. Seeds itself freely, so keep away from other more delicate plants or it will smother them.

Lobelia erinus 10-20x10-15cm (4-8x4-6in) Use the trailing kinds with names like 'Crimson Fountain' and 'White Fountain' or 'Cascade' in containers and hanging baskets. Varieties like 'Cambridge Blue', 'White Lady', 'Rosamund' (purple-red with a white eye) and 'Emperor William' (bright blue), traditionally used as formal edging are also pretty in informal drifts to fill gaps at the front of borders.

WARNING Lobelias are poisonous.

Nemophila menziesii 20x15cm (8x6in) Saucer-shaped flowers, pure sky-blue with white centres. 'Pennie Black' is an unusual and pretty variety, shorter with white-edged black-purple petals. Easy to grow, provided the soil is not allowed to dry out.

Above The nasturtium, *Tropaeolum majus* 'Dwarf Cherry Rose', a form with cerise flowers. Nasturtiums are invaluable plants for poor, stony soils in sunny situations.

Below Mixed sweet alyssum, *Lobularia maritima*, grown en masse in an annual border. Once you have it, it will seed itself year after year.

Above A cultivar of the cornflower, *Centaurea cyanus* 'Blue Baby'.

Above right *Calendula officinalis* 'Geisha Girl', very double with incurved, deep orange petals.

Nigella damascena 45x20cm (18x8in) Love-in-a-mist. Pretty in all its parts. Soft and feathery light green leaves, semi-double flowers surrounded by thread-like green tendrils. Inflated, green, seed pods ripen to buff. 'Miss Jekyll' is sky blue, 'Persian Jewels' are in mixed shades of blue, pink and white. Sow the seeds outdoors in the final position. They will seed themselves thereafter.

Papaver somniferum 75x30cm (30x12in) Opium poppy. Large single and double (peony-flowered) poppies in shades of red, pink, old rose and dusky purple as well as white. The smooth blue-grey leaves and seed pods are decorative, too.

Papaver rhoeas Shirley Series 60x30cm (2x1ft) Poppies with fragile-looking tissue paper petals in red, pink, apricot and white.

Phacelia campanularia 10-20x10-15cm (4-8x 4-6in) Bell-shaped flowers of intense gentian blue. Sow the seeds in the final site. Protect seedlings from slugs.

Below *Lavatera trimestris* 'Silver Cup', an easy to grow member of the mallow family.

Tropaeolum majus Nasturtium, trailing or climbing 20-180cm (8-72in) Unbeatable for quick, cheap and cheerful cover on poor, stony or sandy soil, but in rich soil they will be all leaf and little flower. In mixtures like 'Alaska' (cream variegated leaves, compact, 20cm/8in), 'Gleam' (semi-trailing, 38cm/15in) or 'Climbing Mixed' (1.8m/6ft) the colour range of cream, golden yellow, orange shades and dark reds blends together well. Good individual colours include 'Empress of India', dark velvety crimson flowers and dark foliage, 'Cherry Rose' and 'Peach Melba'. Unfortunately the plants are often attacked by swarms of aphids in late summer.

Annuals for shady sites

Collinsia grandiflora 45x45cm (18x18in). Unusual, seldom-grown plant with white and mauve pea flowers on slender stems. Needs the support of twiggy stems.

Impatiens 20-30x25cm (8-12x9in) Busy lizzie. Water in dry spells. In the shade white and pale shades show best. 'Super Elfin', 'Tempo' and 'Accent' are reliable series of seeds which can be bought as mixtures or in separate colours.

Nicotiana sylvestris 150x60cm (5x2ft). A statuesque tobacco plant. The basal rosette of large, soft green leaves smothers weeds. 9cm/4in-long slender white, trumpet flowers at the top of each sturdy stem. The flowers are fragrant but close up in full sun. Where space is limited, *N. alata* 'Sensation' (75x30cm/ 30x12in) is fragrant and stays open all day, as do *N. a.* 'Domino' and 'Nicki' (both 25-30x25cm/9-12x9in). Colours are lime, white, pink and dark red. The scent is strongest at night, so plant them under a window or near a door.

Biennials for sunny sites

Alcea rosea 180-240x60cm (6-8x2ft) Hollyhocks, traditional cottage garden plants. Single or double flowers on stout upright stems. Colours include white, pale yellow, many shades of pink and crimson, and maroon-purple so dark that it seems black. Unless you prefer the funnel-shaped single flowers, Chater's Double Group is the strain to go for. Ignore freakish dwarf varieties. Hollyhocks suffer from rust, a difficult disease to control.

Bellis perennis 10x10cm (4x4in) Bachelor's buttons. Double pink and white forms of the common lawn daisy.

Dianthus barbatus 15-45x20-30cm (6-18x 8-12in) Sweet william. A short-lived perennial usually treated as a biennial. Dense clusters of single or double flowers in flat heads on strong upright stems. White, shocking pink, salmon pink, scarlet, crimson, blood red, magenta, maroon. Auricula-eyed sweet williams have flowers marked with concentric circles of different colours.

Erysimum cheiri 20-60x30cm (8-24x12in) Wallflower. The scent and rich colouring of wallflowers are an essential part of spring. Choose from taller varieties (40cm/15in) 'Blood Red', 'Ruby Gem', 'Cloth of Gold' 'Primrose Monarch' and 'White Dame'. 'Persian Carpet' is an aptly named mixture of soft colours. Dwarf varieties include 'Orange Bedder' and 'Scarlet Bedder' (25cm/10in high). Siberian wallflowers (*E. allionii*, 30cm/1ft) are brilliant pure orange.

Above The foxglove, *Digitalis purpurea*, will seed itself freely. Dig up seedlings and move them to new positions in autumn. The leaves make good ground cover.

Left *Dianthus barbatus*, sweet william, an old cottage garden favourite.

Onopordum acanthium 180x90cm (6x3ft) A magnificent, dramatic plant needing space. Sometimes called scotch thistle. Huge, serrated silver leaves. Large, purple-pink, thistle flowers on tall branching stems. It will also grow in semi-shade. Self-seeding.

Right Silybum marianum, Blessed Mary's thistle, has beautiful foliage.

Far right Lunaria annua variegata with *Myosotis sylvatica alba*, forget-me-not.

Below Myosotis sylvatica alba, garden forget-me-not.

Silybum marianum 120x60cm (4x2ft) Blessed Mary's thistle. The leaves appeal rather than the violet-pink flowers. Deeply lobed, spiny, dark-green veined and marbled with white in a ground-hugging rosette.

Biennials for shady sites

Digitalis purpurea 100-150x30-45cm (36-60x12-18in) Stately foxgloves for the back of flower borders, groups between shrubs, among old roses or in their native setting of light woodland. Excelsior Hybrids are tall in colours from cream to purple. Foxy Mixed Hybrids Group are shorter, to 90cm (3ft). *D. p.* 'Alba', the white form, and *D. p.* 'Apricot' are worth seeking out. Foxgloves prefer dappled shade. If suited they will seed freely.

Lunaria annua 75x30cm (30x12in) Honesty. The flowers vary from a crude magenta pink to a vibrant purplish red. They are scented and bloom in spring and early summer. The distinctive seed pods are translucent silvery discs. *L. a. alba* has white flowers. *L. a. variegata* has white leaf margins.

Myosotis sylvatica alba 20-30x20-30cm (8-12x8-12in) Forget-me-not. Easy anywhere but partial shade is ideal. They seed themselves like mad but are easy to pull out when not wanted. Pink and white forms are available, but the familiar blue is unbeatable.

Annuals and biennials for difficult sites

CHALKY SOIL *Calendula officinalis*, *Erysimum cheiri*, *Lavatera trimestris*, *Lobularia maritima.*

SANDY SOIL *Antirrhinum*, *Impatiens*, *Limnanthes douglasii*, *Lobularia maritima*, *Papaver rhoeas* (Shirley Series).

SEASIDE *Antirrhinum*, *Calendula officinalis*, *Impatiens*, *Limnanthes douglasii.*

Bulbs

Bulbs are the bravest of plants, thrusting out optimistic shoots long before winter has ended. They are also among the easiest plants to grow: many tolerate shade and competition from other plants, including grasses. Spring bulbs look their best planted in random, natural groups and in drifts on lawns and under deciduous trees.

Later in the year there are bulbs for beds and borders to plant in gaps between shrubs and herbaceous plants, keeping up a constant supply of colourful flowers.

All bulbs need sunlight on their leaves to nourish the bulbs for the next year's flowering, so don't cut the leaves down until they have withered and don't tie them in knots.

A few easy to grow bulb species which give good value in the garden are described below.

Above Crocosmia 'Citronella' flowers profusely in late summer, but needs a warm, sheltered position.

Spring bulbs

Chionodoxa 15x5cm (6x2in) Blue bell-shaped flowers, similar to scillas but lighter blue, and in flower from early to mid-spring. Best in sun.

Crocus (corms) Up to 10x8cm (4x3in) The winter-flowering species, *C. chrysanthus* and *C. tommasinianus* and spring-flowering *C. vernus* ssp. *albiflorus* are more delicate than the Dutch hybrids. The slender goblet-shaped flowers open in response to the sun. White, purple, mauve, blue and yellow. Birds peck at the yellow flowers but leave the others alone. Crocuses need good drainage. Plant under trees, in the open in short grass, or under and around shrubs. *C. speciosus* has pale blue flowers in autumn.

Eranthis hyemalis and *E. h.* Cilicica Group 5x8cm (2x3in) Winter aconite.Cup-shaped bright yellow flowers with ruffs of green leaves. They flower with the snowdrops and like the same conditions.

Galanthus nivalis 10-15x5-8cm (4-6x2-3in) Snowdrop. White flowers delicately patterned with green hang gracefully above narrow grey-green leaves in late winter. In light shade and moist soil snowdrops increase rapidly.

Hyacinthus 20x10cm (8x4in) Like tulips, hyacinths can be grown in pots indoors (buy bulbs that have been specially prepared for forcing) then planted out in the border in sun or light shade. Their flower spikes will be less dense outdoors but they will continue to flower for many years. Some people find the heady scent overpowering in a room but in the open it wafts around deliciously.

Narcissus Height from 10-45cm (4-18in) Daffodils, narcissi and jonquils are all forms of *Narcissus*. There are hundreds of varieties, flowering from very early to very late spring. Except for the choicest kinds, grow them in grass rather than in the border where the dying leaves are unsightly. Avoid those with very large flowers: they look unnatural.

Scilla bifolia and *Scilla sibireca* 10x5cm (4x2in) Intense little gentian blue, bell-shaped flowers in early spring. They thrive and multiply in any reasonable soil in sun or light shade among shrubs or in short grass.

Tulipa Height from 15-90cm (6-36in) Some species are just a few inches tall with delicate flowers of pure, clear scarlet or softly striped yellow and white. Over the centuries breeders have produced stately plants with single or double flowers and striped, crimped or frilled petals as well as the familiar smooth ovals. A rich colour range: glowing red, fiery orange, soft peach and lilac, every shade of pink and yellow, and almost black. Well-drained soil, sun.

Summer bulbs

Agapanthus campanulatus 60-120x45cm (24-48x18in) Hardy in all but the coldest parts of Britain where it is wise to protect with a winter covering of bracken or straw. The grey-green strap-shaped leaves arch elegantly. Loose heads of bluebell-like flowers on stout, smooth stems in late summer. Splendid in formal pots but equally good in the border. Sun, shelter, good drainage.

Allium Onions are members of this family, as are chives. The latter (*Allium schoenoprasum*) has decorative, tubular, grass-like leaves and clusters of tiny purple-pink flowers held in small globes. *A. christophii* 40x15cm (16x6in) has spectacular silvery-mauve spheres of starry flowers up to 15cm (6in) in diameter.

Right *Narcissus cyclamineus*, an early flowering miniature species 15-20cm (6-8in) tall, for sun or partial shade, best in moist soil where it will seed itself.

Far right *Narcissus* 'February Gold', height 30cm (1ft), is one of the earliest to flower and can be forced to flower in pots still earlier.

DESIGN TIPS

- Grow tulips in pots for their first season and plant them out in grass under fruit trees the following autumn.
- Chives make a neat edging to beds and borders.

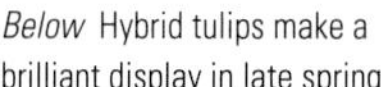

A. giganteum 120x30cm (4x1ft) has tall, densely packed drumsticks of red-purple flowers. Full sun, well-drained soil.

Crocosmia x *crocosmiiflora* 60-150x20-30cm (24-60x8-12in) Montbretia. The hybrids 'Lucifer' (flame red) and 'Emily McKenzie' (deep orange) have large flowers and bring strong colour to the late summer garden.

Below Hybrid tulips make a brilliant display in late spring.

The yellow forms are less hardy. Any soil except heavy clay or bog, sun or part shade.

Lilium Height 60-200cm (2-6ft) There are lilies for most soil types and positions in the garden, but they need good drainage. They are also vulnerable to leatherjackets, mice, rabbits, squirrels, slugs and millepedes (see Chapter 14, Diseases and Pests). This sounds dire, but lilies are so lovely it is worth giving them a try. If your soil is unsuitable, they grow well in pots and tubs.

Lilium candidum 150x20cm (60x9in) Madonna lily. Tall stems of large white trumpets from an evergreen rosette of leaves in midsummer. Slightly alkaline soil, sun.

Lilium regale 150x30cm (5x1ft) Clusters of highly scented, white trumpet flowers streaked with rose-purple on the backs of the petals in midsummer. Sun, ordinary soil.

Mid-century Hybrid lilies are usually trouble-free, flowering early to midsummer in shades of yellow, orange and red. *L.* 'Enchantment' has sturdy stems 90cm (3ft) tall with numerous orange red, outward-facing flowers.

Olympic Hybrid lilies have scented trumpet flowers, white inside and cream, pale green or pink outside. *L.* 'Black Dragon' is purple-red on the outside.

Bulbs for difficult sites

MOIST SHADE *Arum italicum pictum*, *Camassia*, *Galanthus*, *Leucojum*.

COASTAL AREAS *Crocus*, *Narcissus*, *Galtonia*, *Scilla*, *Tulipa*.

SANDY SOIL *Crocus*, *Iris*, *Muscari*, *Tazetta Narcissus*, *Ornithogalum*, *Scilla*.

CHALK AND LIMESTONE *Chionodoxa*, *Colchicum*, *Crocus*, *Cyclamen*, *Narcissus*, *Muscari*, *Scilla*, *Tulipa*.

The Tools of the Trade

If you are gadget-minded, you will end up with as many implements in your tool shed as a top chef has in his kitchen. If you are a tidy gardener, they will be clean, oiled and hung in orderly ranks: a place for everything and everything in its place. At the other end of the scale are the gardeners whose one pair of secateurs is found, after hours of searching, rusting under a rose bush and whose fork has spent the winter stuck in the potato patch.

Equipping yourself for gardening can be expensive. It can also be wasteful: there is such a bewildering array of tools to choose from in catalogues, garden centres and DIY stores that it is easy to be seduced into buying tools which are seldom or never used. The following advice tells you which tools you really need.

It is important that you enjoy using your tools, so comfort is the first consideration. Before you buy, test tools for ease of handling. The shaft of a spade, fork or rake should be the right length so that a stooping posture is avoided; the hilt or handle should be easy to grasp when you are wearing gloves; the weight and balance should feel right.

You want your tools to last, so check that they are solidly made and sturdy.

Essential

The tools listed are the minimum for efficient and happy gardening. First-time gardeners could drop hints to family and friends as Christmas or the retirement party approaches. But if you ask for garden tools as presents, make your choice first, then ask for the brand and model that suits you best. If there is more than one enthusiast in the family, each person should have their own tools if possible.

Safety in the Garden

Hospital casualty statistics show that gardening is a dangerous occupation. Manual tools have sharp points and blades; electric and petrol-powered machines are even more hazardous.

- Wear protective clothing as recommended by the manufacturers of machinery and chemical preparations.
- Have a course of tetanus injections. Keep up to date with boosters.
- Never garden in sandals or flimsy shoes.
- Make sure electrical and power tools are fitted with safety cut-out devices.

Spade

Even if you go in for the no-dig method of gardening (see Chapter 7, Preparing the Ground) you will need a spade to spread any compost, manure and mulching material and to make planting holes for trees, shrubs and large herbaceous plants.

Spades come in three blade sizes:

- Digging spades 29x19cm (11½x7½in).
- Ladies' spades 25x16cm (10x6½in).
- Border spades 23x14cm (9x5½in).

Even beefy male gardeners often prefer a ladies' or border spade for its lightness and manoeuvrability among precious plants.

The blade should be sharp. Forged steel blades can be sharpened when they lose their cutting edge. Some blades have a tread on the upper edge, which makes them slightly heavier but saves feet and footwear.

Of all gardening activities digging is hardest on the back. To avoid backache, make sure your spade has a long enough handle. The standard length of 71cm (28in) is comfortable for people under 1.6m (5ft 4in) tall. If you are taller, look for an extra long handle. They are available up to 90cm (3ft).

The most expensive spades and forks are made of stainless steel and are a good investment if you garden on clay, as the sticky soil does not cling to their shiny surfaces and they do not rust. Tools with blades coated in a non-stick material are also available.

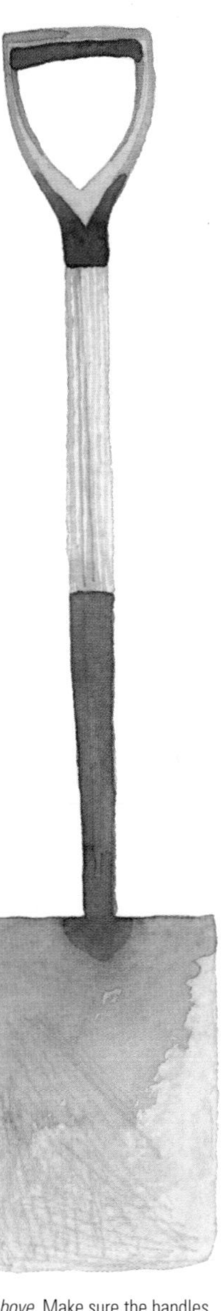

Above Make sure the handles of spades and other tools are a comfortable length for you.

Watering can

A 10-litre (2-gallon) plastic or metal can with a long spout and interchangeable coarse and fine roses (sprinkler heads) is useful for watering seedlings, newly planted plants and vulnerable plants during dry spells. Buy a well balanced one, so you can carry it with one hand when full.

Trowel

This is probably the tool you will use more than any other for weeding and planting. Cheap trowels tend to bend and break easily, so buying stainless steel will save money in the long run. A second trowel with a narrow blade is useful

Below Whether you choose a traditional metal watering can or a plastic one, make sure it is well balanced and easy to carry when full.

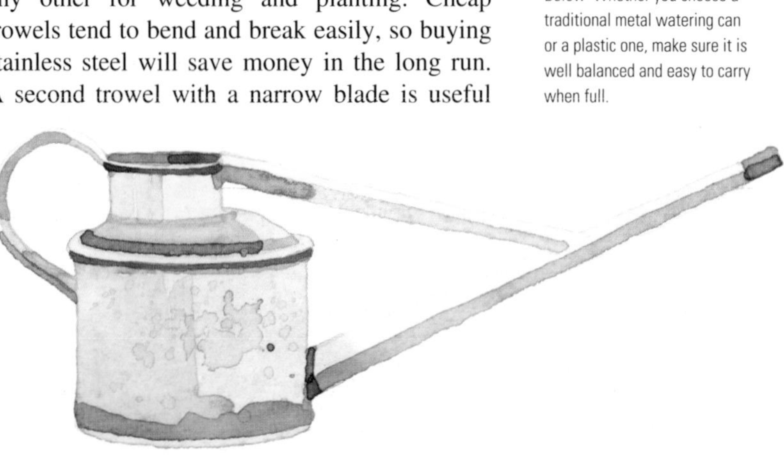

TIPS

- Avoid buying tools with welded joints or short sockets to hold the shaft: their working life is comparatively short.
- Small tools like trowels and secateurs are difficult to find if you have left them lying in the garden. Brightly coloured handles make them easier to spot.

Right and far right Trowels and hand forks may have short or long handles; choose a trowel that feels comfortable to handle and has a sharp blade.

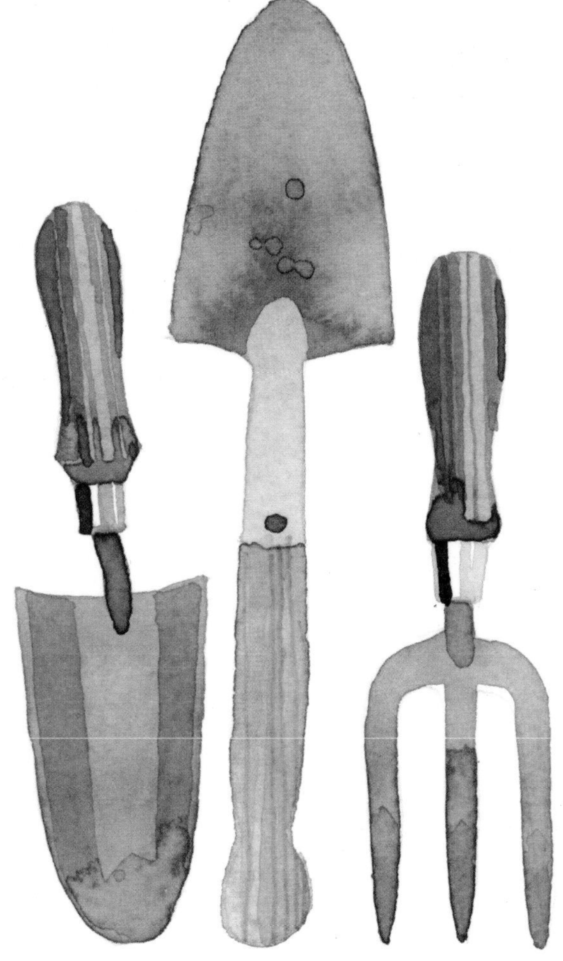

for planting bulbs and for getting out weeds with taproots, like dandelions.

Secateurs

You need a pair of general-purpose secateurs for dead-heading, flower gathering and pruning of branches up to 1.25cm (½in) diameter. Look for handles that are comfortable to grip and will not slip in your hand, make sure that the span of the handles when open is not too wide for your hand, and that the safety catch can be operated with one hand. Secateurs for left-handed people are produced by some manufacturers, and there are secateurs with a ratchet action which are easy to operate if you have arthritic hands or other difficulties.

Below Secateurs should be easy to use when wearing gloves.

Mower

The kind of mower you need depends on the job you want it to perform. A small, hand-operated push mower will cut in widths of about 30cm (1ft), and there are many options between this and a tractor-drawn gang mower for playing fields and parkland. Do you want a striped lawn? If so, choose a cylinder mower with a roller. Are you likely to leave grass rather long before you get round to cutting it? If so, you need a powered rotary mower that can be easily adjusted for height of cut. If you are growing a wild flower meadow, very few ordinary mowers will cope with the main cut. Use a sickle or scythe for small areas. For larger areas consider hiring a reciprocating scythe/Allen scythe, or a strimmer.

Shears

If your garden has a formal hedge or free-standing topiary to clip, shears are essential equipment. They are also invaluable for tidying up grass where the mower cannot reach, against walls and around the base of trees and shrubs, and for clipping over plants like lavender and helianthemums after flowering. Some people even use them to prune roses. Choose shears with comfortable handles and lightweight blades which are notched at the base for cutting individual stems.

Desirable

You don't have to have these tools but sooner or later you will be glad of them.

Fork

Some people prefer a fork to a spade as their all-purpose digging implement. It does less damage than a spade when weeding or cultivating among plants, and can be used for spiking lawns to improve drainage.

Like spades, forks come in three sizes. The smallest and most versatile is a border fork.

Hand fork

A small fork is useful for weeding and for planting out seedlings and other small plants. Hand forks with flat tines are best for most purposes. Long handled, small forks are useful for weeding the backs of borders and for general weeding if you prefer to do the job standing rather than on your knees.

Rake

Use a rake to level soil for seeding and planting. A rake used with a light touch is also useful to remove dead leaves and other debris from beds and borders.

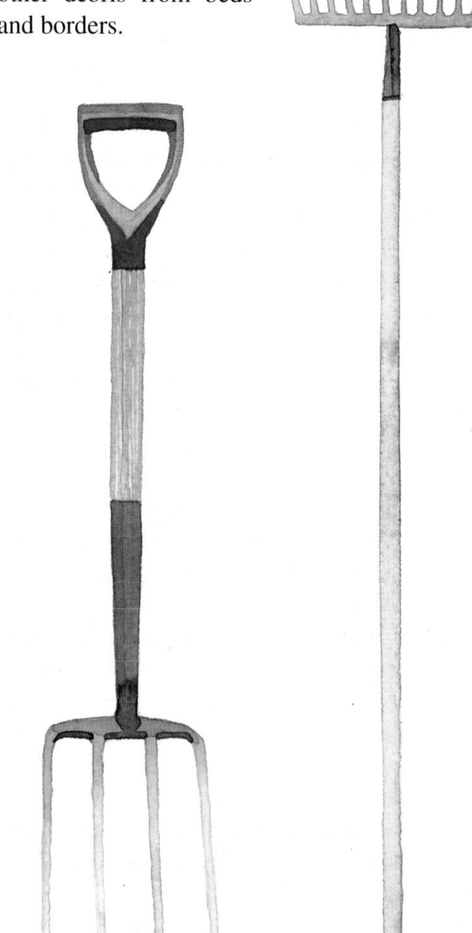

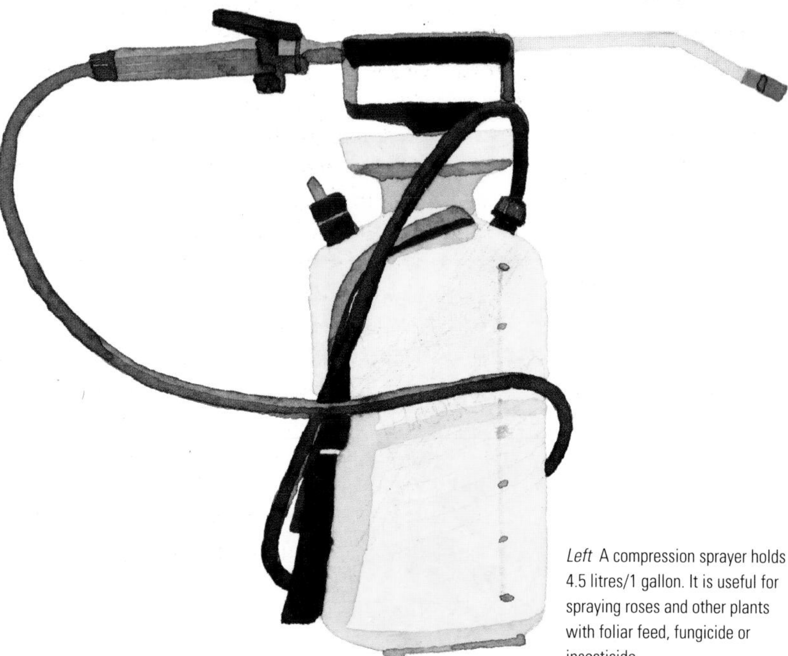

Left A compression sprayer holds 4.5 litres/1 gallon. It is useful for spraying roses and other plants with foliar feed, fungicide or insecticide.

A general purpose rake has a head 30cm (1ft) wide with about 12 teeth. The handle should be long enough to move the rake backwards and forwards without stooping. The norm is 1.5m (5ft), but you may prefer a longer one. The handle should be smooth surfaced so that your hands can move up and down it.

Besom

Just a bunch of birch twigs tied to the end of a pole, the traditional besom broom is still the best and least tiring tool to use for sweeping up leaves.

Sprayer

Hand-operated trigger sprays holding from 0.5-1 litre (1-2 pints) are useful for applying foliar feeds, insecticides or just plain water in a fine mist. Keep several sprayers of the kind used to dampen clothes for ironing, and mix the various products as and when you need them.

In large gardens a compression sprayer (4.5 litres/1 gallon) or a knapsack sprayer (10-15 litres, 2-3 gallons) may be needed.

WARNING *If you use weedkiller it is essential to keep a separate sprayer that is never used for anything else and to empty and wash it immediately after use.*

Wheelbarrow

A barrow makes light work of shifting heavy loads around the garden.

Metal or plastic? Galvanized metal is stronger for carrying heavy loads, but will rust. Prolong its life by treating with anti-rust paint as soon as

Below The traditional besom broom is an excellent tool for sweeping up leaves.

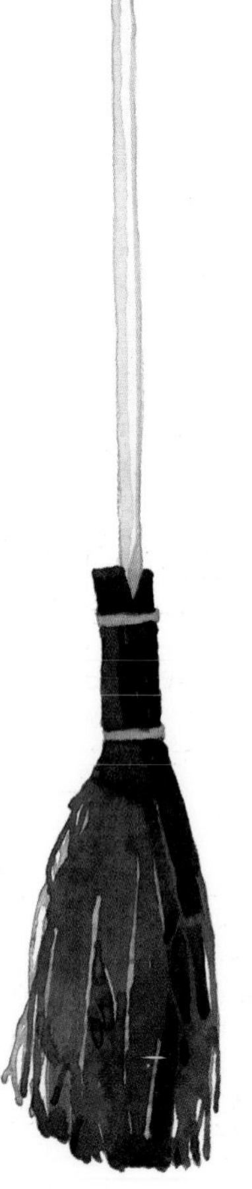

TIPS

• For raking up autumn leaves on lawns an ordinary rake is less efficient than a leaf rake with long, flexible plastic tines, a spring-tined lawn rake or a besom.

• The art of using a wheelbarrow is not to pile it too high. It is better to make two trips than to have your load topple over halfway to the bonfire.

Far right When you buy gardening gloves, try them on to make sure they fit comfortably and are flexible enough to work in.

SAFETY TIP

Small plastic pots or caps placed on the top of bamboo canes help protect eyes and other vulnerable parts.

the first signs appear. Moulded plastic is light but may crack if treated roughly.

One wheel or two? A low, two-wheeled barrow with a handle like a pram is stable and easy to load and push if you are elderly or disabled. But a single-wheeled barrow is easier to manoeuvre in small spaces.

Solid or inflated wheels? Barrows with inflated tyres or ball wheels are better on soft ground as they do not sink in.

A traditional barrow with one solid wheel is fine for most purposes. Check that it is balanced with the weight above the wheel, that the handles are of the right height for you to push it without bending and that the frame does not catch you on the shins when you walk.

Before buying a wheelbarrow, check its width if you have narrow paths or gateways.

Carrying sheet

In small gardens the easiest way to collect and carry leaves, weeds and clippings is on a carrying sheet – a rectangle of woven fabric with a handle at each corner. You dump the material onto the sheet then gather up the four corners to carry it. A plastic bucket or washing up bowl is also useful.

Hosepipe

In all but the smallest gardens, a hosepipe will save time spent lugging a watering can to and from the kitchen sink.

A hosepipe is the best aid to determining curved lines when you are setting out a new bed or an informal pond.

A hose can be fitted with various irrigation attachments (see Chapter 12, Watering).

Pruning saw

Sooner or later you will need a saw to deal with unwanted branches on trees and shrubs. The most versatile is a Grecian saw with a narrow, curved blade and curved handle. It cuts when you pull rather than push it and is easy to manipulate between branches that are close together.

Right Pruning tools: secateurs are essential equipment, and the Grecian saw and long-handled loppers are both useful. A knife is difficult to use for pruning without some practice, but it is useful for cutting string and ripping open polythene bags of compost or fertilizer.

Gloves

Most gardens have a few roses and other prickly shrubs. If you don't want lacerated hands when you prune or train them, you will need a stout pair of gardening gloves. Leather and vinyl-coated fabrics are thorn-proof but inflexible; they make your hands hot and sweaty in warm weather. Cotton gloves are flexible but not thorn-proof. The best compromise is to choose gloves with leather or vinyl palms and fabric backs. Gauntlets with long cuffs protect wrists and lower arms as well as hands.

Many gardening gloves seem to be designed for hands with wide palms and short stubby fingers. Try to find a pair which fit closely but not too tightly and have flexible fingers so that you can feel what you are doing. As with small tools like trowels and secateurs, gloves left lying about the garden are easier to locate if they are brightly coloured.

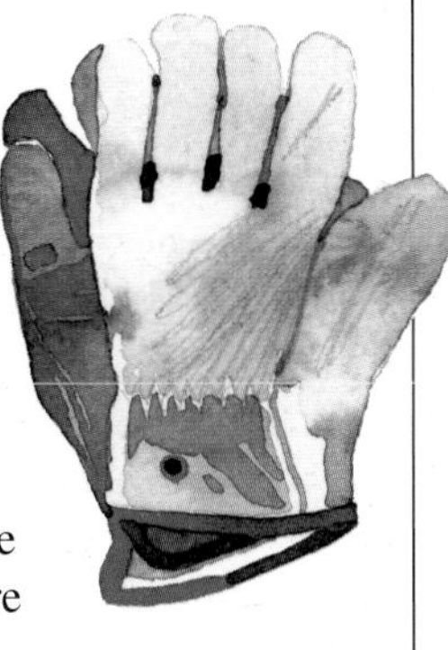

Kneeler

When weeding, kneeling is a less tiring posture than bending or squatting. A cushioned kneeling pad protects trousers and kneecaps from wear and tear on damp or stony ground and protects turf from the impact of bony knees. A kneeling stool with a metal frame is useful if you have difficulty getting down onto your knees or up from them. Knee pads which strap onto your legs are uncomfortable to work in: they are either too tight or they slip down.

Other

BAMBOO CANES of various lengths.

STRING for tying climbers and tall herbaceous plants to supports. Although soft garden twine wears out and has to be renewed more often than wire, it is preferable as wire can damage plants by cutting into the stems as they swell. String is also useful for setting out straight lines in the vegetable garden or, when making borders, paths or hedges.

LABELS of different shapes and sizes. Use unobtrusive aluminium or plastic labels, and renew the lettering when it fades after a few years.

INDELIBLE MARKERS

POTS AND SEED TRAYS are dealt with in Chapter 15, Increase and Multiply.

Optional extras

Hoe

Caution is needed when hoeing out weeds in beds and borders. It is only too easy to root out young plants with the weeds and to chop the tops off emergent bulb shoots. Hoeing too close to shrubs can damage surface feeder roots, and diseases may gain access through resulting wounds. But a hoe is certainly the best implement for weeding between straight rows of seedlings in the vegetable garden.

When choosing a hoe, look for a sharp cutting edge and a handle of the right length: when held upright it should reach to just below your nose.

The swoe is a good all-purpose tool with a triangular blade sharp on all three sides, and the single-bladed Dutch hoe is easy to use without causing damage.

Cultivator

There are various cultivators available with different arrangements of prongs or wheels on a long handle, but the jobs for which they are designed can be dealt with just as easily, efficiently and quickly by a fork and a rake.

Below Hoeing stirs the soil surface, removing weed seedlings.

HOES

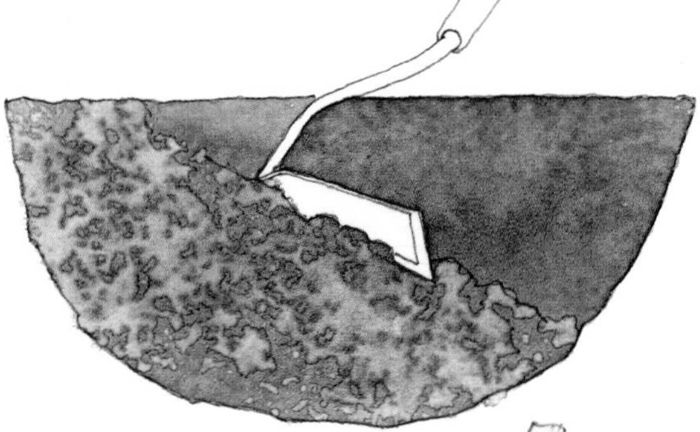

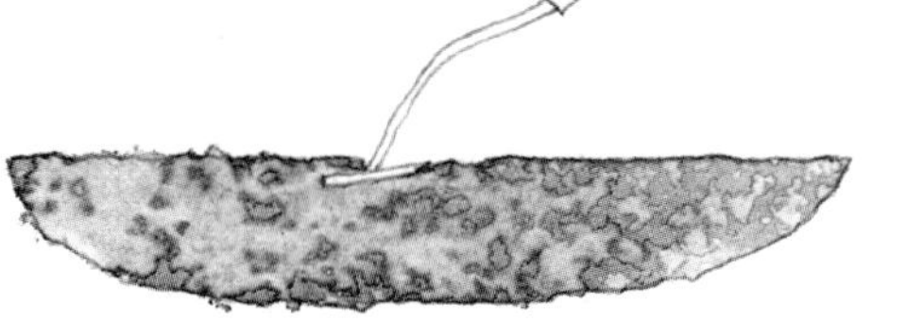

1 The swoe is a relatively modern invention, with a sharp edge on three sides of the blade. It is used with a push-pull action, with the blade horizontal to the soil surface. It may be used for earthing up, and making seed drills, but is most useful for weed control. It is light and easy to use; the narrow blade makes it very manoeuvrable.

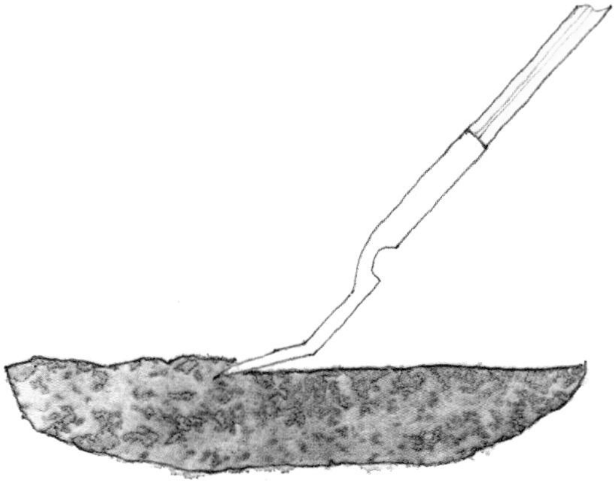

2 The Dutch hoe, or push hoe, is used with a skimming action, keeping the blade horizontal, while the gardener walks backwards. The sharp blade cuts off weeds at the neck.

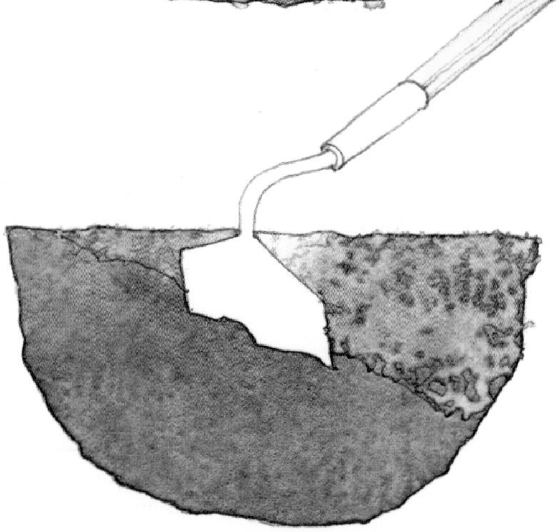

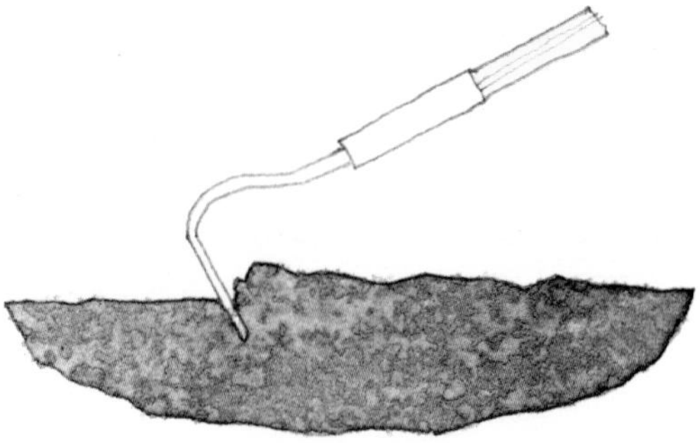

3 The draw hoe is used with a chopping action to break up the soil surface, to chop up weeds, to draw out seed drills and to earth up vegetables such as celery or potatoes. It causes fewer casualties amongst closely spaced plants than the Dutch hoe.

Right Many gardeners have a favourite weeding implement which started its useful life in the kitchen.

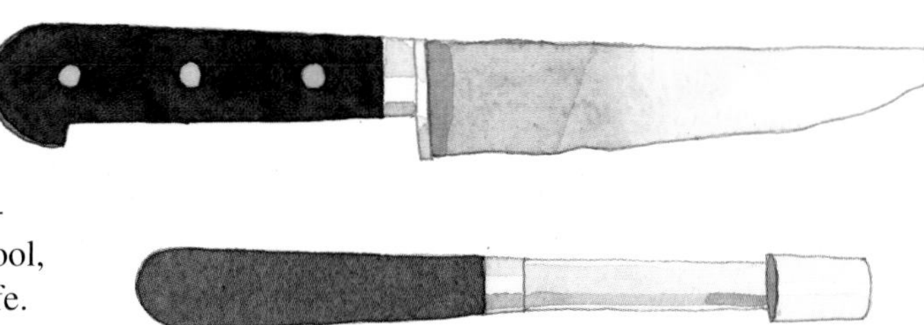

Weeding implements
Special tools are available for weeding in beds, in lawns and between paving. Everyone has their own favourite weeding implement; it may be a purpose-made tool, an apple corer or an old kitchen knife.

Long-handled pruner (lopper)
Like larger, stronger secateurs with long handles for reaching high branches, pruners and loppers are used for cutting branches of between 1.25 and 2.5cm (½in and 1in) diameter. For anything thicker than 2.5cm (1in), use a saw. The long handles and heavy-duty blades make these tools heavy to manipulate above your head and it is sometimes difficult to see what you are doing in a bushy shrub or tree. The easiest lopper to handle is one with a curved blade cutting against a curved groove which holds the branch. Those with a straight blade and anvil have a tendency to slip against the branch.

Bulb planter
If you regularly plant a lot of daffodils or tulips in turf, a long-handled bulb planter is a handy gadget. It takes out cylindrical plugs of soil which are then replaced on top of the bulbs. This only works successfully on moist medium to heavy soil. Sandy or stony soil will not form a satisfactory plug. A short-handled bulb planter is no more efficient than a trowel.

Right A long-handled bulb planter is more efficient than the short-handled type, and saves the back from a good deal of bending.

Sieve
A coarse-meshed sieve is used to eliminate stones and other debris from the soil of seedbeds and planting positions. A finer mesh is used to sieve a thin layer of soil or compost over seeds when sown in trays or in the open.

Knife
Skilled gardeners nearly always use a knife in preference to secateurs for pruning and taking cuttings, and there are special knives for budding and grafting.

A blunt knife or a sharp one in unskilled hands can damage fragile plants. But it is always useful to carry one in your pocket for cutting string, opening up plastic bags of compost and harvesting asparagus and other vegetables.

Long-handled shears
Cheaper to buy and easier to control than a mechanical nylon-line trimmer, these shears have long handles set at right angles to the blades and are used to trim small areas of grass on banks, around trees or at the base of a wall.

Long-handled edging shears
These are designed for one specialist job: trimming the grass at the edges of lawns. They should be light to handle with handles long enough to use without stooping.

Lawn edger
A half-moon blade is attached to a spade handle to make a tool for cutting a neat edge to turf.

Dibber
This is a tool for making small, deep planting holes. For seedlings and cuttings a pencil does the job just as well. A larger dibber may be useful in the vegetable garden, especially for planting young leeks.

Widger
A handy metal implement like a narrow spatula wider at one end than the other. It is used to lift fragile seedlings without damaging the roots and is also a handy weeding tool.

Slasher
This tool is like a shorter, lighter scythe with a blade at right angles to a wooden handle. It is useful for cutting down nettles, thistles and other tall, coarse weeds, but hard to find now because it has been superseded by strimmers and brush cutters. Agricultural suppliers sometimes stock them.

TIP

The quickest way to give the garden a facelift is to trim all lawn edges with edging shears or half-moon blade. Don't be too enthusiastic, though: your lawn will shrink if you are over-zealous too often.

Storing tools

Your choice of tools will be dictated to some extent by how much space you have to keep them in.

If the broom cupboard under the stairs is the only place available, think twice before you go out and acquire a wheelbarrow or a lawn mower, although a small, lightweight mower takes up no more space than a domestic vacuum cleaner, and can be hung from the wall. Hooks to hang tools from can be fixed on the inside of a door as well as on walls. Look for trowels and secateurs which have a looped thong to hang them from. To support a spade or fork, fix two strong nails 5cm (2in) apart, projecting 2.5cm (1in) from the wall.

Additional useful storage space can be provided by a narrow shelf – 15cm (6in) wide is enough – for holding bottles and packets of pesticides and fertilizers and small and medium sized flower pots. Make sure there is at least one shelf high enough to be out of reach of children.

If you have a garage you can probably find space in it for your garden tools. If not, and if there is no suitable space indoors with easy access to the garden, you will want to consider installing a garden shed. Sheds are not beautiful to look at but can be hidden behind a hedge, a trellis of climbing plants, or a group of tall shrubs. If there is room to make a general utility area around the shed, including a compost bin and standpipe, a hard surface of concrete or paving slabs is practical.

If you have plenty of space, put up the largest shed you can afford. You can never have too much storage space, and if the shed is well lit with windows and has electricity installed, you can spend happy hours in it potting and pottering in all weathers.

The use of your shed will be greatly increased if you install a working surface at standing or sitting height. If you are not much of a carpenter, a paper-hanger's trestle table or an old but sturdy kitchen table from the local auction or junk shop will do nicely. Underneath the table or workshelf, large bags of compost, grit and fertilizer can be stored and flower pots and seed trays stacked.

In a small garden it is worth considering using a bunker with a hinged lid instead of a shed: it can do duty as a seat as well as a store. A shoulder-high cupboard built against a wall can also provide unobtrusive storage space.

Regrettably, thieves are aware of the value of garden tools, so doors and windows of sheds and other stores should be securely fastened with lock and key or a sturdy padlock.

TIP

If you are always too tired or too pressed for time to clean your tools and hang them up, keep a large bucket of oiled sand in the garage or shed and stick spades, forks and other tools into it at the end of the day.

Below 'A place for everything and everything in its place' is a counsel of perfection which you may find hard to follow. But a well organized tool shed does save time and temper spent looking for mislaid tools.

SECATEURS
Sharpening secateurs of the blade and half anvil type: carefully observe the number and position of all components before beginning the operation. Dismantle the secateurs, and put all parts in a safe place. Sharpen the blade, on the outer surface only, by drawing a fine tooth file downwards across the cutting edge at an angle of 25-30°. Clean with an oily cloth and reassemble.

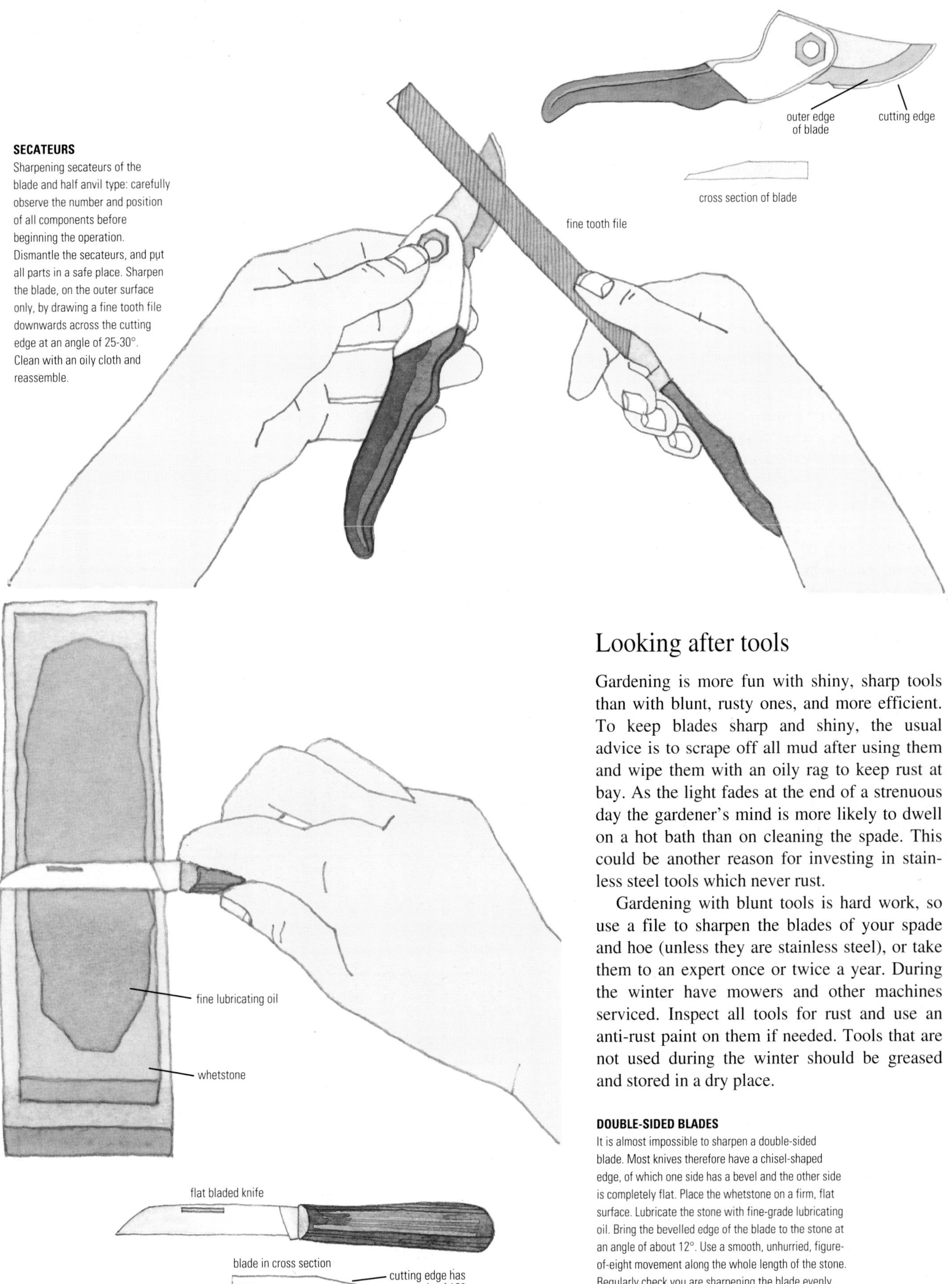

Looking after tools

Gardening is more fun with shiny, sharp tools than with blunt, rusty ones, and more efficient. To keep blades sharp and shiny, the usual advice is to scrape off all mud after using them and wipe them with an oily rag to keep rust at bay. As the light fades at the end of a strenuous day the gardener's mind is more likely to dwell on a hot bath than on cleaning the spade. This could be another reason for investing in stainless steel tools which never rust.

Gardening with blunt tools is hard work, so use a file to sharpen the blades of your spade and hoe (unless they are stainless steel), or take them to an expert once or twice a year. During the winter have mowers and other machines serviced. Inspect all tools for rust and use an anti-rust paint on them if needed. Tools that are not used during the winter should be greased and stored in a dry place.

DOUBLE-SIDED BLADES
It is almost impossible to sharpen a double-sided blade. Most knives therefore have a chisel-shaped edge, of which one side has a bevel and the other side is completely flat. Place the whetstone on a firm, flat surface. Lubricate the stone with fine-grade lubricating oil. Bring the bevelled edge of the blade to the stone at an angle of about 12°. Use a smooth, unhurried, figure-of-eight movement along the whole length of the stone. Regularly check you are sharpening the blade evenly.

Machinery

WARNINGS Motor machinery, whether petrol or electric-powered, is dangerous.

- *Always observe the safety instructions that come with a new machine, and if you hire machinery, check that it is safe to use. Wear the recommended protective clothing. All electrical machinery should be used with an earth leakage trip/safety cut-out device.*
- *Trimmers and brush cutters are dangerous not only to people but also to plants. Careless use of these machines can destroy small shrubs along with the weeds or long grass. If the trunk of a young tree is mutilated by a strimmer, it may die. Even if it recovers, it will probably be scarred for life.*

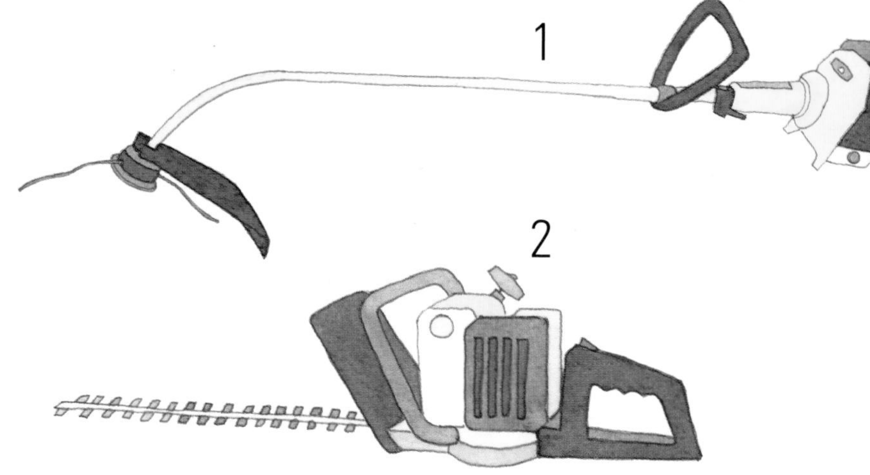

TRIMMERS

1 Nylon-line trimmer (strimmer). Used to cut grass round the stems of trees and shrubs, and in other places where the mower cannot reach, but it is only too easy to damage your plants. A worthwhile investment for larger gardens. In small gardens use hand shears.

2 Powered hedge trimmer. Only worth owning if you have a lot of hedges to trim. Hired machines can be unsatisfactory and downright dangerous.

Mower

Grass-cutting machines vary from electric ones not much bigger than a vacuum cleaner to large tractor mowers. Your choice will depend on your requirements.

Nylon-line trimmer, brush cutter

Trimmers or strimmers have a motor-driven nylon line which rotates so fast that it cuts soft obstacles that come in its path. Lightweight electric machines are suitable for trimming grass in awkward places in small gardens, but cannot deal with anything tougher than grass.

Petrol-driven models are fitted with tougher line and/or a metal blade. They can cut down weeds and those with metal blades can cut through brambles and other scrub plants. They are heavy, noisy and tiring to operate, and for safety reasons goggles, ear-muffs and protective clothing should be worn.

It might be worth buying a brush cutter if you have a garden with extensive wild areas, but for most gardeners it is best to hire one when you have areas to clear. Use shears for trimming grass in places where the mower cannot reach.

Rotavator

Motor-driven cultivators are useful to weed and prepare neglected ground for planting or seeding, but they can be hired and are only worth owning if you have a large vegetable garden needing annual cultivation.

Left A motor-driven cultivator, worth hiring to prepare neglected ground at the outset.

TIPS

- Gardening can be hard exercise: dress in layers that can be removed as you warm up.
- In cold weather wear thin silk gloves under a leather or vinyl pair.

Hedge trimmer

Powered hedge trimmers are extremely dangerous. Do not buy or hire one unless it has a hand guard, a dead man's handle (stops the motor immediately the trigger is released) and two-hand switches, which ensure that the blades will only work when both your hands are on the machine.

If you have more than, say, 25m (80ft) of hedge to cut, a powered trimmer will save time. Where there are extensive hedges at a distance from a mains power point, a petrol-powered trimmer is probably the best choice. But it will be heavier and noisier than an electric one. For small hedges a cordless trimmer, charged from a battery, is a possible option, but it will not cut through thick shoots.

Double-sided blades do the job more quickly than single-sided. A blade 40cm (16in) long is fine for the average user, though a longer blade will be quicker if you have a lot of hedges to cut.

When using a hedge trimmer it is important to wear goggles, ear muffs, thick gloves and stout shoes or boots, preferably with steel toe caps for protection.

Clothes

What you wear when gardening can make a lot of difference to your comfort and safety. Some people seem to manage to stay clean when gardening, but for most of us gardening clothes take a lot of punishment and will end up stained with mud, blood and dandelion juice. So it makes sense to wear out scruffy old clothes in the garden.

When choosing what to save from the jumble sale there are various points to bear in mind. Twigs and thorns snag rough surfaces, so a smooth-textured sweatshirt is more practical than a woollen sweater, and a waxed jacket better than Harris tweed.

Freedom of movement is essential, so you need clothes that are loose enough to allow you to bend easily at the elbows and knees. Except in wet weather, a sleeveless jacket or jerkin is the most practical outer garment, and, since much of a gardener's time is spent kneeling or squatting, loose trousers are more comfortable than tight jeans. But don't wear trousers or jackets and sweaters with flapping loose ends that might catch in machinery.

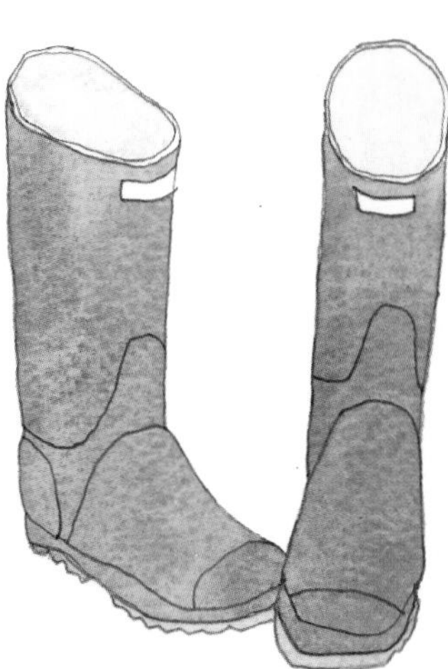

In winter it is obviously important to keep warm: if your back is warm whilst you are digging or heaving sacks of compost, you are less likely to suffer from backache. More body heat escapes through the top of the head than in any other direction, so in cold weather a woolly hat is useful even if it makes you look like a football supporter – there is no room for sartorial vanity in the garden. Keen gardeners in warm waterproof and windproof clothing find that they are able to ignore even the most unfriendly winter weather.

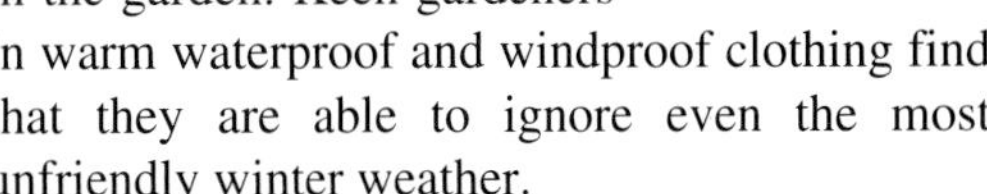

On a hot summer's day, if you can bear to leave your deck chair and iced drink, it is tempting to garden, if not in swimwear, at least in shorts. If you do so, perhaps your legs will be enviably tanned by the end of the day, but they will also be hatched with minor lacerations and probably spotted with midge bites and nettle stings. Trousers and a long-sleeved shirt in cool cotton are more practical, and a hat or vizor to keep the sun off your nose is also advisable.

WARNING *You may not be aware of the strength of the sun, especially on a breezy day. Use sun filter cream or lotion on exposed parts to minimize the risk of skin cancer.*

It is worth repeating that safety is all-important: never garden in flimsy or open-toed shoes, and always use the equipment recommended when operating machinery or spraying weedkillers, insecticides and fungicides.

The whole point of working in the garden is to be able eventually to sit back and admire the results, and allow your friends to share your pleasure. When that time comes it is only fair to the garden to dress with style for the occasion.

Preparing the Ground

If you have moved to a new garden or decided to develop your present garden, you will want to get on with choosing plants and putting them in. But it is worth spending time preparing the ground beforehand. Some plants are going to be in place for many years and you won't get the opportunity to improve soil once they are established. The more trouble you take, the better the plants will grow, and you only have to do it once.

You may not have to do it at all if you have inherited a garden that has been well looked after so that the soil is in good heart and weed-free. But even in such a case, you may want to alter the layout, making new beds for shrubs, perennials or fruit and vegetables out of areas of lawn or rough grass.

Renovating a neglected and overgrown garden will need rather more time and effort, and dealing with a site which the builders have just left is usually the biggest challenge of all.

Whatever raw material you start with, there are several operations to be completed before the ground is ready for the plants, each requiring different techniques and tools.

Clearing the site

WHEN? Getting rid of rubbish left by builders, previous occupants or yourself in a previous, non-gardening incarnation is the first operation, and it can be carried out at any time of year.

HOW? Lurking under brambles there may be enough metal rubbish (bedsteads, old fridges, cookers and the like) to fill a skip. If so, your local scrap-metal merchant may be interested. He probably won't pay you anything for your rubbish, but he might take it away without charging you. Look in Yellow Pages.

If there is a lot of rubbish to shift it may be worth hiring a skip. Otherwise it is a matter of filling your car boot (the bedstead will have to

TIP

If you inherit a neglected, overgrown garden, identify and mark any plants worth saving before you start clearing the vegetation.

Left Even landscape and garden contractors are not always conscientious about how they dispose of their rubbish. If you employ them make sure debris is removed from the site, not buried under your new lawn or flower beds. The best contractors lay boards under concrete mixers and other heavy equipment, to avoid compacting the garden soil more than is absolutely necessary. Ask your contractors to do the same.

Left Rubbish need not always be removed from the site. This limestone scree garden was made with barrowloads of rubble from a demolished shed, providing just the right free-draining conditions for saxifrages, sedums, edelweiss, geraniums and campanulas.

Right Burning is the quickest way to dispose of woody stems, provided bonfires are permitted in your area. Wait till the heap is fairly dry and choose a day when the wind will not blow smoke towards your neighbours.

Far right If there are brambles to clear you will need stout thorn-proof gloves. Use secateurs or loppers to cut the long branches into manageable lengths for the bonfire or skip.

go on the roof) and making as many trips as are necessary to the council tip.

You will need a wheelbarrow, a fork for lifting rubbish, secateurs and perhaps a saw for cutting brambles and other undergrowth into manageable pieces, old newspapers and matches to start a bonfire. Wear stout gloves and sturdy footwear. Lifting heavy items may be a job for two people.

When you have cleared away any surface rubbish and managed to get a fork through the hard crust where the builders mixed their concrete, you will probably find a burial ground for broken bricks, plastic bags, drinks cans and bits of torn timber embedded with rusty nails. It is best to find and clear this kind of rubbish at the outset rather than wait until you are digging a hole to plant a tree.

If you live in an area where bonfires are forbidden, you will have to dispose of the brambles and other weeds by the same method. If bonfires are allowed, make sure the smoke is not a nuisance.

Before lighting a bonfire, check which way the wind is blowing. The quickest way to make enemies of new neighbours is to waft ash and smuts from burning rubbish onto the clean shirts and pillow cases that they have just pegged out. To get a bonfire going, you may have to wait for the rubbish heap to dry out.

It may not be practical to remove rubbish from the site if it has to be carried through a terraced house, or if it is immoveable. Some gardens have concrete air raid bunkers from the Second World War which are so strong that they cannot be broken up. In such cases the bunker or rubbish must be included in the design of the garden. Broken concrete, stones and bricks can be used as foundations for steps, paths or paved areas, or used to make a raised terrace. In an informal garden, rubble can be mounded and covered with topsoil to vary the contours or used as the basis of an area of scree or gravel for alpines and other plants that enjoy a well-drained site. If there is no alternative to burying rubbish, choose shallow-rooting plants to cover that area.

Golden Rules of Ground Preparation

- Be thorough; it will save time and trouble later.
- Check disturbed ground for buried builders' rubbish. It will be more difficult to remove at a later stage.
- Before clearing rubbish, make sure your tetanus inoculation is up to date.
- Let your neighbours know what you are doing. They will be more understanding if you talk to them first.
- Don't let weeds run to seed.
- Let the frost work for you to break down roughly dug soil.

Eliminating weeds

(See also Chapter 11, Weeding.)

WHY? Weeds compete (only too successfully, as a rule) with garden plants for food and moisture. Later it will be difficult to weed between plants without damaging them, so the more weeds you can get rid of at the preparation stage the better.

WHEN? Chemical weedkillers (a translocated weedkiller is preferable: see Chapter 11) work faster and better when the weeds are growing strongly, between spring and mid-summer. Choose a still, clear day; even the gentlest breeze can cause spray to drift onto precious plants. Ideally it should not rain for six hours after spraying, so check the weather forecast (the reason that old gardeners seem to have a sixth sense about the weather is that they listen to the radio).

Spring and early summer is also a good time for digging out weeds by hand; the process of digging and forking will bring dormant weed seeds to the surface and they will quickly start into growth. The weed seedlings can then be hoed off on a dry day.

If you don't have time to dig out weeds before they run to seed, cut down the stems, postponing the weeding operation till later. If you don't do so, the problem will be multiplied many times over.

Above Stinging nettles *(Urtica dioica).* Dig them out (wearing gloves) or use two or more applications of systemic weedkiller. Nettles are a breeding ground for several butterfly species, so if your garden is large enough, leave a large clump in a sunny place. The plant in the foreground is the lesser celandine; often regarded as a weed, it makes pretty ground cover in places where it cannot swamp delicate plants.

TOOLS

- Brush cutter, worth hiring for large areas of brambles, nettles and other scrub and tall weeds.
- Scythe or slasher, will do the same job using muscle-power.
- Gloves (thornproof).
- Rake, to collect debris.
- Wheelbarrow.
- Knapsack sprayer, if you decide to use a chemical weedkiller for large areas, or
- Compression sprayer, 4.5 litre (1-gallon) capacity, for medium-sized areas, or
- Watering can with a dribble bar for any small areas.
- Mechanical rotavator, worth hiring if you do not wish to use chemicals but you have a large area to clear.
- Spade or fork, for hand weeding.

HOW? In large areas, if, for example, you are preparing a new lawn or a vegetable plot, a translocated chemical weedkiller will do the job efficiently. A knapsack sprayer is the most practical method. Be sure to follow the manufacturer's instructions and also to wear appropriate protective clothing. Take care, when you are spraying, that the chemical solution does not soak through your clothing. If, in spite of all precautions, you still get weedkiller on your skin, wash it off immediately under running water.

Later, when the weeds have withered, cut them to the ground. A few weeks later you will probably need to administer a second dose of weedkiller to deal with regrowth of the toughest weeds such as nettles and docks. Don't be in a hurry to get your plants in; it will save you considerable time and effort later if you start with clean ground.

'Green' methods

Many people are uneasy about the dangers of chemical treatments, in the long term to the health of the soil and in the short term to animal and human health. Alternatives are:

HARD LABOUR Dig or fork over the area very thoroughly, removing all roots of perennials to the bonfire and turning over small annuals to

TIP

Catch the weeds before they produce seeds: 'one year's weed, seven years' seed' is part of gardening lore.

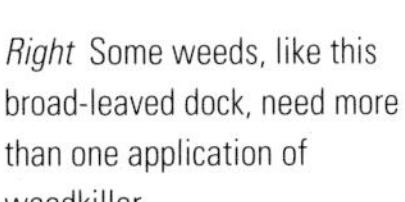

Right Some weeds, like this broad-leaved dock, need more than one application of weedkiller.

Below Thistles are easy to pull up at the seedling stage.

bury them as you dig. If the ground is infested with the creeping roots of ground elder or bindweed, a fork is more efficient than a spade as there is less likelihood of breaking the roots. Take care, though, with pernicious ground elder, bindweed and couch grass: each fragment of root that is left in the ground will almost certainly produce a new plant.

If you are going to clear small areas by digging out individual weeds, do not cut the stems to the ground; the job is easier when there is some top growth to grasp hold of. Brambles, nettles and other vicious weeds will be easier to deal with if you shorten them, but leave 30cm (1ft) or so of stem. Loosen the roots with a fork, then yank them out by hand.

ROTAVATION The mechanical alternative to hand digging is a heavy duty rotavator, which can be hired. A small domestic one will not dig deep enough. Repeated rotavation in warm, dry weather destroys most weeds, including couch grass, by exposing the roots so that they shrivel and die.

However, unless you rotavate four times, the weed problem may be exacerbated; the machine will chop up the roots of couch grass into small pieces, each of which will form a new plant.

- Cut off the top vegetation.
- Rotavate shallowly.
- Rotavate again, deeply.
- After a few weeks couch and other weeds will appear, and a third deep rotavation can take place.
- When the weeds reappear, rotavate a fourth time. At the same time you can add any soil improvers that are needed (see pp.88-9).

WARNING Repeated rotavation of the same ground can produce a hard pan at the depth of the machine's blades, so only use this method once.

BLANKET MULCH If you are not in a hurry, a 'mulch' of old carpet or black plastic left in place for six months is an excellent way to eliminate weeds. Cut them down first with a brush cutter, slasher, mower or shears. Make sure the mulch excludes all light.

Below To some gardeners, this is a weed-infested lawn, to others a species-rich sward.

Digging

WHY? Digging breaks up compacted soil so that the roots of plants can penetrate, worms and other soil-improving creatures can do their work and drainage is improved. It lets air in to speed the breakdown of organic matter, making more nutrients available to plants. Digging is the only way to remove obstinate roots and large stones. It also provides you with an opportunity to add manure, compost and other soil improvers.

WHEN? Let the winter weather do the work, particularly if your soil is heavy clay. In autumn and early winter, turn the soil over roughly, leaving it in sizeable clods. Repeated freeze/thaw cycles break down clods. By the time spring comes the frost, wind, snow and rain will have worked the clods down into a manageable texture. The remaining lumps are easily broken up by bashing with the back of a fork.

Pick a day for digging when the soil is easy to work. The heavier the soil is (that is to say, the greater the clay content) the fewer ideal days there will be. If the soil is too wet, it will stick to your boots and your spade, and lifting a spadeful will be hard on your back and shoulder muscles. Digging and standing on wet soil will cause compaction, which can damage the soil structure permanently. On the other hand, if clay soil is baked dry it will be too hard to get a spade into.

If you miss the chance to dig in the autumn, switch from other gardening jobs during spring and summer to spend twenty minutes digging at any time when conditions are right.

TOOLS

- Rotavator: it may be worth hiring one to cultivate a large area for a lawn, vegetable plot or extensive ornamental beds. It will not dig as deep as a spade, but in one day it can bring hitherto uncultivated soil to an even tilth. But the disadvantage of using a machine is that if there are perennial weeds it will chop up the roots and spread them around. If it is couch or ground elder, each piece will sprout anew.
- Spade: the traditional digging implement, and preferable to a fork in stony ground where the stones can get stuck between the tines of the fork.
- Fork: more manageable than a spade for turning and breaking up heavy soil. Where there are running roots of couch grass or ground elder a fork will get them out without breaking them.
- Timber plank or length of hardboard or fibreboard, to stand on while digging so as not to damage the soil structure.
- Bucket or wheelbarrow, to dispose of weeds, roots and large stones.

HOW? There is a right way and a wrong way to dig. If you use the right technique you will probably still need a relaxing bath at the end of a day in the garden, but at least you will not risk permanent damage to your back.

GENERAL PRINCIPLES Digging is a three-stage technique and at each stage the general principle is to use your body weight rather than your muscles. Work 'backwards' so that you're not treading on dug soil.

TIPS

- Keep a small piece of wood or a flat stone with a sharp edge in your pocket to clean the blade of your spade.
- To dig small areas or dig round existing plants simply take out one spadeful at a time and turn it over in the same hole, chopping it with the spade or bashing it with the fork to break it up.

SINGLE DIGGING

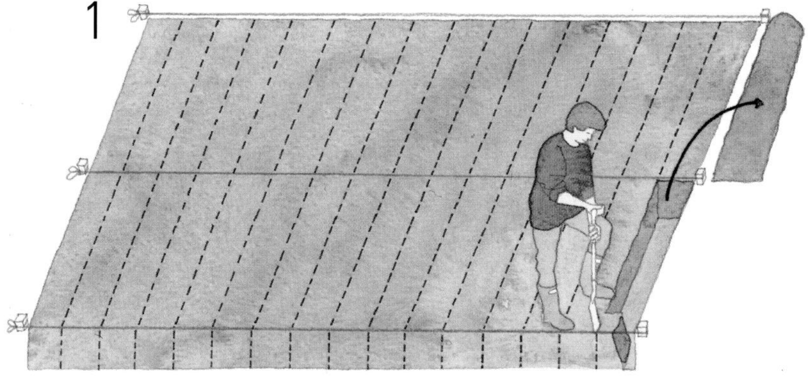

1 Mark out the plot with string lines. If the plot is large, divide it into two halves. Take out a trench, or one spade's depth (one spit) barrow, and 30cm (1ft) wide. In a single-width plot, barrow this topsoil to the other end of the plot. It will be used to fill the last trench dug. In a double-width plot, move the topsoil to the position shown. It helps to place the topsoil on a sheet of polythene.

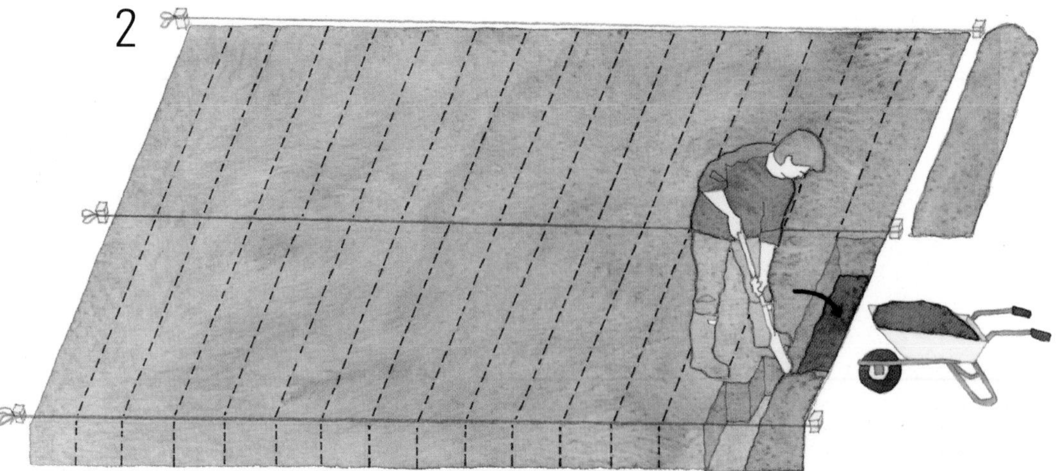

2 Organic matter can be added, either by placing a 2.5-5cm (1-2in) layer in the bottom of each trench, or by spreading it on the surface before you start, so that you turn it into each trench as you dig.

Golden Rules of Digging

- Take small spadefuls – it's quicker in the long run.
- Stop before you feel tired: to begin with, thirty minutes is probably long enough. Don't rush – it is not a competition or test of endurance. Stop and do something else before you start digging again.
- Put the spade in vertically.
- Do not dig when the soil is wet.
- Bend your knees, not your back.

- Cutting the soil: keep the spade vertical and drive it into the soil by leaning on it from above, with one foot on the top of the spade. Don't push it in with your arms and shoulders.
- Lifting the soil: pull the handle towards you and lean on it to lever up a spadeful of soil, bending your knees.
- Turning the soil: straighten your knees, twisting the spade to one side to turn the soil over as you drop it.

SINGLE DIGGING Also known as 'trenching', this is the only method you are likely to need. It is an efficient way to dig over a regular shaped area such as a vegetable plot or a border.

- Dig a trench one spit (the length of the spade blade) deep by about 30cm (1ft) wide.
- Remove the soil from the trench and barrow it to the far end of the plot you are digging.
- If needed, spread organic material or fertilizer in the bottom of the trench.
- Dig along the face of the trench, turning the soil into the trench, thus forming a new trench parallel to the first.
- Continue digging a series of trenches until you reach the end of the plot.
- Fill the final trench with the soil from the first.

3 Working along the face of the second trench, turn the second trench of soil into the first, forming a new trench parallel to the first. For the sake of your back keep the spade blade vertical, and make each spadeful no more than 10cm (4in) wide.

Levelling

WHEN? If you did the sensible thing and dug roughly in the autumn, by spring the frost will have broken the clods down to a manageable texture. All you need do is rake over the area to level out any lumps and bumps and hollows.

- Do your raking when the soil is dry on top but moist underneath.

TOOLS

- Rake. For most gardens an ordinary metal one is adequate. But if you have a large area to prepare, use a wooden landscape rake with a 1m (3ft) wide head.
- Bucket, to collect debris.
- Wheelbarrow, to remove debris.

HOW? If the rake handle is the correct length, there will be no need to bend your back. For most people 1.5m (5ft) is the right length.

- Stand upright and push the rake back and forth in front of you, using long strokes and moving backwards in a straight line. The technique is to push away harder than you pull towards you, and not to lean on the rake, as that will cause the tines to dig in and will interrupt your rhythm.
- At the end of each line you will have raked up a small pile of stones and twigs which you can remove in the bucket.
- When you have raked over the area in one direction, rake it again at a right angle.

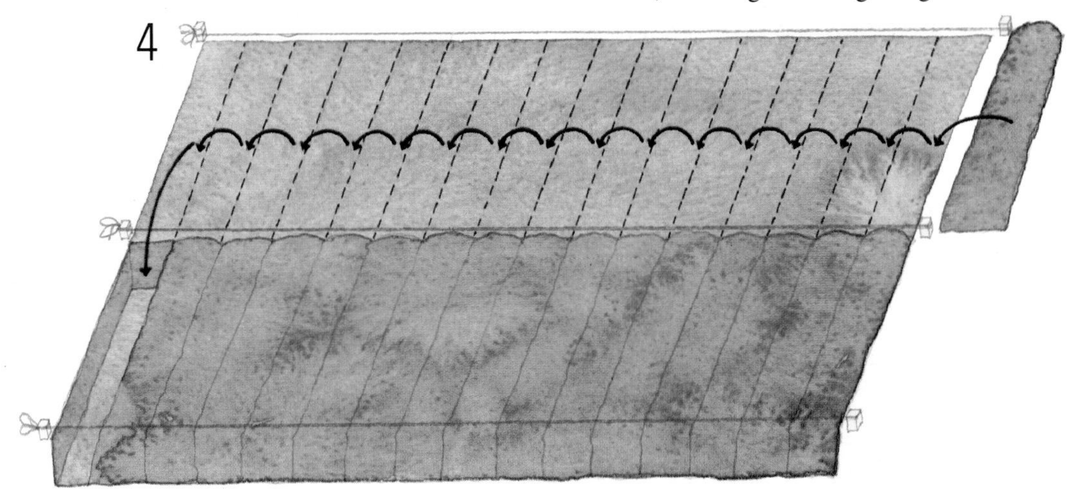

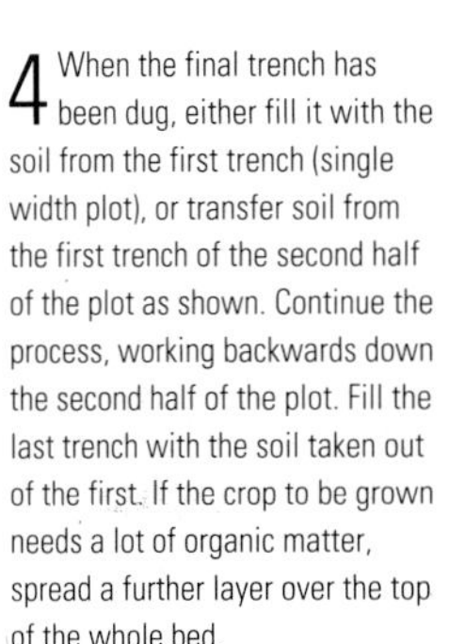

4 When the final trench has been dug, either fill it with the soil from the first trench (single width plot), or transfer soil from the first trench of the second half of the plot as shown. Continue the process, working backwards down the second half of the plot. Fill the last trench with the soil taken out of the first. If the crop to be grown needs a lot of organic matter, spread a further layer over the top of the whole bed.

Improving the soil

(See also Chapter 13, Feeding.)

WHY? Gardening on good, fertile soil is a pleasure, but on problem soils it can be a pain. If your soil is very acid or alkaline, poorly drained, heavy, free-draining or compacted, it is worth taking steps to improve it so that you can grow a wider range of plants.

WHERE? It would be labour-intensive and expensive to treat a whole garden with lime, fertilizer or other soil improvers, and gardeners who make their own compost will know that there is never enough of it. But if you want to grow vegetables or roses on poor soil, it is worth doing all you can to improve it in specific areas.

WHEN? Simply digging heavy or compacted soils will improve them, and if you need to add material, this can be done at the same time, in autumn or early winter. However, if you apply lime to improve the pH (to make acid soil more alkaline), you should not combine it with other improvers. If you are digging in manure, compost or fertilizer in the autumn, wait until February before adding lime.

HOW? Most soil improvers are dug into the top spit of the soil. They can also be spread on the surface as a top dressing: lime will be washed down into the soil by the rain, and organic improvers will be worked into the soil by worms and other useful creatures.

- Different soil types need different treatments. You can discover what category yours is by carrying out the checks described in Chapter 2, Understanding Your Garden.

Problem soils

All problem soils are improved by the addition of bulky organic material to increase their humus content. It comes in the following forms:

- Animal manure, obtainable from farms and stables. Gardening books rightly tell you to use 'well-rotted' manure. This is because fresh manure can damage plants. You can tell if it is fresh by the smell, but if in doubt, stack it, covered with a sheet of polythene to keep the rain out, for a few months before using it.
- Spent mushroom compost, available from mushroom farms. It usually contains chalk or lime which helps correct the pH of acid soil. Avoid using it on very alkaline soils.
- Grass cuttings, free if you have a lawn. Either compost them or dump them on the area you wish to improve and dig them in later.
- Green manuring, where a crop is grown on the site to be improved. The roots of the crop break up and aerate heavy soils, and when the crop reaches a certain stage it is dug or rotavated into the ground, thus adding organic matter and recycling nutrients. It is a useful technique to use on ground that is lying vacant for a season.

The easiest green manure crops to use are those that can be roughly dug in in autumn, leaving the frost to complete the operation. Buckwheat or fenugreek can be sown between March and August and dug in from two to three months later. Alsike clover, bitter lupin and phacelia can be sown in spring and dug in just before they flower. For more information, and seeds, contact the Henry Doubleday Research Association (see p.274 for address).

- Commercial soil improvers and conditioners: branded products are more expensive than any of the above materials, but for small gardens it may be more practical to buy a few bags from a local garden shop.

Right Chicken manure should be used sparingly, and like all organic matter, should be well rotted. It is best to add it to the compost heap rather than spread it direct onto the garden.

Below Organic material spread as a mulch is worked down into the soil by worms.

Below Fenugreek *(Trifolium ornithopodiodes, left)* and Alsike clover *(Trifolium hybridum, right)* are green manure crops, to be dug in a few months after sowing.

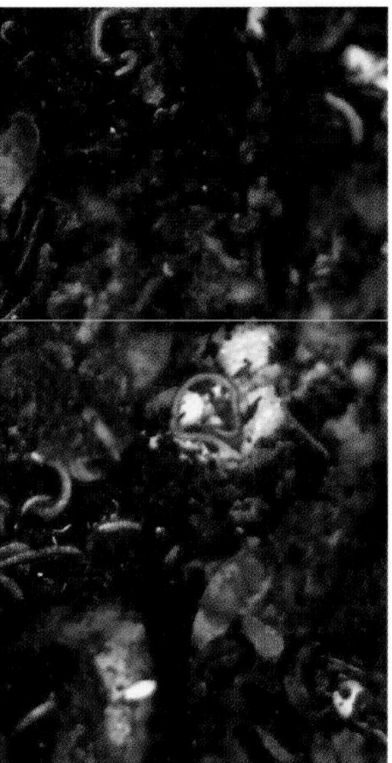

Above Horse manure; dig it in or mulch round shrubs and trees.

CLAY SOIL Clay is fertile but dense and sticky, easily waterlogged, cold and slow to dry out. It dries very hard and deep cracks form. Frost breaks it down very effectively if roughly dug in autumn.

There are various artificial clay improvers on the market but there is no evidence that they are more effective than a combination of coarse, gritty sand and bulky organic matter.

- Bulky organic material: dig in as much as you can get, a bucketful per square metre or yard at least.
- Coarse sharp sand grit, obtainable from builders' merchants, will improve the structure of clay soils if you use enough of it. A 5cm (2in) layer should be spread over the soil and then dug in. The large amount needed makes this only practicable for small areas.
- Lime improves the crumb structure in clay and also raises the pH level, which is very useful on acid clay soils. For rates of application see Chapter 13.
- Gypsum has the same effect as lime without raising the pH level.

SANDY SOIL The attributes of sand are the opposite from those of clay, yet, like clay, it is improved by liberal additions of bulky organic material.

- Cow and pig manure are particularly good as they are sticky and hold the sand particles together.
- Ground limestone: sandy soil is easy to work and warms up quickly in spring, but it drains very rapidly so that nutrients get washed away, leaving the soil acid. It therefore benefits from an application of lime every two or three years. For rates of application, see Chapter 13.

CHALK AND LIMESTONE SOIL Yet again, the all-purpose organic material is the best treatment. In this case it improves the fertility and depth of topsoil and retains moisture.

TIP

Don't add lime or mushroom compost to soil where you intend to grow azaleas or other lime-haters.

PEATY SOIL On peat you can make a marvellous bog garden, but it may be impossible to improve drainage as the water table is probably near the surface.

Peaty soils are usually acid and benefit from lime (see under 'Sandy soil', above). However, on peat the optimum pH for growing vegetables is 5.8 (6.5 on other soils), so test before applying any lime.

POORLY DRAINED SOILS Deep digging and the addition of sharp sand and organic material can improve the drainage in clay soils. More serious drainage problems, on lawns for example, can be solved at a cost by having land drains installed.

The alternative is to live with the problem by growing plants that tolerate such conditions and by building raised beds where you can grow other plants.

Changing the soil

If the soil in your garden really makes you despair, you can replace it in key positions with bought-in topsoil.

The quality varies greatly, so examine it before you buy. It should be free from large stones, lumps of clay and weed roots, and it should not be too sandy. Beware of topsoil that has been stacked high for a long period, as it will have lost its structure.

The no-dig garden

The theory is that walking over the soil and frequent digging spoils the soil structure. Therefore, after thorough initial preparation of the ground, you sit back and let the worms do the work. Worms aerate the soil as they move through it and convert organic matter into humus as it moves through them.

Organic material is applied in the form of a mulch of good compost or well-rotted farmyard manure each year. The mulch will also prevent weed growth, and because digging often causes dormant weed seeds to germinate, the no-dig system should almost eliminate weeds after a few years. The soil will be of such good structure and open texture that those weeds that appear will be easy to remove.

For the system to succeed you must avoid compacting the soil by walking on it, specially in wet weather. Therefore beds should be narrow enough for you to reach the centre without having to step onto them. The ideal is 1.2-1.5m (4-5ft): an arm's reach from either side. The soil builds up a high level of fertility so that plants can be grown closer together.

Planting and Transplanting

Planting is the most satisfying gardening activity. It induces a feeling of benevolence towards each plant; you are ensuring its survival and, as you settle it into its new home, in your imagination the plant and its companions leap forward to their maturity, and your garden is transformed.

If you get your plants off to a good start they will reward you with star performances. If you don't take the small amount of trouble that is necessary, they will probably live but they may not flourish – a permanent reproach.

WHERE? Even the most careful planners are sometimes to be seen wandering around the garden searching for an empty space for an impulse buy from the local nursery or garden centre, or for a plant donated by a friend. If you are not working strictly to a plan, here is a checklist of plant requirements that should be satisfied if the plant is to thrive:

- Shelter from wind or frost or both? Only the hardiest plants will thrive when exposed to frost and dessicating winds. The large leaves of some plants will be torn by strong winds and may scorch in full sunlight.
- Sun or shade? Plants that tolerate 'light shade' will not do well in heavy shade.
- Damp or dry site? If you cannot provide a moisture-retentive soil for plants which prefer it, dig plenty of organic material into the planting hole and apply a thick layer of mulch after planting. Be prepared to water in dry spells. Ideally, plants should be selected to suit your soil type. Even if you are willing to water – a time-consuming exercise – you may well lose an 'unsuitable' plant in the event of a hosepipe ban.

TIP

Although there is a 'right time' for most jobs in the garden, if the choice is between doing it at the wrong time or not doing it at all, it is always worth doing it at the wrong time. This applies especially to planting and transplanting: provided you take extra care the chances of success are good.

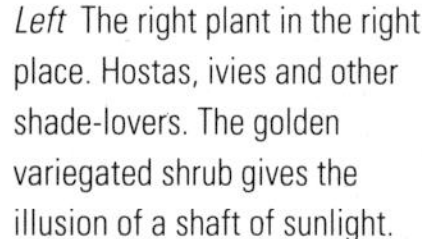

Left The right plant in the right place. Hostas, ivies and other shade-lovers. The golden variegated shrub gives the illusion of a shaft of sunlight.

- Soil type preferred? Check whether the plant needs acid, alkaline or neutral, and light or heavy soil.
- Height and spread? How tall and broad will the plant grow? Will it have enough space to develop to its full potential? You may choose to plant trees and shrubs close together in order to create a shelter belt or hedge, but in general it pays to allow plants space to attain their full size. If you deliberately put a quart plant into a pint space, be prepared to prune it carefully each year and accept the fact that it will never achieve its characteristic form.
- Adjacent plants? Make sure the new plant will not interfere with their growth by casting shade on them, robbing them of moisture and nutrients, or crowding them out. Will its leaves and flowers enhance its neighbours with harmonizing or contrasting colour and texture? You may have to move other plants around to make a good position for the new acquisition.

Above Be aware of the size plants will reach at maturity before you plant them near the house.

Right Willows and poplars have invasive roots and should be positioned well away from buildings.

WARNING *The roots of trees planted too near a building may damage the foundations or interfere with drains and cables. Willows and poplars are particularly dangerous in this respect.*

WHEN? Plants bought in pots can be planted at any time of year provided the soil is not sodden or frozen hard. But if they are planted between late spring and early autumn, they will need regular watering and weeding until established. If you do plant in the summer, remember to keep an eye on the plants and water them if they show signs of stress. Be generous with water to ensure that it penetrates deeply enough to encourage deep rooting. Plants under stress may also be more vulnerable to pests and diseases than plants which have had a chance to establish themselves.

The gardener's life is made easier if both container-grown and bare-rooted plants are put in during the traditional planting season, which is during autumn, winter and spring. The plants can then settle down and form a good root system before summer drought or scorching sun puts them under strain. (There is some evidence that pot-grown plants with well-established root stems stand a better chance of survival.) There are exceptions, though, to this timing:

- Heavy clay soil is cold and may be sodden throughout the winter, making it a struggle for young plants to survive. Therefore on clay, planting is best delayed until spring. The same applies in very cold areas. If in doubt, ask an experienced local gardener's advice. You can dig the holes roughly in autumn, leaving the frost to break up the clods.
- Evergreen shrubs are more delicate than deciduous plants and are best planted in early autumn (October) or late spring (end of April, beginning of May). Stick to spring on clay soil.
- Most bedding plants (biennials and annuals planted for a temporary summer display) are tender and will be killed by frost. They should only be planted out when all risk of frost has passed, in early summer.
- Small herbaceous plants may be lost or devoured by pests during the winter dormant period. They are best kept in a sheltered place until they have started into growth in spring.

Tools and equipment

The tools you need depend on the size of the plant. It is no good taking a trowel to plant a tree or a spade for a primrose.

FOR PLANTING TREES, SHRUBS AND LARGE HERBACEOUS PLANTS

- Spade to dig the hole.
- Fork to loosen the soil.
- Sheet of plastic or hardboard to put the soil on when you dig the hole.
- Watering can (full), or hose.
- Peat and bonemeal and/or compost or manure if appropriate.
- Mulching material.
- Secateurs.
- Labels.

FOR PLANTING TREES The above, plus

- Stakes, ties, rabbit guards and mallet or dumpy sledge hammer.

For small plants:

- Trowel.
- Kneeling pad.
- Watering can.
- Secateurs.
- Labels.

FOR CLIMBING PLANTS As for trees and shrubs, plus canes and string or plastic ties.

HOW? The soil is the most important element to ensure good growth. You need to decide whether you should add organic matter (compost, leaf mould or manure) and/or fertilizer to improve the soil around the new plant. If you have chosen plants especially to suit the site, in a bog garden, for example, or on a hot, dry bank, additives are probably not necessary. On average, fertile soil they are optional and may even hold back plant development.

Recent tests have shown that trees and shrubs planted in ordinary garden soil grow faster and stronger than those in soil with added compost and nutrients. The roots spread further in search of water and nutrients, forming stronger anchorage, whereas if you improve the soil in the planting hole, the roots tend not to move out of it. However, some plants such as roses, which were not included in the tests, are 'gross feeders' and perform best if fed liberally. Also, if your soil is not 'ordinary', for example if it is stiff clay, if chalk is very near the surface or if it is very thin and sandy, most plants will appreciate some extra organic material around their roots.

The most important discovery from the tests was that in all cases plants did better if the soil around the plant was kept weed-free and mulched.

Whether you add anything to the soil or not, there are some general principles that apply to all types of plant.

PLANTING CONTAINER-GROWN PLANTS

1 With a trowel dig a planting hole slightly wider than the plant's pot, and the same depth.

2 Take the plant gently out of the pot, turning it upside down with one hand on the crown of the plant. If the plant does not slide out easily, tap the pot firmly with the trowel.

3 Put the plant in the planting hole, spreading the roots evenly. Ensure that they are not restricted, and that the soil level is the same as it was in the pot. Firm gently with your fingers. Label, and water in thoroughly.

- Water container-grown plants thoroughly an hour or so before planting. Bare-rooted plants should have their roots covered in damp compost or newspaper, or wrapped in polythene until the moment of planting: they must not be allowed to dry out. If the roots are dry or the stems shrivelled, leave the roots to soak in a bucket of water for an hour or two before you plant them.

Right After planting, water gently but thoroughly to settle the roots into the soil and provide moisture.

Below Press the soil really firm around each plant to ensure the roots are in contact with the surrounding soil.

- Dig the planting hole deeper and wider than the plant's root system so that you do not have to bend the roots to fit the hole and so that the roots have well-cultivated soil to grow into initially. An extra 30cm (1ft) all round is about right for trees, 15cm (6in) for most shrubs.
- Make the soil receptive to the roots: when preparing a planting hole, remove stones and roots, and break up lumps of soil. You are aiming at a loose, crumbly texture that is fine enough for the plant's roots to penetrate easily.
- Water the planting hole thoroughly.
- Prune off any broken or torn branches and roots, making a clean cut.
- Untangle the roots of bare-rooted plants and spread them out in the planting hole. This should not be necessary with container-grown plants, but if you find that the roots are tightly matted or spiralling round when you remove the pot, loosen the compost on the outside and gently tease out the roots with your fingers. Cut off any roots that are twisted or very long.
- The finished level of the soil after planting should be the same level as the soil in the container. With bare-rooted plants you can usually see on the plant's stem where the soil came up to in the nursery before the plant was lifted. If in doubt, plant with the soil about an inch above the point where the stem joins the roots.
- When you have covered the roots with soil, press it down really firmly. The most common mistake is not to plant firmly enough. With trees and shrubs this means treading it down with your full weight. Exception: be more gentle on clay soil for fear of compacting it.
- Young plants need plenty of water. After planting, water thoroughly and spread a 5cm (2in) deep mulch around the root area to conserve the moisture.
- In dry weather water the plants regularly for the first season.

WARNINGS - *Never try to pull a plant out of its pot by the stem(s). If the plant is held in the pot by roots spreading out of the holes at the base, cut these off. Hold the pot at an angle nearly upside down with one hand spread across the surface to stop the compost spilling and give the base of the pot a sharp tap with the knuckle of the other hand. The rootball should then fall cleanly from the the pot. If it still sticks, give a much sharper tap with the handle of a trowel.*

- *Never plant in hot, dry weather, and preferably not during the hottest part of the day. If possible, watch the weather forecast and time planting before a spell of rain.*

Trees, including orchard fruit

Trees come in various sizes: the smallest are transplants, then whips, feathered, light standards, standards, heavy standards, extra heavy standards and semi-mature specimens which go up to very large sizes indeed.

It is tempting to go for a standard tree for instant impact. But there is a lot to be said for planting small: transplants and whips establish quickly. They do not need staking and many species will reach the size of a standard in five years. During those years (a short time in the life of a garden) you will get a great deal of pleasure out of watching their development.

Staking

If you decide on a standard tree it will need initial support. Feathered trees only need support on very windy sites. The purpose of the stake is to hold the stem of the tree vertical until it can stand on its own, and to prevent the roots being disturbed when the wind rocks the tree.

The Victorian method, using a tall stake to just below the first branch of the tree, is still common practice. However, by restricting the sway of the tree's stem in the wind, high staking encourages growth of the stem diameter above the tie at the expense of growth of the lower stem. This makes the tree vulnerable to wind damage when the stake is removed.

Modern practice advocates a stake not more than one-third of the height of the tree's stem, usually just 60cm (2ft) above the ground. It holds the roots firm but allows the stem of the tree to bend in the wind, which helps strengthen it. Movement of the tree's stem produces chemical responses which encourage root growth and increase the diameter of the stem.

Light standards and standards need a sturdy stake with a sharpened point at one end. A larch pole is suitable, a bamboo cane is not: if the stake is inadequate, you will find the tree is holding up the stake instead of vice-versa.

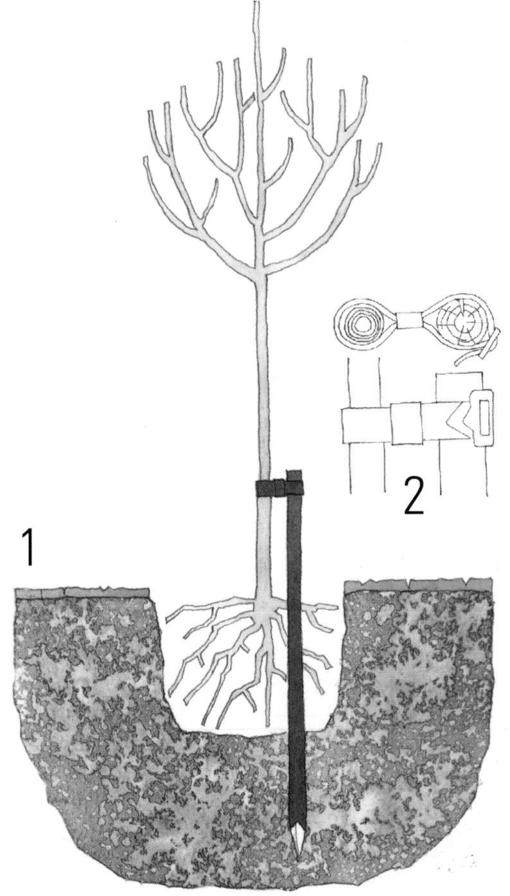

STAKING

1 A softwood stake of about 1.5m (5ft) long and 7.5cm (3in) in diameter is adequate for light standard and standard trees. Drive the stake into the bottom of the planting pit, so that about 60cm (2ft) stands above soil level. Do this before you plant, to avoid damage to the tree roots. Position the stake close to the trunk and on the windward side. The top of the stake should reach to one-third of the stem's height. Place the tree into the pit. Check that the trunk is vertical. Spread the roots evenly, so they do not curl round or double back on themselves. Replace the top soil in layers, firming gently. Ensure that the final soil level at the base of the trunk is the same as it was in the pot or in the nursery.

2 Secure the tree to the stake with a rubber tree strap. Place the strap around the trunk and thread the free end back through the spacer. Adjust so that the trunk is firmly held. Attach to the stake with the buckle on the side furthest from the trunk. The strap should be 2.5cm (1in) below the top of the stake.

Heavy standards need two posts, one each side, and anything larger should be planted by a specialist and secured with guy wires underground to anchor the root ball as well as stakes above ground to hold the trunk in place.

You will need ties to fix the tree to its stake. Rubber straps with buckles and an adjustable stay between tree and post are unobtrusive, long-lasting, easy to handle and can be adjusted as the girth of the tree's stem expands.

It is important to check stakes and ties regularly, and to loosen ties before they restrict the expanding stem. It is also essential to remove the stake and tie as soon as the tree is firmly anchored. If the planting hole was properly prepared and the tree correctly planted this will be by the end of the first growing season.

1 Breaking up the soil at the bottom of a planting hole helps drainage and makes it easy for roots to penetrate. Remove big stones or roots.

2 Adding a mixture of soil and compost will give the young tree a very good start. On richer soil you can leave out the compost.

3 It is important to plant trees at the same depth as they were in their container or in the nursery. You can use a cane to check the level.

4 Don't be afraid to stamp the soil in really firmly; it brings the roots in close contact with the soil and prevents wind-rock and frost lifting.

3 Heavy standards need the support of two stakes with a crossbar. Plant the tree, then drive in stakes, approximately 1.8m (6ft) long, 60cm (2ft) from the trunk. Position them so that when you attach the cross piece, it will be close to the trunk with sufficient room for the tree tie and spacer. Knock in the stakes, leaving 60cm (2ft) of their length above soil level. Nail the tie to the cross piece and then nail the cross piece, 7.5x4cm (3x1½in), to the stakes. Thread the free end of the tie through the spacer and secure the tree to the cross piece, firmly but not too tightly.

4 On windy or sloping sites, a short stake at an angle will give additional support. Insert the stake after planting. Use a stake about 1.8m (6ft) long, with a diameter of 5cm (2in). On the side opposite to the direction of the prevailing wind, drive the stake into the ground to 60cm (2ft) of its length, 80cm (32in) from the base of the trunk at an angle of about 60°. Attach to the tree at just over one-third of the stem height, using a rubber strap.

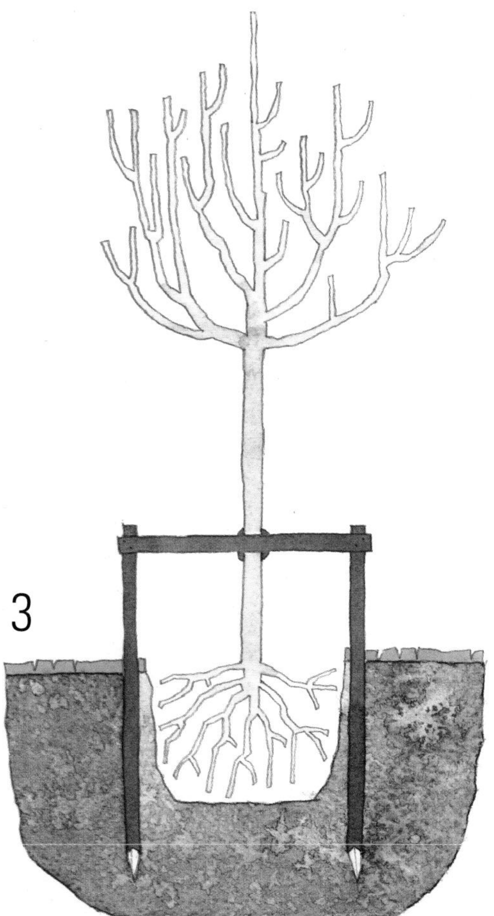

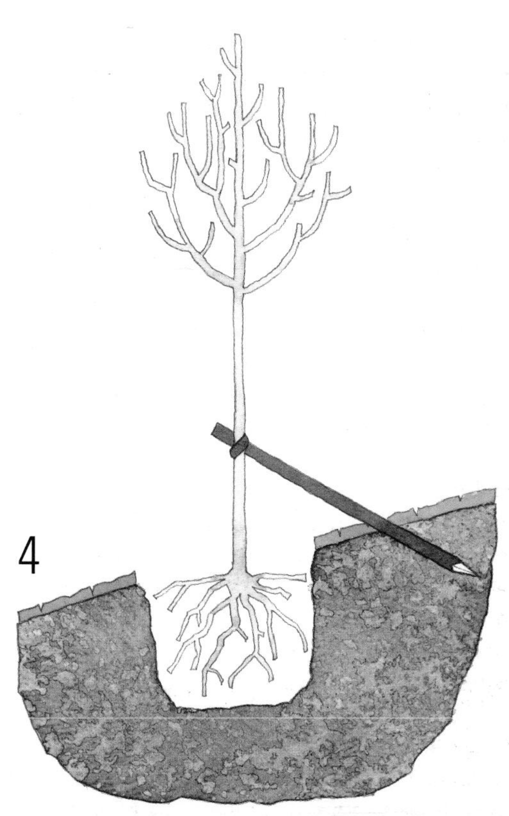

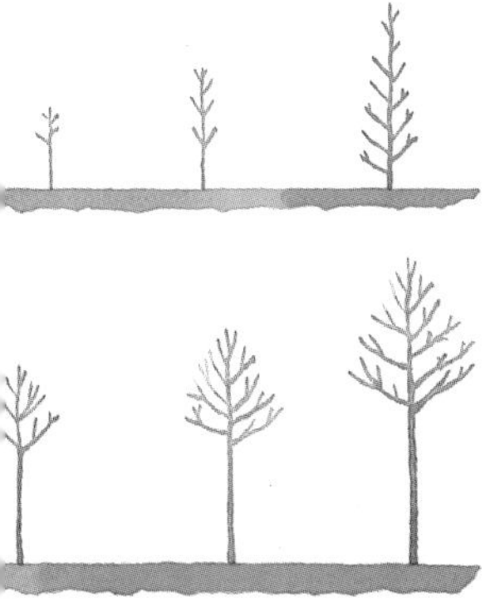

TREE SIZES
Trees are available from nurseries in these sizes: *(top left to bottom right)* transplant, whip, feathered tree, light standard, standard, heavy standard.

Remove the stake at the beginning of the second season so that the tree has a season to further establish itself before the onset of winter gales. If you are uncertain whether the tree has made firm anchorage, shake it. If this does not displace the crown or lead to movement of the roots at soil level, it is time to remove the stake.

WARNING *If the stem of a tree is chafed or strangled by the tie holding it to a stake, it will be permanently disfigured.*

HOW? If you are planting in grass, cut out a circle of turf (1m/3ft diameter for trees, 60cm/2ft for most shrubs).

- Dig a hole 15cm (6in) wider and deeper than the rootball, placing the topsoil on a plastic sheet or board. If you reach subsoil, dig it out and replace with topsoil from elsewhere.
- With a spade or fork, break up the soil at the bottom and sides of the hole.
- Drive the stake in either vertically or at an angle of 45° so that one-third of its length is below ground.
- Water the hole and let the water drain away.
- This stage is much easier if two people do it together. Remove the tree from its container or if bare-rooted from under cover, and with secateurs prune off any damaged or extra-long roots.
- One person should hold the tree vertical, close to the stake. The stake must be on the windward side of the tree, otherwise the tree will be blown against the stake and its bark damaged. The second person spreads the roots out evenly and uses the spade to half fill the hole with soil. The tree-handler can shake the tree gently. This helps the soil settle round the roots.
- The spade handler firms the first layer of soil by treading it lightly, adds the rest of the soil and treads it well in all round the tree.
- A rabbit guard, if needed, is then wrapped round the tree's stem and the tree is secured with a tie to the top of the stake.
- Use secateurs to prune off any damaged shoots and remove any weak or crossing branches.
- Finally, water copiously around the whole root area, then mulch with mushroom compost or other mulching material.
- In dry weather, water regularly, giving each tree at least 10 litres (2 gallons). The frequency and quantity of water required will vary according to soil type and weather conditions.

Shrubs, including fruit bushes

Follow the general principles given above, using a trowel for small shrubs and a spade for larger plants. There is usually no need to stake shrubs except those trained or grafted as standards (with a single stem, like a miniature tree), and large specimens being transplanted. Don't forget to water and mulch.

Climbers

In a small garden you can grow many more plants if you make full use of vertical space by growing climbing plants up walls and fences, on arches, pergolas or posts, and even into trees.

Supports for climbers

A few plants, like ivy or *Hydrangea petiolaris* (climbing hydrangea), are self-clinging. In the wild they hoist themselves towards the light up tree trunks or cliffs by means of tiny suction pads or rootlets growing out of the stems. They will do the same up a wall, fence or pillar. The only help they need is a cane leant against the support to guide the early shoots in the right direction. In the wild they also creep along the ground and can be used as ground cover in the garden too.

Others need the support of trellis or wires, and it is important to install the support before you plant.

Plants which climb by twining or by means of tendrils clasping the support need to be tied to it initially, but once they get going can climb without help, although they will give better coverage if, when they are putting out new shoots, you coax them in the right direction. In this category are wisteria, vines, honeysuckle, clematis. These plants can also scramble through shrubs or trees, but it is important when positioning them to match the vigour of the host to that of the climber, or you will find the host strangled to death.

Other plants, like roses, make their way in the wild by hooking their thorns onto other plants, and these need tying in to a supporting frame. Types of support include:

TRELLIS Square or diamond mesh constructed from timber treated with preservative. Trellis can either be painted or left to weather to an unobtrusive silvery grey. If it is painted, avoid using any shade of green paint except the very darkest or an olive-khaki shade.

DESIGN TIP

Bright green paint never looks right against the subtle and varied greens of foliage. The same applies to plastic mesh: black is more unobtrusive than green, and plain galvanized wire is more discreet than wire coated with green plastic.

Below Climbers can be grown on free-standing arches and arbours as well as on walls and fences.

Above *Lonicera periclymenum* (honeysuckle) climbs by twining its shoots round the support. In time it will grow dense enough to hide the supporting wire or trellis.

Below Climbers should be tied in with string or plastic, not wire which strangles the branches as they grow fatter.

WIRES Galvanized or plastic-covered to prevent corrosion, stretched horizontally under tension at intervals of 30cm (1ft) and attached to the wall or fence with vine eyes.

CHAINLINK Fence panels or panels of plastic mesh or chicken wire.

Whatever support you use, it is important to fix it about 2in (5cm) out from the wall. If the wire or trellis is tight up against the wall, neither plant tendrils nor wire or string ties will be able to pass behind it. Climbing plants will also be healthier if the air can circulate behind them. It is a good idea to fix trellis or wire mesh panels to the wall with hooks so that the whole panel, with the plant attached, can be lowered when the wall needs pointing or repainting.

Some climbing plants are annuals, like runner beans and sweet peas. Others are perennials which die down in winter. They do not have to have permanent support but can be grown up wigwams of bamboo, screens of nylon netting or other temporary structures.

HOW? Make the planting hole at least 45cm (18in) out from the wall. The soil close to the wall will be poor, dry and may be full of mortar rubble. Also, the roots and swelling main stems of strong climbers like wisteria can damage a wall in time.

- Mix a bucketful of compost and a good handful of granular fertilizer (see Chapter 13, Feeding) into the soil at the bottom of the hole.
- If the plant arrives tied to a cane, do not untie it until after planting. If it has several strong shoots, push a cane for each shoot into the planting hole, leaning the canes against the wall or fence that the plant is to be trained on. The canes should make a fan shape.
- When you put the plant into the hole, lean it at an angle towards the wall or support. Spread out the roots.
- Backfill the hole with more of the soil and compost mix. Tread the soil firm.
- After planting, untie the stems from their cane, separate them gently if they are twined around each other and train each shoot to its new cane and, if the shoots are long enough, to the main support structure, tying them at strategic points as necessary.
- Cut off any weak or damaged shoots. Water well and mulch.

Climbers can be tied to their supports with plastic-covered wire, with patent plastic ties, with raffia or with jute garden string. I prefer to use string, as it is less likely than wire to damage swelling stems by cutting into them. On the other hand, it does need renewing more frequently. Try to use reef knots that can be undone easily later.

Special case: clematis

Clematis often performs disappointingly. To give of its best it needs special treatment when planting.

- Dig a hole 60x60cm (2x2ft).
- Fork two or three handfuls of bonemeal into the bottom of the hole. Cover with 15-20cm (6-9in) of well rotted manure or compost.
- Half-fill the hole with soil mixed with peat and bonemeal.
- Plant the clematis with its rootball 5-8cm (2-3in) below soil level, burying some buds or leaf joints. If necessary, lay the plant on its side to achieve this: roots will form on the buried stem and new shoots will grow from below ground level.
- Cover with soil and firm carefully.
- Cover the root area with tiles or a paving slab to keep the roots cool, or use mulch 8cm (3in) thick.
- Never let the roots dry out.

Perennials and biennials, including vegetables

The technique is the same whether you are planting ornamental flowering plants or vegetable crops, whether you have bought the young plants or seedlings or whether you have raised them yourself and are moving them from trays or a seedbed (see Chapter 15, Increase and Multiply). You can also move self-seeded plants like foxgloves or forget-me-nots to new positions.

WHEN? Most perennials and biennials can be planted in autumn, when the soil is still warm, or spring, but there are some perennials which are not one hundred per cent hardy, and it is safer to plant them in late spring.

- Perennials for spring planting include *Agapanthus*, *Alstroemeria*, *Artemisia arborescens*, *Crocosmia*, *Lobelia cardinalis* and hybrids, *Penstemon* and *Zantedeschia*.

WHERE? Between shrubs in mixed beds and borders, in a border devoted to herbaceous plants or in containers. Whichever is the case, the soil should have been dug over earlier, thoroughly weeded and any organic material already added.

Above and opposite far right Plant flag irises *(Iris germanica)* with the top half of the rhizome exposed. Dig a shallow planting hole and make a mound of soil at the centre. Cut back the leaves to about 10cm (4in) and put the rhizome on the mound. Spread the roots evenly. Cover with soil to half the rhizome's depth. Firm and water in.

Left *Alstroemeria* Ligtu hybrids will spread freely if planted in spring in a sheltered, well-drained position.

DESIGN TIP

Plant perennials in bold clumps or drifts of five or more of a kind. Odd numbers give a more natural effect; three plants are adequate in small borders.

Above *Agapanthus campanulatus* 'Isis' flowers in late summer and associates well with fuchsias. It is an excellent plant for containers. Vulnerable to frost, it should be planted in spring rather than autumn.

Right Plant perennials in bold groups at the correct distance apart. *Salvia nemorosa* are grouped at 45cm (18in) apart. The violet flower spikes contrast vividly with the leaves of a golden acer.

HOW? Most of these are small plants when young and can be planted with a trowel rather than a spade, using your hands rather than your heel to firm the soil round each plant, and a watering can with a rose attachment rather than a hosepipe to water them in. Most perennials are best planted with the base of the plant level with the surrounding soil, but these have special requirements:

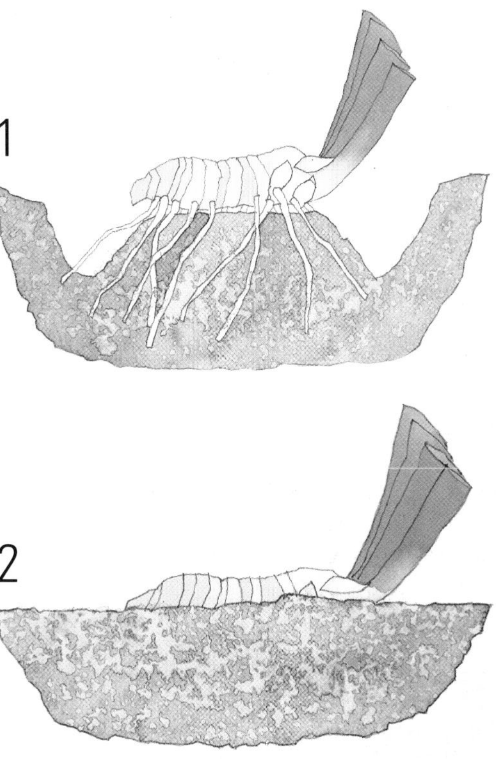

- Flag irises (*Iris germanica*, shown above) like their rhizomes to be baked in the sun. Dig out a wide, shallow planting hole, make a low mound in the middle and rest the iris rhizome on the mound, spreading out the roots on either side (1). The rhizome should be pointing south to get the maximum sunlight. Then cover the roots and the lower part of the rhizome with soil and firm it (2). The central ridge of the rhizome should be showing above the soil. Unlike most perennials which are planted in early autumn or spring (or year-round if bought in containers), irises get off to a good start if planted in July or August, after flowering.
- Paeonies can prove a disappointment, producing few flowers or none. More often than not the reason is that they have been planted too deep. They will reward you if you plant the crowns with the buds just showing above the surface, and certainly no deeper than 2.5cm (1in). They will go on getting better and better if you prepare a deep, wide planting hole, adding plenty of organic material. Mulch annually with manure or compost.

Annuals

Half-hardy annuals

These include *Antirrhinum* (snapdragon), *Impatiens, Lobelia,* marigold (African and French), petunia, *Salvia*, stock, *Nicotiana* (tobacco plant) and *Zinnia.* They can be grown from seed at home or bought at various stages of growth from plugs (small seedlings with their roots filling a little wedge-shaped plug of compost) to plants in full flower.

Plants in full flower are best avoided: they are past their best by the time you plant them. Buy whilst they are still in bud.

Hardy annuals

Best grown from seed in their final flowering position, as most of them do not take kindly to being transplanted. Among them are cottage garden favourites *Alyssum,* pot marigold, cornflower, larkspur, love-in-a-mist, poppy, sweet pea and *Nasturtium.*

WHERE? Most annuals prefer a sunny position, but busy lizzies and *Nicotiana* are happy in shade. Half-hardy annuals are great stand-bys for filling gaps in summer borders, for formal bedding schemes and for window boxes, pots and hanging baskets.

Hardy annuals are ideal for a quick effect in a new garden and to fill gaps between newly planted shrubs. In the latter case, don't plant them too close to the shrubs or they will soon swamp them.

Above Petunias are ideal for pots and window boxes as well as in the border. The silver leaves of *Helichrysum petiolare* tones down the petunia's vibrant magenta.

WHEN? The seed of half-hardy annuals is sown in the greenhouse (or on the kitchen windowsill) in February or March (see Chapter 15, Increase and Multiply). After pricking out and growing on they can go out into the garden towards the end of May or in June. Plugs are best bought early (during April) and grown on in trays or pots indoors (greenhouse or windowsill) until the end of May. When the time comes, plant when the soil is moist but not saturated. If you do

Left Lathyrus odoratus. Not all sweet peas are fragrant. Make sure you buy scented varieties.

TIPS

- Bedding plants raised or bought in degradable fibre pots are more expensive but get off to a good start as their roots are not disturbed.
- Don't worry if you are late sowing annuals. They will just start flowering a few weeks later than those sown earlier.

PLANTING ANNUALS

1 With a trowel, dig out a hole just big enough to hold the plant roots comfortably.

2 Lift the plants gently from the tray, one at a time, using a trowel or widger.

3 Put the plant in the planting hole, disturbing the roots as little as possible. Plant with the neck at or just below the soil level. Firm gently with the fingers, and water in thoroughly with a fine rose.

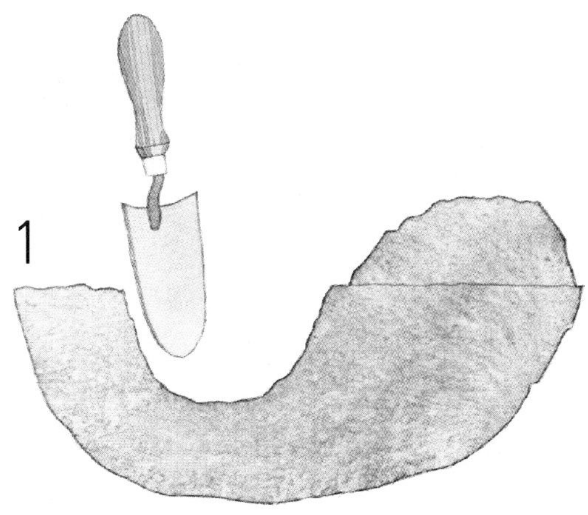

your planting on a dull day or in the evening, the plants will not suffer stress from strong sunlight and will have a night in which to recover.

Don't be tempted to buy half-hardy plants as soon as they appear in shops and garden centres, which is often ridiculously early. They should not be planted outside until all risk of frost is past, and even if there is no frost, chilly nights will set them back.

Hardy annuals are sown in the open in March and April.

TOOLS

- Fork to break the soil down if the site has not been prepared in advance.
- Trowel: a narrow bladed trowel is the best tool for planting most bedding plants.
- Widger: for seedlings and small plants the broad end of a widger is useful.
- Watering can with a fine rose.

HOW? Bedding plants are fragile and the less they are handled the better. I find it easier not to wear gloves for this rather delicate operation.

- Water plants thoroughly in their trays or pots. Leave to drain for an hour or so.
- Make sure the soil where the plants are to go is moist, weed-free and without stones or lumps.
- Keep the tray of plants in the shade, even if it is only the shade cast by the wheelbarrow, and only lift out one plant at a time.
- First make a hole just large enough to receive the plant, then lift the plant carefully with the trowel or widger, disturbing the roots as little as possible. Slide the plant into the hole and firm the soil around it gently with your fingers.
- Water thoroughly. Keep an eye on the plants and in dry weather water daily until they are growing strongly.

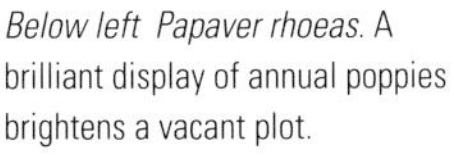

Below left *Papaver rhoeas*. A brilliant display of annual poppies brightens a vacant plot.

Below centre *Centaurea cyanus* 'Polka dot'. Cornflower seeds are available in mixed colours as well as the traditional blue.

Below right *Calendula* 'Fiesta gitana'. Double marigolds in mixed shades.

Bulbs and corms

I enjoy bulbs more than any other kind of plant, indoors and out. Once the first shoots of snowdrops and aconites have broken the earth's crust, the rest of the spring bulbs follow thick and fast: crocuses, daffodils, scillas, *Chionodoxa*, anemones, hyacinths, fritillaries and tulips.

WHERE? Most spring bulbs will grow up through turf and other low ground cover. Underneath deciduous trees, where grass grows sparsely and the sun shines through when the trees are leafless, is an ideal situation.

But beech trees, and evergreens such as yew and holly, cast such dense shade that only the bravest bulbs will survive. Hardy cyclamen, *Cyclamen coum*, *C. hederifolium* (*C. neapolitanum*) and *C. purpurascens* (*C. europaeum*), tolerate these conditions. The small pink or white flowers appear in autumn before the leaves. In winter the heart-shaped leaves form a dense carpet; they are dark green and some are prettily marked and marbled with silvery white.

Some miniature narcissi and the little February-flowering irises, *Iris danfordiae* and *I. reticulata*, do not like competition and are better off at the front of the border or in a rock garden. They like well-drained soil and are happiest on chalk or limestone.

Small bulbs can be planted to grow up through low ground cover such as thymes, prostrate campanula and creeping sedum. Larger bulbs planted between herbaceous perennials will fill the gaps until the leaves of the perennials have developed. Use stately crown imperials (*Fritillaria imperialis*), tulips and hyacinths.

Summer-flowering bulbs, such as lilies and alliums, are a valuable component of herbaceous and mixed borders.

Left Cherry blossom, daffodils and tulips make a spring display.

Most bulbs appreciate good drainage but do not like very dry conditions. One that will thrive in a dry, sunny place is *Triteleia laxa* (*Brodiaea laxa*). It has heads of starry mauve-blue flowers in late spring and early summer.

WHEN? The earliest bulbs to be planted are the autumn-flowering crocuses and colchicums. They should go in towards the end of summer (July to August). If left till later they will already be putting out shoots, as they start flowering in early autumn. Next come all the spring bulbs except tulips. Tulips should not be planted until November as early growth is vulnerable to frost. Choose a time when the soil is not wet and sticky but is moist enough not to crumble as you lift it.

TOOLS

Everyone has their favourite bulb-planting tools:

- Spade to lift turf when planting bulbs in lawns, orchards or meadows. Make sure the blade is sharp.
- Long-handled bulb planter for planting daffodil and tulip bulbs in close-mown turf. Short-handled bulb planters are less useful: the twisting action needed to operate the planter puts a strain on the wrist.

BULB PLANTERS

Bulb planters come in two basic sorts. Long-handled ones usually have a footrest and place less stress on the wrists when twisting to cut out a plug of turf. Short-handled ones may cause strain on the wrist but can be perfectly adequate on light soils.

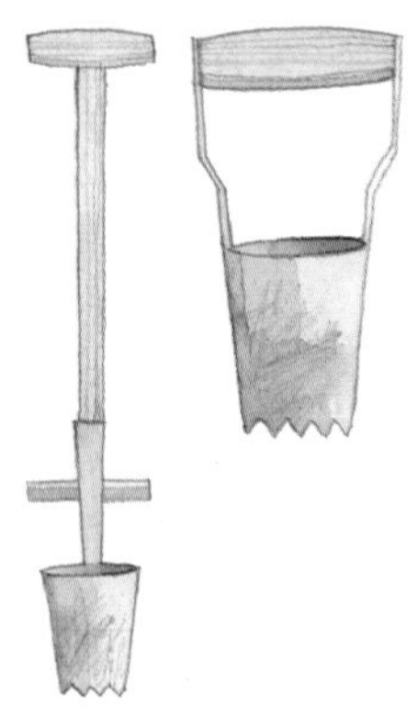

TIPS

- It doesn't seem to matter if you are late getting bulbs planted. I have planted daffodils as late as February, and they flowered at the normal time. However, if you are late they may have started sprouting, and care is needed to avoid damaging the shoots.
- With some bulbs and corms it is difficult to see which way up they should be planted. With cyclamen, look for traces of roots at the base. With others, if in doubt plant them on their sides – not ideal, but better than upside-down.
- Dig in plenty of grit before planting lilies, and sit each bulb on a handful of grit or course sand. If drainage is poor, the bulbs will rot.
- Grass must not be mown until the bulb foliage has died down, so if necessary allow gaps between groups of bulbs so that paths can be mown through the long grass.

Left A few yellow and white intruders give a more natural look to this carpet of early-flowering *Crocus tomasinianus* 'Whitewell Purple' in grass under trees.

- Trowel for planting small bulbs. A narrow trowel is useful. I have seen an apple-corer recommended, to be used in the same way as the larger bulb planter, but I have not tried it.
- Widger for planting small bulbs.
- Labels and an indelible marker to mark the position of bulbs in borders, so that you do not dig them up when planting something else.

PLANTING BULBS

1 The bulb planter cuts out a cone-shaped plug of earth, and the bulb is placed in the bottom of the hole.

2 The cone-shaped plug is then replaced on top of the bulb.

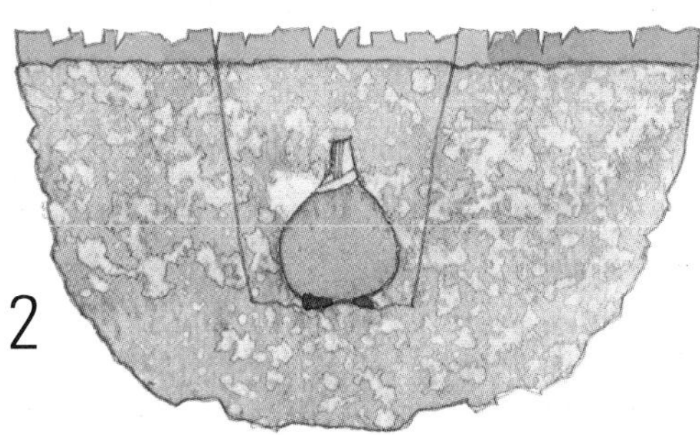

- Black cotton. Birds like to peck at crocus flowers; they seem to go mostly for the yellow ones. They can be deterred by stretching above the bulbs a network of black cotton (invisible except close up), wound onto short sticks.

HOW? Bulbs in grass should look as if they came there naturally. Scattering them in handfuls and planting where they fall is the easiest way to get this effect. If you are planting the bulbs by lifting turf and placing them underneath, try to make a random effect with some bulbs closer together than the 'correct' planting distance and some further apart.

In beds and borders bulbs look best in groups or drifts. At the front of borders they look best curving in and out between groups of other plants rather than as an even edging.

Planting bulbs in turf

HOW?
- With a spade, cut a rectangular panel of turf vertically to the required depth on three sides.
- Slide the spade under and fold back the turf.
- If the ground under the turf is compacted, loosen it with a fork.
- Scatter the bulbs, turn them point uppermost.
- Fold the turf back over them and tread it down gently.

Alternatively, use a trowel or bulb planter to take out a plug of soil to the correct depth, drop the bulb in and replace the plug.

Recommended Planting Distances

Recommended planting distances are not mandatory, but are a useful guide to spacing the plants so that they do not crowd each other.

Distances for the more popular bulbs are listed below with planting depths for 'ordinary' soil. In light, sandy soil they should be planted a little deeper and in heavy clay soil not as deep.

A general rule is to plant bulbs from two to three bulb widths apart and cover them with two to three times their own depth of soil.

	Distance apart	Depth
Anemone	10-15cm (4-6in)	4-5cm (1½-2in)
Chionodoxa	5-10cm (2-4in)	5-8cm (2-3in)
Colchicum	23cm (9in)	8-10cm (3-4in)
Crocus	8-10cm (3-4in)	5-8cm (2-3in)
Cyclamen	10-15cm (4-6in)	Exception to the rule: the corms should be barely covered
Endymion (bluebell)	10-15cm (4-6in)	10-15cm (4-6in)
Eranthis (winter aconite)	8cm (3in)	2.5cm (1in)
Fritillaria meleagris	10-15cm (4-6in)	10-15cm (4-6in)
Fritillaria imperialis	23-40cm (9-15in)	20cm (8in)
Galanthus (snowdrop)	8-15cm (3-6in)	2.5cm (1in)
Hyacinthus	15-23cm (6-9in)	13-15cm (5-6in)
Iris (miniature)	5-10cm (2-4in)	5-8cm (2-3in)
Lilium	depends on species	
Muscari (grape hyacinth)	8-10cm (3-4in)	8cm (3in)
Narcissus (including Daffodil)	10-20cm (4-8in)	15cm (6in) most varieties
	5-8cm (2-3in)	8cm (3in) miniatures
Scilla	8-10cm (3-4in)	5-8cm (2-3in)
Tulipa	15cm (6in)	15-30cm (6-12in)

Bottom right A fine display of Dutch crocuses at Kew Gardens, London. Birds peck the flowers of yellow crocuses, but this white and mauve scheme is unscathed.

Moving mature plants

Sooner or later you will want to move plants. If you move house (and garden) there is no reason why you should not take a few favourite plants with you. Or perhaps you are altering the layout of a garden, or rationalizing a garden that has become overcrowded. You may want to correct earlier mistakes, such as planting sun-loving plants in a shady position. Sites which started out sunny sometimes become shady when neighbouring plants grow out to overhang them.

Five years or so after planting, your original planting scheme may become overcrowded; most gardens reach a stage when gardening is more a matter of taking plants out than putting them in.

Large shrubs and trees

Before attempting to undertake this major operation, consider whether moving is the best solution to your problem. Stricter pruning may serve instead. Tired, old plants, or those that have developed an undesirable shape from being crowded out on one side, are not worth saving: get rid of them.

If you have a choice of what to move from an overcrowded border, move smaller, younger plants in preference to mature ones; they have a better chance of survival.

Don't try to move fast-growing, short-lived shrubs like *Buddleja, Ceanothus,* and *Cistus.* The following are also difficult to move successfully: *Colutea, Genista, Gleditsia, Robinia, Ulex, Wisteria.* Conifers don't like being moved except when small.

WARNING Moving trees or large shrubs is heavy work and may need two reasonably strong people. If in doubt, call in a professional who will have the right equipment.

WHEN? Least stress is suffered by a plant if it is moved during its dormant period: between late autumn and early spring for deciduous trees and shrubs. At this time of year the roots are not feeding and there are no leaves to suffer stress from sun, wind or frost. Evergreens are best moved in early autumn or late spring when the soil is warm and the roots can put on immediate growth.

Pick a calm day when the soil is moist but not wet. Water the plant copiously for a few days before you move it.

TOOLS

- Spade: make sure the blade is sharp.
- Fork.
- Secateurs.
- Pruning saw.
- Strong string.
- Knife.
- Large sheet of hessian or polythene on which to lift the plant.
- Sheet of hessian or polythene to hold soil from the planting hole.

HOW? The aim is to cause the minimum stress to the plant. Its roots should be disturbed as little as possible and it should be out of the ground for the shortest possible time.

- Prepare the new hole, digging out an area twice as wide as the root spread of the plant and the same depth. Pile the topsoil on a plastic sheet beside the hole. Remove any large stones, and if you hit subsoil, remove that and bring enough topsoil from elsewhere in the garden to make up the bulk. Fork over the bottom of the hole to loosen the soil and fork in one or two spadefuls of compost or manure with two handfuls of bonemeal.

TIPS

- Don't be put off if you can only move plants at the 'wrong' time. The chances of success are reasonable if the job is done correctly and if aftercare is conscientious.
- The chances of moving large trees (up to 5m/15ft tall) and shrubs (up to 2.5m/9ft) successfully are improved if they are prepared by root pruning in advance. This can be done in spring and the plant moved in autumn, or in autumn to move it a year later.

Below *Buddleja globosa* is difficult to move successfully. It grows fast, so scrap it and start again.

- Water the hole copiously and allow the water to drain away.
- With secateurs and/or pruning saw, tidy the plant by cutting out dead wood, removing weak branches and shortening any ungainly shoots.

MOVING A SHRUB

1 Before moving a shrub, prepare a new planting hole twice as wide as the root spread of the plant, and as deep. The root area will be equivalent to the spread of the branches. Fork over the bottom, adding compost or well-rotted farmyard manure. Water the hole, and allow the water to drain away.

1

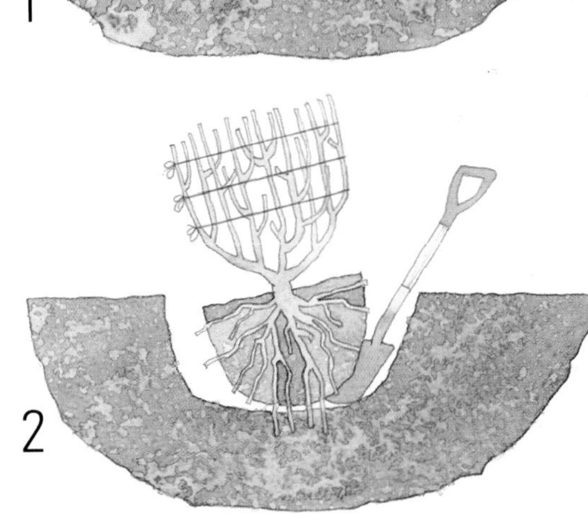

2 Cut out all dead and weak wood, and cut back the remaining growth to about 45cm (18in). Tie the branches together with soft string. Dig out a circle around the root ball, cutting through large roots with secateurs or pruning saw. Cut through the roots under the shrub by chopping with a spade.

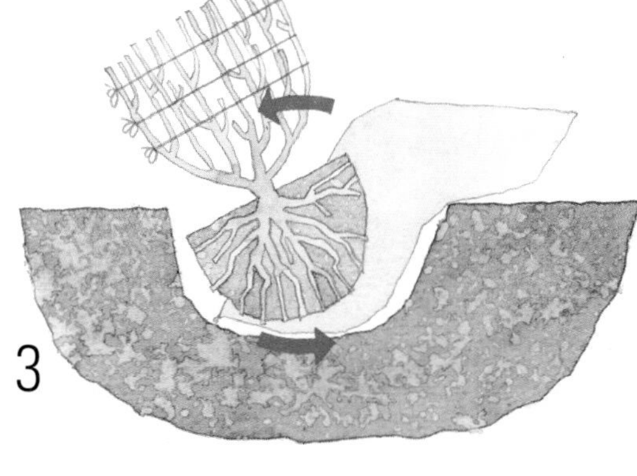

3 Rocking the plant gently, ease a sheet of polythene or hessian beneath the root ball. Wrap the entire root ball in hessian, and tie firmly around the base of the stem. Carry the plant by the root ball; do not lift it by the stem.

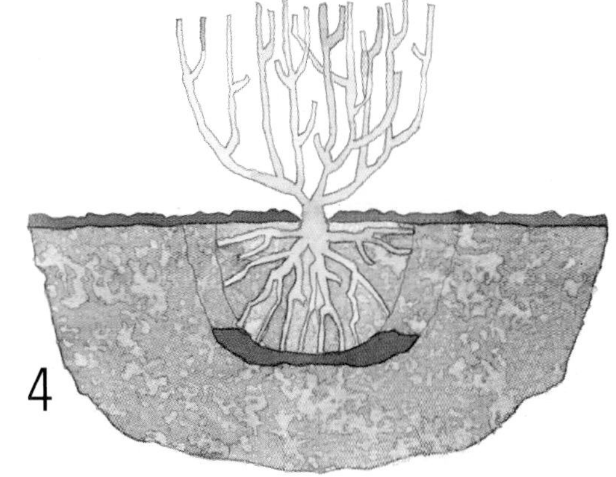

4 Put the plant in its new hole. Ease out the hessian from beneath it. Back fill with topsoil, and firm in with your feet. Make sure the new soil level is the same as the old. Water thoroughly, and apply a mulch. Water thoroughly in dry spells until growing strongly.

- Using string, tie the branches as upright and tightly as possible without damaging them. This will make the plant easier to handle and prevent branches being broken in transit.
- To dig up the shrub or tree, first dig out a circle around the root ball. The diameter of the trench will be about as wide as the spread of the branches. You can get away with a smaller circle, but the wider you can manage, the more roots will be preserved. However, plants with large, widely spaced roots positively benefit from root pruning as the process encourages new feeding roots to develop. Use a sharp spade and chop cleanly through any roots you encounter. Use secateurs or a pruning saw to sever thicker roots. Then use the spade to cut underneath the plant, cutting roots as necessary. You may need to lean the plant from side to side to complete this stage of the operation. Do resist the temptation to yank it out by hand: it will tear the roots.
- With the plant still in its hole, ease the hessian or polythene sheet under the rootball, rocking the plant to and fro until it is in the centre of the sheet. Pull the edges of the sheet up round the stem and tie them to it. Lift the plant by the sheet, not by its stem. If it is very heavy two people can lever it up using a spade or fork at opposite sides.
- Put it into the new hole, adjusting the soil level to match the level in the previous position. Untie the sheet and ease it out from under the rootball.
- Backfill with topsoil, treading it in firmly.
- Water thoroughly and spread a 5cm (2in) layer of mulch.
- If the plant needs support, do not damage the root system by driving stakes through it. Make a triangle of stout pegs around the plant and anchor the stem to them with guy lines threaded through lengths of plastic hose to protect the stem.
- If you are moving the plant in summer, spray it with a diluted solution of non-fungicide wallpaper paste to prevent water loss through the leaves.
- Keep an eye on the plant until it is growing well. Water (but do not drown) it in dry spells. The leaves of evergreens may become desiccated. If necessary, put up a windbreak made of plastic mesh on the vulnerable side and spray the leaves with water daily for a week or two after moving. Continue with this if the leaves wilt or look dull. Stress may cause evergreens to lose some or even most of their leaves but this does not mean the plant is dead. Wait and see if new leaves appear the following spring before you give up on it.

Herbaceous plants

Preferably in autumn or spring, prepare a hole, dig up the plant, drop it into the hole and firm the soil around it. This is a perfect chance for you to remove any roots of bindweed, couch grass or ground elder that have might have invaded the plant's own root system. In fact, it is sometimes necessary to move an entire herbaceous border simply in order to get rid of these pernicious weeds.

You may want to take the opportunity to divide established plants and make a number of new young plants. Follow the instructions for propagation by division in Chapter 15, Increase and Multiply.

Bulbs

Normally, bulbs are planted in autumn when they are dormant. However, if you want to move some, even if you remembered to mark their position when they were in flower, you are likely to damage the bulbs with spade or fork when lifting them. It is best to lift them when the flowers have faded but the leaves are still visible.

Next season's flowers depend on nourishment taken in through the leaves, so do not cut them off. There are two options:

- Dig them out carefully, keeping as much soil on the roots as possible, and replant them in plastic pots. Keep them watered and feed with liquid fertilizer once a fortnight until the leaves have died. Then clean off the soil and lay them in trays in a cool, dry place. When dry they can be bagged up and stored in cool, dry, dark conditions till planting time in the autumn.
- Lift plants carefully with leaves intact, divide up crowded clumps and replant in the new site immediately, adding a top-dressing of bonemeal. Water them in dry spells until the leaves have died down.

Above Transplanting a mature *Mahonia*. A trench is dug out round the root ball and the roots are cut as necessary, using sharp secateurs or pruning saw.

Root pruning

Root pruning is used prior to moving large trees and shrubs. Done in autumn or early winter, it encourages new roots to grow, making it easier for the plant to establish itself when moved. It is also used as a remedial treatment for established fruit trees which are making a lot of vigorous top growth at the expense of fruit production.

When planting bare-rooted trees and shrubs (including roses), or when moving plants from one part of the garden to another, any roots that are damaged should be cut off neatly and cleanly. Very long roots can be shortened and crossed roots removed. The idea is to end up with an untangled, evenly distributed network.

Far left If you are moving herbaceous plants, such as *Helenium*, rather than transplant the entire clump, remove the most vigorous shoots from the outside of the clump and plant them. Throw away the tired, woody centre.

Left Lifting tulip bulbs after flowering: dig the bulbs out carefully with a spade or fork. Cut off the seed heads. Heel in or put in pots or trays of compost. Wait until the leaves die before drying off and storing until planting time in the autumn.

ROOT PRUNING

1 Mark out a circle of about 90cm (3ft) in diameter around the base of the tree using a dibber and string line.

2 Dig out a trench about 30cm (1ft) across, and 45cm (18in) deep, exposing the roots. Remove the soil carefully to avoid – as far as possible – disturbing the slender fibrous roots through which the tree feeds. Cut large, woody roots with a pruning saw. Replace the soil and firm it with your feet. The following spring feed and water the tree in dry spells.

HOW? Dig a trench 45cm (18in) deep and about 30cm (1ft) wide around the trunk of the tree. Keep it about 90cm (3ft) away from the trunk.

- Remove the soil carefully to expose the roots of the tree. There are two kinds of roots, the thin fibrous roots by which the plant feeds, which should be disturbed as little as possible, and the thick, woody roots, which anchor the tree.
- Sever the thick roots and cut the downward-growing roots from below.
- Replace the soil and firm it down.
- Stake the tree to prevent wind rock.
- The following spring, feed and water the tree in dry spells.

Note that some experts recommend root pruning in two stages, trenching and cutting a semi-circle one year, and dealing with the other half the following year.

1

2

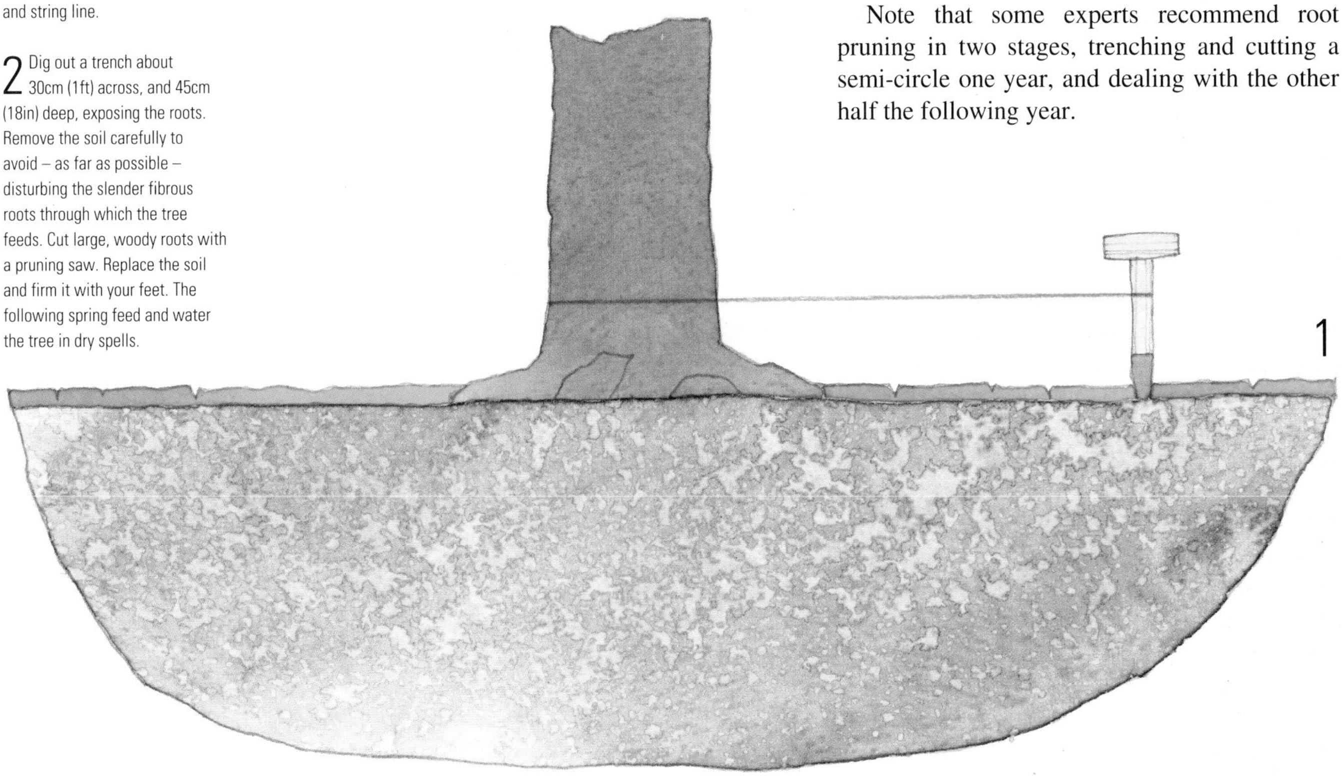

Lawns

This chapter explains how to make and maintain a lawn, but it also offers alternatives. Many gardeners take it for granted that a lawn is the best covering for vacant ground in the garden. But other choices are sometimes more satisfactory. If your garden is small, turf may get too much wear and tear to survive; a mowing machine occupies much-needed storage space, and it hardly seems worth the trouble to mow a pocket handkerchief of grass; in dense shade, grass will never thrive.

If these are your problems, it is worth considering alternatives. Sparse grass infested with moss can be replaced by ground cover plants, paving, gravel or a combination of all three. Moss can be treated as an asset and augmented with ferns and other natives of damp shade. In sunny places scented lawns can be planted with camomile or thyme. Instructions are given at the end of this chapter.

Good drainage is a prerequisite for a decent lawn. Visible signs of poor drainage are moss, algae in the form of black or green slime, and lichens. On an existing lawn the cause of poor drainage may be compaction due to excessive rolling in the past or just many years of foot traffic. If so, renovation (see below) will solve the problem.

However, if water is held on the surface because the soil is heavy clay or because there is a layer of impervious rock or an iron pan below the surface, it is essential to install drainage before you make a new lawn, and with existing lawns it is probably worth starting again from scratch. To find out, do the soil and drainage tests described in Chapter 2, Understanding Your Garden. It may be enough to break up the subsoil with a subsoiling machine but such machines are large and can only operate in areas with wide access. The installation of land drains is a skilled job and it is best to pay for some professional assistance.

Making a new lawn

Turf or seed

The first decision to take is whether you are going to lay turf or sow seed. Turf is expensive but instant (although ideally you should not walk on it for a month after laying), and can be laid at almost any time of year. Apart from the cost (about ten times as much as seed), the only snags are that turf should be laid within 24 hours of delivery and that it is heavy, so you may find it difficult to handle if you are not strong.

Turf is easy to lay in straight lines, but if your lawn is to have curved and undulating edges, it will be easier to seed it. The two main problems with seed are that it needs protecting in the early stages from birds, cats, dogs and people and that the lawn is vulnerable to weeds at the beginning.

WHERE? Plan your lawn so that no one part of it gets excessive wear: avoid grassing right up to doors or French windows and avoid frequently used routes, such as from house to garage or from kitchen to compost heap. In such places grass soon wears down to bare mud, so they are best paved or gravelled. If you like the appearance of grass paths, make them wide enough to avoid getting worn down. Be aware that narrow grass borders between flower beds and hard-surfaced paths are labour-intensive to look after.

DESIGN TIP

If a conventional weekly mowing regime is too time consuming, some areas can be cut infrequently to form a meadow with close-mown paths winding through it.

Below The perfect lawn makes the perfect foil for the flower or shrub border, but its creation and maintenance will be time consuming (and may well become an obsession).

WHEN? Turf can be laid at any time provided the ground is not frozen or waterlogged, but grass seed is best sown in spring as soon as the soil has warmed up. The season for sowing continues until early summer, but the later it is left the more likely it is that regular watering will be needed. Lawns can also be sown in late summer/early autumn. As spring is a busy time in the garden, the ground preparation can be done in advance on mild winter days.

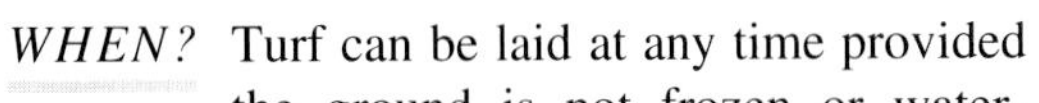

On very weedy ground it would be best to spend an entire season clearing the ground, but for that you need patience.

LEVELLING

1 For small areas and for those not intended for fine lawns, levelling can be done by eye, but small hollows may show uneven growth, and pronounced bumps will be scalped by the lawn mower. For a perfectly level lawn, mark out the area in a grid pattern, driving in stakes at 2m (80in) intervals.

2 Lay a plank across the top of the stakes and, using a spirit level, drive them in until they are perfectly level.

3 Tie string tightly between the stakes, about 2.5cm (1in) below the top of the stakes. Keep this measurement consistent, so that strings are level.

4 Rake over the soil so that it is level with the string. Use the back of the rake to push the mounds into hollows If the surface is very uneven, use topsoil from elsewhere to level it.

5 On very uneven ground you may have to move considerable quantities of soil. Level the stakes with a spirit level as before, and tie string tightly between them. Using a spade, transfer bumps to hollows as necessary.

6 Once the surface has been made roughly level, complete the operation using the back of a rake.

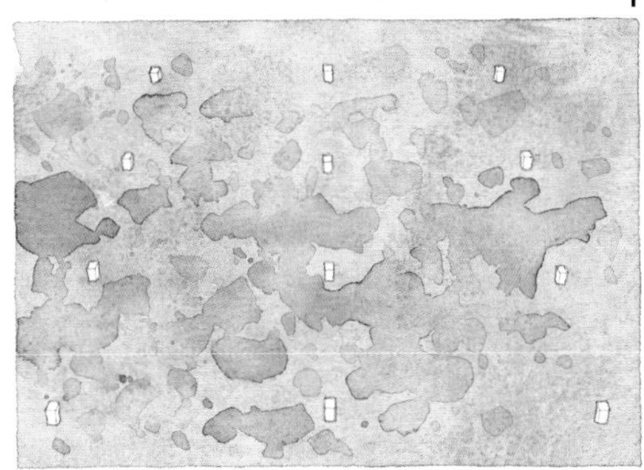

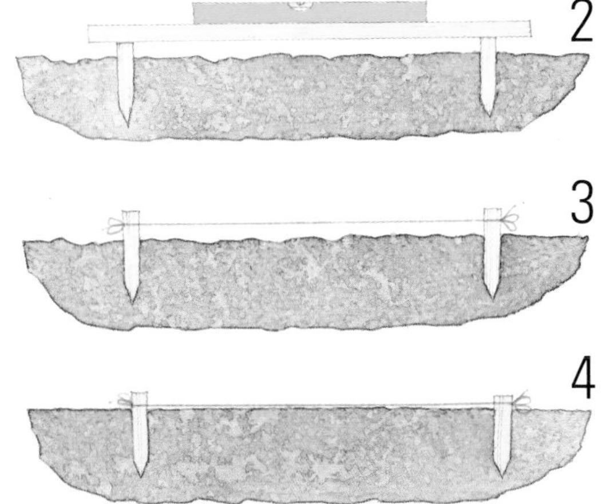

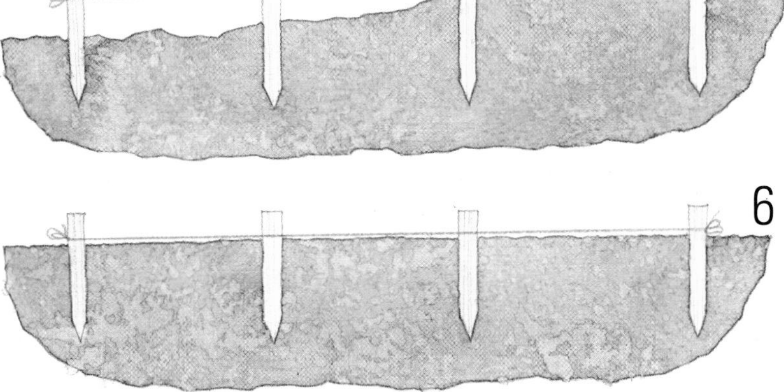

Ground preparation

If the ground is well prepared, the lawn will last as long as you do. Preparation is the same for turfing as for seeding.

TOOLS

- Weedkiller, if you don't object to using chemicals.
- Sprayer or watering can with dribble bar to apply weedkiller.
- Rotavator: the area will have to be dug over, so for all but the smallest lawns it is probably worth hiring a machine for a day. The alternative is a spade and/or fork.
- Rake to obtain a fine tilth.
- Bucket to discard stones into.
- Wheelbarrow to cart the stones away.
- Fertilizer to help the grass establish.

WEEDING By far the easiest method is to spray with a systemic weedkiller containing glyphosate which will kill all vegetation, including couch grass (also known as twitch). The best time to spray is when the weeds are growing strongly. In areas infested with couch and other perennial weeds, such as dandelions, docks, thistles and nettles, it is a good idea to wait for a second growth of weeds to appear and spray again. A third treatment may even be necessary.

If you do not like to use chemicals, the no-work weed-killing method is to cover the area with old carpet or with black plastic weighted down round the edges and leave it for six months. The alternative is to dig the plot by hand, forking out all roots, especially the thin, white roots of couch.

LEVELLING AND MAKING A TILTH Do the final preparation immediately prior to turfing or seeding on a day when the soil is slightly damp but not so wet that it sticks to your shoes or boots.

- Roughly rake over the surface, removing stones and other debris as you go. I find it easiest to put them into a bucket beside me, and when it gets heavy transfer the contents to a wheelbarrow.
- If you want a level lawn, use the back of the rake to push soil from bumps into hollows. In informal gardens with gentle slopes it can be more attractive to leave the natural contours than to flatten them, but small mounds and steep slopes will impede the mower.
- Firm the ground by treading it with small steps and even pressure with the heels. After firming, correct any bumps and hollows.
- Scatter a general granular fertilizer at 50g per sq m (1½oz per sq yd). Rake gently to and fro until you have made a good tilth – tilth means a fine, crumb-like surface.

Laying turf

Two kinds of turf are available:

MEADOW TURF Cut from fields by farmers or by developers preparing sites for building, this is not usually the romantic mix of grass and wild flowers that the word 'meadow' conjures up. It is more likely to consist mainly of coarse, fast-growing rye grass and will probably include weeds. But it is hard-wearing and usually cheap. It usually comes in rolls 40cm (16in) wide and 137cm (54in) long. They are thick, heavy and awkward to handle.

PURPOSE-GROWN TURF Specially grown for sale to gardeners and landscapers, easy to lay and usually more expensive. Two main types are available, hard-wearing turf for general use combining fine grasses with coarser ones, and ornamental turf with fine-leaved grasses only. The latter is only suitable for bowling greens and lawns which are more for looking at than walking on. Turf consisting of shade-tolerant grasses is available from some suppliers.

See the turf before you buy. Reject turf growing unevenly with any thin patches, turf growing in clay soil, turf with yellow leaves or weeds in it and turf which falls apart when you unroll it.

Small quantities can be picked up from local garden centres and DIY stores. Local suppliers will usually deliver and may lay it for you at a price. National firms selling purpose-grown turf have local depots or sell through local garden centres and stores.

WHEN? Any time, provided the ground is not frozen or too wet.

TOOLS

- String and pegs to mark out straight lines.
- Hosepipe to mark out curves.
- Plank to stand on.
- Half-moon cutting tool or sharp spade.

HOW?

- Mark out the area to be turfed with string and pegs or, if the lawn is to have a curved outline, with a hosepipe (or a length of heavy rope) laid on the ground.
- If appropriate, lay the first turf along the straight edge of a path or paving. Lay a line of turfs, butting them tight up against each other, as they will shrink slightly. If the ground is uneven, or the turfs of uneven thickness, adjust this by adding or taking away soil under them as you go.
- When you have laid the first line, put the plank over it and kneel on the plank to lay the next. Stagger the joints as you would if building a wall.
- If the edges of the lawn are curved, lay the turfs to beyond the curved edge and cut round the edge with a half-moon or sharp spade after the turfing is complete.
- Tread the turf down gently to be sure it is in contact with the soil beneath it.
- Water thoroughly with a sprinkler, making sure the water goes through the turf to the soil below. In dry weather water regularly, especially along the joints in the turf.
- When the grass is growing, mow to a height of 2.5cm (1in) until the turfs have knitted together. Thereafter mow once a week during the growing season to a height of 1.5cm (1/2in).

LAYING TURF

1 Avoid using small sections at the end of the row; they tend to disintegrate. Use sieved topsoil to level out any irregularities beneath the surface as the lawn is laid. A top dressing of fine topsoil should be applied when laying is complete, and brushed into crevices to help the turves knit together quickly and evenly.

Above Turf is delivered in rolls like short lengths of carpet. Check that the grass looks dense and healthy and reject any that has turned yellow.

Sowing grass seed

As with turf, ornamental seed mixes of fine grasses without rye grass (often described as 'front lawn' seed) and hard-wearing mixes with rye grass ('back lawn') are available. Some producers also supply special shade mixes.

For hard-wearing lawns look for mixes containing modern, fine-leaved varieties of rye grass.

WHEN? From early to late spring or from late summer to early autumn. Pick a dry day when the prepared soil is fairly dry.

TOOLS

- Seeding machine For large areas it may well be worth hiring a wheeled seeding machine.
- Plastic bowl for smaller areas. If you broadcast the seed as in the hymn 'We plough the fields and scatter. . .', a washing-up bowl is as good a container as any.
- Strip or roll of plastic to define the edge of the lawn and prevent the seeds from falling beyond it.
- Rake.
- Netting (optional) with fine mesh to protect the seed from birds and cats, and pegs to fix the netting.

HOW?

- Lay the plastic strip round the perimeter of the lawn.
- Measure the area of the lawn in square yards or square metres.
- Weigh out the correct quantity of seed as recommended on the packet, or at 50g per sq m (1½oz per sq yd), which includes some for the birds. Divide the seed into two halves.
- If you are using a machine, put in half the seed and sow in parallel lines. Then sow the other half at right angles to the first.
- If you are broadcasting the seed by hand, start by marking off two or three square metres. Measure the correct quantity of seed for this small area and scatter half the seed, walking backwards as you go. Then scatter the other half, walking at right angles to the first lot. This test area will help you to gauge how big a handful you need to achieve the correct distribution. Once you have got the hang of it, put the seed in your bowl and scatter merrily.
- Rake over the area very lightly to partly cover the seed, hiding most of it from the birds.
- Cover with netting (optional).
- If rain is forecast, pray that the forecasters have got it right. If not, water with a fine sprinkler. Tiny blades of grass should begin to cast a faint green haze over the area after two or three weeks – less in warm conditions. The young shoots are very drought-susceptible, so if there is no rain, it is important to water regularly until the grass is growing strongly.
- When the grass is 4-5cm (1½-2in) long (ornamental grasses) or 6.5-7.5cm (2½-3in) long (hard-wearing grasses), you can cut it, keeping it at a height of 2.5cm (1in) for the first few cuts and never lower than 1.25cm (½in).
- Keep off the grass for six months (ornamental grasses) or three months (hard-wearing grasses). The following spring, feed with fertilizer.

2 If your lawn edge is curved, lay the turfs so they extend beyond the final edge. Mark the curve with rope or hosepipe, and cut the turf with a sharp spade or half-moon cutter. Make sure you are not left with small sections of turf at the edge of the lawn.

Renovating and maintaining a neglected lawn

If it is in a really terrible state, weedkill the existing grass and other vegetation, tackle the drainage problems and start again from scratch. If it looks rescuable, proceed as follows.

Diagnosing the problem

Bare patches are one of the commonest problems. They may be caused by too much wear, outside a door for example, at the top and bottom of steps, along the edge of a border or where a path has been worn along a frequently used route across the lawn. These are problems that will not go away. Either resign yourself to patching the worn areas with new turf every year or replace the worn grass with flagstones or, in the case of a path, gravel or stepping stones set into the lawn.

Under trees the shade and rainwater dripping down make it difficult for grass to survive. You could try turfing or seeding with a special shade grass mix, or plant an area of shade-loving ground cover.

As already mentioned, if there is more moss than grass in a lawn it is usually a sign of poor drainage. Moss-killers (Lawnsand, for example) may keep the problem at bay, but in my experience they do not even do that. Before ripping through the lawn with a subsoiling machine, or before installing land drains, try a programme of aerating and scarifying (see below) for two years running. You should really do it every year as routine maintenance.

Weeds in the lawn such as daisies, buttercups, dandelions, plantains, lady's slipper and speedwell are not a sign of anything except that your lawn needs weeding. I have a weakness for them, because lawn weeds were the first flowers that I could name in my childhood: 'Daisies are our silver, buttercups our gold. . .' But I know that most people prefer an unbroken green sward to a spangled one.

Patching worn areas

- Fork over the top few inches, working in 70g per sq m (2oz per sq yd) of general fertilizer.
- Rake to a fine tilth.
- Scatter the appropriate mix of grass seed (see above) evenly.
- Rake it in lightly.
- Water the areas regularly until the grass is growing well.
- You will probably need to fence off the area to prevent it being walked on.

Alternatively, patch with turf bought in or lifted from elsewhere in the garden.

Scarifying

Scarecrows scare, scarifiers scarify. A scarifier is a machine which scratches up and rakes out moss and other lawn debris known as thatch. Motorized scarifiers can be hired. The job (a tedious one) can also be done by hand with a spring-tined rake. It is important to kill moss with a chemical moss-killer before you start, otherwise you are just spreading it. If you scarify by hand you should rake vigorously in two directions, one at 30° to the other. Collect up and burn the thatch that you have removed.

WHEN? The best time for these operations is early autumn, when the grass can recover and put on some new growth before the arrival of winter. Perfectionists scarify once a month.

Aerating

This means spiking the lawn to let air in and improve drainage.

WHEN? Aerating is best done in early autumn, after scarifying. On ground that is badly compacted, give it another go in late spring.

HOW? In small areas it can be done with a garden fork.

- Push the fork in vertically for about 15cm (6in), angle it back slightly to open up the holes, then pull it out.
- Work backwards to avoid treading on the area you have treated, pushing the fork in at 10cm (4in) intervals.

For larger areas special machines can be bought or hired.

TIPS

- Golf clubs and other sports centres will sometimes allow members to hire machines for scarifying and aerating, and the groundsmen to operate them.
- During a drought avoid putting the grass under stress: mow less frequently with the blades set higher than usual. Leave the clippings lying on the ground to form a light mulch.

Below This once beautiful close-mown lawn has been badly worn by the passage of many feet.

Above A lawn spangled with daisies, speedwell and buttercups can be just as attractive as one manicured to bowling green standard.

Weeding

Tall weeds, like nettles and docks in neglected grass areas, will disappear if the grass is cut short regularly for a season. If lawn weeds such as buttercups and plantains are present and the grass has grown long through neglect, treat the area as follows.

WHEN? Between late spring and early autumn, while the grass is growing strongly.

TOOLS

- Mower or scythe.
- Granular fertilizer, and an applicator or a plastic bowl.
- Weedkiller and sprayer, or watering can with dribble bar.
- Grass seed for bare patches.

HOW?
- Cut the grass to about 5cm (2in).
- Feed it with a general fertilizer.
- Two weeks later, apply a weedkiller designed for use on lawns.
- After the weeds have died, seed any bare patches that have appeared.

The only alternative to using weedkiller is to grub out all the weeds by hand with whatever implement suits you best. Large patches that consist more of weed than of grass can be lifted like turf, using a sharp spade. A long-handled bulb planter may be useful for tap-rooted weeds like dandelions and docks, an apple corer for smaller weeds.

After a summer spent eliminating weeds it pays to scarify, aerate and feed in the autumn. There are 'weed and feed' products available, which do both jobs at the same time.

Right In neglected grassland, docks *(Rumex obtusifolius)* and other tall weeds can be eliminated by regular mowing for a season.

Feeding

Every time you cut grass you are removing the nutrients that have been taken up by the blades of grass, and unless you restore nutrients from time to time, your lawn will starve. The easiest and cheapest way to do this is to leave the clippings on the ground to decay and feed the grass. If you mow little and often, as the counsel of perfection recommends, the effect will not be unsightly.

To revitalize tired lawns and to maintain healthy lawns, the experts recommend two doses of fertilizer, one in late spring/early summer, the other in early autumn. An overdose will kill the grass, so it is worth using a wheeled spreader which distributes the fertilizer evenly. These gadgets can be hired, but if you care about your lawn you will probably want to buy one.

Watering

Grass growing vigorously is less susceptible to invasion by weeds and moss. To help it hold its own against them, make sure that the grass is not dry at the roots by using a sprinkler in dry weather during the growing season. After several drought years in a row one feels guilty about using water for such a frivolous purpose, and during a drought it may not be allowed anyway.

Conserve moisture by top-dressing lawns on light soils with a thin layer of sifted garden compost. Brush it in lightly.

Alternatives to grass

In sun

CAMOMILE (*Chamaemelum nobile*) The most famous camomile lawn is at Buckingham Palace. It covers a large area and must have been a nightmare to weed in its early years. Once established, camomile makes a dense sward in which few weeds can get a roothold. But for the first year or two it needs a lot of attention. Hand-weeding camomile is time-consuming but pleasurable. The fresh green feathery foliage makes a soft cushion to kneel on, and the scent is soothing.

Camomile will stand being stepped on from time to time, but will not survive frequent foot traffic. It is best suited to small areas, around a seat in a herb garden or rose arbour, or for forming a chequer-board pattern with paving slabs. It must have a sunny site and a free-draining soil.

The non-flowering variety 'Treneague' is the best to use as its habit is low and dense. Trim it over four or five times a year to prevent long, bare stems developing. Flowering kinds need cutting more often. Small areas can be trimmed with shears. Larger camomile lawns can be cut with a mower (the blades set high) or a strimmer.

To plant a camomile lawn, prepare the site as if for a grass lawn. Tuck in the little plants 15cm (6in) apart for quick results, 30cm (1ft) apart if you are prepared to wait a little longer and want to save on the cost of the plants. Water during dry spells and weed as necessary. Camomile is quite fast growing and, if planted in the spring, the plants should knit together to form a sward by the autumn.

CLOVER During dry summers the patches of green in a brown lawn are clover. It is a more drought-resistant plant than grass, needs mowing

Golden Rules of Maintaining Lawns

Remember, prevention is better than cure.

DO

- Mow little and often. Mow hardwearing lawns once a week with the mower blade set at 2.5cm (1in) and ornamental lawns twice a week at 1cm (½in).
- Scarify and aerate at least once a year.
- Feed in spring.

DON'T

- Subject areas to unreasonable wear.
- Walk on the lawn when it is frozen or under snow.
- Scalp the lawn by mowing too close.

Above The perfect lawn demands constant attention to detail. It needs to be well fertilized, to replace the nutrients that are taken away in the clippings at every mowing.

Above Turf on narrow paths wears out quickly and is best replaced with paving in places where space is as restricted as it is under this rustic arch.

less often and is hard-wearing. I have not yet experimented with it, but I think it is a promising lawn plant. The main problem in establishing a clover lawn would be eliminating the grass: if the area is too large for hand-weeding, use the chemical preparation Weedol.

DAISIES Like clover, daisies are such persistent weeds in grass lawns that, on the principle of 'If you can't beat 'em, join 'em', I speculate on the possibility of making an all-daisy lawn. Daisies (*Bellis perennis*) are lime-lovers whereas lawn grasses will not tolerate large doses, so liberal applications of lime will encourage the daisies and discourage the grass.

THYME A carpet of thyme has much the same attributes and requirements as camomile, and can be planted the same way. Choose creeping, low varieties like *Thymus pseudolanguinosus*, which has tiny woolly grey leaves and mauve flowers, *T. serpyllum albus* with white flowers, *T. s.* 'Annie Hall' (pale pink) or *T. s. coccineus* (dark red). A mixture of these three will give a tapestry effect. By the way, bees love thyme, so don't tread on the carpet in bare feet.

In shade

MINT (*Mentha requienii*) This very low creeping mint with tiny leaves and tiny mauve flowers colonizes damp, shady places and does not mind being trodden on occasionally. However, it dies back in winter, so cover won't be permanent.

MOSS In damp, shady places where moss has taken over, keep the moss and eliminate what is left of the grass. A carpet of moss has a soft, alluring texture and can vary in colour from brightest emerald to subtle olive.

Right A camomile lawn is invitingly green and soft and its clean, fresh fragrance is delicious.

PART 2

LOOKING AFTER YOUR GARDEN

Plants that are well cared for will reward you with spectacular flowers and prolific crops of fruit. They are also less susceptible to pests and diseases than neglected plants. Understanding the principles of good maintenance, and acting on them, adds to the creative pleasure of gardening. This part explains the principles and takes you through their practical application step by step.

Pruning

A mystique has developed around the subject of pruning, so that even some experienced gardeners are daunted by it. But it is surprisingly difficult to kill a plant by incorrect pruning, and once you understand the logic behind techniques and timing, the application of common sense and sharp tools will ensure good results.

The reasons for pruning

Pruning is the removal of parts of a plant in order to channel the plant's energy in the direction you wish it to take. The term 'pruning' is most often used with reference to shrubs, but the same principle applies to cutting branches from mature trees (tree surgery) and to clipping hedges and topiary. A broad interpretation of pruning also includes the dead-heading of roses, the removal of old stems from herbaceous plants and the mowing of grass. It is usually the growth above ground that is pruned, but some plants, such as old fruit trees, can benefit from pruning of their roots. Pruning is carried out either to improve the health of a plant or to manipulate its performance in the garden.

Left On trees, diseased or unwanted branches should be removed with a clean cut, leaving intact the collar where they join the main stem.

For health

- To remove dead, diseased or damaged branches. Disease will spread if not checked, and dead or damaged branches provide opportunities for pests and diseases to enter the plant.
- To stimulate growth. Some plants will grow with renewed vigour if some or all of their branches are cut back. Removing some entire branches lets light and air into the centre of a bush, encouraging new, healthy growth.
- To increase stability. Lopsided or top-heavy plants are vulnerable to strong winds. Their shape can be corrected by careful pruning. Old shrubs which have become leggy and ungainly often respond well if they are cut back radically.

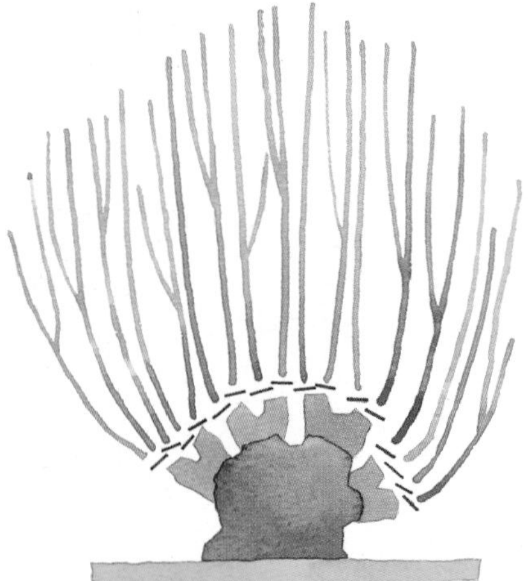

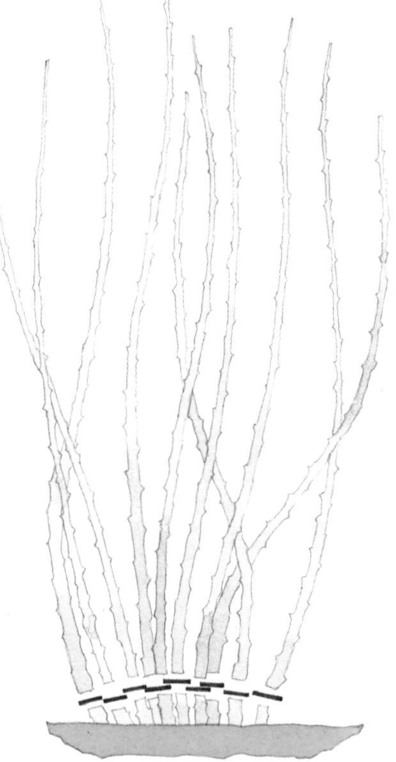

PRUNING FOR SPECIAL EFFECTS

1 Coppicing (stooling) trees and shrubs. This is a simple technique to encourage new growth with brightly coloured winter stems. Do it every year, or every other year, in early spring, just before growth resumes. On planting, cut all shoots back hard to within 7.5-10cm (3-4in) of the base. In subsequent years, simply cut back all main stems to within a few centimetres of the base, cutting out weak, spindly growth completely. Species that can be coppiced for winter stem effects include *Cornus alba*, crimson stems; *Cornus alba* 'Sibirica', scarlet stems; *Cornus stolonifera* 'Flaviramea', yellow to olive-green stems; *Salix acutifolia* 'Blue Streak', blue-white bloomed, deep purple stems; *Salix alba vitellina* 'Britzensis', bright orange-scarlet stems; *Salix alba vitellina*, egg-yolk yellow stems; *Salix daphnoïdes*, purple-violet stems; and *Salix irrorata*, white-bloomed, purple stems.

2 Pollarding. Trees grown for winter stem colour can be allowed to form a woody trunk to the desired height, before cutting back on an annual basis, as with coppicing. This technique is known as pollarding.

3 Cutting down. Some species grown for winter stem colour do not form a trunk, but instead form clumps by means of suckers. Cut back the previous year's stems to within 2.5-5cm (1-2in) of ground level annually in early spring, as or just before growth resumes. Some species, which are not grown specifically for stem colour, but which nevertheless have attractively coloured young stems, can be cut back to ground level using the one-in-three rule (see p.122); so that they produce a proportion of new growth every year. Species that can be cut to the ground for winter stem effects include *Rubus thibetanus*, blue-white bloomed, purplish stems; *Rubus cockburnianus*, brilliant white-bloomed, purplish stems; *Rubus phoenicolasius*, red bristly stems. Species cut to ground using the one-in-three rule include *Leycesteria formosa*, sea-green stems; *Kerria japonica*, bright emerald-green stems.

Right A well pruned hybrid tea rose bush. Weak stems have been removed at the base. The remaining stems are shortened to about 23cm (9in), with sloping cuts above outward-facing buds.

DESIGN TIP

Box, *Lonicera, Santolina* and other evergreen or ever-grey plants, clipped to form mounds or cones, give a firm structure to mixed planting schemes.

For performance

To encourage bigger crops of flowers and fruit. You may wish a plant to put all its energy into producing numerous flowering and fruiting shoots. This is usually achieved by light pruning at the tips of the plant's shoots. When large blooms are required for showing, there are pruning methods to ensure that quality rather than quantity is achieved.

To induce a second crop. If plants like *Helianthemum* (rock rose) and *Nepeta* (cat mint) are cut right back after flowering, they will grow new shoots and flower again in the same season.

To reduce size. Most plants are at their best if allowed to grow naturally, and planting should be planned to allow sufficient space to reach their mature size without restraint. However, that is not always possible, and it may be necessary to prune a tree or shrub to prevent it crowding out its neighbours, encroaching on a path or robbing house windows of light.

Creative pruning

To improve shape. Pruning young trees and shrubs to build up a framework of relatively few, strong branches pays dividends. It ensures good health and a graceful shape in later life.

To change shape. Pruning, sometimes with the aid of training wires or frame, can produce a plant that grows in an artificial shape. Forest trees such as beech, hornbeam or yew trimmed to form hedges are a common example. Yew, box and other bushes can be clipped into geometric or fantasy topiary figures; fruit trees can be trained as fans, espaliers and cordons; limes, hornbeams and other trees can be entwined to form screens on stilts, known as stilt hedging. The fashion for training plants into ornamental shapes for the formal garden was popular in Roman times and again in the sixteenth and early seventeenth centuries, and is currently enjoying a revival.

For special effects. Willows such as *Salix alba vitellina* and *Salix alba vitellina* 'Britzensis' ('Chermesina') and some *Cornus* (dogwood) varieties are grown for the winter effect of their colourful stems and are pruned in spring to encourage vigorous new growth each season. Some trees, including *Catalpa bignonioïdes* and *Paulownia tomentosa,* will produce huge leaves, double their normal size, if the trees are treated as shrubs and cut back hard in spring. This involves sacrificing the flowers as this form of pruning produces a fresh crop of immature stems each season and they never have a chance to reach the stage of flowering.

Below To keep topiary immaculate, trim with sharp shears or an electric hedge trimmer two or three times a year from mid- to late summer. Even if you only cut once a year it is important not to miss a year or your topiary will become misshapen. Yew *(Taxus baccata)* and box *(Buxus sempervirens)* for large pieces, *Buxus suffruticosa* for small topiary and edging) are best for complex shapes. For quicker results use privet *(Ligustrum ovalifolium)* or small-leaved ivies.

WHEN? The vast majority of plants: immediately after flowering. This ensures that the plant has time to produce new flowering stems in time for the following season.

- Plants that are grown for their fruits, whether edible or ornamental: after fruiting, usually winter or spring.
- Plants that flower in late summer and early autumn: spring rather than immediately after flowering. Pruning so late in the season would encourage tender, soft young shoots, which could be damaged by winter frosts.
- At planting time: most plants, whether planted bare-rooted from autumn to spring or from containers all year round, need some tidying up of the top growth, and sometimes the roots.

Guide to pruning times

SPRING (mid-March to early April)

- Bush, shrub, climbing and standard roses (see Chapter 19, Growing Roses).
- Shrubs which flower in the late summer or autumn: *Buddleja,* deciduous *Ceanothus*, *Fuchsia, Hydrangea,* winter jasmine.
- If not done in autumn, cut down stems of herbaceous perennials.

LATE SPRING

- As they finish flowering, prune *Forsythia, Ribes, Spiraea, Viburnum.*

SUMMER

- As they finish flowering, prune *Cytisus* (broom), *Deutzia, Genista, Helianthemum, Philadelphus,* rosemary, *Santolina, Syringa* (lilac), *Weigela.*
- Some fruit and ornamental trees should be pruned in summer, following the old rule 'stone fruit in summer, pip fruit in winter'. Cherries, plums, peaches and almonds are best pruned between mid-May and mid-July, the season when there is least risk from silverleaf and die-back diseases. See 'Special cases', p.130.

LATE SUMMER (August-September)

- Trim evergreen hedges: box, yew, privet.
- Prune rambler roses. See p.242.

AUTUMN (and/or spring)

- Cut down stems of herbaceous perennials except those with ornamental seedheads.
- Prune roots of old, unproductive fruit trees if necessary.

Care of Pruning Tools

DO

- Store them in a dry place where they will not rust.
- Put them away clean.
- Oil the joints from time to time.
- Keep cutting tools sharp: they will be much easier to use and do a better job. Either keep a whetstone to do the job yourself (see Chapter 6, The Tools of the Trade) or take your tools to a specialist at least once a year. Most firms that service mowing machines are equipped to sharpen hand tools as well. A friendly butcher who is prepared to sharpen your kitchen knives may also be willing to do secateurs and pruning knives.

DON'T

- Leave them out of doors.

Left Old, neglected fruit trees can be brought back to health and productivity by fairly drastic pruning. Use a bow saw to remove thick branches.

Right Wisteria often fails to flower if left unpruned. In late summer cut the long, whippy shoots back by three-quarters, except for those needed to form the plant's framework. In winter cut back again, leaving two or three buds.

Below A selection of pruning tools. Long-handled loppers *(left)*, Grecian saw *(left foreground)* and secateurs *(centre foreground)* are essential equipment.

WINTER

- Fruit trees and bushes producing pip fruits. See 'Special cases', p.130.
- Remove dead and diseased branches of trees and shrubs.
- Cut hazel branches for use as pea sticks and supports for herbaceous plants.

LATE WINTER (February)

- Some clematis types. See 'Special cases', p.130.
- Shrubs grown for their colourful stems, such as *Cornus alba* and *Salix*.

Tools

It is important to have the right tool for each job. If you try to cut through a branch of half an inch diameter with a pair of secateurs, you will ruin the secateurs and probably the tree as well. You may also strain your wrist or shoulder. It is worth investing in the best tools you can afford.

- Gloves.
- Secateurs.
- Knife: if you are confident of your skill in using it.
- Scissors: short-bladed household scissors are useful for jobs that are too fiddly for secateurs, such as dead-heading, cutting out spent stems of small herbaceous plants, trimming cuttings, cutting flowers for the house, cutting string, etc.
- Shears: essential for trimming hedges and topiary.
- Long-handled pruner/lopper for branches that are too high to reach with secateurs.
- Pruning saw to prune out branches more than 2.5cm (1in) thick on trees or large shrubs.
- Mechanical hedge trimmer: only if you have a lot of hedge. Observe safety rules strictly.

General principles of pruning

If you understand the basic rules of pruning, your common sense will tell you how to apply them when you are faced with pruning an unfamiliar plant.

Above all, prune cautiously. It is very easy to remove a branch, but it is impossible to put it back again.

Start with a mental picture of what you want the plant to look like and when. Between each cut, step back and take a good look at the plant from all angles, so that you can see what is needed to develop an even and graceful shape.

Removing unwanted branches

The old-fashioned method of cutting branches off flush with the stem they are growing from is now known to be positively harmful. It renders the wood more vulnerable to wound parasites and wood decaying organisms.

Trees and shrubs have a series of natural defenses to prevent the infection of wounds; the most important is situated at the branch collar (where the branch joins the parent main stem). For the tree to heal itself quickly and effectively, it is important not to cut into the collar.

Dead-heading

Your garden will look more attractive if you remove the stems of shrubs and herbaceous plants when the flowers have faded. But there is another reason for cutting off the faded flowers on shrubs and cutting out the spent stems of herbaceous plants, biennials and annuals: the objective of the plant is to reproduce itself by developing ripe seed, and when it has accomplished this task, it will stop flowering and die down. But if you prevent it from reaching the seed stage by cutting off the flower stems, it will try again, by producing a fresh crop of flowers.

Hard pruning

The harder you prune, the more vigorous the new growth. Severe pruning can also be an effective last resort to renovate a sickly shrub.

TIPS

- All plants will get away better after pruning if their root area is kept free of other plants, eliminating competition.
- Some plants have statuesque or filigree winter shapes, or ornamental seedheads. Leave them uncut to decorate the garden in winter, to cut for the house and to spray for Christmas decorations. Allow seedheads to develop and ripen if you want to collect seeds for propagation.

THE ONE-IN-THREE RULE
Many shrubs produce their best display on young, vigorous wood; removing one stem in three helps ensure regular replacement of flowering wood. Use the system to remove weak or badly placed growth, and keep the bush within bounds, with an open, airy centre. Begin pruning when specimens have had three or four years to establish themselves. In subsequent years, take out a third of the old wood annually. If shrubs need further tidying, cut the remaining stems back by up to one-third of their length. First stand back and examine the overall balance of the shrub, and earmark likely branches for removal. Take out the oldest wood first, cutting back almost to ground level. Treat weak growth in a similar fashion. If the shrub still looks crowded, take out some branches, open up the centre of the bush, cutting to a promising new growth bud. Sometimes buds will not be apparent, and you may have to tidy back the stub, once new buds have broken out.

Above Lavender can be kept dense and bushy by clipping after flowering. Remove flower stems and straggly growth but avoid cutting into old wood.

Above and below To encourage strong stems and big flowers, buddlejas can be cut back in early spring to 5-8cm (2-3in) of the old wood.

STOOLING Those shrubs grown principally for their colourful bark in winter should also be pruned hard. To make sure they produce plenty of strong stems the whole bush can be cut down to within a few centimetres of the ground. This is known as stooling. Nervous gardeners can compromise by cutting down just half the shrub's stems, leaving the new wood produced in the previous season but the prizes will go to the bold gardener.

POLLARDING is a similar technique used to control the growth of trees: all the branches are cut back to the main trunk every few years. It is the method used traditionally on willows to produce plenty of long, flexible young stems to weave baskets, furniture and fencing. In the garden pollarding should be the last resort for trees which have outgrown their position.

Removing suckers

Some choice varieties of trees and shrubs (many roses, cherries, crab apples, lilacs and rhododendrons) are grafted onto the rootstock of a common, stronger variety. Sometimes unwanted shoots of the host plant grow from below the graft joint or from the roots underground. These must be removed as they will eventually take over the ornamental grafted plant.

If the suckers are above ground, cut them off flush with the stem of the rootstock. If underground, scrape away the soil till you reach the point where the sucker is attached to the root and tear it off by twisting and pulling.

With some shrubs, the natural habit of growth is to produce suckers: that is one of the ways they reproduce themselves. Lilac, *Viburnum farreri* and some species of roses are examples. If unchecked, they will form dense thickets with few flowers, so it is usually best to remove all but a few of the suckering stems.

Renovating old plants

When a shrub has become unattractively sparse and leggy or, at the other extreme, very bushy with thin twigs which do not flower, it is worth trying the drastic measure of cutting it down to within 30cm (1ft) of the ground. Ancient roses often respond well.

If the job is done in early spring and the plant is fed and watered generously, it may take on a new lease of life, putting out strong new shoots. Over the next few years it can be trained into an attractive shape.

Such severe pruning is a kill or cure method. Do not be too upset if the plant dies. It is worth trying to revitalize and reshape a poor specimen but not worth shedding tears over it if the rescue operation fails.

Pruning trees

Health hazards are diseased branches, overcrowded branches, dense twiggy growth which robs the crown of light in its centre, and crossing branches which rub against each other, creating a wound where diseases and pests can enter.

You can probably deal with small trees yourself, using a lopper or saw, and observing the general principles described above.

WARNING Ornamental cherries may bleed when cut. To avoid trouble later, identify future problems early and rub off unwanted growth buds while they are new.

Aftercare

When you prune a plant, you are administering a shock to its system and asking it to work harder to produce new growth. It will need extra food and water to help it recover from the shock. When pruning takes place in spring or summer, feed the plant immediately, water it and weed and mulch the whole root area. Make sure it continues to get enough water throughout the growing season. Give winter-pruned plants the same treatment in spring when they start into growth after their winter dormancy.

Trees

Trees should be allowed to develop naturally, and pruned only when necessary for their health or in order to maintain a well-balanced shape.

WARNING *Amateur tree surgery has led to many accidents, all serious and some fatal. Pruning mature trees is a specialized and dangerous job and should be left to a professional expert.*

If a tree that needs pruning is too big to reach from the safety of the ground or if you are in any doubt whatsoever, employ a professional. The Arboricultural Association can supply a list of qualified and approved tree surgeons. Beware of cowboys: they may leave you with a mutilated tree, and they are not always adequately insured against third party risk.

The leading stem

All trees (and some shrubs) develop by producing a single 'leading' stem (the trunk) which grows taller each year, with side branches developing from it. You can control the growth of the tree by manipulating this 'leader' and its branches. If you want the tree to develop to its full height and potential, make sure the leader has no competition.

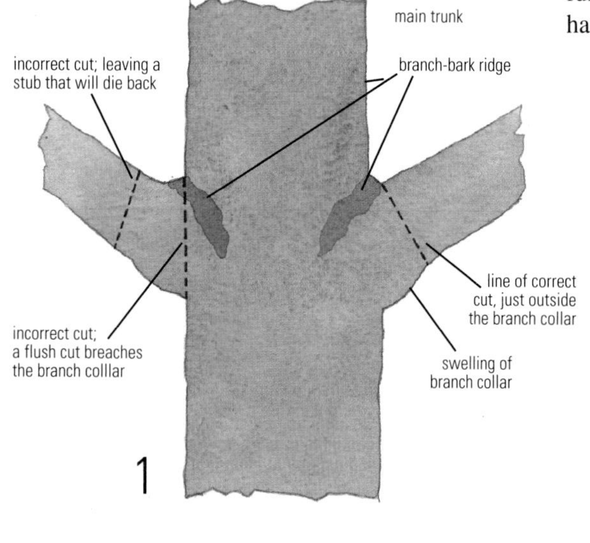

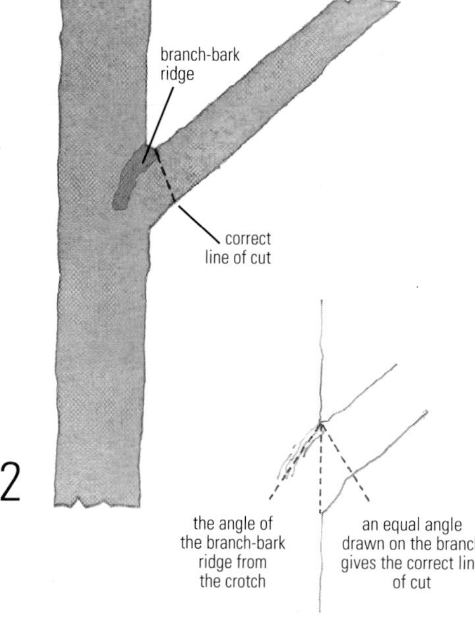

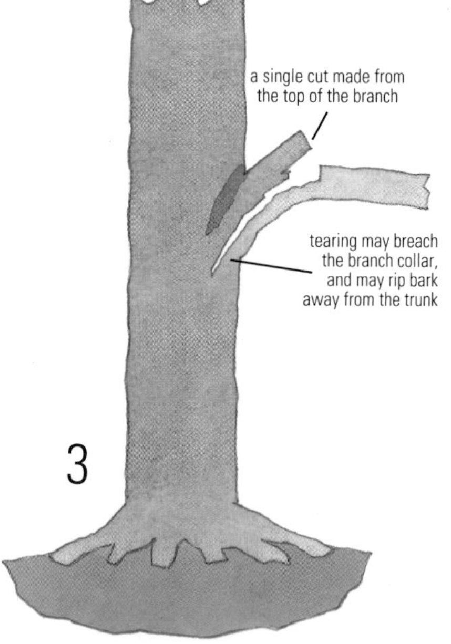

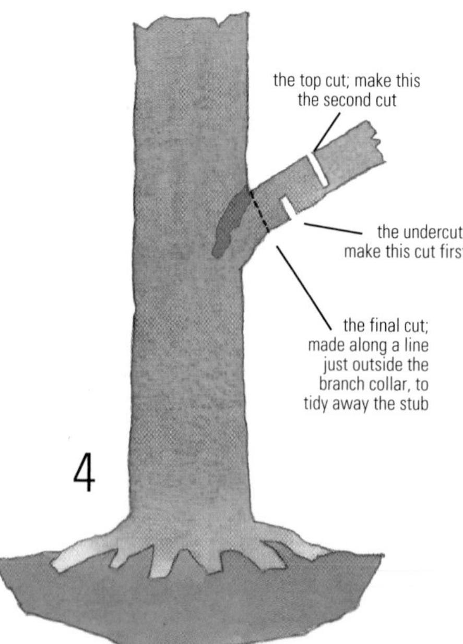

REMOVING UNWANTED TREE BRANCHES

1 It is usually quite easy to see the swelling of the branch collar where a large branch joins the main trunk. When removing branches, do *not* cut into the collar, which will breach a tree's natural defences, or leave too long a stub which will die back.

2 On small branches the branch collar is seldom obvious, but at the branch base you will see a wrinkle of bark known as the branch-bark ridge. Observe the angle that it makes from the crotch into main stem. Make your final cut at an equal and opposite angle to this on the branch.

3 A branch removed with one cut will tend to tear along the grain of the wood, pulled down by its own weight before the cut is complete. This may extend into the trunk and breach the branch collar. Do not attempt to remove large branches from mature trees or any branches that cannot comfortably and safely be reached from the ground. If in *any* doubt, consult a professional tree surgeon.

4 Using a bow saw, make an undercut at a convenient distance from the branch collar, no more than one third through the branch, to avoid pinching the saw blade. Make a top cut at a distance away from the undercut that corresponds to the width of the branch, and deep enough just to overlap. The branch will then tear away without breaching the collar. Cut the remaining stub away with a cut that extends from the crotch along a line on the outside of the collar. For convenience, this final cut may have to be made from beneath the branch. Very small branches that can be comfortably grasped with one hand may be removed with just one cut. Using a bow saw or pruning saw, and supporting the branch with your free hand, make the cut from below the branch upwards towards the crotch, taking care not to breach the branch collar.

Watch your trees, and if any of them begin to fork at the top, cut off one side of the fork stem so that only one leader remains. Conversely, if you want to restrict the height, to make it easier to collect the harvest from a fruit tree, for example, or to stop a hedge of conifers at the required height, or to create a bushy head, cut the leader out at the spot from which the top branches grow.

The only other pruning attention a young tree needs is a careful assessment of its shape each year. The aim is to end up with even growth all round; to ensure this, ungainly or over-vigorous branches can be removed.

Trees that are planted too close to buildings may need cutting back. Prune so that the shape remains symmetrical and natural, removing some branches at the main stem and shortening others.

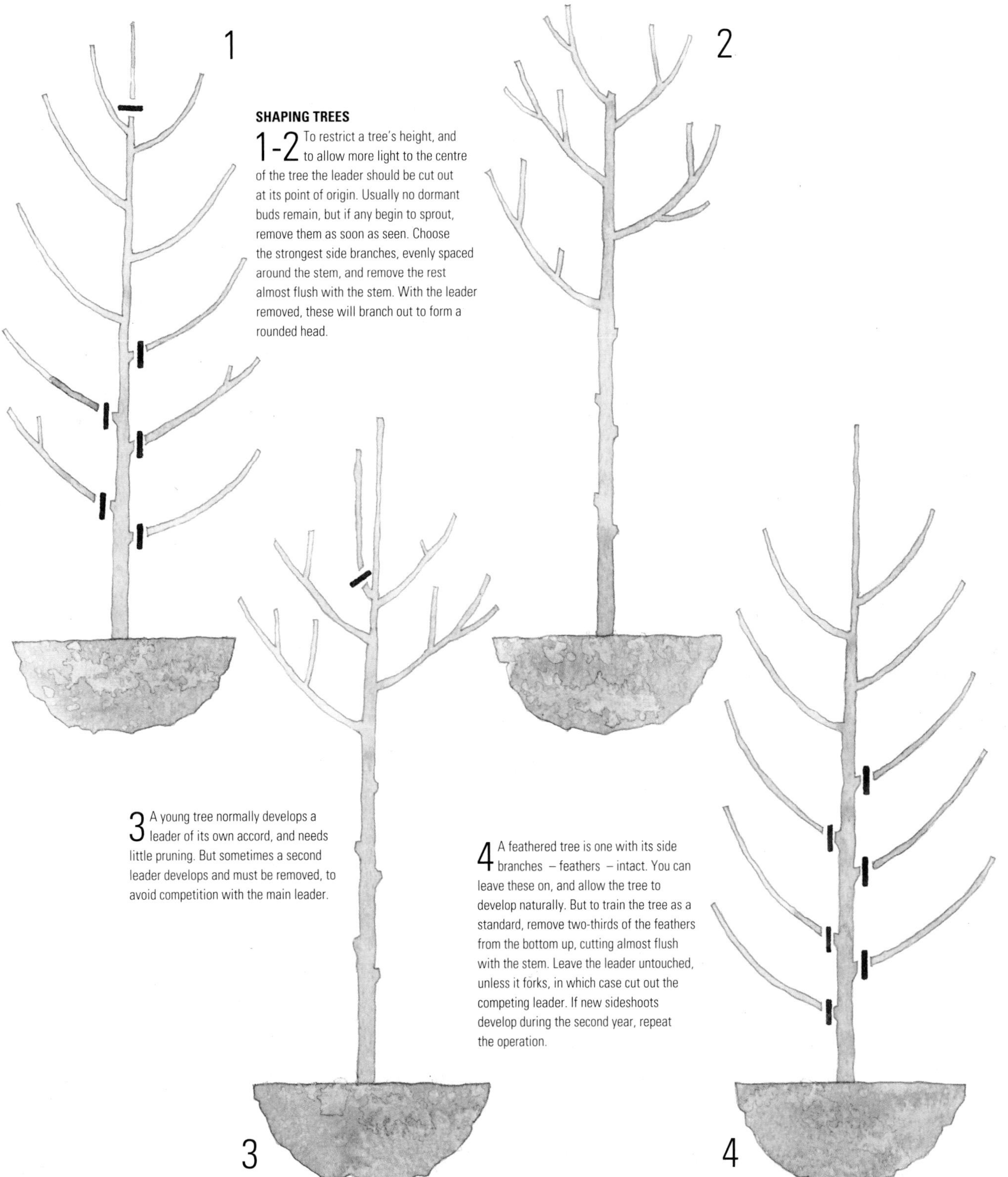

SHAPING TREES

1-2 To restrict a tree's height, and to allow more light to the centre of the tree the leader should be cut out at its point of origin. Usually no dormant buds remain, but if any begin to sprout, remove them as soon as seen. Choose the strongest side branches, evenly spaced around the stem, and remove the rest almost flush with the stem. With the leader removed, these will branch out to form a rounded head.

3 A young tree normally develops a leader of its own accord, and needs little pruning. But sometimes a second leader develops and must be removed, to avoid competition with the main leader.

4 A feathered tree is one with its side branches – feathers – intact. You can leave these on, and allow the tree to develop naturally. But to train the tree as a standard, remove two-thirds of the feathers from the bottom up, cutting almost flush with the stem. Leave the leader untouched, unless it forks, in which case cut out the competing leader. If new sideshoots develop during the second year, repeat the operation.

Deciduous shrubs

If you inspect your shrubs carefully every year to see if pruning is necessary, it will save a lot of trouble in the long run. Pruning a dense, neglected shrub is a real battle, and if it is a thorny subject like a shrub rose, you will not only look as if you have been dragged through a hedge backwards; you will have been.

To prune shrubs, follow the general principles outlined above. The only possible area of confusion is in the timing. This is determined by whether the plant bears its flowers and fruit on old wood (stems which were produced in the previous year or in earlier years) or new wood (stems produced earlier in the same year).

When pruning, remember your objective: to make a shapely shrub with strong young branches spaced out enough to let light and air into the centre.

Shrubs that flower on old wood

Prune immediately after flowering. Most shrubs which flower on old wood are spring or early summer flowering. By the time the flowers are fading it is easy to distinguish between the old wood on which the flowers bloomed, with its hardened brown or grey bark, and the new green shoots which have not borne flowers.

In addition to pruning for health as already described, these shrubs benefit from the removal of stems which have flowered, so that the plant can put more vigour into the development of the new shoots which will flower the next year. If the new shoots have plenty of light and air, they will grow and ripen well and reward your care by flowering well the following year. Examples include *Forsythia, Spiraea, Ribes, Deutzia, Philadelphus,* rosemary and *Weigela.*

- If the stems become overcrowded, remove some of the oldest (they will have rougher, more faded bark than younger branches) at ground level or at the point where they shoot from the parent stem.
- Remove weak or particularly spindly shoots and crossed branches that are rubbing against each other.
- Observing the one-in-three rule, remove most of the stems which have borne flowers, always cutting just above an outward-facing bud.
- Look carefully at the shape of the shrub and finish by doing any cosmetic pruning to improve its appearance.

Left Ribes sanguinem 'Brocklebankii' flowers in early summer on wood formed the previous year. Prune immediately after flowering.

Left Unlike many evergreen shrubs, if rosemary *(Rosmarinus officinalis)* becomes overgrown and leggy it can be cut back hard and will shoot from old wood.

TIP

On some plants, such as fuchsias, all top growth is killed off by frost, except in mild climates. To prune them simply cut off all the dead wood at ground level. New shoots will appear from under the ground.

RENOVATING AN OLD LILAC

1 During winter months, when the plant is dormant, cut all old growth back to within 30-60cm (1-2ft) of ground level. Do not expect blooms this first season. Apply a generous mulch of garden compost or well rotted manure, and water freely in dry weather.

2 During the first season, the stumps will throw out a number of new shoots. In spring or summer, select the strongest shoots that are best placed to give a well balanced specimen, and remove the rest. Rub off any new buds developing on the stump. During subsequent seasons, remove any further new shoots. Lilac blooms on the previous season's wood, so you may get your first crop of blossom the following year.

2

Shrubs that flower on new wood
In flower from midsummer onwards on stems formed in spring of the same year. Examples include *Buddleja, Fuchsia, Hibiscus syriacus, Lavatera thuringiaca, Leycesteria formosa, Phlomis fruticosa* and *Perovskia atriplicifolia*.

If left unpruned these shrubs tend to make a network of ever more spindly twigs with ever fewer and smaller flowers. The pruning objective is to produce new and vigorous flowering stems each year.

In early spring, prune for health, as discussed on p.118.

Cut back all the remaining stems to within two or three buds of the old wood.

Evergreen shrubs

WHEN? The same general principles apply to evergreens. The best time to prune is late spring or early summer (the second half of May in Britain), when the new season's soft young shoots have begun to harden up. If you prune earlier more young shoots will develop and will be vulnerable to late frosts. Finish pruning evergreens soon after midsummer or the new growth will suffer frost damage.

*WARNING Some plants will die if you cut back into old wood, for instance broom (*Cytisus*), lavender, sage, rue.*

RENOVATING OLD SHRUBS

Neglected shrubs often form a dense tangle of growth and bear only a few small flowers. Many shrubs respond well to brutal pruning – they have the capacity to break buds from old or very old wood.

1 Shrubby species, like *Philadelphus*, can become congested with old twiggy growth. In winter, cut the old twiggy growth to the base, and remove half of the stouter old stems at the base. Leave any promising new growth alone. Mulch generously, and water during dry periods in the following growing season.

2 During the growing season, a few flowers will be carried on old laterals, and new growth will emerge from the base. This will flower the following summer. During the next winter, remove all old wood, and any weak, twiggy growths produced during the summer. Aim to leave a balanced framework of last year's and the previous year's growth. During the following summer, last year's growth will produce strong, flowering side-shoots. When you have re-established a healthy framework of young wood, resume pruning on the one-in-three principle.

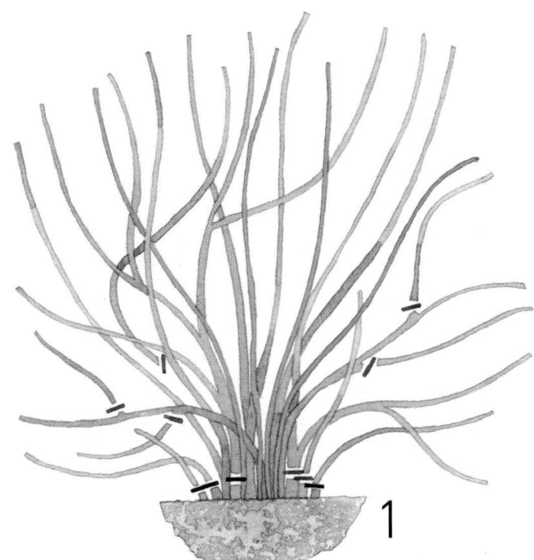

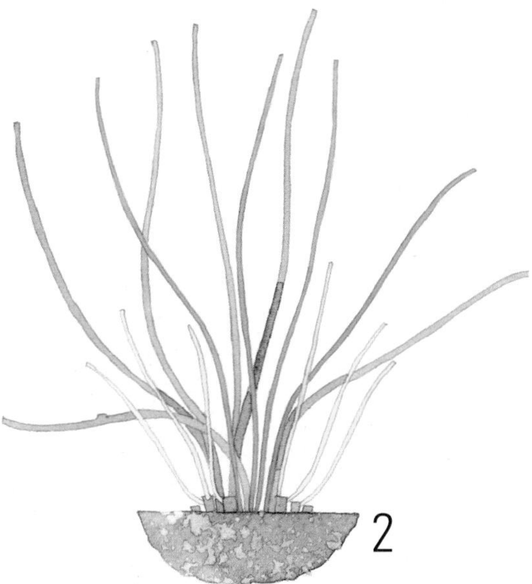

Formal hedges and topiary

WHEN? Established, slow-growing evergreen hedges of yew, box or holly should be trimmed in late summer or early autumn. Fast-growing evergreen hedges (privet, *Lonicera,* Leyland and Lawson cypress, *Thuja*) will need trimming two or three times between early summer and autumn. Do the job when they are looking untidy.

Deciduous hedges made of beech, hornbeam, hawthorn (also called quickthorn), blackthorn (sloe) and field maple should be cut at the end of summer.

Formal edgings, like lavender, *Santolina* and hyssop, and flowering hedges, for example *Berberis, Escallonia,* purple-leaved *Osmanthus* and *Prunus,* should be trimmed immediately after they flower.

Hedges grown for their decorative display of berries should be pruned in winter (for instance, *Cotoneaster*) or spring (*Pyracantha*).

TOOLS

- Power-driven hedge cutters are labour-saving if you have extensive hedges to trim.
- Hand-operated shears should be comfortable to handle, sharp and should have a notch at the base of the blades for cutting through hardened branches.
- Secateurs may also be needed.
- String guide-line the same length as the hedge, attached to a stick or cane at each end, will help you to cut a straight and even line. Perfectionists use a timber template made in the desired profile of the hedge.
- 'Donkey' for collecting the clippings. This is a flat groundsheet with handles at the four corners. Lay it at the base of the hedge so that the clippings fall on it, moving it along as you work. When it is full you pick up the load by the handles and transfer it to a wheelbarrow or directly to your bonfire site.
- Rake for stray clippings.

Above Provided you choose the right plants, topiary creations are limited only by your imagination. But a herd of elephants needs a lot of space and time-consuming maintenance.

HOW? A well trimmed hedge is a fine sight. To achieve it you need sharp tools and a patient, methodical approach.

You will only get good results if the plants which compose the hedge are healthy and strong. As with the grass on a lawn, every time

Golden Rules of Pruning

DO
- Always have sharp tools.
- Have bright coloured tools so that you can find them if you leave them lying about the garden.
- Burn all dead or diseased prunings.
- Observe pruning principles when cutting flowers and foliage for the house.

DON'T
- Be scissor-happy. Stand back and look between cuts.
- Try to fit a quart into a pint pot: allow enough space around your shrubs and trees for them to develop to their natural size. Plants hacked back to fit a space that is too small are a sorry sight.
- Try to cut an inch-thick branch with your rose secateurs.
- Cut into old wood on brooms (*Cytisus*), lavenders, *Buddleja, Fuchsia,* winter jasmine.

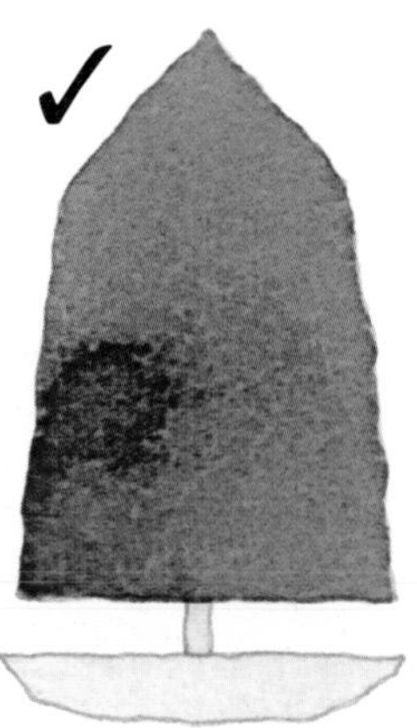

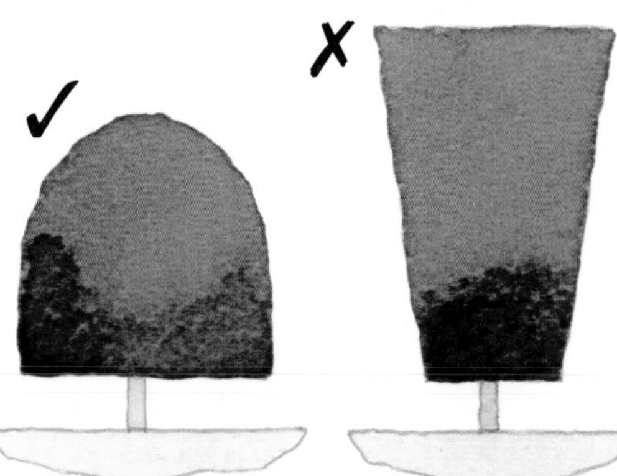

CUTTING HEDGES
The side of a hedge should be cut with a 'batter', an outwards slope from top to bottom. This allows light to reach the bottom of the hedge, encouraging dense growth.

DESIGN TIP

Hedge tops can be cut flat or rounded, or treated ornamentally with castellations, finials or even peacocks or pussy cats if you have topiary ambitions.

you cut a hedge or a topiary bush, you are removing great reserves of food that the plants have put their energy into producing, and asking them to start all over again. Unless you make fresh food supplies available in the form of fertilizer and water, the plant cannot replenish the growth that you have removed.

To be the right shape, hedges that are higher than 1.2m (4ft) should be shaped with a 'batter'. That is to say, the sides should slope slightly so that the hedge is narrower at the top than at the base. This allows light to get to the base, preventing it from becoming sparse and leggy. It also helps to prevent snow damage, when the weight of the snow can cause the hedge to splay outwards at the top and become misshapen.

- Keep a space of 50cm (20in) clear of planting on each side of your hedges to give access for cutting them.
- Fix string guide-lines in place, one at the base and one at the top of the hedge.
- Using a motor-powered cutter or shears, trim first one side, then the other, then the top. Trim to two or three inches shorter than the width and height that you require, to allow for growth during the coming season.
- Gather up the cuttings and burn them.
- After cutting, fertilizer should be applied to encourage new growth and, if water supplies permit, the roots should be kept moist in any dry spells.

Large-leaved hedges such as laurel and *Aucuba* are best trimmed with secateurs because leaves cut in half by shears are unsightly. Perfectionists also use secateurs on holly.

Above right A simple but effective design of geometric shapes.

TIP

Newly planted hedges should be lightly trimmed three or four times a year to encourage them to thicken up. In the long run, this makes a far better hedge than the less time-consuming method of leaving it to reach the required height and width before you start cutting it.

Renovating old hedges

Most hedges that have outgrown their space or become straggly can be restored to a manageable size and dense growth by cutting them down ruthlessly to about 50cm (20in) from the ground and feeding with fertilizer or manure. This is best done in spring, with a full season's growth to come. This treatment usually succeeds with privet and *Lonicera nitida* but conifers (except yew: see below) and lavender will not respond to this treatment since they usually will not break easily from old wood. Unkempt old conifer hedges are best rooted out. Lavender is quick growing, and if cuttings are taken from an old hedge, the new one will look good in about three years.

Far right A topiary 'figure' reminiscent of a chess piece.

Below A spiral cone take time, patience and a steady hand.

Renovating a yew hedge

Old yew hedges are worth taking some trouble over. They may have been in your garden for a hundred years or more, and can be restored to their former glory and manageable dimen-

sions in a few years without sacrificing any of their height.

HOW? In late spring cut all branches on one side of the hedge right back to the trunk. It is nerve-racking to do this but new growth will sprout from the trunk and after three or four years it will look like a hedge again.

- Cut the top to whatever height you wish it to remain at.
- Feed with manure or granular fertilizer and water in dry spells. This is important as it is a shock to the plants' system to lose so much all at once.
- After a two-year recovery period, cut the other side of the hedge right back in the same way, feed and water.

Special cases

Some plants have a reputation for being difficult to prune correctly. The job may seem daunting the first time, but when you have done it once you will be perfectly confident thereafter.

Tree fruit

Free-standing apple, pear and plum trees that are producing plenty of fruit can be let well alone. Just remove diseased, crossing, weak or unwanted branches during winter for pip fruit, summer for stone fruit, observing the general pruning principles. Poor performers may be rescued by root pruning (described in Chapter 8, Planting and Transplanting).

Sometimes established fruit trees are too productive, bearing quantities of undersized fruits which weigh the branches down. This can be corrected by removing some of the fruit buds. The problem here is how to tell a fruit bud from an ordinary growth bud which will produce a new shoot. Fruit buds are usually fatter and more rounded and stand out from the parent shoot on short, gnarled spurs. You can see them quite distinctly in late winter.

Prune newly planted fruit trees and bushes with three aims in mind:

- To develop a plant of the required shape. Where space is limited this may be a cordon, espalier, arch or a fan against a wall.
- To keep the shape open enough to allow light in to ripen the fruit.
- To encourage fruit to form. Fruit buds form more readily if the branches of young trees are trained horizontally, as with espaliers or fans. On trees and bushes in the open, branches are sometimes bent out and tied to canes.

In either case, pruning consists of removing unwanted growth shoots but leaving fruit buds.

Soft fruit

RASPBERRIES bear fruit on shoots (known as canes) which grew from the base of the plant in the previous season. After harvesting the crop, cut the woody canes that have fruited down to the ground leaving the new green shoots to bear next year's crop.

BLACKCURRANTS Each year thin out the bushes by removing enough of the old fruited shoots to keep an open bush. The old shoots are hard and dark brown to black, the young ones a lighter brown and smoother and more flexible.

RED AND WHITE CURRANTS, GOOSEBERRIES In winter cut back the main shoots by about half, to an outward-facing bud, and cut the lateral shoots back to within two or three buds of the parent stem. Old bushes may need some branches to be removed completely to keep the bush open.

Left An apple tree trained and pruned 'festoon' style; decorative and productive.

Below Apples trained and pruned as cordons, forming a useful barrier where space is limited.

For different methods of training fruit trees and bushes and for fruits not described here, see Chapter 16, The Kitchen Garden.

Roses

See Chapter 19, Growing Roses.

Clematis

Pruning clematis is another task which alarms the inexperienced gardener. The purpose is to induce the plant to put out vigorous flowering shoots and to keep the flowers at a level where they can be enjoyed. Left unpruned, most clematis hybrids would produce flowers well above eye level where only a few passing birds and butterflies could appreciate them.

The pruning process is straightforward. The difficulty comes in recognizing which type of clematis you are looking at in your garden, as different types need different pruning.

> *DESIGN TIP*
>
> If you can't make up your mind whether you prefer pink- or white-flowered *Clematis montana*, grow both and let them intertwine.

Above *Clematis* 'Perle d'Azur'. Prune hard in winter.

Above *Clematis tangutica.* Decorative seedheads. Pruning optional in late winter.

Below *Clematis alpina* 'Frances Rivis'. Minimal pruning.

Below centre *Clematis orientalis* 'Bill Mackenzie'. Decorative seedheads. Pruning optional in late winter.

Below right *Clematis* 'Ville de Lyon'. Prune hard in winter.

MINIMAL PRUNING

The following wild species and their hybrids can be left alone. To keep them in bounds, tidy them after flowering every few years .

Clematis alpina, C. a. 'Columbine', 'Frances Rivis', 'Pamela Jackman', 'Rosy Pagoda', 'Ruby', 'White Moth'. The hanging, lantern-like flowers appear in spring. *C. alpina* seldom climbs higher than 2.5m (8ft).

C. armandii Large evergreen leaves, white scented flowers, grows to 12m (30ft).

C. cirrhosa Evergreen, white flowers in winter, grows to 5.5m (15ft).

C. flammula Scented, small white flowers mid-summer to early autumn, grows to 10m (30ft).

C. macropetala Like *C. alpina* but grows taller (to 4.5m/12ft) and flowers a little later. Varieties include 'Maidwell Hall', 'Markham's Pink', 'Snowbird' and 'White Swan'.

C. montana Smothered in late spring with white or dusky pink, four-petalled flowers smelling of vanilla, grows to 12m (40ft). Varieties include 'Alexander', 'Elizabeth', 'Freda', *grandiflora,* 'Marjorie', 'Mayleen', 'Pink Perfection', var. *rubens,* 'Tetrarose'.

DRASTIC PRUNING

It is tempting to plant clematis in spaces which are too confined for them. *C. montana*, often planted on a trellised porch, is a triffid and will outgrow its station and cover the roof of a two-storey house. Where it is given space, up a yew tree or a Leyland cypress, for example, it needs no pruning at all. In other situations, like all clematis, it can be cut back ruthlessly after flowering and if the main stem is cut to within 30cm (1ft) of the ground it will be up and running gamely the following season. This treatment may be necessary if the wall it is grown on needs repointing.

HARD PRUNING IN WINTER

(any time up to the end of February)

Clematis which flower on the current year's new growth are cut down to just above the lowest pair of leaf buds on each stem. If left unpruned, all the flowers will be out of sight at the top of the plant.

'Bill Mackenzie' Yellow flowers, fluffy seed-heads, midsummer to autumn, to 4.5m (15ft).

'Comtesse de Bouchaud' Mauve pink, mid- to late summer, to 2.5m (8ft).

'Ernest Markham' Petunia red, midsummer to early autumn, to 3.5m (12ft).

'Etoile Violette' Deep purple, mid- to late summer, to 3.5m (12ft).

'Gipsy Queen' Violet purple, midsummer to early autumn, to 3.5m (12ft).

'Hagley Hybrid' Shell pink, mid- to late summer, to 2.5m (8ft).

'Huldine' Pearl-white with pale mauve bars, mid- to late summer, to 4.5m (15ft).

'Jackmanii' Deep violet, mid- to late summer, to 6m (20ft).

'John Huxtable' White with green stamens, midsummer to early autumn, to 2.5m (8ft).

'Lady Betty Balfour' Royal blue, early autumn, to 4.5m (15ft).

'Madame Edouard André' Wine-red, mid- to late summer, to 2.5m (8ft).

'Margot Koster' Mauve-pink, mid- to late summer, to 2.5m (8ft).

'Niobe' Deep black-red, mid- to late summer, to 2.5m (8ft).

'Perle d'Azur' Sky blue, midsummer to early autumn, to 3.5m (12ft).

'Rouge Cardinal' Crimson, mid- to late summer, to 2.5m (8ft).

tangutica Yellow flowers, seedheads, later summer, to 4.5m (15ft).

'Victoria' Heliotrope, mid- to late summer, to 3.5m (12ft).

'Ville de Lyon' Carmine, midsummer to autumn, to 4.5m (15ft).

viticella and Viticella Group, including 'Abundance', 'Alba Luxurians', 'Kermesina', 'Purpurea Plena Elegans', 'Royal Velours', 'Viticella rubra'. Small nodding flowers, pinks, reds, purples, mid- to late summer, to 3.5m (12ft) or more.

LIGHT PRUNING IN WINTER

Many clematis varieties, including those with the largest flowers, flower on wood made in the previous year. Prune them lightly by cutting back any dead growth and removing weak shoots. If you get it wrong and cut them to the ground, the worst that can happen is that you will lose a year of flowering and know better next time.

'Beauty of Worcester' Double blue flowers followed by single, mid- to late summer, to 2.5m (8ft).

'Duchess of Edinburgh' Double white, mid- and late summer, to 2.5m (8ft).

'Elsa Späth' ('Xerxes') Deep violet blue, mid- to late summer, to 3m (10ft).

'Henryi' Cream, mid- to late summer, to 3m (10ft).

'H.F. Young' Wedgwood blue, early to midsummer, to 3m (10ft).

'Lady Northcliffe' Wedgwood blue, mid- to late summer, to 1.8 m (6ft).

'Lasurstern' Lavender blue, mid- and late summer, to 3m (10ft).

'Lord Nevill' Dark blue, mid- and late summer, to 3m (10ft).

'Marie Boisselot' ('Madame le Coultre') White, mid- to late summer, to 3.5m (12ft).

'Mrs Cholmondeley' Lavender blue, early to late summer, to 3.5m (12ft).

'Nelly Moser' Mauve with lilac bar, early and late summer, to 3m (10ft).

'Prince Charles' Mauve-blue, mid- to late summer, to 1.8 m (6ft).

'Richard Pennell' Rosy purple, early to midsummer, to 3m (10ft).

Light pruning in winter *(clockwise, from top left): Clematis* 'Duchess of Edinburgh'; *Clematis* 'Henryi'; *Clematis* 'Lasurstern'; *Clematis* 'H. F. Young'.

Light pruning in winter *(clockwise, from above)*: *Clematis* 'The President'; *Clematis* 'William Kennett'; *Clematis* 'Nelly Moser'; *Clematis* 'Silver Moon'; *Clematis* 'Mrs Cholmondeley'.

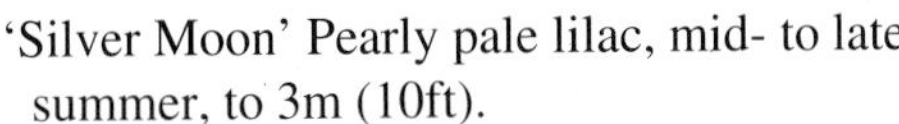

'Silver Moon' Pearly pale lilac, mid- to late summer, to 3m (10ft).
'Star of India' Purple with red bar, mid- to late summer, to 3.5m (12ft).
'The President' Deep purple blue, mid- to late summer, to 3m (10ft).
'Vyvyan Pennell' Violet-crimson double, early to mid- and late summer, to 3m (10ft).
'William Kennett' Lavender blue, mid- to late summer, to 3m (10ft).
'Xerxes' See 'Elsa Späth'.

Right *Chaenomeles speciosa*. After flowering, prune to tidy up and tie in. In winter cut new growth back to a flower bud.

Below right *Cytisus scoparius*. Immediately after flowering cut back the flowered shoots. Do not cut into old wood.

Chaenomeles

Once known as japonica, the flowering quinces have edible fruits and flower prolifically from the first mild winter spell until late spring. The quality of flowers is increased if all shoots are cut back in winter to a flower bud.

Cytisus scoparius

European broom and its hybrids will become leggy if not pruned annually. After flowering they can be clipped over with shears, removing the flowered shoots to within a few centimetres of the main branches. But avoid cutting into the old wood or you may kill the plant – so start as you mean to go on.

DESIGN TIP

Plant clematis where they can ramble through shrubs which have finished flowering.

Weeding

Weeding can be a pleasurable and soothing occupation. It puts you in touch with the fine details of your garden. You would not normally crawl round the garden on your knees, and the weeding posture gives you a chance to enjoy the intricate shapes and delicate markings of leaves and flowers. You can watch the bees and other insects at work and release the scent of plants like thyme and camomile as you brush against their foliage.

Clearing weeds

WHY? A weed is a plant growing where you do not want it. Plants that are conventionally accepted as weeds arrive by seeding themselves or by creeping under the fence from neighbouring gardens or fields and hedgerows. Garden plants may also seed themselves in unwanted places. Other plants, acquired from the garden centre as 'weed-smothering ground cover' may themselves become weeds. They certainly smother other weeds, but can also smother choice but weaker garden plants.

Weeds should be removed for three reasons:

- They are unsightly. Buttercups or yellow dandelions may look appropriate in an area of rough grass. But in a carefully planned, blue and white border they become weeds.
- They rob more fragile garden plants of food, water and light.
- Some are hosts for pests and diseases.

Newly planted trees and shrubs grow stronger and faster if the area of soil around the roots is kept completely free of other plants. If you want your plants to thrive, eliminate competition.

Above Stinging nettles: large colonies are best treated with a systemic weedkiller.

WHEN? Before you plant make sure that the ground is free of weeds. It will save a lot of trouble later on. Starting with clean ground will not prevent annual weed seeds from blowing in, but it ensures the absence of those pernicious perennial weeds which increase by means of creeping underground roots and stems.

Bindweed, couch grass and ground elder are the bane of any gardener's life. They entangle their roots with those of your choicest plants so that you cannot dig them out without damaging your favourites. Once you have an infestation, the only way to get rid of them is to dig up all your plants and start again.

- Among plants in established beds hit the weeds as early in their life cycle as possible.

TIP

When hand-weeding, take the opportunity to lift and transplant self-sown seedlings of garden plants.

Far left Docks: if you don't have time to dig them out, cut down the flower heads before they go to seed.

Left Trees and shrubs will establish better if the ground around their roots is kept free of competition from weeds.

Above right Ragwort is poisonous to livestock, so get rid of it before it spreads to neighbouring fields.

Deal with weeds before they seed themselves, or there will be hundreds more to deal with the following year. Weed seeds germinate at all times of year, so remain vigilant.

- Get into the habit of carrying a weeding tool in your pocket or garden basket so that you can remove weeds whenever you see them.
- If you have large areas to weed, choose a day when the soil is moist enough to release roots easily, but not so wet that the roots are clogged and you compact the soil by treading on it.

Hand-weeding

Even in well-mulched beds, some hand-weeding will be necessary. Weeding by hand is by far the safest way to remove competition among small, delicate plants.

Golden Rules of Weeding

DO

- Weed ground thoroughly before you plant.
- Make maximum use of ground cover plants.
- Mulch.
- Get at weeds when they are young.
- Weed when the soil is neither too dry nor too wet.
- Burn the tops of weeds that have run to seed and the roots of perennial weeds.
- Wear protective clothing when spraying.

DON'T

- Allow weeds to seed themselves, specially docks, thistles, grasses and ragwort. If you don't have time to weed before it happens, slash the tops off with a slasher or billhook, or cut them down with a strimmer, and remove debris.
- Spray on a windy day.

TOOLS

- Border fork for large weeds.
- Hand fork.
- Narrow-bladed trowel.
- Widger or old kitchen knife.
- Gloves for dealing with prickly plants and for all garden work, if you prefer protected hands.
- Kneeling mat or knee pads – not essential, but a kneeling posture is the most comfortable and the least hard on back muscles.
- Bucket, bowl or basket to put the weeds in.

HOW? I prefer using bare hands to pull out small weeds and only resort to a tool for more obstinate ones with deep, penetrating roots, such as dandelions.

- Tackle a small area at a time and clean it thoroughly. The sight of a really tidy patch provides an incentive to continue with the work.
- Remove the roots of weeds completely. It is frustrating when stems break off leaving the roots in the ground. To avoid this, weed when the soil is neither too wet nor too dry.
- Hold the weed firmly where the stems meet the roots and pull up, easing the roots out with fork or knife at the same time.
- Take a bowl, bucket or basket round with you and drop the weeds into it.
- When the container is full, empty it onto the compost heap or bonfire.

WARNING *Do not put weeds that have gone to seed or weeds with invasive roots like ground elder, couch grass and bindweed on the compost heap.*

Hoeing

WHY? The quickest way to get rid of weeds that are still at the seedling stage is with a hoe. It is easy to damage young garden plants at the same time, but hoeing is an excellent method in vegetable and nursery beds between rows, or among roses or other shrubs where there is no underplanting.

WHEN? Hoe while weed seedlings are still small. The surface of the soil should be dry and the sun shining so that it withers the weeds before they take root again. In wet conditions weeds have an amazing ability to re-establish themselves.

HOW? Stand upright, holding the hoe in a relaxed grip. The hoe should have a long enough handle to wield it without bending your back.

- Move the blade gently to and fro, teasing the surface of the soil without digging into it.
- Skill rather than muscle is needed and will come with a little practice. The aim is to expose the roots of weed seedlings.
- When you encounter a large weed, jab at it with the hoe's blade just below the soil surface. Even persistent perennial weeds will succumb if their tops are repeatedly chopped off.

Chemical weedkillers

It is not known what long-term effects some chemicals have on the soil's fertility and on the environment in general. But the frequency with which seemingly totally safe and effective products are withdrawn from the market illustrates the difficulty of recommending specific chemicals.

There are different chemicals for different purposes, and they act in different ways. For example, lawn treatments kill weeds but do not harm grass; other preparations will kill grasses without harming shrubs and perennials. When you choose a product, read the label to make sure it is recommended for your purpose.

Weedkillers are applied either as granules or diluted and watered on to the plants to be treated. They can be used as an overall treatment or applied to groups of weeds among other plants, or as spot treatment to individual weeds.

CONTACT weedkillers kill the parts of the plant which they touch. Annual weeds will die if a contact weedkiller is sprayed or watered on to their leaves; perennials and shrubby weeds will suffer a setback but will probably eventually recover.

SYSTEMIC (TRANSLOCATED) weedkillers enter the plant through the leaves and work down to the roots, killing the whole plant. They are effective against shrubby weeds like brambles and elder as well as perennials. Persistent weeds need several applications a few weeks apart.

RESIDUAL weedkillers are applied to the soil; they prevent weeds germinating and remain in the soil for some time. Some shrubs and perennials are sensitive to residual weedkillers. They are used most safely where no plants are grown, on paving, paths and drives.

WARNING Follow the manufacturer's instructions to the letter. Always wear protective clothing. If, in spite of all precautions, weedkiller is splashed on to your skin, make for the nearest tap and rinse under running water.

TOOLS

- Sprayer if you use liquid weedkillers: hand-held for targeting individual weeds or groups of weeds, knapsack spray for large areas.
- Protective clothing: waterproof gloves for spreading granules; waterproof jacket and trousers or a boiler suit, and waterproof boots and gloves for spraying; and goggles to protect eyes.

WHEN? Only spray on a windless day. This is not just for the sake of your own plants; if spray drifts on to your neighbours' gardens, you may be legally liable for any problems it causes.

- Choose a day when no rain is forecast for at least six hours.
- Spray when weeds are growing strongly.

HOW? Calculate the area to be treated and mix quantities accordingly, so that you won't have an excess to dispose of.

- Make sure that your sprayer is clean and that the spray nozzle is not blocked. Test it with water before you mix the weedkiller.
- Wearing waterproof gloves, mix the spraying solution precisely according to the manufacturer's instructions, measuring accurately. Don't add 'one for the pot'; overdosing is certainly wasteful and possibly harmful.

Left A draw hoe *(left)* and a Dutch hoe *(right)*. Most gardeners find the Dutch hoe easiest to work with when weeding.

TIP

Small, hand-held sprays are available. Use them to target individual weeds in beds or lawns.

Above Grass treated with systemic weedkiller before preparing a new shrub bed.

Left If there is an ash tree in or near your garden, unwanted seedlings will spring up all over the place. Make sure they don't get a chance to grow into saplings.

WARNING Don't mix a cocktail of chemical weedkillers unless recommended to do so by the instructions.

HOW? Partly fill the sprayer with water before you add the chemical, a basic precaution against splashing undiluted chemical on your face or in your eyes.

Pour the chemical carefully, holding the container so that it pours slowly and smoothly rather than glugs and splashes out.

Top up with more water to the required level.

Avoid stepping on areas treated with weedkiller (unless you want to decorate your green lawn with a trail of brown footprints).

Watch what you are doing. Just a few drops of weedkiller on the leaves can kill a perennial plant and deform a shrub for a season.

Spray any weedkiller left over on a patch of bare soil. Do not pour it down the drain.

Wash out the sprayer thoroughly and put the weedkiller away in a safe place, well out of reach of children and preferably securely under lock and key.

WARNING Don't hoard chemicals from year to year. Many local authorities will collect waste garden chemicals: contact the environmental health officer who will need to know the name of the chemical you want to dispose of.

Weed prevention

The ideal that all gardeners aim for is a completely weed-free garden. But weeding the garden is like painting the Forth Bridge: before you have finished weeds have crept in again at the place where you started.

It is worth repeating that weeds should never be allowed to seed themselves, and that it saves a lot of trouble if you can deal with them at the seedling stage. But if you want to achieve weed-free beds with minimum effort, it can only be done by preventing weeds germinating in the first place.

Ground cover

'Ground-cover' plants hold weeds at bay by acting as a living mulch. They are shrubs or perennials with leaves which cover the ground so densely that weeds stand little or no chance.

There is a very wide choice of such plants available, so that it is possible to make a labour-saving garden using nothing else. Some plants do the job only too well, smothering any less aggressive garden plants as well as weeds, but those listed below behave well. As with other mulches, you must start with clean, weed-free ground. It will also be necessary to mulch between the ground-cover plants for the first one or two seasons, until the plants have grown enough to join up and form a complete carpet.

Right Ground cover: the large leaves of *Persicaria bistorta* 'Superba' and *Hosta sieboldiana* var. *elegans* prevent weed germination by excluding light.

Ground-cover plants

FOR VIRTUALLY ANY SITE *Alchemilla mollis,* prostrate cotoneasters, *Epimedium, Geranium macrorrhizum, Hedera* (ivies), *Hypericum calycinum, Mahonia aquifolium, Polygonum* (creeping varieties), *Rubus tricolor* (needs space), *Stachys olympica, Vinca* ssp.

MOIST, SHADY SITES *Ajuga reptans, Bergenia, Hosta, Prunus laurocerasus, Pulmonaria, Waldsteinia.*

DRY, SHADY SITES *Acanthus spinosus, Brunnera macrophylla, Euphorbia robbiae, Heuchera, Lamium, Pachysandra terminalis, Sarcococca, Tiarella.*

DRY, SUNNY SITES *Anaphalis, Aubrieta, Hebe, Helianthemum, Nepeta, Phlomis, Potentilla, Salvia, Santolina, Senecio, Thymus.*

Mulching

The most important aid to weeding is the mulch. It is important, too, in other aspects of gardening. You will find mulches and mulching mentioned in Chapter 7, Preparing the Ground, Chapter 8, Planting and Transplanting; Chapter 12, Watering; and Chapter 13, Feeding.

If you don't like using chemical weedkillers, mulching is an excellent, labour-saving way to clear the ground before planting: the three types of mulch described below, blanket mulch, organic mulch and cleansing crops, all give good results.

Once an area has been cleared of weeds, it can be kept clean more or less permanently if a sheet of black polythene or polypropylene is pegged down to cover the whole of the bed or border. Shrubs and other plants are then planted through criss-cross slits cut in the fabric. The appearance of beds mulched in this way can be improved by a thin layer of crushed bark or gravel.

Among established plants you can save a lot of the time and trouble spent weeding, feeding and watering if you get into a routine of mulching when you tidy the garden in autumn or spring. According to what material is used, a mulch will fulfil one or more of the following functions:

(1) Suppress weeds by excluding light.
(2) Conserve moisture in the soil by slowing evaporation.
(3) Insulate plant roots, keeping them warm in spring and autumn, cool in summer.
(4) Improve soil texture: organic mulching material is eventually worked into the soil by worms.
(5) Provide nutrients: plant food from organic mulch is gradually washed down to the plants' roots.

Mulching Materials

Organic	Functions	Comments
Garden compost	1, 2, 3, 4, 5	Free but difficult to make enough.
Mushroom compost	1, 2, 3, 4	Not for lime-hating plants.
Leaf mould	1, 2, 3, 4, 5	Free but difficult to make enough.
Well-rotted farm manure	2, 3, 4, 5	Often carries weed seeds, adding weeds rather than reducing them.
Granulated/chipped bark	1, 2, 3, 4	Expensive but attractive.
Grass clippings	1, 2, 3, 4, 5	Free. Don't use if it contains seeds of daisies and other weeds, or if the lawn has been treated with weed killer. Avoid mulching with grass clippings in wet weather: a soggy mat will form, reducing soil aeration.
Cocoa shells	1, 2, 3	Expensive but the most effective.
Inorganic	**Functions**	**Comments**
Black polythene	1, 2, 3	
Woven polypropylene	1, 2, 3	Permeable to air and water, so better than polythene, but more expensive.
Old carpet	1, 2, 3	Free.
Newspaper	1, 2, 3, 4	Free.
Gravel	1, 2, 3	

Above Chipped bark makes a long-lasting, weed-smothering mulch.

The main types of mulch are:

BLANKET MULCH If time is on your side, and you are patient, mulch with strong polythene sheets firmly pegged or weighted down to prevent the wind lifting them. After six months all the vegetation underneath will be dead. Old carpet is also recommended for this purpose. Ugly black polythene, carpet or newspaper mulch can be hidden by a thin layer of bark or gravel.

TIPS

- Protect the roots of slightly tender plants from frost with a 15cm (6in) layer of organic mulch.
- In strawberry beds and other vegetable plots cover the whole area with woven polypropylene and plant through slits cut in it.
- Carry on mulching through the summer by tipping grass cuttings round shrubs and trees every time you mow.

ORGANIC MULCH The same result can be obtained by applying a really thick mulch of lawn mowings over ground elder and bindweed: 30cm (1ft) is not too deep, as it must exclude all the light and air that the weed plants need. It makes a messy gunge which is unattractive but worth putting up with.

CLEANSING CROPS Certain crops are effective in eliminating most weeds from the site where they are grown, by excluding all light. In vegetable gardens areas where potatoes and Jerusalem artichokes have been grown are fairly weed-free, and it is well worth growing them for a season on sites intended eventually to host ornamental plants.

Tagetes minuta, a plant of the marigold family, is used by organic gardeners to control weeds. Three to four months after sowing, the roots exude a substance that deters celandines, couch grass, creeping buttercup and ground elder.

WHEN? The perfect time to mulch is late spring, when the soil has warmed up and the shoots of bulbs and herbaceous plants are showing above ground. In practice, this is the busiest time in the garden, so you may find it suits you better to mulch in autumn or on mild winter days.

Mulch after a spell of wet weather when there is plenty of moisture in the soil. Never mulch onto dry soil – instead of conserving moisture the mulch will prevent it penetrating the soil.

Trees and shrubs can also be mulched at the time of planting, between autumn and spring.

HOW?

- Remove weeds, dead leaves and any other debris.
- Apply fertilizer if needed.
- If you are using organic mulch spread it 5-10cm (2-4in) deep over the ground, putting it under branches and leaves.
- Don't take mulch right up to the stems of plants and don't cover young shoots.
- Inorganic mulches: carpet can be cut with a Stanley knife or heavy duty scissors. Lay it with the pile facing down. Polythene (strips or sheets bought specially, or old fertilizer and compost bags) should be pegged down or weighted with bricks or large stones. Lay whole newspapers slightly overlapping and cover with a thin layer of organic mulch or gravel.

Below The mulch on this border of moisture-loving plants keeps it weed-free and conserves moisture. As the plants mature they will form increasingly effective ground cover.

Recognizing weeds

Good weeds

Many weeds are pretty plants and would be cherished as wild flowers if they were not a nuisance. Their crime is being too successful, but they need not all be banned from the garden if suitable homes can be found for them where they will not encroach on other plants. A daisy-spangled lawn can be as attractive as one that looks like a billiard table: it is just a different concept. The white foam of cow parsley under trees is a happy harbinger of summer days but in a border it will soon take over and become a menace. Even a nettle patch has its value, as food and breeding ground for butterflies, provided it can be controlled.

As well as those mentioned above, 'weeds' that are attractive in the wilder parts of the garden include the lesser celandine. Its glossy, heart-shaped leaves make an excellent ground cover under trees in the spring and are followed by prolific flowers like yellow stars. In early summer the leaves as well as the flowers die down, leaving behind it no trace until the following spring.

There are numerous wild flowers to grow at the margins of the garden which are too aggressively successful to be anything but weeds in beds and borders: rosebay willowherb, cow parsley, betony, moon daisy (ox-eye daisy), speedwell, meadow buttercup, soapwort, violet, white deadnettle, clover, yarrow.

Bad weeds

WORST Couch grass, ground elder, bindweed.

Although the last two are attractive in leaf and flower, all three must be eliminated at all costs. This is easier said than done, as their roots sometimes run too deep to be forked out and are often entangled with those of garden plants. A thick mulch helps to bring the roots nearer the surface, where they can be got at. For complete eradication the only effective method is the 30cm (1ft) mulch described on p.139, or spot treatment with a systemic weedkiller brushed on to the leaves, but this will need to be repeated several times in a season and for more than one season.

ALMOST AS BAD Nettles, docks, thistles, Oxford ragwort (poisonous to livestock).

These weeds are usually found growing in rough grass areas. Get rid of them by mowing the grass short for a season. If they appear in beds and borders, these are the options:

- Cut them down several times during the growing season, or
- Fork or dig them out by hand, or
- Spot-treat with weedkiller.

Grassland weeds which are a problem in lawns are discussed in Chapter 9, Lawns.

SEEDLINGS OF TREES AND SHRUBS Sycamore, ash and elder are the worst offenders. Keep a beady eye out for them and catch them when young: a 1m (3ft) high tree sapling growing up through a prize shrub is almost impossible to remove without spoiling the shrub.

TIP

Keep a colony of nettles in a sunny place if you want to provide food for the caterpillars of Peacock, Red Admiral and Tortoiseshell butterflies.

Below All these plants are potential weeds, but they are pretty enough to be welcomed into the garden, provided they are restricted to their own area.

BINDWEED
Bindweed will twine to the top of a shrub, throttling young stems as it goes. It can be eradicated at the planning stage by deep mulching for a season or more. Among established plants it is impossible to dig out its deep, running roots completely. Hold it at bay by pulling out the stems with as much root as you can get at, every time a shoot appears. This will gradually weaken it.

COUCH GRASS, CREEPING TWITCH
The thin white rhizomes are impossible to dig out without breaking them, and each broken piece will make a new plant. Best treated with a systemic weedkiller.

CREEPING BUTTERCUP
Moves fast by means of over-ground runners, but can be up-rooted quite easily with the aid of a hand fork or trowel.

DANDELION
The important thing is to get to dandelions before they seed. If you don't have time to do a proper weeding job, pick off or mow off the flowers before seedheads form.

CLEAVERS, GOOSE GRASS
The stems, sometimes metres long, leaves and seeds are all covered in tiny prickles, making the plant cling to one's clothing or to animals' fur. The stems are easy to pull out of other plants but it needs a delicate touch to bring the roots out with the stems.

HORSETAIL
Horsetail is very persistent and resists chemical and hand weeding. For complete eradication try a deep, light-excluding mulch for two or three seasons running. A quicker alternative is to grass over the affected area and keep it close-mown for a season.

RAGWORT
Common ragwort (and the similar Oxford ragwort): it is important to prevent Oxford ragwort seeding if your garden is near agricultural land, as the weed is poisonous to grazing animals. Use weedkiller or dig out the plants individually.

Watering

Plants can live without soil if they are given artificial nutrients but they cannot live without water any more than we can. Even in the desert regions of the world the survival of plants depends on water. Cacti, agaves, aloes and other succulents have become adapted to take up the precious moisture when it is available and store it in their fleshy stems, leaves or roots over long periods. Some of these plants can be grown out of doors in mild areas and will even tolerate some frost, but must have good drainage, as a combination of cold and wet will kill them.

Other plants need more water than is naturally available in most gardens. Their natural habitat is the rain forest and they also need a consistently high temperature to survive.

Apart from aquatics, which live in water, and bog plants, which are adapted to waterlogged conditions, garden plants are just as unhappy with too much water as they are with too little, hence the need for reasonable drainage to prevent roots from drowning after heavy rain.

Even in the most benign climates, droughts occur from time to time. At such times plants lose more water through their leaves than they can take up from the soil. Their leaves begin to wilt, giving out a distress signal to which the gardener should respond by giving water, or the plant will eventually die of dehydration. Generally, watering is only necessary when plants show signs of stress.

For some gardeners, watering is an obsession. The great variety of watering gadgets available on the market bear witness to this. If you become a martyr to watering you will find it very time-consuming and, when your local council slaps on a hosepipe ban just when your garden most needs water, you will have used the time to no avail.

The sensible approach is threefold:

- Study local conditions: if the soil in your garden is free-draining or if it is in an area of low rainfall, choose drought-tolerant plants.
- Make the best possible use of rain.
- Do your utmost to improve the water-holding capacity of soil by incorporating organic matter and by mulching.

Golden Rules of Watering

DO
- Mulch to keep the moisture in the soil.
- Choose drought-resistant plants on sandy and chalky soil.
- Water newly planted plants thoroughly, then mulch them.
- Watch plants for signs of stress during drought.
- Use a fine spray to water seedlings or small delicate plants.
- When you water, water thoroughly.
- Water in the evening.
- Target the root zone.

DON'T
- Go out leaving the sprinkler running.
- Allow plants in containers to dry out.
- Water plants that do not need it.

TIP

Conserve rain water and make your own liquid fertilizer by sinking a sack of farmyard manure in a water butt or tank.

Knowing your climate

It is possible that we may have to change our ideas about rainfall in the light of global warming. But if serious climate changes are happening, they are happening very slowly in gardening terms. Until now, and probably for some time to come, when there are several seasons of excessive drought, the balance is usually redressed by excessive rainfall in subsequent years so that the average rainfall over a decade is fairly constant. Of course that is no comfort during the drought years, and if you live in an area of relatively low rainfall you may have serious problems.

The amount of rain that falls annually is not the same as the amount available to the plants in your garden. That will depend on the frequency of the rain. Rain that falls little and often throughout the year, as in Britain, is more useful to many plants than a rainy season followed by several months of reliable sunshine. In Britain the centre and east of the country gets the same amount of rain as the south of France. But because the south of France has long, hot, dry summers, the vegetation is very different. The use that plants are able to make of the rain

Left A well placed water butt collects rain from the roof gutters.

Drought-tolerant plants *(top to bottom)*:

Ceanothus needs sun and shelter, preferably from a wall.

Cytisus battandierei, the pineapple-scented broom, also needs the protection of a south- or west-facing wall in most areas

Dianthus (pinks) and border carnations like a hot, dry position, as do many other grey-leaved plants.

Iberis sempervirens, candytuft, is a dense, low-growing evergreen, happy in well-drained, poor soil in full sun.

Vinca minor 'Variegata', the lesser periwinkle, is a tidier plant than *Vinca major*. Both make effective ground cover in dry shade.

also depends on whether the local soil retains water or loses it rapidly through drainage and evaporation.

The climate chart on p.33 shows the rainfall in Britain and Europe. But, even within your garden, there will be variations:

- Less rain will reach borders on the sheltered sides of walls or hedges.
- Much more water will be lost through evaporation in open, windy spaces than in sheltered, shady ones.
- The water-retentive quality of the soil may vary from one part of the garden to another.

Choosing the right plants

If your garden is in an area of comparatively low rainfall or on rapidly draining sandy soil, you will have to accept that some of your favourite plants will need special attention in the way of soil improvement before planting and watering afterwards. It makes sense to group them together so that, rather than spread your manure or compost so thinly that it has no effect, you can use it to make a separate bed for special plants. Also, whether you use a watering can or an automatic irrigation system, it saves time (and water) to keep those plants most in need of water in one group. Outside this area, stick to plants that are tolerant of dry conditions.

Drought-Tolerant Plants

SHRUBS FOR DRY, SUNNY POSITIONS
Abelia, Artemisia, Atriplex, Berberis, Buddleja, Caryopteris, Ceanothus, Ceratostigma, Cistus, Colutea, Convolvulus cneorum, Cotoneaster, Cytisus (broom), *Escallonia, Genista, Hebe, Hypericum, Kolkwitzia*, lavender, *Olearia, Perovskia, Phlomis, Phormium, Phygelius, Potentilla, Ribes* (flowering currant), *Romneya*, rosemary, *Salvia* (sage), *Sambucus* (elder), *Santolina, Senecio, Spartium junceum* (Spanish broom), *Spiraea, Yucca*.

PERENNIALS FOR DRY, SUNNY POSITIONS
Acanthus, Achillea, Alstroemeria, Anaphalis, Bergenia, Crambe, Crocosmia, Dianthus, Echinops, Euphorbia myrsinites, Gypsophila, Helianthemum, Iberis, Iris, Kniphofia (red hot poker), *Nepeta* (catmint), *Papaver, Penstemon, Pulsatilla, Sedum, Sisyrinchium striatum, Stachys olympica, Thymus, Verbascum*.

SHRUBS FOR DRY SHADE
Amelanchier, Berberis, Buxus (box), *Cotoneaster, Euonymus, Hedera* (ivy), *Ilex* (holly), *Mahonia, Pachysandra, Prunus laurocerasus, Rubus tricolor, Sambucus, Skimmia, Vinca*.

PERENNIALS FOR DRY SHADE
Ajuga, Alchemilla, Bergenia, Brunnera, Iris foetidissima, Lamium, Liriope, Pulmonaria.

Many of the plants listed above have evergreen grey leaves. By using them you are allowing the conditions in your garden to dictate the planting design, which is just as it should be.

Conserving water

In the soil

There are various ways to make the most of available water:

HUMUS I must emphasize yet again the importance of organic material (humus). It holds water like a sponge, making it available to the roots of plants as and when they need it. Artificial 'sponges' are also available. They are granules of a water-holding gel to be mixed with soil or compost. Although too expensive for general use, they are effective for keeping growing media moist in containers. In beds and borders add humus in the form of organic mulch.

MULCHING This, the most important of all gardening aids, is as valuable for conserving water in the soil as it is for suppressing weeds. Different mulching materials are discussed in detail in Chapter 11, Weeding. A good mulch prevents moisture escaping from the soil through evaporation and helps rain to penetrate the soil gradually and gently, lessening the risk of soil being washed away in a downpour. It is no use putting down a mulch over dry soil; if you can, before mulching wait until there has been enough rain to saturate the soil. In dry spells give lawns a mini-mulch by leaving the grass collecting box off the mower.

SLOWING DOWN DRAINAGE If you have very free-draining soil you can improve small areas by restricting the speed at which rainwater drains through it. Lay a layer of polythene (old fertilizer bags will do) 45cm (18in) below the surface if you intend to grow shrubs. 30cm (1ft) is deep enough for perennials. Spike the polythene with a garden fork to allow some drainage or you will end up with stagnant porridge.

When planting shrubs and trees, lay a piece of turf upside down, or a thick layer of newspaper, at the bottom of the planting hole.

In containers

Plastic containers retain more moisture than terracotta ones. If you find plastic aesthetically offensive, it helps to line clay pots with polythene, leaving a drainage hole at the base, or to drop a plastic pot into a clay one. Water-retentive granules can be added to the compost in Gro-bags, pots, tubs and hanging baskets.

Collecting rainwater

Good gardeners save water. At times of serious drought the use of hosepipes and sprinklers is often banned, so it pays to have your own precious supply.

The run-off from the roof into the house gutters can be diverted into a water butt. Modern

BASIN PLANTING
In dry areas, or on very freely draining soils, you can target the root area by 'basin planting'. Make a ridge about 7.5cm (3in) high around an area about 75cm (30in) in diameter. Water will then percolate directly to the roots below. The same technique can be used for shrubs and perennials, using smaller basins.

Below To conserve rainwater, pipe the run-off from roofs or paved areas into an ornamental pond.

TIP

Keep the ground around your plants weed-free to ensure that there is no competition for available water.

Right An antique pump gives access to rainwater stored in an underground tank.

Below right A plastic water butt.

plastic butts are obtainable from DIY stores in various sizes. Traditional oak butts are more expensive but more picturesque. You will also need a plumbing gadget to channel the down-pipe into the butt and a hacksaw to cut the downpipe.

Alternatively, the run-off could be piped to a galvanized metal tank in the greenhouse or vegetable garden, or into an ornamental pond. The garden designer and writer Gertrude Jekyll used to have 'dipping pools' at strategic points in the garden. They were square or circular and had stone steps descending into them so that, when the water level was low, you could step down to fill a watering can.

Butts, tanks or other water containers above ground level should have opaque lids. If light is excluded, algae cannot grow and the water will stay clear. A lid will also prevent small creatures falling in and drowning.

The water supply

In small gardens it may be simple to fill watering cans at the kitchen sink (check that it is large enough and the taps are high enough) or to attach a hose to the cold tap every time you want to water the garden.

But if this is inconvenient or if you need a secondary water source, for example near the vegetable garden or greenhouse, you will want

to install a standpipe out of doors. This is best done by a qualified plumber. Check that the tap is a convenient height for filling cans and, in order to avoid standing in a pool of liquid mud every time you fill a watering can, make a gravel-filled soakaway under the tap or at the very least put down a few concrete slabs.

Effective watering

It is a waste of water as well as your time to water indiscriminately. Use the water on those plants that need it most. In a drought, water the following:

- Newly planted trees and shrubs for the first two years.
- Herbaceous perennials for their first season.
- Bedding plants for at least the first six weeks after planting.
- Plants growing in containers.
- Plants against house or garden walls.
- Vegetable crops: keep an eye on beans, celery, cucumbers, courgettes and marrows, peas, onions and tomatoes, in particular.
- Seeds, seedlings and cuttings in the greenhouse or on the windowsill.
- Any plants showing signs of stress: look for leaves losing their lustre or wilting.

WARNING *The following plants are specially drought-susceptible: fibrous-rooted* Begonia, Camellia, Godetia (Clarkia), Hydrangea, Impatiens *(busy lizzie),* Lobelia, Mimulus, Nemesia, Nemophila, Rhododendron, *silver birch,* Viburnum *(some),* Viola.

- There is no real need to water lawns. Grass is very resilient, and although it turns brown in a drought, it will green up again when the next rain comes.

WHEN? The best time of day to water is the evening. The plants have the cooler night to refresh themselves and less water is lost by evaporation.

- Some plants need copious amounts of water at particular times in their development: clematis and roses when they are forming their flowers; broad beans, courgettes, sweetcorn and all bush and tree fruits when the fruits begin to swell.
- As for frequency, the standard advice is that it is better to give plants a lot of water once a week than a little water more frequently. Of course nature doesn't know about this and sometimes waters little and often with short showers. A small quantity of water only penetrates the top few centimetres of soil. It will not reach most plants' roots and encourages new roots to form near the surface where they will be more vulnerable to drought.
- Newly planted bedding plants and plants in pots and hanging baskets need watering daily, and in very hot weather twice a day.

These shrubs are susceptible to drought. When you plant them dig in plenty of peat, compost or leaf mould, and apply a deep mulch every spring:

Above left Camellias are good plants for pots and tubs. Make sure the compost never dries out.

Opposite Astilbes and hostas need moist soil and will grow in bog conditions.

Below left Hydrangeas enjoy the light shade of woodland glades and a moist root run.

Below Rhododendrons are woodlanders, and thrive in acid, moisture-retentive soil.

Tools and equipment

WATERING CAN It is not worth having anything smaller than a 10-litre (2-gallon) can even in the smallest garden. Plastic cans are lighter than metal but not so long-lasting. Buy one that is well-balanced and can be carried with one hand.

PLAIN HOSE Nothing is more frustrating than the hosepipe which will not quite reach its target. An optimistic extra tug will jerk it off the tap, and an attempt to direct its jet with a thumb over the outlet will give you, not the plants, a soaking. Before you buy a hose, check the length you need.

A plain hose has many uses. Hand-held it can be used to water individual plants and with a sprinkler it can cope with large areas. You can also wash your car or your dog, top up a fish pond, fill a paddling pool and put out a fire.

LEAKING OR SEEP HOSE (not to be confused with a plain hose that has sprung a leak) Designed so that water seeps gradually from its surface, it is laid on top of the soil or buried to supply water directly to the roots of plants. Using T-joints, complex systems can be constructed to cover large areas. They can be left *in situ* and turned on to seep as required. They take anything from 6 to 75 minutes to deliver 7.5 litres per metre (1½ gallons per yard) run, depending on the water pressure.

TAPS Nowadays taps are available with timing devices so that you could go away for a fortnight leaving your leaking hose to water the garden at planned intervals. What if the weather changes and rain buckets down for the fortnight? That problem is solved by fitting a moisture sensor to tell the electronic timer what is happening in the soil.

SPRINKLERS A professional irrigation consultant will devise a sophisticated, custom-made system. Sprinklers can be timed to pop up out of the ground like the joke fountains Renaissance princes installed in their gardens to soak their unwary guests. Look under 'Irrigation' in Yellow Pages.

HOW? The objective is to get the water to the roots of the plants that need it.

- To do this accurately and economically for young trees, shrubs and climbers, sink a 23-30cm (9-12in) length of drainpipe into the soil next to the plant and pour the water into it. By this method the water gets straight to its target. A plastic flowerpot with a large central hole or a plastic bottle with the base cut off can be used in the same way.
- Install the water container at the time of planting or you risk damaging the plant's roots. In rapidly draining ground, target the root area by making a ridge of soil around each plant to form a shallow basin.
- Watering with a can is easiest with the rose removed and the can held low so that the spout is close to the ground and the water does not splash. Try to get a steady flow and avoid pouring water so hard as to disturb the soil.
- When watering small plants keep the rose on the spout or you may find that you wash the plants out of their holes.
- If you have a lot of plants to water, use a hosepipe rather than a watering can.

Water quantity

Give plants enough water to penetrate to the plant's lowest roots over the whole root area.

- Depending on the size, trees and shrubs need 5-20 litres (1-4 gallons) each.
- For more shallow rooting plants use about 10 litres (2 gallons) to each square metre/yard; more on sandy soil and in hot weather.
- Pots and tubs should be watered evenly until water seeps out at the base.

Desperate measures

In a serious drought when the use of hosepipes is banned, none of these systems is any comfort as you watch your plants shrivel. Save the day by recycling washing up and bath water.

TIPS

- During a drought cut lawns with the mower blades high and leave the cuttings on the lawn as a mulch.
- You can check whether you are giving enough water by digging down with a trowel to see how deep the water has gone.

Feeding

Like all living things, in order to survive, plants need water and food. The food is present in the soil and is taken up in the moisture absorbed by the plant's roots. In nature the food supply is constantly replenished by the recycling of leaves and other dead and decaying matter to form humus. But in gardens we usually prevent this from happening by tidying up dead leaves and weeds, so it is sometimes necessary to compensate for our tidiness by adding organic matter in the form of manure, leaf mould or compost. If they are not readily available, or if we are in a hurry for results, we can also use natural fertilizers in a concentrated form, or artificial fertilizers manufactured to chemical formulae. The need is greatest on free-draining, sandy or stony soils, where the rain washes down the nutrients so that plant roots cannot reach them.

It is easy to set up a simple feeding routine and well worth the short extra time spent on it for the reward of healthy plants and the pleasure you will get from their flowers and fruit.

The balanced diet

Plant foods are described in terms of their chemical composition. There are three essentials:

NITROGEN (chemical symbol N) helps stems and leaves to grow.

PHOSPHATES (P_2O_5) help the roots.

POTASH (K_2O) encourages a good crop of flowers and fruits.

All three are needed for balanced growth. General fertilizers containing these three components are described in shorthand as NPK (Nitrogen, Phosphates, Potash). The ratio of the three components is always described in the same order even when the letters are omitted, for example 3:6:9 means 3 parts of nitrogen to 6 parts of phosphates and 9 parts of potash, and is printed on the packets of artificial fertilizers.

As well as the big three (NPK), plants need the following:

- Calcium (Ca), often lacking in acid soils. It can be supplied in the form of hydrated lime. Don't add lime if you grow heathers and other acid-loving plants. They need very little calcium.
- Magnesium (Mg), sometimes lacking on sandy or peaty soils. It is specially important for roses and tomatoes, and is an added ingredient in some general fertilizers: look for the Mg content on the ingredients list.
- Sulphur (S), another essential which is contained in Growmore and other fertilizers.
- Trace elements (iron, manganese, boron, molybdenum, zinc, copper) are essential for healthy plants, but only in minute quantities. An overdose of any of them can do more harm than good. Trace elements are usually available in sufficient quantities in manure and compost and in most commercial fertilizers. You will need to add them only if you have identified a shortage. Warning signs of these deficiencies are illustrated on p.152.

Organic Magic

COMFREY A 'magic' plant which makes instant compost. If the leaves are cut and left overnight to wilt they can be laid directly as a mulch round shrubs and perennials, at the bottom of planting holes or in trenches for vegetable crops. Comfrey's deep roots bring minerals to the surface in its leaves which have a higher potash content than farmyard manure.

Symphytum x *uplandicum* (Russian comfrey) is the one to grow, preferably in a sunny, separate bed, as it can be invasive. Dig in plenty of manure and feed with a high-nitrogen fertilizer in spring and you will be able to cut several crops each year.

VERMICOMPOST Worm casts from worm-worked plant and animal wastes are available from organic suppliers.

Left The leaves of comfrey make instant cut-and-come-again compost with a high potash content.

Opposite Compost in the early stages of decomposition.

TIP

The greater the humus content of your soil, the less extra food your plants will need.

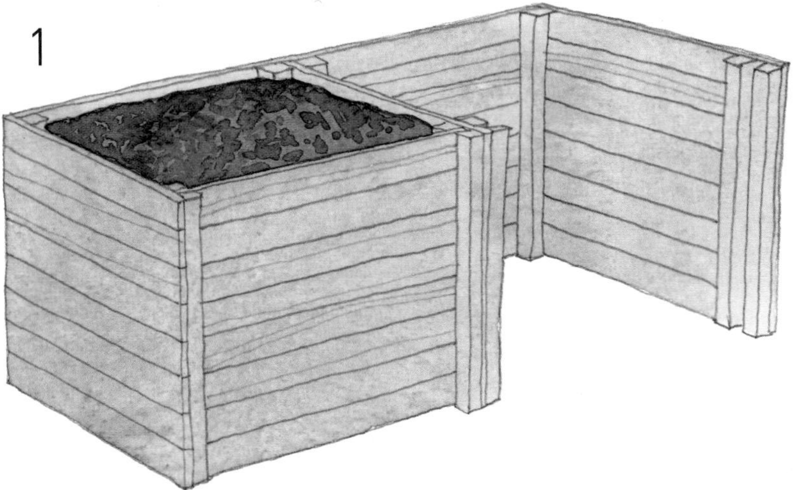

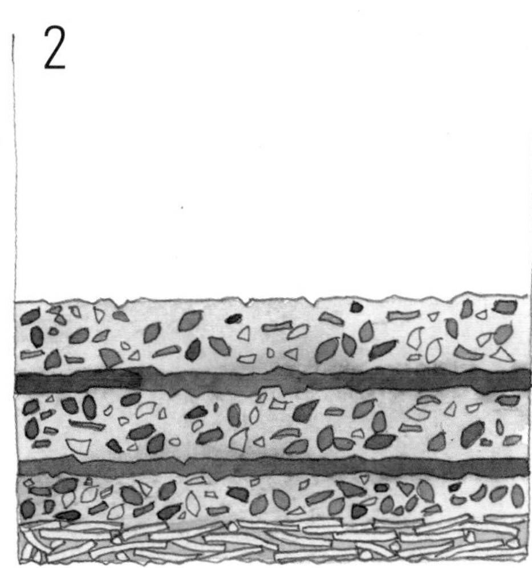

MAKING COMPOST

1 In a shady sheltered site, use a double bin. One bin matures while the second bin is filled.

2 Build the compost in layers: fibrous stems at the bottom so air can circulate; then a 15cm (6in) layer of refuse, one part green leaves, grass and soft kitchen refuse mixed with two parts carbon-rich stuff: straw, shredded newspaper, fibrous stems, contents of vacuum cleaner; then 2.5cm (1in) of soil and/or manure. Repeat until the bin is full. Cover bins. After about four months the compost should be dark, crumbly and smell clean.

A plant on a nutrient-deficient diet may not die but it will sicken and cease to develop to its full potential.

Types of fertilizer

Artificial fertilizers

Quick and easy to apply, artificial fertilizers come in liquid, powder and granular forms. For most garden plants Growmore granular fertilizer, which has equal amounts of each food (NPK 7:7:7) is effective and safe. Some growers consider that the ideal is to have more potash than nitrogen.

WARNING *Too much nitrogen makes plants put out lots of leafy shoots at the expense of flowers and fruit.*

Organic fertilizers

LEAF MOULD The best long-term, slow-acting improver for all soils and particularly sandy soil and heavy clay. You can never have too much. Don't waste fallen autumn leaves by burning them. Collect them into a wire netting enclosure in the darkest shade of your garden. The leaf mould will be ready to use the following autumn. It is acid, so fork it in or use it as a mulch on lime-hating plants. For general use on acid and neutral soils, add 140g lime per sq m (4oz per sq yd).

GARDEN COMPOST Properly made, provides nutrient-rich, texture-improving humus. Like leaf mould, you can never make enough. Ignore complicated recipes involving lime and other activators.

WARNING *Do not put cooked food or bones on the compost heap; it will attract vermin.*

SPENT MUSHROOM COMPOST A good substitute for home-made compost, but avoid using it among lime-hating plants like rhododendrons, azaleas and summer-flowering heathers.

ANIMAL MANURES Horse is best but not easy to come by, and pig (NPK 0.48:0.58:0.36) is better than cow, which has very little potash.

BLOOD, FISH AND BONE An organic fertilizer commercially available in concentrated form as powder or as granules. Its NPK proportions vary with different makers, so check before you buy.

WARNING *Spread grass cuttings in thin layers or mix with other material; if packed too densely it will turn into an evil-smelling sludge.*

Choosing and using fertilizers

Farmyard manure, composted household and garden waste and leafmould are 'natural' plant foods with one great advantage over manufactured fertilizers: they supply organic bulk to improve the texture and water-holding ability of the soil as well as nutrients to feed the plants.

WARNING *Manure usually contains weed seeds, and if you are not very careful, home-made compost may have the same problem.*

ORGANIC OR ARTIFICIAL FERTILIZERS? Concentrated organic plant foods are available for gardeners who lack space to make their own compost and do not have access to farmyard manure. If you object to using chemical products in your garden, they may be the answer. Most artificial foods are faster acting and many are less expensive. Some organic fertilizers (bone meal, dried blood, hoof and horn) do not contain potash (K). It can be added either in the form of wood ash or in a mulch of spent mushroom compost.

FAST OR SLOW-RELEASE? Fast-acting types of fertilizers should be applied little and often, otherwise nitrogen may be wasted, as it is quickly washed away by the rain or by overwatering. However, some artificial fertilizers contain nitrogen which is released slowly, giving a balanced feed for a whole season. Bone meal is a natural, long-lasting source of nitrogen with a high phosphate content that promotes root growth.

TOP DRESSING OR BASE DRESSING? A base dressing is mixed with the soil before sowing or planting. A top dressing is spread on the soil surface. It can be worked into the top layer of soil either with a fork or a hoe, or left to be washed in by the rain. You will need both at different times.

SOLID OR LIQUID? Concentrated fertilizers come as granules. Liquid fertilizers are bought as concentrates to be dissolved in water and applied with a watering can or a hose-end dilutor (a special gadget that fits onto a hosepipe). The nutrients become quickly available to the plant.

FOLIAR FERTILIZERS Liquid food sprayed onto the leaves of the plant to supply instant nutrients. They are a good rescue device for ailing plants which may have poor root systems.

Buying fertilizers

MANURE Can usually be bought direct from the source, from stable or farm.

Fresh manure can damage plant roots, but well-rotted manure is seldom available, so make sure you have somewhere to store the fresh stuff for a few months. It can be added in layers to a general compost heap or stacked separately. Signs that manure has rotted down are absence of smell and the presence of plenty of worms.

ARTIFICIAL FERTILIZERS These are cheapest bought in large quantities. Granular and powder products can be stored for more than one season. Allotment societies and gardening clubs often bulk-buy for distribution to their members.

Applying fertilizers

WHEN? In spring or autumn when you plant or sow crops, a base dressing of manure or Growmore (all-purpose artificial fertilizer) should be dug or forked into the soil.

- Every spring thereafter a mulch of manure or one top dressing of Growmore is enough.
- Roses, fruit trees and tomatoes are greedy and will respond to extra feeds containing potash for more prolific flowers and fruit.

TOOLS

To spread manure or compost:

- Wheelbarrow.
- Spade or fork.

To scatter granular fertilizers:

- Container such as a plastic bowl or old saucepan.

TIPS

- Fast-acting plant foods are useful when quick results are needed in the case of vegetables or annual and biennial flowers in containers or hanging baskets.
- Organic liquid food can be made at home by soaking a sack of manure in a tank or water butt.
- To find a supplier of manure, look under the Farm and Garden small ads in your local newspaper or try Yellow Pages under Riding Schools and Stables, Horse Trainers, Dairy Farmers or Cattle, Horse, Pig or Sheep Breeders.

Below Some plants have evolved in regions where the soil is stony and lacking in nutrients. In the garden they prefer a starvation diet: for example, *Rosmarinus officinalis* and *Alyssum saxatile*.

Right Phlomis fruticosa, Jerusalem sage, is an evergreen shrub used to the harsh conditions of its native Mediterranean climate. The leaves are densely covered in fine hairs which protect them from dessication in strong sunlight. It prefers a dry site.

- Either your hands or a small container from which to scatter the granules.

Liquid fertilizers:

- Watering can with a medium spray rose.
- A stick to stir the solution if using powder.

Foliar feeds:

- Mist sprayer. For small quantities, a 1-litre, or 1.5-pint, hand-operated spray; for a lot of plants, a pump-action spray. Never use a sprayer that has had weedkiller in it for any other purpose.

Getting the right amount

GRANULAR COMPOUNDS Instructions will be for grams per square metre (g per sq m) or ounces per square yard (oz per sq yd). If you are not sure what a square metre or yard looks like, mark it out on the ground before you begin.

Spread the granules by hand; an average handful weighs 70g (2oz). But who has an average hand? If you weigh out a handful, you can adjust by taking bigger or smaller handfuls. If you have huge or tiny hands, take a jamjar or yoghurt pot and fill it with the required weight of fertilizer. Mark the level on the container in felt pen and use the mark to measure out the correct amount per sq m or sq yd.

Scatter the granules as evenly as you can over the ground, leaving a few inches clear around the stem of each plant and brushing off any granules that fall on the leaves.

LIQUID FERTILIZERS Water onto moist soil at the recommended rate. In dry weather, water beforehand.

FOLIAR FEEDS Apply with a fine spray on a dull, still day. Evening is a good time as the wind often drops at the end of the day.

MANURE, COMPOST OR LEAF MOULD Dug in as part of the autumn preparation programme for vegetable plots or new shrub and flower beds. In spring use as a mulch. The worms will do the digging, and if you apply the mulch after a long spell of sustained rain, it will release its nutrients slowly throughout the growing season, suppress weeds and conserve moisture in the soil.

WARNING When following instructions on the packet, it is a mistake to add 'just a little bit extra', as too rich a diet may give your plants indigestion, and it is a pointless waste of resources.

Golden Rules for Feeding

DO

- Follow the maker's instructions when using commercial products.
- Rescue plants showing signs of stress by giving a quick foliar feed.
- Remember that dry roots cannot feed. Make sure your plants have adequate water at all times.

DON'T

- Feed nitrogen to any plants after midsummer. It will encourage lush new growth just in time for the first frosts to destroy it.
- Over-feed. Some plants have adapted in the wild to dry sites on poor, stony soil and flower best under these conditions in the garden. They include many Mediterranean plants such as *Acanthus, Artemisia, Convolvulus cneorum*, lavender, *Cistus*, rosemary, sage, *Santolina, Phlomis*.

Special diets

Sometimes an all-purpose fertilizer is inappropriate or insufficient. Special ingredients may be needed to correct a deficiency in the soil or to cater for the special needs of certain plants.

Lime

In Chapter 7, Preparing the Ground, we looked at the acid/alkaline balance of soils, measured in terms of pH, and considered the need to add lime to some soils:

- To correct acidity.
- To provide calcium.
- To help break up clay soil.
- To increase the activity of worms and essential soil bacteria.

EXCEPTIONALLY ACID SOIL (pH 4.5 – 5.5) This has one advantage: a small group of lime-hating (calcifuge) plants will thrive on it: azaleas, camellias, blue-flowered hydrangeas, rhododendrons and most heathers. A number of other choice shrubs like the same conditions.

If you want to grow lime-hating plants, don't add lime to the soil. But to increase the range of plants and to grow a reasonable lawn, lime should be added.

SLIGHTLY ACID SOIL The range of plants that do well is extended with a soil of pH 5.5 – 6.5 and includes most fruit, potatoes and roses. This is also the ideal pH value for lawns.

NEUTRAL SOIL (pH 6.5 – 7.3) This is the gardener's dream, supporting the widest range of plants. Lime-haters will grow if plenty of peat is added when planting. Lime is washed out of the soil every time it rains, so even neutral soil needs an application of lime every few years just to maintain its neutrality.

ALKALINE SOIL (pH 7.3 and above) Restricts the plants that can be successfully grown to those liking lime. Don't add more lime.

Above For tomatoes in Gro-bags, use a proprietary high-potash liquid feed according to the instructions on the bottle.

ADDING LIME

Ground limestone or chalk is available packaged in bags from garden centres and horticultural suppliers. Hydrated lime (slaked lime) sounds wet but is a very fine dry powder obtainable from builders' merchants. Unless used very

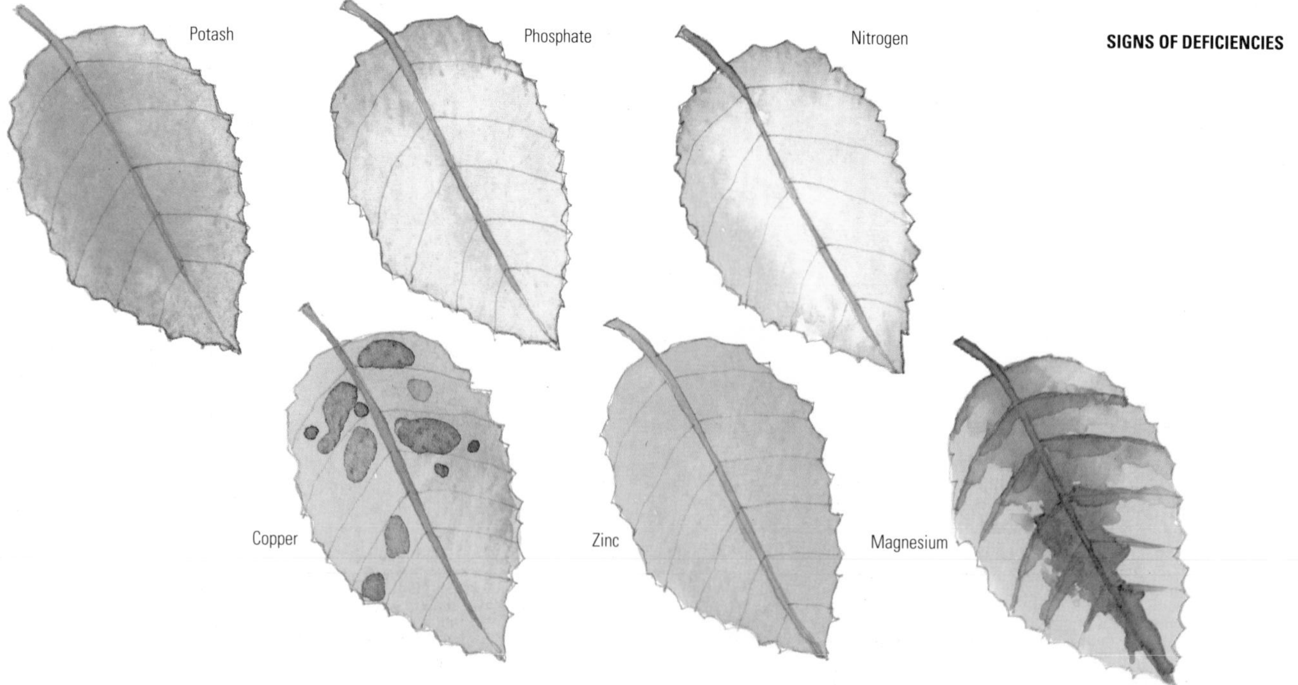

SIGNS OF DEFICIENCIES

Medicine for Sick Plants

When plants look miserable or fail to flower, it may be due to mineral deficiency. If you can diagnose it you can probably cure the sickness.

This table lists plant symptoms and first aid – don't be daunted.

Problems are unlikely to occur if you choose suitable plants for your soil, plant them carefully and stick to a regime of spreading a general fertilizer in spring followed by a mulch.

Stunted growth, pale sickly leaves

- Nitrogen (N) deficiency, most likely on sandy soil or in areas of high rainfall. Apply nitrogen-rich fertilizer such as dried blood (organic), nitrate of soda, nitrochalk or sulphate of ammonia.
- Calcium (Ca) deficiency, most likely on acid or potash-rich soil. Apply lime.
- Sulphur (S) deficiency. Will not occur if you use Growmore or other fertilizer which contains sulphur.

Stunted roots and stems, purplish tinge to leaves, low fruit yield

- Phosphates (P) deficiency. Prevent by adding bone meal (organic) when planting and top dressing in spring with Growmore. First aid: apply Superphosphate.

Edges of leaves yellow then brown, low fruit yield, usually on sandy soil

- Potash (K) deficiency. Prevent by top dressing of Growmore in spring. First aid: water with liquid fertilizer or spray on foliar feed containing nitrate of potash. Phostrogen or products sold as rose or tomato food are suitable.

Yellow or brown patches between leaf veins

- Magnesium (Mg) deficiency, which can be caused by excessive liming or occur on chalky soil. The organic remedy is foliar feeding with Epsom Salts diluted 30g (1oz) to 10 litres (2 gallons) of water. Or use a chemical liquid feed containing magnesium (Mg) such as liquid Growmore.
- Manganese (Mn) deficiency (leaves yellow but not brown between veins; usually on chalky soil). Humus and artificial fertilizers contain all the necessary trace elements but manganese can be locked in by calcium. Use a foliar feed containing trace elements.

Young leaves yellow or yellow-green

- Iron (Fe) deficiency, most common on lime-hating plants and in roses grown in alkaline soils. Water with Sequestrene as first aid, avoid adding lime and add plenty of humus for long-term soil improvement.

Dieback – young shoots die back from the tips
(usually on fruit and vegetables grown in sandy soil)

- Zinc (Z) deficiency. Use a foliar feed containing trace elements. Mulch with organic material such as mushroom compost.

Dieback plus brown spots on leaves (fruit and vegetables on sandy soil)

- Copper (Cu) deficiency. Use a foliar feed containing trace elements. Mulch with organic material.

TIP

Commercial brands of rose food such as Toprose are just as good for fruit as they are for roses. Special tomato food is also exactly the same formula.

carefully, it can scorch foliage. It should be added in autumn, after digging.

Traditional husbandry with a three-year crop rotation involves liming the plot intended for brassicas (cabbages, sprouts, cauliflowers, broccoli). Once every three years is also adequate for ornamental beds unless the soil is sandy, in which case every two years is preferable. Clay soil can go for five or six years without liming. Don't use lime around lime-hating plants and don't apply hydrated lime in excess of 500-600g per sq m (12-16oz per sq yd) at any one time. If more is needed add it the next autumn.

WARNINGS • *Do not combine lime with manure, compost or fertilizer and do not use it where you intend to grow potatoes.* • *Adding lime can bring an initial crop of weeds.*

HOW MUCH LIME TO USE

(Amounts given below are per sq m/sq yd.)

	Limestone	Hydrated lime
pH 4.5-5.5 clay		
Peat	1200g/34oz	900g/26oz
Loam	800g/23oz	600g/17oz
Sandy soil	420g/12oz	315g/9oz
pH 5.5-6.5 clay		
Peat	600g/17oz	420g/12oz
Loam	420g/12oz	315g/9oz
Sandy soil	270g/8oz	200g/6oz

LIVING WITH LIME

My advice to anyone with alkaline soil who wants to grow lime-hating plants is, don't even try. But if you really hanker after azaleas and camellias, grow them in tubs, pots or raised beds filled with lime-free (ericaceous) compost.

I have seen Epsom Salts recommended to neutralize the lime, but I have not tried it. The dose is 28g (1oz) in 10 litres (2 gallons) of water for an area of 1.7 sq m (2 sq yd).

Individual plants can be dosed with Sequestrene (sequestered iron) and thereafter watered with cold tea.

Potash (K)

Roses and fruit trees and bushes need two high-potash feeds a year to give of their best.

Use potash-rich tomato or rose food as a top dressing in spring and again around rose bushes at the end of the first flush of flowers in midsummer. The second application for fruit should be when the small fruits begin to swell.

Tomatoes in Gro-bags are best fed with a weak solution of tomato or rose fertilizer every time they are watered. The same applies to cucumbers, peppers and aubergines, and to some greedy flowers like chrysanthemums and dahlias, especially if grown for showing.

Nitrogen (N)

For lush green lawns the objective is strong, healthy leaves, so a fertilizer with a high nitrogen content brings the best results. 'Weed and Feed' products do both jobs at the same time. Use when the grass starts to grow in spring.

Diseases and Pests

In most gardens and greenhouses, diseases and pests seldom create serious problems; they just cause temporary disfigurement. Learn to differentiate between serious and cosmetic damage. But if you are aware of them, you can prevent them if possible, and identify and treat them when necessary. Treatment will only be needed occasionally if you ensure that your plants are strong and healthy and therefore resistant to pests and diseases. It also helps to keep your garden reasonably tidy and therefore inhospitable to them. Good hygiene should be at the forefront of plant health management.

Some varieties of ornamental plants, fruit and vegetables are notoriously susceptible to disease, whereas others have disease resistance bred into them. Disease-resistant strains are usually described as such in catalogues since it is a good selling point. It makes sense to prefer these to others, even if they cost a little more.

Left Black spot on variegated ivy. Ivies can be affected by a number of fungi causing leaf spots. Cut out affected leaves or, if severely affected, spray with benomyl.

Above Botrytis cinerea, grey mould, attacks many plants, especially those that are damaged or growing in cold, damp and overcrowded conditions.

Fungal diseases

The diseases described here are those most commonly encountered in gardens.

Blackspot

See Chapter 19, Roses. Other plants also have fungi that cause spotty leaves, but they are seldom serious.

Botrytis (grey mould rot)

A disease of the greenhouse, for which there is no organic remedy. Spray with a fungicide containing benomyl, thiophanate-methyl or carbendazim.

Clematis wilt

This disease has gardeners wringing hands or gnashing teeth (according to their temperament).

DIAGNOSIS Apparently healthy shoots on clematis plants suddenly wilt from the tips of the shoots back to the main stem. Eventually the whole plant appears to have died. Don't despair. You have probably only lost one year's flowering. The whole plant is seldom killed and new shoots will come from below ground the following season.

PREVENTION Clematis wilt is less likely to develop if the plants are planted 10cm (4in) below the level of the pot they come in. Spraying with Bordeaux mixture or benomyl will help prevent the disease.

TREATMENT There is no cure except to cut the affected parts right out. Look out for signs

Prevention

Strong, healthy plants are less vulnerable than those under stress from drought or insect infestation. General preventive measures include weed control, because weeds can act as hosts to the fungi; planting at the correct distance, because overcrowding encourages fungi; cutting down perennials at the end of the season and clearing debris from beds; watering during dry spells. In the greenhouse, hygiene, tidiness and ventilation are all-important.

When you are using chemicals in the garden, safety is essential. Follow to the letter the instructions on packets and bottles, including those concerning storage. Wear rubber gloves when spraying and keep pets indoors.

If you don't want to use pesticides, watch out for insects and remove them by hand.

In addition:

- Keep flower pots and equipment clean, only use sterile composts.
- Make sure young plants are planted correctly and give them the necessary aftercare, feeding and watering when required.
- Start spraying roses and other vulnerable plants before signs of infection appear.
- When you water greenhouse plants, water from below as much as possible: diseases can be spread by splashes onto the leaves.
- If the weather is mild, put affected plants outdoors for an airing on a breezy day. Spray off visible colonies of whitefly with a jet of water.
- Tidy up dead leaves and other debris and burn prunings from affected plants to prevent bugs and diseases breeding.
- When you spot a problem, treat it without delay.

of wilt and, as soon as you detect it, cut back into healthy growth. New healthy shoots may develop to replace those removed.

Damping off

One of the most troublesome greenhouse diseases, for which there is no remedy: soil-borne fungi cause seedlings to wither and die. Prevent damping off by using clean pots and trays and sterile compost. Sow seeds thinly. As an additional precaution against the disease, before sowing water the compost with Cheshunt compound (fungicide).

Grey mould

DIAGNOSIS This is the disease that in a wet summer causes rose buds full of promise to turn into soggy brown lumps before they open. Raspberries and strawberries are susceptible in wet weather.

TREATMENT To prevent mould developing, spray strawberries with a systemic fungicide as the flowers start to open, and thereafter once a fortnight. Pick off affected fruit to prevent the disease spreading.

TIP

In autumn, remove the fallen leaves of diseased or pest-infested plants, so that the pests and diseases have no winter refuge.

Opposite, left Grey mould rot, *Botrytis cinerea*, on grapes. Hygiene and good ventilation are essential. Spray fortnightly, from blossoming to three weeks before harvest.

Right Damping off of seedlings is almost inevitable when seeds have been sown as thickly as this.

Honey fungus

The words can reduce the strongest gardener to a gibbering wreck. His or her first reaction to the news is to give up, move house and start all over again.

There are two reasons why the identification of honey fungus throws gardeners into panic. First, by the time an identifiable symptom has appeared the plant is already under sentence of death. Not only will the affected tree or shrub almost certainly die but the disease may already have spread to neighbouring plants, putting them too on the danger list. Gardening is not without its heartbreaks and the news that you will lose one and perhaps more mature trees is cause for deep despair.

The second reason for panic is that there is no known remedy except to grub up and burn all affected plants including their roots, and sterilize the soil or replace with new soil before planting afresh. However, some strains of honey fungus are less virulent than others and have a long-term presence in gardens where little damage is evident.

DIAGNOSIS Look for signs of honey fungus if the leaves of trees or shrubs colour and fall prematurely in autumn, or if branches die for no apparent reason. An exceptionally heavy crop of fruit can also be a sign. If you know that honey fungus is already present in your garden, check trees and shrubs from time to time.

Pull off a section of bark at the base of the trunk or main stem. You are looking for a thin layer of white or cream papery growth between the bark and the trunk. If long, black 'bootlaces' are also present, you have honey fungus. In the autumn this may be (but is not always) confirmed by the development of flat-topped, honey-coloured toadstools at the base of the tree. They will turn black with the first frost.

SUSCEPTIBLE PLANTS

- Climbers: hop, wisteria.
- Conifers: cedar, Japanese cedar, Lawson cypress, Leyland cypress, monkey puzzle, pine, Serbian spruce, wellingtonia, western hemlock, western red cedar.
- Deciduous trees: apple, birch, cherry, elm, maple, rowan, pear, plum, walnut, willow.
- Herbaceous plants: strawberries.
- Shrubs: azalea, blackcurrant, buddleja, cotoneaster, flowering currant, gooseberry, lilac, privet, raspberry, rhododendron, rose, viburnum.

NON-SUSCEPTIBLE PLANTS

- Climbers: clematis, honeysuckle, ivy.
- Conifers: Douglas fir, fir, incense cedar, juniper, larch, yew.

> *TIP*
>
> To test whether the ground is clear of honey fungus, try planting strawberries: if honey fungus is still present they will die within three months.

Below Honey fungus spreads through the soil by means of the black or dark brown 'bootlaces' known as rhizomorphs, which also invade beneath the bark, as shown here.

Bottom Honey fungus toadstools can appear at any time between midsummer and midwinter. They often disappear with the first frosts.

Above Sycamores are susceptible to several fungi, most of which cause only cosmetic damage. Spraying is not practicable on large trees. On small trees, collect and burn fallen leaves, and spray with Bordeaux mixture.

Right Chrysanthemum wilt can be identified by cutting through the stem well above ground level. The wilt fungus causes brown discoloration in the conducting vessels of the stem.

Below Leek rust fungus is worst in mild damp autumns, and on nitrogen-rich soils. Good drainage and crop rotation help reduce infection.

- Herbaceous plants (except strawberries).
- Deciduous trees: beech, box, elder, black walnut, false acacia, hawthorn, hornbeam, sweet chestnut, *Ailanthus*.
- Shrubs: bamboo, *Berberis*, blackthorn, box, cherry laurel, elder, *Elaeagnus*, holly, *Mahonia*, *Helianthemum*, *Cotinus*, stag's horn sumach, tamarisk.

PREVENTION Honey fungus often attacks the stumps of felled trees before it moves on to living plants. It is a wise precaution to remove and burn stumps and their roots.

TREATMENT Chop down the affected plant and remove and burn the stump and roots. In the case of a tree this probably means hiring a qualified tree surgeon with a winch to pull the stump out, or a mechanical stump grinder.

To prevent any rhizomorphs (the bootlaces) in the soil from spreading to healthy plants nearby, you can drench the area with the chemical preparation Armillatox.

If you do not want to take such drastic measures as uprooting all affected plants, an alternative is to make a *cordon sanitaire* around the area, sterilizing the soil and planting non-susceptible species.

The soil can be sterilized with a 2 per cent solution of formalin and left for six weeks before replanting.

To test whether the ground is clear of the fungus, try planting strawberries: if there is any honey fungus still present they will die within three months.

Mildew

DIAGNOSIS White deposit on leaves.

SUSCEPTIBLE PLANTS Powdery mildew attacks roses, apples, forget-me-nots, Michaelmas daisies and, in the vegetable department, courgettes, gooseberries, grapevines and peas. It thrives in dry weather. In warm, damp weather downy mildew can appear on young brassica plants, lettuce, onions and spinach. Greenhouse plants are particularly susceptible to both powdery and downy mildew.

TREATMENT The usual advice is to prune out and burn all affected shoots to prevent the disease spreading. But what if you are then left with no plant at all? At least pick off the affected leaves if you can reach them, then spray with a fungicide such as Tumbleblite or Nimrod T. Bordeaux mixture is organically approved. In the greenhouse, use mancozeb or propiconazole.

Rust

DIAGNOSIS Rust which appears as brown, red, or orange spots on the underside of leaves, can be as lethal to herbaceous plants as honey fungus is to trees.

SUSCEPTIBLE PLANTS *Antirrhinum* (snapdragon) and hollyhocks. Rust also occurs on anemones, bluebells, carnations, fuchsias, irises and sweet williams. Shrubs and trees that can be affected are birch, box, *Hypericum*, *Mahonia*, poplar, rose, rowan and willow.

TREATMENT Spray with a fungicide. If the disease persists uproot and destroy the plant.

Wilts

The fungi that cause plants to wilt and die can affect other plants besides clematis. They are carried in the soil and can be prevented to some extent by thorough cultivation and by rotation of crops in vegetable gardens.

Pests: insects above ground

An enormous number of creatures damage plants above (and below) the ground. Fortunately not all of them are to be found in every garden. Some only attack certain species, others are only a problem in certain years and others do no serious harm. The most common and most troublesome pests are listed below.

Many insects damage and sometimes destroy plants by feeding on their leaves and young shoots. Some, including aphids, cause additional harm by transferring viruses when they suck the plant's sap, or by making wounds through which diseases can enter.

Insect pests can be controlled to some extent by bird and insect predators, and strong, healthy plants can fight back, so a good feeding, weeding and watering regime will help them survive the damage.

Aphids (including greenfly, blackfly)

There are numerous different aphids that feed on different plants. They feed on the sap of soft young shoots, distorting the plant, causing leaves to curl and sometimes preventing flowers and fruit from developing. Aphids also excrete sticky honeydew which attracts sooty moulds, and they can transmit virus diseases. They multiply rapidly, and unless you are prepared to rely on natural predators, aphids should be dealt with before they increase to potentially damaging numbers.

PLANTS AT RISK In the ornamental garden: beech trees, flowering cherries, roses, *Pyracantha, Philadelphus, Chrysanthemum*, conifers, honeysuckle, nasturtiums, shirley poppies. In the vegetable garden: broad beans, brassicas, carrots, lettuces, potatoes. Fruit trees and bushes: apples, cherries, plums, currants, raspberries, strawberries.

Above A colony of grey-green cabbage aphids. They overwinter as eggs on brassicas, so remove plants as soon as they have finished cropping.

DIAGNOSIS Many aphids such as greenfly and blackfly are easily visible on the young shoot tips of rose bushes, broad beans and other plants. On currants and on fruit trees some aphids produce blisters on the leaves or cause the leaves to curl.

TREATMENT The damage done by most aphids can be unsightly but is usually not permanently harmful to the plants. Spray with a product specific to aphids that does not harm ladybirds or bees, such as ICI Rapid. The active ingredient is pirimicarb. This information will be on the label. On fruit trees, a tar oil winter wash can be applied to kill overwintering aphid eggs.

NATURAL PREDATORS Ladybirds, lacewings and hover flies.

Caterpillars

Butterflies and moths lay their eggs on leaves or stems and the eggs hatch into caterpillars; these will chomp their way through the leaves of the host plant until they are ready to form a pupa, from which, in time, a butterfly or moth will emerge.

DIAGNOSIS Most caterpillars are visible on the leaf surfaces or on the underside of the leaves. The browntail, lackey moth and webber moths weave fine silky mesh around their feeding area. Luckily this is not usually fatal, but it weakens plants, is unsightly and spoils or reduces any food crops.

TREATMENT The standard 'green' advice is to pick off the caterpillars by hand and 'destroy' them. An organically approved alternative is to spray with *Bacillus thuringiensis* available under brand names Bactospeine, BT4000 or Dipel. When one or two branches of a shrub or tree are affected, those branches can be pruned off and burnt. Winter moths can be deterred by grease-

Left There are at least seven species of aphids that attack roses, including rose aphids, which are large, dark green or pinkish brown, and at their worst in late spring and early summer.

Below Caterpillars are a nuisance not only because of the damage they cause, but also because they leave unpleasant detritus behind them (known politely as frass).

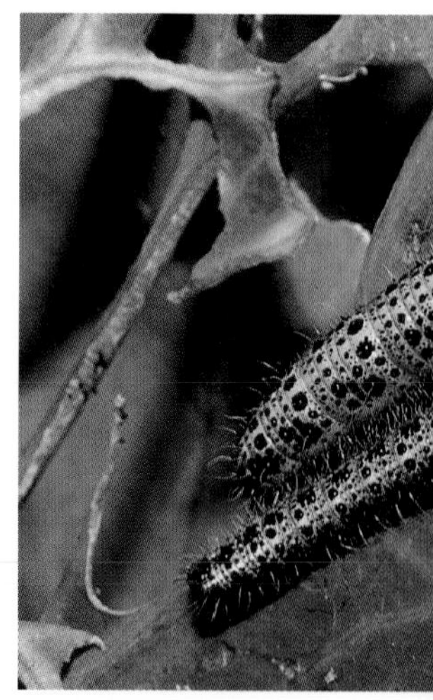

Caterpillars' Favourite Foods

Many caterpillars are specialist feeders: the larva of the cabbage white butterfly and cabbage moth on brassicas (the cabbage family), for example, and that of the codling moth and tortrix moth on apples and sometimes on pears.

Other 'bad' caterpillars include:	Feeding on:
Angleshades moth	Herbaceous plants, especially chrysanthemums
Browntail moth	Hawthorn, roses, cherries and brambles, usually in coastal areas in the south and east
Buff tip moth	Roses and other shrubs and trees, but usually only affects individual branches
Carnation tortrix moth	Outdoor shrubs and greenhouse plants, feeding on shoot tips and flower buds
Lackey moth	Trees and shrubs, including fruit trees and roses
Magpie moth	Trees and shrubs, especially gooseberries and currants
Webber moth	Shrubs, mainly hawthorn and privet
Winter moth caterpillars	Fruit trees, especially apples, pears and plums, damaging the flowers and so reducing the crop
Sawflies – several species feed on different plants	Solomon's seal, gooseberry or currant tree

TIP

Rule-of-thumb guide to soil pest identification: creatures that move fast are likely to be beneficial predators; slow and sluggish creatures tend to be pests.

banding or the application of tar oil wash (see p.166). Set pheromone traps for codling moth.

NATURAL PREDATORS (parasitoids) include ichneumon flies, and braconid and chalcid wasps. A small caterpillar population is acceptable to most gardeners and provides food for birds, so there is no need to take any action unless you get a serious infestation.

Leaf miners

These insects mine or burrow into leaves on various plants including aquilegia, laburnum, lilac or privet. Some make a tracery of fine lines, others make spiral blotches and others produce single blotches. The spots, blotches or small blisters made by leaf miners can be mistaken for evidence of fungal disease because the insect is rarely visible. They do no serious damage and usually need not be treated.

Slugs and snails

With aphids, these are the commonest pests in the garden. They are also the most destructive.

DIAGNOSIS You will soon know if you are plagued with them: they devour succulent leaves at great speed leaving a tell-tale trail of silvery slime behind them. They are most active in spring and autumn when conditions are mild and moist, and snails prefer alkaline soil as they use the lime to make their shells. During the day they rest up under pots, stones and debris. The only thing to be said against mulching is that the mulch provides a home for slugs and snails.

TREATMENT You can discourage the pests by making sure they have no hiding place. Clear away pots, leaf litter and other rubbish. Dig the ground in autumn to expose slugs and their eggs to frost, drying winds and predators.

Minimize slug damage by not planting their favourite food plants – hostas, clematis, delphiniums, hollyhocks, hyacinths, irises, lilies, lupins, pansies, primulas and tulips. Instead, plant shrubs and perennials with aromatic leaves, or with spiny or hairy stems and leaves. If your garden is overrun with slugs, young shoots can be protected with 10cm (4in) sections cut from clear plastic bottles. When the new leaves have toughened up they will have less allure for slugs and snails.

Don't bother with traps like 'slug pubs' (yoghurt pots half full of beer sunk into the ground) and grapefruit halves. They will only make a negligible impact on your garden's slug colony and will catch more friends like earthworms than enemies.

Slug pellets are the only effective death-dealers. Some brands are based on aluminium sulphate and are unlikely to harm birds or animals. Those which are poisonous to birds and animals are treated with chemicals to deter animals and are coloured blue to deter birds. Pellets should be scattered thinly round vulnerable plants, not left in a heap. There is no point in using them in dry weather. The best time is on a warm, damp evening, initially in spring, repeating the treatment after rain if there are signs of slug damage.

NATURAL PREDATORS Birds, hedgehogs, frogs and toads.

Woodlice

These mini-armadilloes live in damp, shady places and come out at night to feed mainly on decaying plant material. They also nibble at roots, stems and leaves, particularly in greenhouses and frames, but do little damage.

Far right Slugs cause damage with rasping tongues combined with insatiable appetite. Night hunting with a torch and pointed stick is a satisfying occupation for aggressive gardeners.

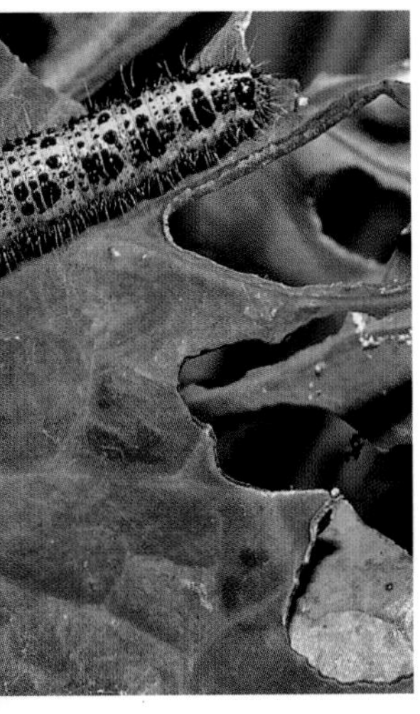

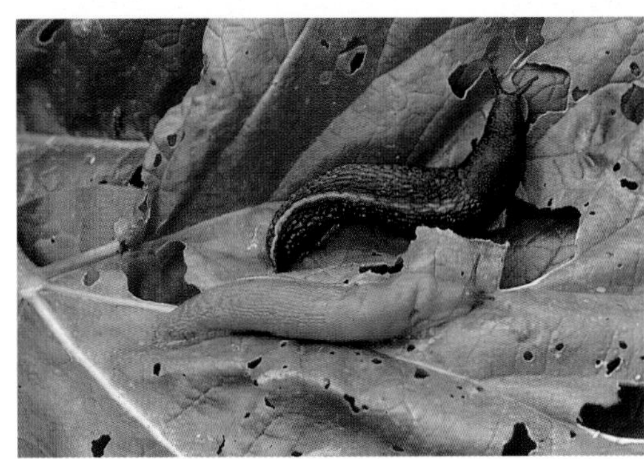

Pests: underground insects

If a plant is dying and you can find no cause above the ground, the damage is probably taking place below the surface. Roots and bulbs as well as stems, leaves and fruit sometimes come under attack. Dig the plant up and inspect its roots or bulb for damage. You may catch the little blighters causing it.

Most soil pests inhabit ground which has not been cultivated for several years. Regular digging or forking in autumn helps to get rid of them by exposing them to predators and the weather. In vegetable plots it helps to rotate the crops (see Chapter 16, The Kitchen Garden).

Ants

If you find an ants' nest under an ailing plant, the ants are not eating the roots. They damage the plant by disturbing the soil or compost and letting too much air in.

DIAGNOSIS If annuals or perennials wilt for no apparent reason, look for ants in the soil around them. A small heap of fine soil is sometimes found in beds or on lawns, with ants busy in it.

TREATMENT The ants' nest can be watered or dusted with pirimiphos-methyl or permethrin. Organic gardeners use a combination of pyrethrum and derris diluted and poured into the nest, or an old-fashioned recipe of icing sugar mixed with borax in equal parts.

Cutworms

These are the stubby brown caterpillars of the turnip moth, the heart and dart moth and the yellow underwing.

DIAGNOSIS Cutworms attack the stems of herbaceous plants and annuals, and young seedlings at ground level, sometimes severing the stems completely. They also attack root vegetables.

TREATMENT Do your utmost to lure a hedgehog into your garden. Winter digging helps by exposing cutworms to frost and presenting them as food for birds. If you turn up cutworms when digging, destroy on sight. The chemical remedy is to spray vulnerable plants with a pesticide containing pirimiphos-methyl or to treat the soil with chlorpyrifos plus diazinon.

Top A disturbed ant hill; the mass of eggs is laid by a single queen, and serviced by workers.

Above Cutworms, the caterpillars of various moths, are aptly named; they cut through the stems of young plants at ground level. They can be active at almost any time of year.

Eelworms (nematodes)

These pernicious microscopic creatures feed on, and can kill, many plants. They also spread diseases among plants.

DIAGNOSIS Signs of attack by eelworms on phlox include small, rough yellow patches

Left Narcissus stem eelworm causes distortion of the leaves and flowers, and affected bulbs are brown and soft. If cut across with a knife, they reveal brown rings of dead tissue.

Above right A leather jacket, the below-ground, larval stage of the crane-fly. Most common on newly cultivated land and in lawns. They feed in autumn and spring on plant roots.

spotting the leaves, narrow leaves and swollen stems. Onions and other alliums show soft and swollen leaves and stems. Many annuals and perennials, especially begonias, chrysanthemums and *Anemone* x *hybrida* are vulnerable to leaf and bud eelworms which cause brown-black patches between the veins of leaves. The bulbs of daffodils and bluebells can become infested leading to distorted growth. The potato cyst eelworm attacks potatoes and tomatoes. The plants turn yellow and die from the lower leaves up. The roots are covered in white, yellow or brown cysts.

TREATMENT Crop rotation and regular digging help to prevent eelworm. There is no chemical treatment, and the only remedy for infested plants is to dig them up and burn them.

Leatherjackets

The larvae of daddy-long-legs (crane flies) eat the roots of annuals, bulbs and vegetables and sever the stems. Brown patches on lawns may be due to them eating the grassroots.

DIAGNOSIS Affected plants may turn yellow, wilt and die. Leatherjackets are easily visible in the soil: they look like stubby, legless, grey-brown caterpillars about 2.5cm (1in) long.

TREATMENT Leatherjackets are pests of undisturbed ground, so regular cultivation will help reduce the problem. To bring them to the surface on lawns, water thoroughly and cover the bare patches with black polythene. After four hours hundreds will have emerged. If you can't face destroying them with a roller or mowing machine, let the blackbirds and starlings do it. Or treat vulnerable plants with pirimiphos-methyl, or soil with chlorpyrifos plus diazinon.

Slugs

See 'Pests: insects above ground', p.159, for diagnosis and treatment.

Wireworms

The larvae of the click beetle feed on plant roots, killing small plants and ruining potatoes and other root vegetables.

DIAGNOSIS Tunnels about 3mm (1/8in) bored into potatoes and roots are a sign of wireworm activity. The 'worms' are thin, orange-yellow and up to 2.5cm (1in) long, with three pairs of legs at the head end. They mostly inhabit undisturbed ground, especially grassland, preferring the top 7cm (3in) of the ground in spring and moving down in winter to a lower level between 45 and 90cm (18-36in).

TREATMENT Regular cultivation reduces the wireworm population. It pays to harvest root crops as soon as they are ready: don't leave them in the ground to feed the pests. However, when bringing former grassland into cultivation for the first time, it may be worth planting a crop of potatoes in order to attract wireworms: when the potatoes are thoroughly infested, dig up and burn the entire crop.

Right Wireworms are the soil-dwelling larval stage of click beetles, about 2.5cm (1in) long, tough and yellow- or white-skinned, they attack the roots of many vegetables and ornamental plants.

Pests: mammals

Badgers

If your garden is on a badger's regular nightly path it can create mayhem, crashing through fences and hedges. Badgers may also rip up lawns in search of the chafer larvae that they feed on. They are legally protected, so the best thing you can do is be proud of your own badger and protect its route. This may mean altering the layout of the garden so that vulnerable plants are not at risk.

Cats

Nobody objects much to their own cat scratching up the odd seedling or rolling on the catmint. It is the neighbours' cats that are the problem. Cats prefer dry soil as a toilet area, so keep your seedbeds and special areas watered. The acceptable alternative to a well-aimed catapult is a short blast from the hosepipe if you happen to be holding one in the right place at the right time. You can protect newly sown areas or vulnerable seedlings with a network of black cotton or by laying round or over them prickly branches of rose, holly or berberis.

Deer

You may be troubled by deer if your garden is adjacent to woodland or parkland. They eat almost any vegetation they encounter, including rose bushes, and destroy trees by rubbing their antlers on the bark. The culprits are usually roe and fallow deer which formerly graced the parkland of country houses and are now wild in the woods. Deterrent sprays have to be renewed frequently, as does lion dung which is sometimes recommended to keep deer away!

The only sure way to keep deer out is with a fence at least 2m (6ft) high. It may be worth talking to the landowner about culling the deer.

Dogs

Owners of unruly dogs have only themselves to blame. Dogs should be trained from puppyhood

Above Grey squirrels dig up and devour bulbs and corms, damage young shoots and buds, take fruit and berries, and strip the bark from twigs and branches. Fruit cages and netting can protect plants above ground, and a layer of wire netting laid over bulbs at planting time acts as a deterrent.

Left The mole's powerful digging claws make tunnels that undermine the roots of any plant that gets in its way.

not to defecate in the garden (this means a daily walk), not to dig holes and not to cross flower beds. However, dogs cannot be trained not to urinate when they need to. Unless you are prepared to follow your pet round with a watering can to wash the affected area, be prepared for scorched patches on the lawn from a bitch and damaged foliage on plants where a dog has lifted his leg. Unforunately the next dog that comes along will use the same place, compounding the problem.

It is sometimes difficult to train guests to prevent their pet from romping over your plants. If friends' and neighbours' dogs are a recurrent problem, the only answer is to put up low fences around beds and borders.

Grey squirrels

Squirrels can kill young trees by stripping the bark. They also dig up bulbs and steal fruit from the garden. Trees should be protected with plastic tree guards or a circle of wire netting. A resident cat and dog will help to deter squirrels.

Mice and voles

They eat seeds and small bulbs. If you don't have an active cat, and don't mind death-dealing, catch them with old-fashioned guillotine mousetraps baited with chocolate or cheese for mice, carrot or apple for voles. Or use humane mousetraps; set the captives free several hundred yards away from your garden. Check traps regularly or the mice will die of starvation, a worse fate than the guillotine.

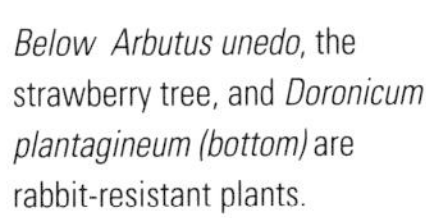

Below *Arbutus unedo*, the strawberry tree, and *Doronicum plantagineum (bottom)* are rabbit-resistant plants.

Moles

They convert even the most unpromising soil into rich, fine crumbs, but although molehills make wonderful potting compost, moles seriously disfigure lawns. There is a tradition (but no proof) that caper spurge (*Euphorbia lathyrus*), wormwood (*Artemisia*) and rue deter moles. Plant them round the perimeter of the garden to prevent moles entering.

There is no reliable way to get rid of moles except by trapping or by poison. The latter is the more humane method of the two.

Rabbits and hares

Dear little bunnies can do untold damage to succulent young plants, although once plants are well established they don't seem so interested.

Young trees can be protected with plastic spiral guards wrapped round their trunks or by corrugated plastic sleeves anchored to wooden stakes, which can be also be used on shrubs of upright growth. Vegetable plots or the whole garden can be fenced with fine mesh wire netting 1.2m (4ft) high. The bottom 15cm (6in) should be bent at right angles and buried at a depth of 15cm (6in). The 90cm (3ft) showing above ground can be hidden by a hedge or informally grouped shrubs.

Right Rabbits and hares damage young trees by stripping the bark from the stems or trunks. Protect by using spiral tree guards or wire netting.

If they persistently defeat your barricades, try growing plants from the following list which seem to be able to survive rabbits:

RABBIT-PROOF TREES AND SHRUBS *Arbutus, Aucuba, Berberis*, birch, *Buddleja*, box, *Ceanothus*, dogwood, *Cotoneaster, Daphne mezereum, Elaeagnus pungens* 'Maculata', *Gaultheria*, gorse, *Hydrangea*, holly, *Laburnum*, lilac, honeysuckle, *Olearia*, tree peony, *Philadelphus, Rhus, Ribes*, rose, rosemary, *Sambucus, Skimmia, Spiraea*, yew, *Viburnum lantana, Viburnum opulus*.

RABBIT-PROOF PERENNIALS *Aconitum, Anemone, Aquilegia, Aster, Astilbe, Bergenia, Campanula lactiflora, C. latifolia, Convallaria, Corydalis, Cynara, Digitalis, Doronicum, Epimedium, Euphorbia, Geranium* (cranesbill), *Hellebore, Hemerocallis, Hosta, Iris, Kniphofia*, lupin, *Miscanthus, Nepeta*, peony, *Papaver, Phormium, Polygonatum* (Solomon's seal), *Polygonum, Romneya*, London pride, *Salvia* x *superba, Sedum spectabile, Stachys byzantina (olympica), Trollius*.

Natural pest control

There is a lot of animal life in the garden; the list of garden pests, some of which can damage plants beyond the point of recovery, is dauntingly long; so it is good to know that not all creepy crawlies in the garden are enemies.

Four-legged friends

HEDGEHOGS eat various ground-dwelling pests including cutworms and slugs. You may not know of your hedgehog population, as they only move about at night. They live (and from November to March hibernate) under hedges or in piles of leaves and logs. It is only too easy to roast hedgehogs in a bonfire, so if possible shift the bonfire pile before you light it and rescue any that you find.

Below left Hedgehogs feed on a variety of ground-dwelling pests.

Left The seven-spot ladybird and its larvae are ravenous consumers of aphids.

Below The centipede, a fast-moving predator of a number of soil-dwelling pests.

SHREWS also feed on ground pests but you are even less likely to see a shrew at its meal than a hedgehog.

FROGS AND TOADS eat slugs, flies and other insects. Both need water in which to breed. The smallest pool will do, but it must have gently sloped sides for easy access and dense vegetation overhanging it to provide cover from preying birds. To start a froggery, ask the local wildlife trust how to obtain spawn in spring.

Feathered friends

Birds figure on the pest side of the balance sheet as well as the useful side; bullfinches nip off the buds of ornamental cherries and fruit trees, pigeons go for cabbages and other vegetables, blackbirds and others for soft fruit and small birds for yellow crocuses.

But who would want a silent garden? Listening to birdsong is one of the pleasures of gardening. And in most gardens you don't have to be at work for long before your own personal robin adopts you.

Most birds feed on garden pests and the 'best' in this respect are song thrushes, which eat slugs and snails when they cannot get worms, and blue tits, which go for caterpillars, aphids and leaf miners.

If you encourage these you will have to put up with the bullfinches and blackbirds as well, but it is a price worth paying. Too much tidiness deters birds.

Creepy crawlies

Without insects for them to feed on there would be no birds, and without insects to pollinate the flowers there would be no fruit, so pest control should never be a matter of eliminating everything that creeps or flies. Some insects are also useful in controlling other more harmful creatures.

GROUND BEETLES AND CENTIPEDES eat slugs, soil grubs and woodlice, although they also prey on worms, the gardener's greatest friends.

SPIDERS catch pests as well as other innocent insects.

HOVERFLIES (wasp lookalikes, but smaller), lacewings and wasps all prey on aphids.

LADYBIRDS are the stars of the show, known and loved by us all. Both the larva and the adult are voracious consumers of aphids: they can eat five hundred per day and more.

TIP

Contrary to popular belief, bread and milk is not good for hedgehogs. To keep hedgehogs around put out tinned pet food – but not too much or they will not be hungry for slugs. If you or your family think of keeping a hedgehog as a pet, be warned that the appealing creature is full of fleas.

Right The caterpillar of the large cabbage white butterfly is the natural prey of a parasitic braconid wasp.

Below *Viburnum opulus* 'Compactum' fruits abundantly.

Legless friends

EARTHWORMS do not feed on pests but I mention them here because they are among the most beneficial creatures in the garden. If you have plenty of worms in the soil you need hardly worry about digging or drainage – they will do it for you, collecting organic material from the surface and burrowing down into the soil with it, thereby helping to make humus, aerating the ground and making the humus more accessible to plant roots. Encourage a worm population by providing organic mulches and liming every few years to provide the slightly alkaline soil in which they thrive.

SLOWWORMS are neither worms nor snakes but legless lizards up to 30cm (1ft) long. In my childhood small boys coveted them as pets but most girls avoided them as if they were cobras. Slugs are their favourite diet and they live in leaf litter, drystone walls or compost heaps.

To Encourage Birds

- Leave hedges and climbing plants bushy to provide nesting places.
- Plant *Berberis, Pyracantha, Viburnum, Cotoneaster*, ivy and elder to provide berries for winter food.
- Provide nesting boxes for bluetits positioned between 2 and 5m (7-16ft) above the ground.
- Install a bird table for the winter, but remember that birds need water as well as food. Stop feeding in late spring so that they can reciprocate your kindness by switching to a diet of pests.

Right Earthworms aerate the soil and help to break down and incorporate organic matter.

Non-chemical pest control

Predators

Set a bug to catch a bug is the theory. The natural predators recommended so far, such as birds, frogs, toads, ladybirds and other insects, are already present in most gardens and just need encouragement to stay there and breed, or to come over the fence from next door.

If you decide to rely on biological rather than chemical pest control, it is vitally important to give this encouragement: if you have already zapped your aphids with chemical warfare, there is no incentive to the ladybird to settle down in your garden and raise a family. You may have to be prepared to let the pest populations build up so that they provide a sufficient food resource for predators, in turn, to build up their populations. It can take two or three seasons to achieve this natural balance, so be patient.

WARNING Avoid using chemical pesticides which kill predators along with the pests. Use selective products.

To build up natural predator populations, make sure the plants which they feed and breed on are in your garden. For example, the predators which eat aphids on roses or beans can be lured to the relevant part of the garden with tansy to attract ladybirds, cosmos for lacewings, and parsley, fennel and dill for hoverflies.

Predator insects can also be artificially introduced with the sole purpose of getting rid of pest insects, but this is only practical in the relatively small and enclosed area of a greenhouse.

Tricks and traps

If you have decided to eschew the use of chemicals, there are other aids to pest control in addition to natural predators.

GREASEBANDS The trunks of fruit trees (and other affected deciduous trees) are encircled with a sticky band 15cm (6in) wide, at 45-120cm (18-48in) above ground level. Put greasebands on in early autumn, remove and burn them in spring. They prevent the wingless female winter moths from climbing trees to lay their eggs. Greasebands can be bought from most garden shops.

HORTICULTURAL FLEECE A light film of spun polypropylene is an effective barrier against flying pests such as cabbage root fly and carrot root fly. The fleece allows water and light through, so it can be left in position until the crop is harvested.

PHEROMONE TRAPS Sticky traps baited with synthetic female hormones lure male codling moths, thus preventing them from mating. The traps are hung from the branches of apple and pear trees in late spring or early summer.

Above A pheromone trap for codling moths.

Below A grease band on a fruit tree.

TAR OIL WASH An old remedy for orchard pests, applied in winter at the same time as pruning. The washes do not discriminate between pests and good insects, but bees are safe as they are not around at that time of year.

DISEASE- AND PEST-RESISTANT STRAINS Some strains of plant are more resistant than others, and plant breeders are always striving to make them more so. Look for them when you are ordering seeds or buying seedlings.

Companion planting

Traditionally, certain plants are grown beside others to deter pests, and 'old wives' tales' are often based on sound practices which have stood the test of time. Serious research into this aspect of horticulture is in its infancy, so it is difficult to point to firm evidence that the old wives (and old husbands) are right. But it is worth experimenting.

Below Horticultural fleece makes a barrier against carrot root fly.

Right Wire netting protects against squirrels.

Below A spiral, plastic tree guard protects the vulnerable bark of young trees from rabbits and hares.

Nasturtiums are thought to act as a decoy for woolly aphids on apple trees, and marigolds *(Tagetes sinuata)* to protect potato crops from eelworm. Garlic is traditionally planted among roses to ward off greenfly.

Recently scientists have begun to take companion planting seriously and have conducted some interesting experiments: they have shown that if onions and carrots are grown side by side, carrot fly and onion thrips are both reduced.

Scientists have also discovered that *Tagetes patula* and *Tagetes erecta* (French and African marigolds) produce root exudate that reduces eelworm (nematode) populations, so the old wives were right. To be effective, the marigolds should be sown as a mass crop for a season and then dug in.

Organic pesticides

Traditionally, pyrethrum and derris are used. Both are available as dust or in liquid form, but they are indiscriminate, poisoning ladybirds, bees, hoverflies, frogs and toads as well as pests.

Chemical pest control

Sometimes weather conditions and other factors combine to produce an infestation amounting to a plague of one pest or another. At such times it may be advisable to resort to chemical control. Insecticides act in one of three ways:

- Insect-contact: the chemical attacks the pest directly.
- Leaf-contact: the chemical coats leaves and stem and the bugs are killed when they chew the leaves.
- Systemic: the chemical penetrates leaves and enters the sap. Insects hidden inside the leaves and those that are visible on the outside are killed. Of the three, the systemic method is the most effective.

Predators to Control Greenhouse Pests

Recent research has had some success in finding ways of controlling insect pests by introducing predators which attack them. Some garden centres sell them or they can be obtained from specialist organic suppliers. Set predators to work as soon as the pest appears.

- The larvae of ladybirds (Cryptolaemus montrouzieri) eat mealy bugs, which attack pot plants and vines.
- Encarsia formosa, a small parasitic wasp, kills whitefly, one of the commonest greenhouse pests, by laying its eggs in their larvae.
- Phytoseiulus persimilis, another predatory mite, gobbles up red spider mites.
- Heterorhabditis controls vine weevil.

Right Mealy bugs, so called because their bodies are covered in powdery white meal. They protect themselves with a waxy substance that makes control with contact chemicals difficult. Systemics are more effective.

When buying insecticides, read the label on the pack. Choose a product that deals with the particular pest you are troubled by and, if possible, does not harm other benign creatures. The pack will also tell you how long after use it is safe to harvest food crops. Those pesticides that do least harm to other living things are listed below. Please note that all these chemicals are toxic to fish.

PYRETHRUM Recommended by organic gardening organizations. It is derived from the plant *Pyrethrum,* kills on contact and becomes harmless within hours. Effective against aphids, caterpillars, spider mite and whitefly. Harmful to bees, so use after they have gone to bed or when they are not flying.

FATTY ACID SOAPS Gardeners used to make up their own mixes of soap or detergent but it is now illegal to do so. Commercial products containing fatty acid soaps are approved for organic gardening. They kill aphids, whitefly and spider mite but not the useful ladybirds and hoverflies.

PIRIMICARB Kills aphids but not bees, ladybirds, lacewings or most other insects.

BIOALLETHRIN, PERMETHRIN, PIRIMIPHOS-METHYL Used in different combinations and do not distinguish between pests and predators.

Increase and Multiply

I grew it myself: these are words that will make a gardener's heart swell with pride. Propagation, the reproduction of plants by seeds, cuttings or other methods, is one of the most creative activities for gardeners. It is the most economical way to stock your garden with plants and have a surplus to give to friends and charities, or swap with other enthusiasts.

All plants have a limited lifespan and, by propagating from your favourites in good time, you can have replacements ready when they finally succumb to a hard frost or to old age.

Growing from seed

We saw in Chapter 3, Understanding Plants, that each seed contains all that is needed – except water – to start a young plant into growth. When the seeds are in contact with moist soil or compost, germination occurs and growth begins.

Secrets of success are gentle, minimal handling of fragile seedlings, and good light but not direct sunlight from germination onwards.

Sowing seeds in trays

Most seeds need a constant temperature for successful germination. Sowing in trays enables them to be grown in a greenhouse, cold frame or indoors until the seedlings are ready to plant out in the garden. Even seeds which readily germinate out of doors have a better chance in clean compost than outdoor soil where weed seeds are present.

WHEN? The instructions on seed packets include sowing times.

- Half-hardy (not completely frost-proof) annuals or tender perennials are sown in late winter (February to March in Britain) or early spring (March to April). These include *Alyssum*, *Impatiens* (busy lizzie), *Lavatera, Lobelia*, French and African marigolds, *Nicotiana* (tobacco plant) and *Petunia*. With this timing they are ready to be planted out in the garden in early summer when all risk of frost is past.
- Perennials and biennials such as foxgloves, wallflowers, Canterbury bells, hollyhocks and sweet williams are sown in early to midsummer. In the first season they make roots and leaves and they flower a year later.

WHERE? Most seeds germinate at a temperature between 15°C and 20°C (59-68°F). If you don't have a greenhouse you might consider investing in an electrically heated propagator. However, a windowsill or table in a light position is adequate and, if it is in a room that you use every day, you won't forget to keep an eye on the seed trays and water them when needed. Make sure the seed trays are not in direct sunlight, which quickly shrivels tender young seedlings.

SOWING SEEDS IN TRAYS

1

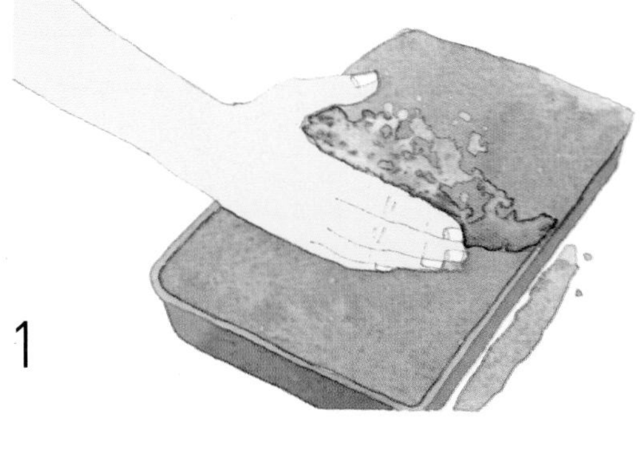

1 Fill the tray with seed compost so that it is slightly mounded above the sides of the tray. Level it off with the edge of a presser board, or with your hand.

2

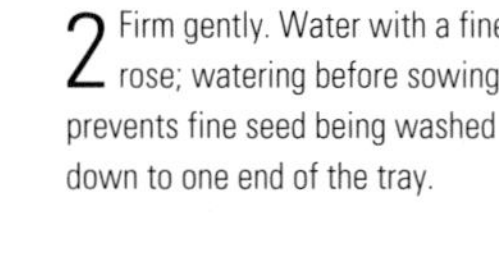

2 Firm gently. Water with a fine rose; watering before sowing prevents fine seed being washed down to one end of the tray.

3

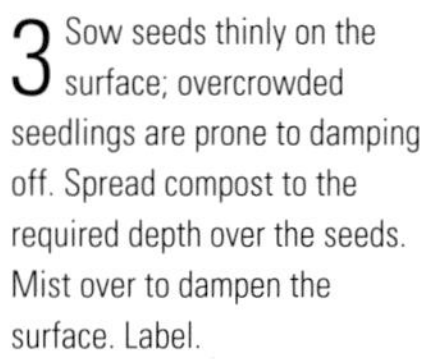

3 Sow seeds thinly on the surface; overcrowded seedlings are prone to damping off. Spread compost to the required depth over the seeds. Mist over to dampen the surface. Label.

4

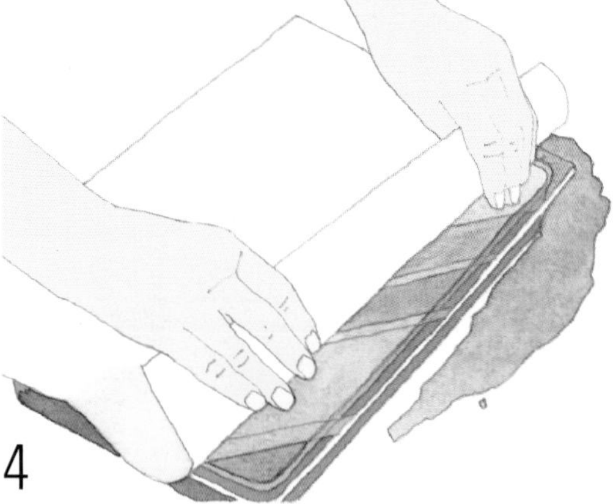

4 Cover with glass or cling film. Turn daily to avoid build-up of condensation. Lay a sheet of newspaper over the top; some seeds will only germinate in the dark. Newspaper also protects emerging seedlings from scorching or baking in strong sunlight.

TIPS

- Collect seeds from your favourite plants. You may even find that by a genetic accident of cross-pollination you have produced a hitherto unknown hybrid in your garden.
- If you only want a few plants from large seeds like sweet peas, courgettes or beans, sow them in small plastic or fibre pots. Store surplus seeds in the freezer.

Golden Rules of Cleanliness

This caution applies to all propagation techniques carried out indoors. Infant plants are vulnerable to pests and diseases, so if you don't observe basic rules of hygiene when sowing seeds or taking cuttings, be prepared for a high failure rate.

The rules are:

- Keep your greenhouse and workbench (or kitchen table) clean. Pests and diseases can lurk in dirty nooks and crannies. Washing down all surfaces in the greenhouse or potting shed with disinfectant is a good indoor winter job.
- Keep pots, seed trays and other equipment clean by scrubbing them out with detergent before storing them.
- Use sterile compost. Ready mixed composts and peat and sand bought in sealed bags are already sterile. If in doubt, after filling pots or trays water them with Cheshunt compound.

TOOLS

- Plastic seed trays. They can be used again and again; a standard tray measures 35x20cm (14x 8in). Half- and quarter-sized trays are readily available and very useful if you don't have unlimited space.
- Multi-purpose compost to fill your trays.
- Watering can with a fine rose.
- Mist sprayer.
- Roll of clingfilm or a pane of glass or perspex big enough to cover the seed tray.
- Labels.
- Indelible pencil or marker pen.

HOW?

- Fill a seed tray with compost and level it off.
- Firm it lightly with a flat block of wood roughly the same size as the tray or with the back of your hand.
- Water thoroughly and leave to drain. Don't leave watering until after the seeds are sown; even with the finest rose the seeds seem to get washed to one end of the tray where they grow overcrowded and prone to disease.
- Shake the seeds out of the packet into the palm of one hand.
- Using thumb and forefinger of the other hand sprinkle small seeds thinly on the surface of the compost. It may help to mix fine seeds with silver sand for more even distribution. Very tiny seeds sometimes come in little plastic tubes and can be tapped gently out. Large seeds can be placed individually at even spacings in trays or three or four seeds to a 9cm (3½in) pot.

WARNING It is a waste of seed and time to sow too thickly: the seedlings will grow too close to prick out easily and will be susceptible to fungal disease. The surpluses of many types of seed can be stored in the fridge until next year.

- Cover the seeds with compost to the depth indicated on the seed packet, using a 3 or 6mm (⅛ or ¼in) mesh sieve if possible. Tiny seeds should not be covered at all.
- Water the surface with a mist sprayer.
- Label each tray with the name of the plant and date of sowing.
- Cover the tray with clingfilm or a sheet of glass or perspex to keep the moisture in. Some seeds need to be in the dark, for instance *Gazania, Nemesia* and *Verbena*, so cover their trays with black polythene or several sheets of newspaper.

AFTERCARE The seeds should germinate in two to twenty-eight days, depending on the species.

- When seedlings appear remove the glass or clingfilm and make sure the tray gets plenty of light.
- Water often enough to keep the compost moist, but do not saturate it. Overwatering is a common cause of failure.
- When two or three pairs of leaves have formed, prick out the seedlings into trays or pots (see below).

SOWING SEEDS IN ROWS

1 Fork over the seed bed, pulling up all weeds as you go. Rake to a fine tilth.

2 Pull a string line taut between pegs along the row, and using this as a guide, make a furrow of the appropriate depth with a stick or dibber. Sprinkle seed thinly in the furrow, or space at recommended distances.

3 Use a rake to cover the seeds with soil. Label the row with name and sowing date. Water thoroughly.

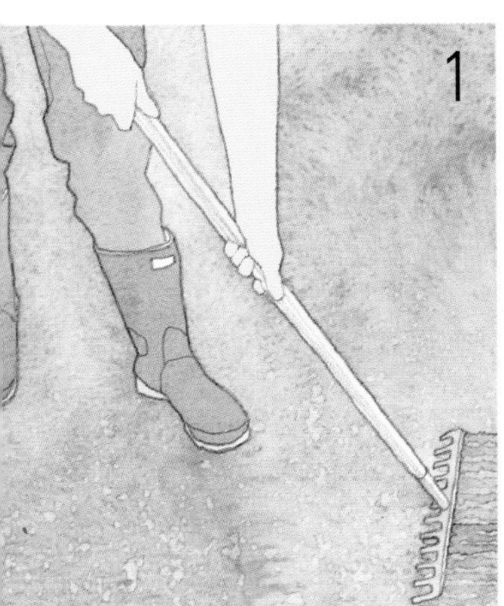

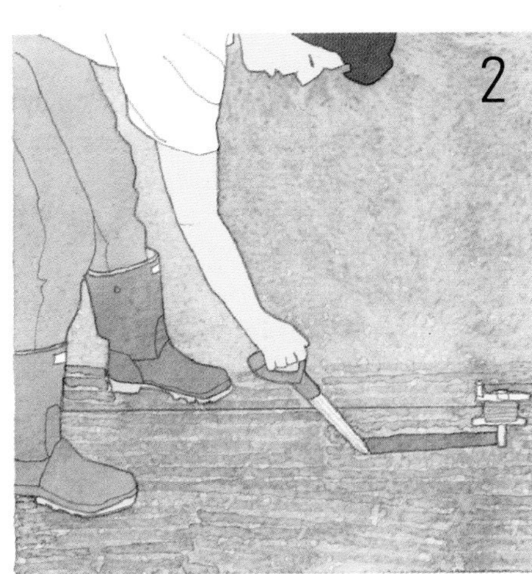

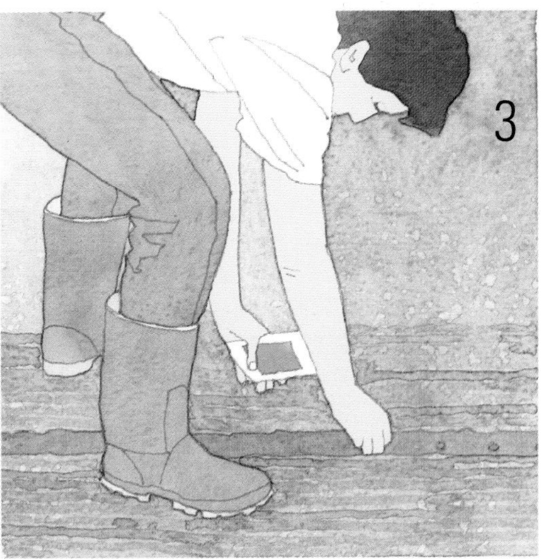

Pricking out

WHY? As seedlings grow, they will crowd each other and become thin and leggy unless they are spaced out in new trays of compost or in individual pots. The delicate process of moving them from their original trays is called 'pricking out'. If your seedlings were sown in pots there is no need to prick them out. You can thin them out by gently removing all except the strongest plant, firm the compost round it, water and leave it to grow on until the time is right to plant it in the garden.

WHEN? Seedlings are ready to prick out when they have two or three pairs of leaves, usually from two to three weeks after they have germinated.

WHERE? Work in a shady, sheltered place so that minimum stress is caused to the plants, and at a table of a comfortable height so that minimum stress is caused to your back. It is a good job to do indoors when it is raining.

TOOLS

- Seed trays or pots, used to accommodate the seedlings.
- Multipurpose compost to fill the trays.
- Pencil or smooth stick of equivalent diameter.
- Watering can with fine rose.
- Widger, or its equivalent: a rigid plant label or a wooden iced lolly stick are about the right size and shape.

HOW?
- Water the seedlings an hour or two in advance.
- Fill the trays or pots with compost, level them, water and leave to drain.
- Using the unsharpened end of a pencil make holes in the compost, evenly spaced at about 5cm (2in).
- Using the widger, label or lolly stick, gently lift up a small clump of seedlings out of the seed tray.
- Take one seedling at a time, holding it by one leaf between thumb and forefinger, and lower it into the hole made by the pencil. Always handle seedings by the leaves, never by stem or roots as they are very fragile.
- Using the pencil, gently firm the compost round its roots.
- When the tray is full, water with a fine rose and put it in the greenhouse or on the windowsill.

Left Lettuce seedlings before and after pricking out.

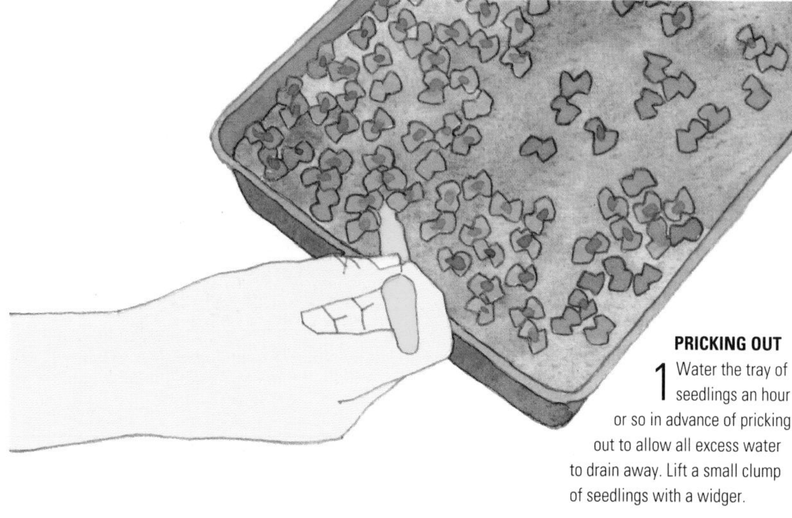

PRICKING OUT

1 Water the tray of seedlings an hour or so in advance of pricking out to allow all excess water to drain away. Lift a small clump of seedlings with a widger.

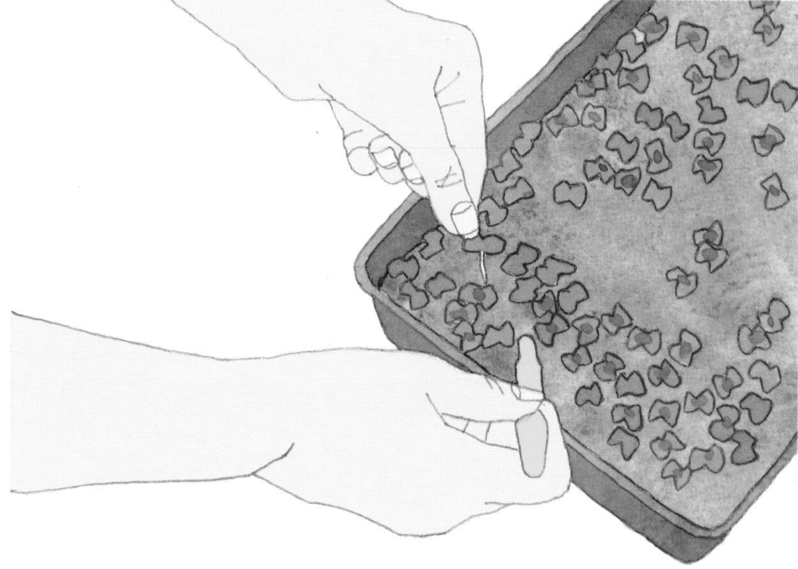

2 Separate out one seedling at a time. Hold the seedling by its leaves.

Potting on

Before they are ready to go out into the garden, the plants that were pricked out may need moving again to give each plant root and air space to develop. Following the pricking out technique, space them further apart in more trays or give each seedling a small pot to itself.

Hardening off and planting out

Plants grown indoors need to be gradually acclimatized before they will thrive outside. When the plants look sturdy and the weather is mild, introduce them to the outdoors over a two-week period. The traditional method is to move them in their trays or pots from the greenhouse to a

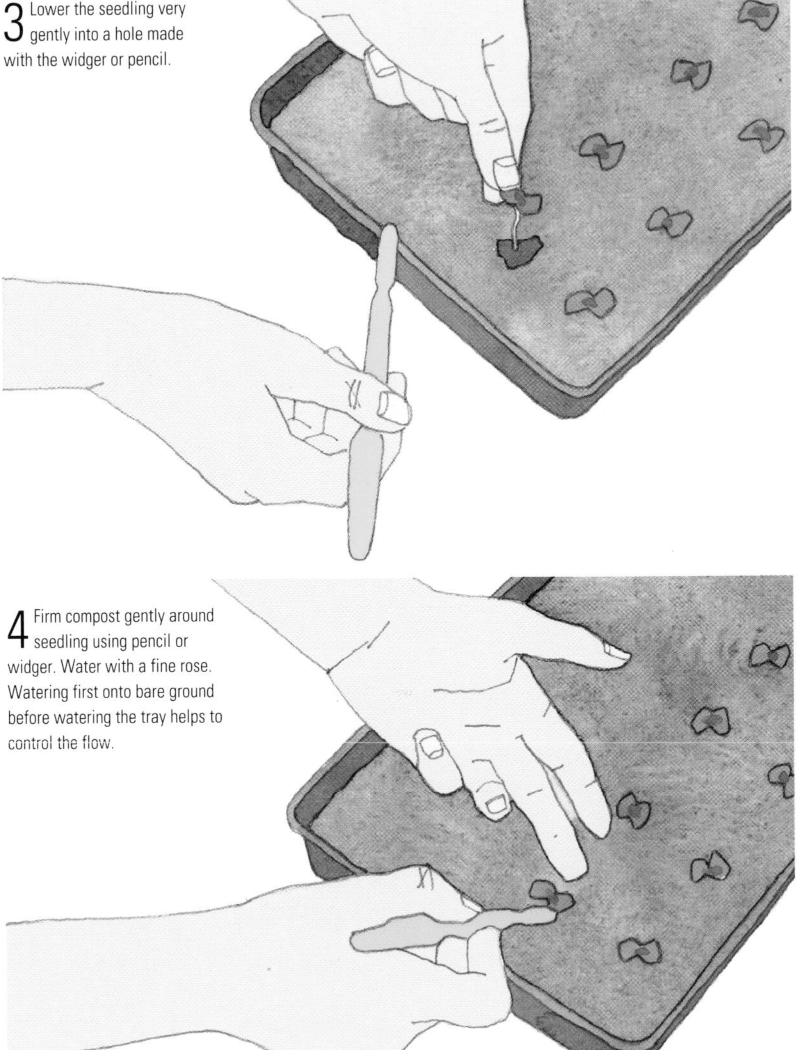

3 Lower the seedling very gently into a hole made with the widger or pencil.

4 Firm compost gently around seedling using pencil or widger. Water with a fine rose. Watering first onto bare ground before watering the tray helps to control the flow.

garden frame with a glass cover. Each day the frame is opened a little wider and finally removed completely. If you do not have a frame, put the plants outdoors in a sheltered place for a few more hours each day. Bring them back in at night until there is a spell of mild weather. After hardening off the plants can be planted outside.

WARNING *If you buy summer bedding plants rather than raising them from seed yourself, the chances are that they come straight out of the protected environment of a greenhouse or polythene tunnel. It is therefore a wise precaution to harden them off before planting them.*

WHEN? Wallflowers, forget-me-nots and other hardy biennials which are to flower the following year should be transplanted to their final positions in autumn. Meanwhile, if they were grown in trays, they can be planted out for the summer in rows in a vacant plot as soon as they are sturdy enough.

Summer bedding plants should be planted in early summer when the risk of night frosts is past. If possible wait until rain is forecast and plant in the evening so that the plants can recover overnight.

WHERE? Use your home-grown herbaceous perennials as part of a permanent planting scheme.

TOOLS

- Trowel, narrow-bladed if you have one.
- Widger, for very small plants like *Alyssum* and *Lobelia.*
- Watering can with a coarse rose.
- Plastic or nylon wind-break mesh, and canes to hold it in place, are optional extras on very windy sites.

HOW? Before planting, water the trays and leave to drain for a few hours. This applies to bought plants as well as home-grown.

- Make sure the site is free of weeds and large stones. If it was not dug or forked over in the autumn, fork it lightly to a depth of 15cm (6in).
- With trowel or widger lift the plants from the tray one at a time, keeping as much soil round the roots as possible. If the tray has become a continuous mat of roots, separate the plants by chopping between them with the blade of the trowel and gently tease out the roots of each plant.
- With a trowel dig a hole the right size to receive the plant, put the plant in, replace the soil round it and firm it round the roots with your hands.
- For the planting distances, consult the table on p.173.
- Water thoroughly.

AFTERCARE Keep the plants watered and weeded. When they are growing strongly mulch the soil between them.

Pinching out (stopping)

If you want dense, bushy plants instead of tall, thin ones it helps to nip out the soft growing tips between finger and thumb. This is a form of pruning: by removing the leading shoot you are encouraging side shoots to develop.

Plants which benefit from pinching out include wallflowers (pinch out tips when the plants are about 15cm (6in) high, chrysanthemums, pot marigolds and *Pelargonium* (bedding geraniums).

Do not pinch out plants such as antirrhinums, foxgloves, hollyhocks and stocks which flower on strong central stems.

DESIGN TIP

For spring- and summer-flowering annuals and biennials, plant them in formal flower beds, pots and tubs, hanging baskets, window boxes. Use them to fill gaps between newly planted shrubs, as underplanting in rose beds, and as edgings to beds and borders.

Sowing seeds outdoors

WHERE? Biennials and perennials can be sown in trays or in rows in a seed bed outdoors and transferred to their final sites in autumn. Some annuals do not transplant well and should be sown where they are to flower, or in degradable fibre pots made of compressed peat or other material that breaks down in the soil.

The following should be sown straight into final positions: borage, cornflowers, *Clarkia, Eschscholzia, Limnanthes*, opium poppy, Shirley poppy and *Phacelia.*

WHEN? Follow the instructions on the seed packet. Wait until the soil has warmed up before sowing annuals. If spring is late, sow slightly later. Pick a day when the soil is moist but not wet, or water the ground the day before you sow.

TOOLS

- Fork or spade if the site was not dug in the autumn.
- String line, with a stick at each end if you are sowing in rows.
- Rake.
- Watering can with a fine rose.
- Labels.
- Pencil or marker.

HOW?
- If not done the previous autumn, fork over the area, weeding as you go.
- Rake to a fine tilth (like breadcrumbs).
- If you are sowing in rows, peg the string line taut along the ground and draw out a furrow of the required depth against the string using a stick or the corner of a rake or hoe.
- Sprinkle the seeds sparsely and evenly along the furrow or space out individual seeds equally.
- Gently rake soil back over the seeds.
- Label the rows and water thoroughly using a fine rose.

Alternatively you can broadcast the seeds:
- Prepare the ground in the same way.
- Rake the ground in one direction.
- Scatter the seeds.
- Rake them in gently at right angles to the first.

Thinning out

Seedlings sown out of doors do not need pricking out but they do need space to develop. When they become crowded, remove the weakest, leaving the strong plants with a few centimetres of space around them. With your fingers firm the disturbed soil around their roots. Repeat the thinning process from time to time as necessary. The thinnings need not all be discarded, but can be planted out in a new row.

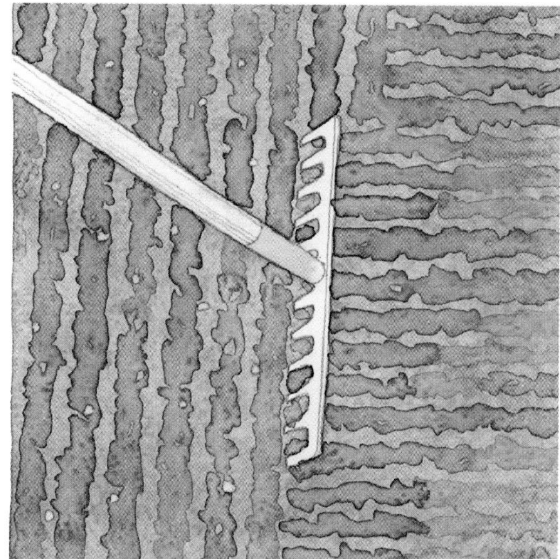

BROADCASTING SEEDS

1 Soil preparation for broadcasting is the same as for sowing in rows. Rake the soil to a fine tilth in one direction. Scatter the seed evenly over the surface.

2 Cover the seeds with the rake, raking in a direction at right angles to the first raking.

TIP

Disappointing results are often due to overcrowded plants. Make sure you thin out or transplant to the correct distances.

Self-Seeding: Plants for Free

In the garden many plants will do the job of sowing the seeds for you if you leave the seedheads to ripen on their stems. If you start with just one of these plants, you will find that by the following spring it is surrounded by seedlings. This is known as self-seeding. If you allow self-seeded plants to grow unchecked they will give an informal, natural look to the garden. If you prefer a more controlled design, all you need do is lift them and transfer them to their new home or leave a few in position, pulling out the rest to allow the chosen few space to develop. Other plants produce seeds that are carried on the wind and may germinate in unexpected places.

Examples include poppies (*Papaver* and *Meconopsis*), foxgloves (*Digitalis*), columbine (*Aquilegia*), honesty (*Lunaria*), *Verbascum*, *Viola,* valerian, *Alchemilla mollis*, forget-me-not (*Myosotis*), polyanthus, wallflowers (*Cheiranthus*), love-in-a-mist (*Nigella*), pot marigold, *Limnanthes douglasii*, some campanulas, Jacob's ladder (*Polemonium*), hardy cyclamen and *Sisyrinchium striatum.*

Plants to Learn With

If you lack confidence, start with a packet of mustard and cress, but the following selection of plants will provide a good introduction to sowing seeds. When in doubt follow instructions on seed packets.

The following abbreviations are used in the 'Type' column: P=perennial, B=biennial, A=annual, or perennial treated as annual.

Plant	Type	When to sow	Where (under glass = greenhouse or windowsill)	Height/final planting or thinned out distance apart	Flowering or harvesting
Alcea (hollyhock)	P (short-lived)	Jan-Feb	Under glass in pots to flower same year	1.35-2.7m (4.5-9ft)/ 38-60cm (15-25in)	June-Sept
		May-June	Outdoors *in situ* to flower following year		
Alyssum	A	Mar-Apr	Under glass in trays	8-10cm (3-4in)/15-20cm (6-9in)	May-Sept
		Apr-May	Outdoors		
Antirrhinum (snapdragon)	A	Feb-March	Under glass in trays	45cm (18in)/30-54cm (12-18in)	July-Oct
Beans (French and runner)	A	Apr	Under glass in pots	45cm-2.5m (18in-8ft)/ 23-60cm (9-24in)	July
Broad beans [1]	A	Nov-Dec or Mar-May for succession	Outdoors *in situ*	90cm (3ft)/15cm (6in) apart in double rows, 60cm (2ft) between rows	Late June through July
Carrot	A	Mar-July in succession	Outdoors *in situ*, sun or part shade	Sow thinly in rows 30cm (1ft) apart; pull baby carrots to thin crop	Successively, June-Oct
Centaurea cyanus (cornflower)	A	Sept or Mar-Apr	Outdoors *in situ*, sun	30-90cm (1-3ft)/23-38cm (9-15in)	June-Sept
Cheiranthus [2] (wallflower)	B	May-June	Outdoors in nursery bed, sun, plant out in autumn	30-60cm (1-2ft)/30-38cm (12-15in)	Apr-June
Cosmos	A	Mar-May	Under glass	75cm (30in)/60cm (2ft)	July-Sept
		Apr-May	Outdoors in mild climates		
Courgette, marrow [3]	A	Apr-May	Under glass in pots	Sprawling/1.2m (4ft)	July-Oct
Digitalis purpurea (foxglove)	B	May-June	Outdoors in nursery bed, part shade, plant out in autumn	Thin to 15cm (6in) apart, 90-150cm (3-5ft)/38-60cm (15-24in)	June-July
Hesperis matronalis (sweet rocket, dame's violet)	B	Apr	Outdoors in nursery bed in sun	Line out 15cm (6in) apart, 60-90cm (2-3ft)/45cm (18in)	June
Lavatera trimestris [4]	.	Sept or Apr	Outdoors *in situ*, sun	60-90cm (2-3ft)/45cm (18in)	July-Sept
Lettuce	A	Apr-Aug in succession	Outdoors *in situ* or in nursery bed, sun or part shade	15-30cm (6-12in)/23-30cm (9-12in)	June-Oct
Limnanthes douglasii (poached egg flower) [5]	A	Sept or Mar	Outdoors *in situ*, sun	15cm (6in)/10cm (4in)	June-Aug
Lobelia erinus	A	Jan-Mar	Under glass	10-20cm (4-8in), trailing/10cm (4in)	May-Oct
Lunaria (honesty) [5]	B	May-June	Outdoors in nursery bed, light shade, plant out Sept-Mar	75cm (30in)/60cm (2ft)	Apr-June, followed by seedpods
Myosotis [5] (forget-me-not)	B	Apr-May	In trays or outdoors *in situ*, light shade plant out Sept-Oct	15-30cm (6-12in)/15cm (6in)	Apr-Jun
Nasturtium	A	Apr	Outdoors *in situ*, sun, poor soil	25-200cm (10in-7ft)/38cm (15in)	June-Sept
Nicotiana (tobacco plant)	A	Feb-Apr	Under glass	60-90cm (2-3ft)/30cm (1ft)	June-Sept
Nigella [5] (love-in-a-mist)	A	Mar, or in mild climate autumn	Outdoors *in situ*, sun	60cm (2ft)/23cm (9in)	June-Aug, earlier if autumn-sowed
Papaver (poppy) [6]	A B	Mar-Apr or Sept (A), May-June (B)	Outdoors *in situ*, sun	60-75cm (24-30in)/30cm (1ft)	June-Aug
Pea and sweet pea [7]	A	Sept-Oct or March	In trays under glass or outdoors *in situ*, sun	Up to 3m (10ft)/15cm (6in)	Peas: July-Aug, sweet peas: June-Sept
Petunia	A	Mar-Apr	Under glass	23-38cm (9-15in)/30cm (1ft)	June-Oct
Radish	A	At 3-week intervals from March on	Outdoors *in situ*, sun, or light shade	7-15cm (3-6in)/thin by pulling when roots are big enough to eat	May onwards
Spinach	A	At 3-week intervals from Mar-July	Outdoors *in situ*, light shade	30-45cm (12-18in)/thin to 15cm (6in) apart, then to 30cm (1ft) apart	May-Oct
Spring onion	A	July-Aug for spring, Mar for summer	Outdoors *in situ*, sun	Rows 15cm (6in) apart, no thinning needed	Mar-May, or May-end June
Stock, ten-week	A	Feb-Mar, or May	Under glass early spring, outdoors late spring	30-60cm (1-2ft)/30cm (1ft)	June-Aug, or July-Sept

[1] Winter-sown crop protects other crops from wind and frost. After harvesting cut tops down, leaving roots in soil to release nitrogen.
[2] When plants are 15cm (6in) high, pinch out tips to get bushy plants. [3] Water copiously in dry spells. Pick courgettes 10 to 15cm (4 to 6in) long. [4] Water in dry spells. Cut early in the day for crisp fresh salads. [5] Self-seeds freely. [6] Most species self-seed.
[7] Plants sown outdoors in autumn need protection with cloches in cold areas. Keep on picking sweet peas to encourage more flowers.

Increasing by division

This is the easiest way to increase your stock of herbaceous perennials. The idea is to break up a mature plant into several pieces each with roots and shoots. Each piece makes a new plant and the tired centre of the original plant is discarded. Success is guaranteed with almost all clump-forming herbaceous perennials, provided you choose plants that are mature enough to produce several rooted shoots. Some plants like *Ajuga,* London pride and strawberries do the job for you by producing offsets (separate little plants).

Besides perennials, there are some shrubs which grow in clumps or produce suckers which can be divided: bamboos *(Arundinaria), Clerodendrum, Gaultheria, Hippophaë, Hypericum calycinum, Kerria japonica, Pachysandra, Pernettya, Phormium*, raspberries, *Rhus*, *Ruscus* and *Vinca.*

Note that suckers on grafted trees and shrubs, including many roses, are offshoots from the rootstock and will reproduce the rootstock and not the grafted plant.

WHY? With many herbaceous plants division is not even optional: it is compulsory if you want to maintain a healthy stock. These plants produce strong young shoots at their perimeter and after a few years the centre or crown of the plant deteriorates.

Lifting and dividing plants provides a good opportunity to pick out the roots of ground elder, couch grass and bindweed, which tend to tangle with the roots of garden plants.

By dividing herbaceous perennials every few years you can increase your stock by at least five to one and probably more.

WHERE? If you are replanting the divided plants in the same place you can do the dividing on the spot. Otherwise dig the plant or plants up and move them to a working area with a hard surface and access to water.

WHEN? In theory, at any time. In practice it is usually done in autumn or spring as part of general tidying up of beds and borders. On heavy clay it is best left until spring. There are optimum times for different plants:

After flowering, plants with fibrous crowns: *Alchemilla, Aubrieta, Campanula, Geranium,*

TIP

If you are buying perennials, it is more economical to buy one large plant in a 1.5 or 2 litre ($2\frac{1}{2}$ or $3\frac{1}{2}$ pint) pot, and immediately divide it into half a dozen plants, than to buy six small plants in 9cm ($3\frac{1}{2}$ in) pots.

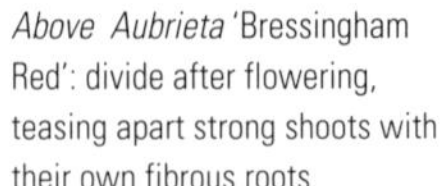

Above Aubrieta 'Bressingham Red': divide after flowering, teasing apart strong shoots with their own fibrous roots.

Left Kniphofia 'Atlanta': divide in spring, using a knife or sharp spade to chop through the fleshy crowns.

DIVISION

1 Cut down top growth to about 10cm (4in) in height, to reduce water loss.

2 Lift the plant with a fork or spade, and shake off as much loose soil as possible.

3 Wash off the remaining soil in water so that you can see where promising new growth emerges from the roots.

4 Gently tease apart rooted sections with strong growth buds by hand, or cut into sections with a sharp knife.

5 Replant the sections, so that the final soil level is the same as it was when you lifted the plant. Firm gently and water in thoroughly.

6 Plants with fleshy crowns, such as *Hosta*, can be cut into sections with a sharp knife, so that each section has at least one 'eye'. Large clumps may need to be cut up with a sharp spade.

1

2

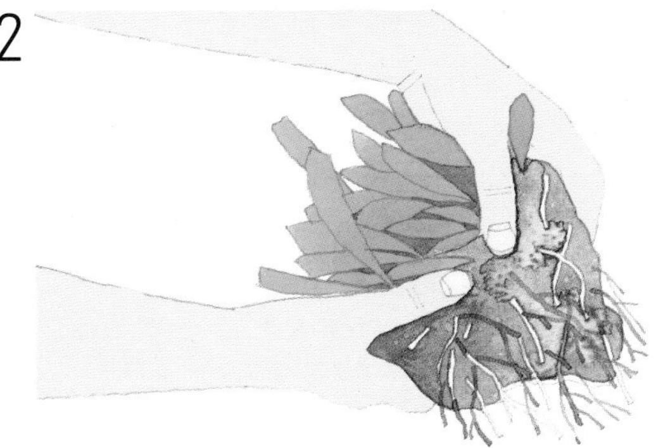

3

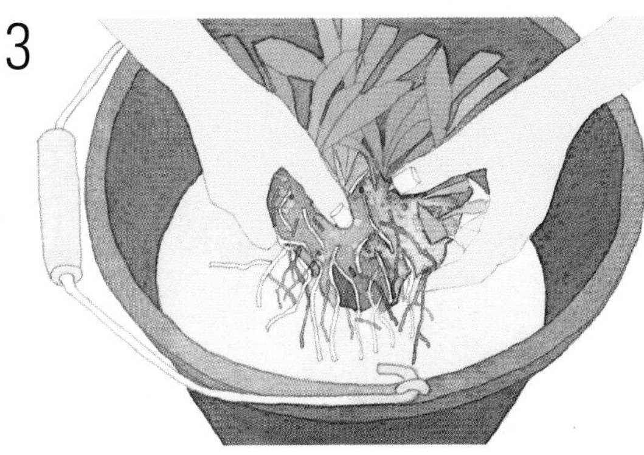

4

5

Hemerocallis, *Leucanthemum* (formerly called *Chrysanthemum*), lupin, *Polemonium*, scabious and *Veronica*; rhizomes: *Bergenia* and *Iris*.

- In spring when dormancy ends and new shoots develop, plants with fleshy crowns: *Astilbe, Delphinium, Hosta* and *Kniphofia*.

TOOLS

- Secateurs.
- Spade or fork, two forks for large plants.
- Medium-sized knife.
- Trowel.
- Watering can.

HOW?
- Cut down stems and leaves to about 10cm (4in).
- Dig the plant up and shake off as much soil as possible. If necessary wash the roots under a tap or in a bucket of water so that you can see where the new shoots are.
- Break up the plant into several pieces each with plenty of roots and one or more strong shoot. With small plants this can be done with your hands. Fleshy crowns can be cut with a knife. Large plants like hostas are more unwieldy. Lie the plant on its side, preferably on a hard surface. Drive a sharp spade through the centre then subdivide the halves in exactly the same way or with a knife. Don't worry if you break off a few shoots – it is inevitable. Another way of dividing large clumps is to insert two forks back to back into the centre and lever the clump apart.
- In all cases throw away the woody centre of the plant.
- Replant the divisions immediately and water them well.
- Pot up any surplus divisions to grow on and give away.

WARNING *Increasing plants by division is easy but there are exceptions: do not try dividing* Alstroemeria, Centranthus *(it will seed itself anyway),* Dianthus, Diascia, Gypsophila, Penstemon.

6

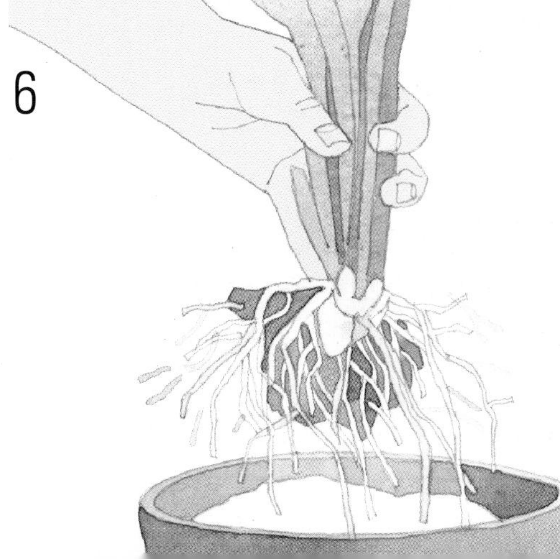

Taking cuttings

Propagating plants from cuttings is not just for experts. Some plants are trickier than others but the basic technique is always the same: you push a stick into the earth and wait for it to grow roots at the bottom and new leaves at the top.

WHY? You can reproduce shrubs or trees more quickly from cuttings than seeds.

- Many plants do not 'come true from seed'. That is to say, the seedlings may not have the same characteristics as the parent plant. So if you want to produce a true replica of the parent plant (its clone), take cuttings.
- Large numbers of a particular plant for, say, a lavender hedge or box edging are expensive to buy. If you take cuttings instead you will have your hedge for the price of two or three plants.
- Cuttings are easy to swap. If a friend admires a shrub in your garden you can offer a cutting.

WARNING *Never take cuttings from someone else's plant without permission. It is a form of theft.*

Stem cuttings

Cuttings can also be taken from leaves and roots, but stem cuttings are the easiest and most commonly used. There are three main types each requiring different growing conditions.

SOFTWOOD CUTTINGS The soft young tips of the current season's shoots. They are at a stage of rapid growth and are the quickest, but not the easiest, to root. Being soft and immature, the shoots wilt easily and are more susceptible to pests and diseases.

SEMI-RIPE CUTTINGS (also known as semi-hardwood, and the easiest to succeed with) The wood has begun to ripen but has not yet become hard. Semi-ripe shoots are still in active growth.

HARDWOOD CUTTINGS are shoots cut when the wood of the stem has hardened.

Cuttings can be taken at three different points on the stem:

NODAL CUTTING A node is the slight swelling at the junction of leaf and stem. The stem is cut straight across about 2.5mm (1/8in) below a node, preferably using a scalpel. Used for softwood, semi-ripe and evergreen cuttings.

HEEL CUTTING A heel cutting may be a softwood or semi-ripe cutting. Select a strong young side-shoot and pull down sharply so that it separates from the parent stem with a heel of tissue. Use a sharp scalpel to trim the ragged 'heel'.

INTERNODAL CUTTING Using sharp secateurs, cut straight across the stem half way between two nodes. Used for semi-ripe and hardwood cuttings, including clematis and fuchsias.

Taking softwood cuttings

WHERE? Cuttings need a warm and humid atmosphere, under polythene or mist in a clean greenhouse, or propagating frame, or indoors under polythene bags.

- Cuttings need light but not direct sunlight.
- Choose a table or workbench in a cool, shady place to prepare and pot the cuttings.

WHEN? Choose a day when you will not be interrupted: it is important to get the cuttings from the parent plant into the growing medium without delay.

- Greenhouse plants: any time of year.
- Outdoor plants: from early to midsummer, depending on the species. Take cuttings when the first flush of growth is under way. Shoots should be firm and turgid, and will snap easily.

TOOLS

- Secateurs or a sharp knife.
- Polythene bag to keep cuttings fresh. If there is to be any delay add damp moss to the bag.
- Sharp knife or scalpel to trim the cuttings.
- Flowerpots, or a propagating frame with its own tray. Square flowerpots are easier to store than round ones; a 10cm (4in) diameter pot will take between four and eight cuttings.
- Rooting medium for filling the pots: half peat and half coarse sand or perlite is reliable.
- Pencil to use as a dibber.
- Watering can with fine rose.
- Fungicide to prevent diseases.
- Cover to maintain humidity round the potted

TIPS

- All cuttings will stay fresher if taken early in the morning when they contain the maximum water levels in their cells.
- Don't be disappointed if some of your cuttings fail; 50 per cent is a good strike rate.

STEM CUTTINGS

1 Nodal cutting. With a scalpel cut the stem across at about 2.5mm (1/8in) below a node, the slight swelling at the junction of leaf and stem. Use for softwood, semi-ripe and evergreen cuttings.

2 Internodal cutting. Using sharp secateurs cut straight across the stem between two nodes. Use for semi-ripe and hardwood cuttings.

3 Heel cutting. Select a strong, young side-shoot and pull down sharply so that it separates from the parent stem with a heel of tissue. Trim off ragged edges with a scalpel. Use for softwood or semi-ripe cuttings.

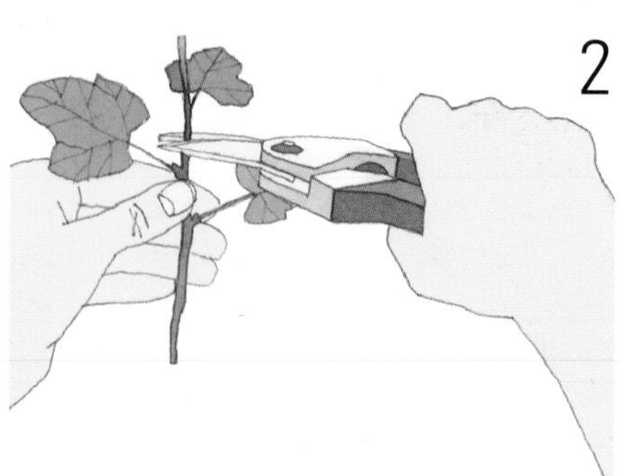

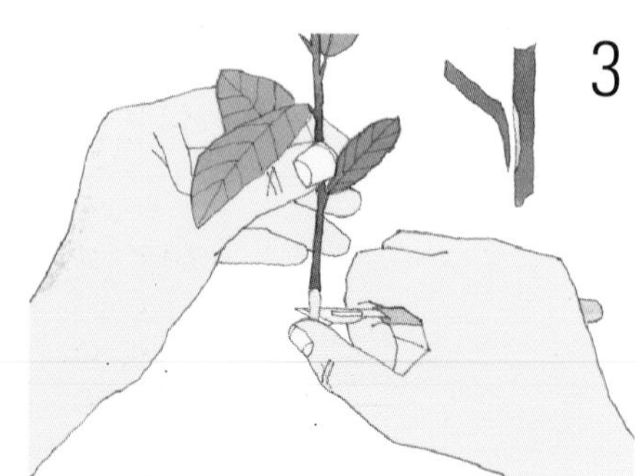

SOFTWOOD CUTTINGS

1 Trimming a cutting. Trim to about 15cm (6in) long, cutting just below a node. If the cutting material is less that 10cm (4in) long, take a heel cutting and trim the heel with a sharp blade. If it is too long, trim off the top of the stem. Remove leaves from the bottom one-third of the stem.

2 Potting up cuttings. With a dibber or pencil make a hole in the compost and insert the cutting to the depth of the bottom leaves. Push the compost back round the stem with the dibber. Make sure the leaves of each cutting do not touch.

cuttings. If you don't have a propagating frame or cold frame, a glass fish tank or clear polythene bag are good substitutes. Polythene bags need rubber bands to hold them in place. Cuttings in round pots can be covered with wide-necked jam jars or the bottom half cut from a clear plastic bottle.

HOW? • Counsel of perfection: prepare the parent plant by pruning it hard in early spring to encourage lots of strong young shoots.
• Fill the pots with the rooting medium.
• Water thoroughly and allow surplus to drain.
• Early in the morning, take cuttings from your chosen plants. Select strong, disease-free shoots preferably without flowers or flower buds. They are fragile, so handle them as little as possible and deal with small batches so that they don't have time to wilt. The average length for cuttings is 10cm (4in) but they can be as short as 5cm (2in) and as long as 15cm (6in). If in doubt cut a complete branch and select individual shoots at the workbench or kitchen table. As you collect them put the cuttings or branches in a polythene bag to keep them fresh.

Preparing and potting the cuttings

Deal with the cuttings one at a time, leaving the rest in the polythene bag. discard any that show signs of wilting.

HOW? • With a scalpel cut the stem across about 2.5mm (1/8in) below a node.
• Trim off the leaves from the bottom two-thirds of the stem. The ideal cutting has four leaves.
• Dip the cut end in fungicide.
• Using a pencil make a hole in the compost and insert the cutting with half its stem buried.
• Gently firm the compost round it.
• Add more cuttings till the pot is full. Leaves should not touch each other.
• Water in with a fine rose.
• Label with the plant's name and the date.
• Either place the pots together in a propagating frame or cover each pot with a polythene bag fastened round the pot with a rubber band. The polythene must not touch the leaves, so support it with wire hoops or three or four short sticks.
• Softwood cuttings root best if given gentle heat at the roots (15-24°C/59-75°F depending on the species) with the top kept cool, conditions that can be produced within a mist propagator. Next best is a shelf above a radiator giving off the right heat (beware of baking the cuttings).
• To shorten your odds in the race between rooting and rotting, mist with fungicide weekly.

Hardening off and potting on

If new shoots appear from the stem or tip, the cutting has probably rooted. If roots appear in the holes at the base of the pot it certainly has.

HOW? • As soon as the roots have appeared start hardening off (acclimatizing) the plants by gradually removing the polythene cover or glass.
• Polythene bags can have a few holes cut in them and the rubber band securing them can be removed.
• After a few days move each cutting to a pot of its own containing multi-purpose compost.
• At this stage plants are often killed by overwatering or under-watering and they wilt if exposed to sunlight or if kept in a hot greenhouse. Gradual acclimatization to normal garden conditions is the aim. The compost should be kept moist and the plants should have plenty of light without standing directly in the sun. Continue to spray with fungicide.

Taking semi-ripe cuttings

WHEN? The wood of the shoots will have begun to change colour and to harden but it should still be flexible and bend under pressure. Most plants are at this stage between midsummer and early autumn (July to September in Britain).

TOOLS

Tools as for softwood cuttings, but also:

- Hormone rooting powder, which helps roots to form (optional but it enhances the chances of success with some plants). It loses its power quickly so don't keep it more than one season.
- Jam jar or other container of water if you use rooting powder, to moisten the stem before dipping it in the powder.

HOW? Follow instructions for softwood cuttings. On large-leaved plants, reduce the leaf area by cutting off half of each leaf crosswise. This reduces moisture loss.

Semi-ripe cuttings are less fussy about environmental conditions than softwoods and most can be rooted without bottom heat. They can be left uncovered in a greenhouse or frame or in the house, but in that case they should be sprayed with a mist of tepid water twice a day.

They may take several months to root. If they are deciduous, they will lose their leaves in autumn. It doesn't mean they are dead, so don't chuck them out. But do remove the dead leaves to avoid diseases.

Taking hardwood cuttings

WHEN? Hardwood cuttings are best taken in autumn just after leaf-fall or in early spring just before the leaf-buds break. Ideally, prepare the plant a year in advance by hard pruning to encourage robust new growth.

WHERE? Hardwood cuttings can be grown in a sheltered bed out of doors, preferably a site that is sunny for at least part of the day, with space for a trench or row of trenches, perhaps in the vegetable garden. The cuttings will occupy it for a year. If wind is a problem put up a mesh windbreak.

TOOLS

- Spade.
- Secateurs.
- Coarse sand.

HOW? The cuttings should be a little longer than those of soft or semi-hard cuttings, 15-30cm (6-12in), and ideally of about pencil thickness.

To Take Large Numbers of Cuttings for a Hedge or Edging

- Take the cuttings in autumn, as already described.
- Make bundles of from 10 to 20 cuttings secured with rubber bands.
- Bury them in a box of sand with just the tips showing.
- Leave them for the winter in a sheltered place or cold frame.
- In spring inspect them. Those that have formed calluses at the base will develop roots and can be planted. Throw the rest away.

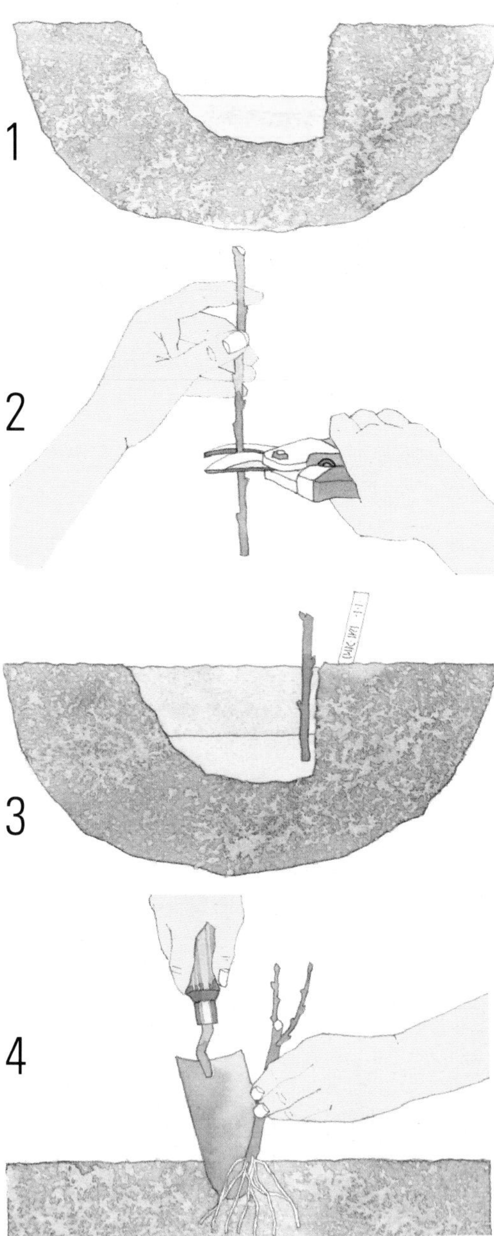

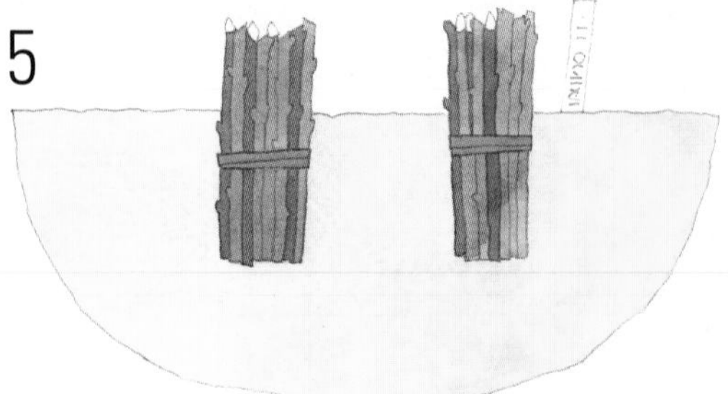

HARDWOOD CUTTINGS

1 In the open garden or in a cold frame, prepare a trench with one side vertical 15cm (6in) deep with a 5-7.5cm (2-3in) layer of sand at the bottom.

2 Prepare cuttings with a sloping cut at the top just above a healthy leaf bud and a straight cut 15cm (6in) below at the bottom.

3 Insert the cuttings against the vertical side of the trench with the bases in the sand and the tops 2.5-5cm (1-2in) above ground level. Backfill with soil and firm with the foot. Label. During winter, re-firm if the frost lifts the cuttings.

4 In spring the cuttings that have taken will come into leaf. Weed and water them during summer. In autumn, lift and transplant them to their permanent positions or pot up and grow on for planting out in the following spring.

5 To grow large numbers of plants, take cuttings in the autumn. Secure bundles of 10-20 with a rubber band and put in sand in a box or cold frame. In spring, if they have formed calluses at the base, line them out in a trench. They should form healthy root systems by autumn.

Above Escallonia 'Apple Blossom': take semi-ripe cuttings in late summer.

Right Cytisus 'Porlock': not reliably hardy. Insure against loss by taking cuttings in late summer.

Below Genista tinctoria (Dyer's greenwood): semi-ripe cuttings, late summer.

Bottom Hebe: semi-ripe cuttings, late summer.

- With a spade dig a trench about 15cm (6in) deep with one side vertical.
- Cover the base of the trench with sand.
- With secateurs cut suitable stems from the plant, at least as thick as a pencil.
- Near the tip of the stem, just above a leaf-bud, make a cut sloping upwards in the direction of the bud. Make this cut low enough on the stem to remove any soft wood at the stem's tip.
- Cut straight across the stem near the base. This cut need not be at a node.
- On evergreens remove all but the top three or four leaves.
- Set out the cuttings against the vertical face of the trench 10-15cm (4-6in) apart with the slanted tip 2.5-5cm (1-2in) above the ground.
- Backfill the trench and firm it round the cuttings with your foot.
- In spring those that have taken will begin to grow. Keep them weeded and watered through the summer.
- Transplant them to their final positions in autumn.

Plants to learn with

The following plants root fairly easily from cuttings, but do not expect 100 per cent success: *Buddleja*, box, *Caryopteris, Choisya, Cistus, Escallonia, Euonymus, Forsythia, Genista, Griselinia, Hebe, Hedera, Hydrangea, Hypericum, Jasminum, Laburnum*, lavender, *Ligustrum* (privet), *Lonicera nitida, Olearia*, passion flower, *Philadelphus, Phlomis*, poplar, *Potentilla, Ribes*, sage, *Sambucus nigra, Santolina, Senecio, Spiraea, Weigela*, willow.

Layering

You may have noticed with some shrubs or climbing plants with low branches that where a branch touches the ground roots develop. As with self-seeders, this plant is doing the job of propagation for you. All you need do is cut the rooted section loose from the parent plant and pot it up or replant it straight into the garden. Make sure you cut a section of stem with a few buds on it: these will produce the new shoots. Many plants layer themselves naturally. With others it is simple to give them a helping hand.

The propagation methods described here are the simplest and most generally used. If you have success with them and get bitten with the propagating bug you will want to try your hand at leaf cuttings and various ways of grafting. The techniques are more easily demonstrated than described, and the best way to learn is to attend one of the demonstrations arranged by horticultural colleges and clubs.

WHY? It is the easiest way to propagate many climbing plants and a number of shrubs too. You need no special equipment or housing for the plants.

WHERE? Close to the parent, because the new plant remains attached to the parent until it is strong enough to detach.

WHEN? In autumn or early spring.

Below Lilacs are easy to increase by layering. This one is *Syringa* 'Souvenir de Louis Spaeth'.

Right Thymes spread naturally by layering. Help them by spreading a thin layer of soil or potting compost over the plant.

Far right Deciduous and evergreen azaleas can be increased by layering.

TOOLS

- Secateurs.
- Spade.
- Peat and grit.
- Stiff wire.
- Wirecutter.
- Watering can.

HOW? Some plants (ivies, thyme) root so easily from layers that all you need do is lay a branch or shoot on the ground and weight it down with a stone. With other plants success is more likely if you do as follows:

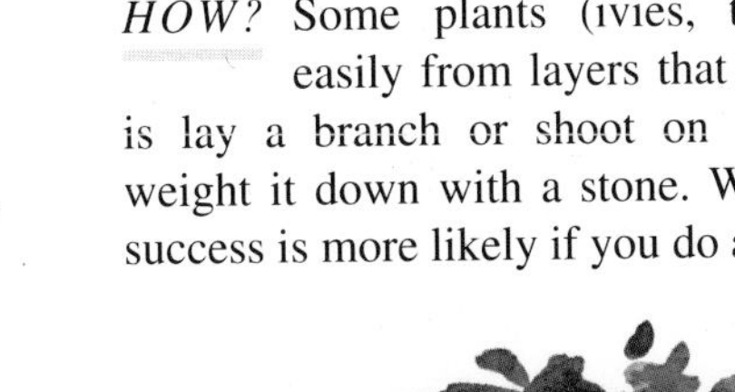

LAYERING

1 Simple layering.

2 Wounding to encourage rooting: with a sharp knife, cut a sliver of stem, about 3cm (1½in) long, at a shallow angle. Hold the wound open with a matchstick. Peg down and bury with soil.

3 Some plants, especially those of the bramble family, will root naturally at their tips. This can be encouraged by tip layering. Proceed as for simple layering, but in this case bury the tip of the plant just beneath the surface of the soil.

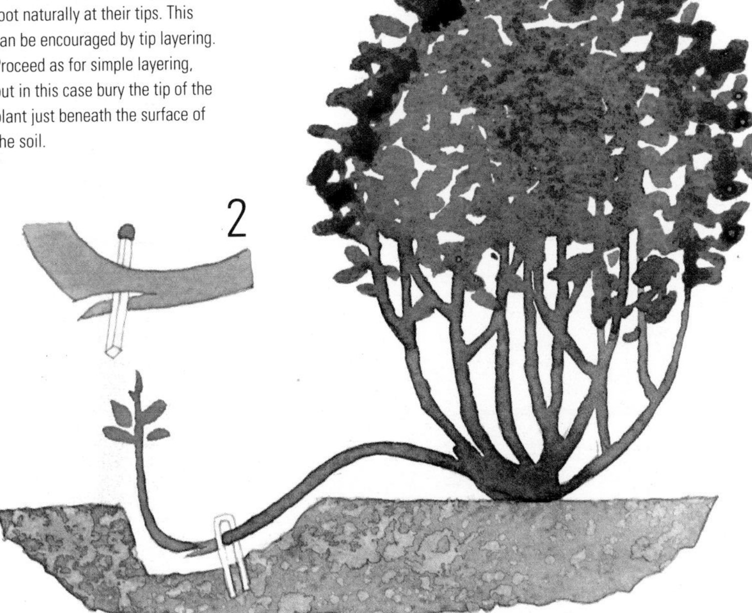

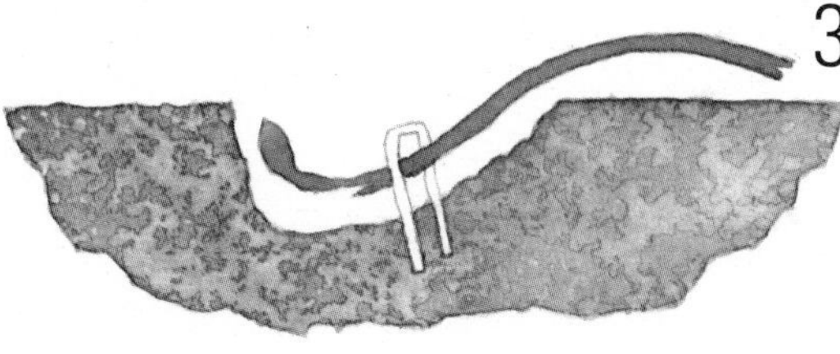

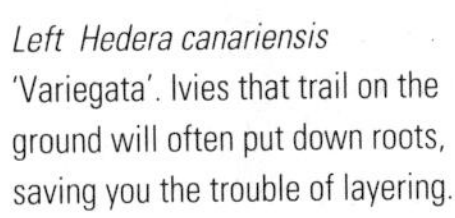

Left Hedera canariensis 'Variegata'. Ivies that trail on the ground will often put down roots, saving you the trouble of layering.

- In the spring before you carry out the layering, prune the lower branches of the parent to produce strong new growth. Feed it with Growmore, and water if necessary.
- To provide good rooting conditions fork peat and grit into the soil around the plant.
- Choose a long, strong young shoot near the base of the plant. Bend it down to the ground, taking care not to snap it.
- Mark a spot on the ground 22cm (9in) in from the tip of the shoot. At that spot dig a trench 15cm (6in) deep with the side furthest from the plant straight and the near side sloping.
- On the selected shoot trim off the leaves and sideshoots except for those at the tip.
- Lay the shoot in the trench with 22cm (9in) of the tip bent up against the straight side. With plants that are difficult to root it helps to slit halfway through the stem at an angle; hold the slit open with a matchstick.
- Peg the shoot down with bent wire.
- Return the soil to the trench, burying the stem. Firm by treading gently.
- Water well.
- When a good root system has formed (usually by the following autumn), sever the new plant from its parent.
- After three or four weeks, dig it up and replant it.

Plants to learn with

SHRUBS *Amelanchier,* evergreen azalea, *Camellia, Cornus, Cotinus coggygria,* fig, *Forsythia,* lilac, *Pieris,* thyme.

CLIMBERS *Campsis, Celastrus,* ivy, jasmine, evergreen honeysuckle, *Parthenocissus, Schizophragma, Vitis, Wisteria.*

PART 3

BECOMING A SPECIALIST

Sooner or later you will probably become interested in a particular type of plant or style of garden. This part explains how to make a start with areas which need special expertise, such as the kitchen garden, the rose garden and the water garden.

The Kitchen Garden

Nobody would pretend that there is any economic gain in growing your own vegetables. On the contrary, if you calculated the time taken to produce a cauliflower or a pound of carrots from your garden, you would find that the home-grown product costs a great deal more than the supermarket version.

But it is not for that reason that gardeners grow vegetables. It is because vegetables that have come straight out of the soil into the pot taste incomparably better; and because if you grow your own broad beans, courgettes and carrots, you can pick them when they are tiny (it is worth committing infanticide on these three crops for the tenderness and flavour).

Many of the varieties of fruit and vegetables available from greengrocers and supermarkets have been chosen for their high yield and for their uniformity of size and colour. The home grower can choose the varieties with best flavour and plan crops to ripen in succession.

There is an additional satisfaction in achieving even partial self-sufficiency, dating perhaps from time immemorial when Adam and Eve delved or from when our hunter-gatherer ancestors first discovered how to grow crops.

Choosing a site

You don't have to have a separate kitchen garden to grow vegetables, or an orchard to grow fruit. If you only need small quantities, instead of growing them in rows, you can grow them in groups among ornamental plants. Some vegetables are themselves ornamental and contribute to the overall garden scene (see list below). In small gardens make the most of vegetables that grow vertically, such as runner and other climbing beans, peas, tomatoes, courgettes and squashes.

Fruit bushes and trees are decorative enough to grow anywhere, contributing blossom in spring and colourful fruits in late summer and autumn. If space is limited, grow dwarf forms or train the plants cordon- or espalier-fashion to form fruitful barriers between one part of the garden and another.

If vegetables and fruit are your priority, you may want to reverse the usual ratio and, rather than a flower garden with some vegetables, go for a vegetable garden with some flowers. Such gardens, laid out in ornamental formal patterns, have become fashionable since the 1980s and are usually described as *potagers* (French for vegetable garden). They can be very decorative, but there is a lot still to be said for the traditional vegetable plot and to some eyes the symmetry of neat rows of vegetables is easily as pleasing as a more elaborate design. Flowers can be added among the cabbages or bordering the paths to make a garden in the country cottage style. Making best use of available space whichever style you choose is dealt with under 'Preparing the plot', p.186.

Try to give your vegetables the best site in the garden. All too often they are banished to a shady, stony corner so that flowering plants can have pride of place. But most vegetables and fruit do best in an open, sunny site with good soil, and will reward you all the more if you provide it.

Above Wigwams of climbing beans, almost too pretty to confine to the vegetable garden.

Try to make the site accessible from the kitchen. A walk to the furthest corner of the garden to cut a cabbage in winter, in the dark, in the rain, takes the fun out of growing your own produce.

WHEN? The keen vegetable gardener who prides himself on never needing to patronize a greengrocer only gets a real break from his plot in winter, and even then should be spending the days when conditions are right preparing the ground for next season. The busiest time is from early spring, when the first seeds are sown, to early summer, when the first crops can be harvested. In autumn the ground is

Below The ornamental vegetable garden or *potager* combines vegetables with herbs and other flowering plants.

Above Neat rows of vegetables in beds surrounded by hard paving or gravel paths, which make maintenance and access easier.

prepared for the following spring, and crops to overwinter, such as broad beans and spinach, are sown. Other crops may also be sown under the protection of cloches.

Techniques for planting and growing vegetables are similar to those for ornamental plants (see Chapters 8, Planting and Transplanting, and 15, Increase and Multiply). Those that need different treatment are listed under 'Choosing vegetables', below. Most vegetables are either hardy or half-hardy annuals, or are treated as such. In order to achieve a succession of crops, seed-sowing times are more flexible than with ornamental plants. Salad crops (lettuce, beetroot, radish and Chinese leaves) can be sown outside successively from spring until late summer.

Perennial vegetables (for instance asparagus, globe artichokes, rhubarb, sorrel and seakale) can be planted in spring and should have a plot set aside specifically for that purpose, since they are not included in rotation plantings.

Tools and equipment

There is no need to invest in special tools for the vegetable garden if you already have the basic armoury described in Chapter 6, The Tools of the Trade. However, these optional extras will be particularly useful:

- Hoe: for weeding between rows and for drawing out shallow trenches when sowing seeds. A swoe is a good all-purpose hoeing tool.
- Garden line: as a guide to planting in straight rows, a nylon line on a reel with its own metal pegs is more efficient than bits of string knotted between two sticks.

The following rate as equipment rather than tools, but sooner or later you will probably find that you need them:

- Stakes to support a permanent wire framework for raspberries or espaliered fruit trees: angle-iron painted in matt black is the least obtrusive material. Metal is also the most enduring material to use for a permanent fruit cage. Sturdy larch poles can also be used. When choosing sizes remember that, to make a reliably stable support, one-third of the stake should be buried in the ground.
- Wire: galvanized or plastic-coated wire to stretch between stakes.
- Bamboo canes: 2.5m (8ft) canes to make wigwams for climbing beans.
- Shorter canes: useful to support nets for climbers including peas, and as temporary protection for soft fruit.
- Nylon netting: netting with a wide, square mesh can be used stretched between canes to provide a climbing frame for peas, beans and sweet peas. To protect your crops from birds 2cm (3/4in) of netting needs to be draped over a frame. Avoid visually intrusive bright green netting and use black, if you can find it, or a dark green variety.

Preparing the plot

Recently there has been a trend away from the traditional way of growing vegetables lined out in rows with space to walk between the rows. This method is now considered wasteful of space and walking between rows consolidates the soil, ruining its structure. It is more efficient to have a number of permanent beds with permanent paths between them. The vegetables are planted in blocks with an equal distance between each plant so that there is less competition for nutrients, light and water. Their leaves act as weed-smothering ground cover. Manure and compost are concentrated on the beds, not wasted on the space between them, and over the years fertility is built up.

If, in addition, the beds can be raised 25-30cm (9-12in) above the level of the path, drainage is improved and the soil warms up quicker in the spring. The raised beds can be contained with timber planks, a few courses of bricks or breeze blocks, or with stacked turves. Topsoil is dug out along the paths and used to build up the raised beds. Paths between beds can be brick, flagstones, concrete, gravel, mown grass or just trodden earth, according to your taste and budget. If you adopt this method the beds need not be rectangular but could be circular or wedge-shaped.

But it is essential that the beds are narrow enough for the gardener to reach the centre from the path for cultivating, weeding and harvesting. A convenient width is between 90 and 150cm

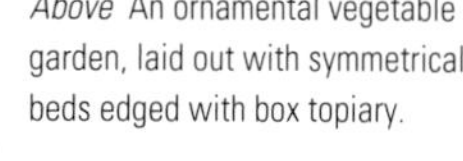
Above An ornamental vegetable garden, laid out with symmetrical beds edged with box topiary.

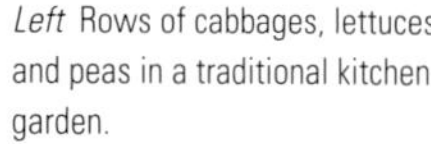
Left Rows of cabbages, lettuces and peas in a traditional kitchen garden.

Right Lettuces planted at fortnightly intervals.

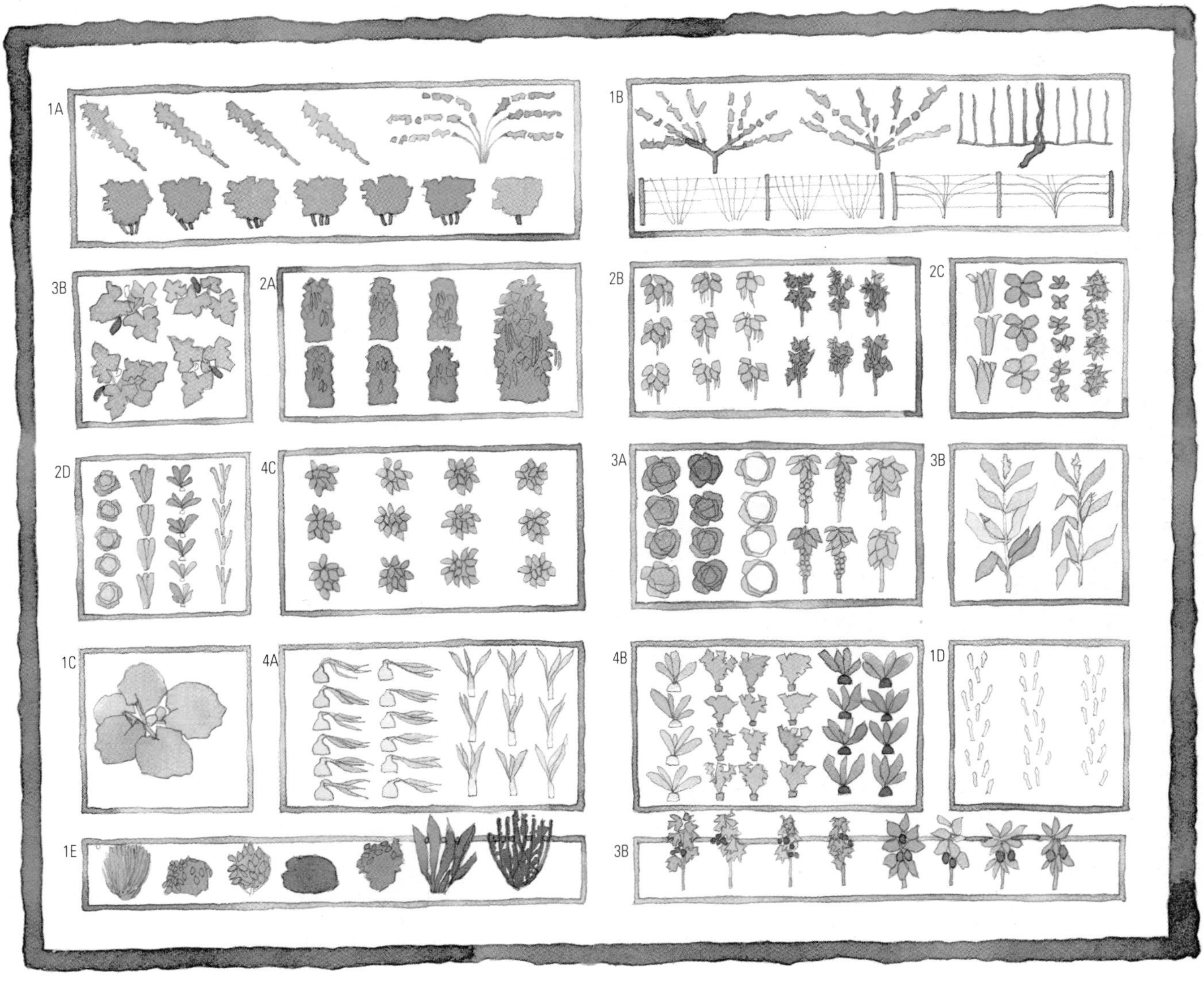

THE KITCHEN GARDEN

A kitchen garden worked by the no-dig system on either a three- or four-year crop rotation:

1 Permanent crops
A: cordon apples, loganberries, currants and gooseberries
B: peaches, apricots, vine, raspberries, blackberries
C: rhubarb
D: asparagus
E: herbs

2 Legumes and salads
A: peas, runner beans
B: French beans, broad beans
C: Chinese vegetable
D: English salad

3 Brassicas
A: cabbages, cauliflowers, sprouts, broccoli
B: summer crops followed by spring cabbage – courgettes, sweet corn, peppers, aubergines

4 Roots
A: onions, leeks
B: turnips, parsnips, beetroot
C: potatoes

(3 and 5ft), and the beds can be of any length that suits the site. Paths should be at least 30cm (1ft) wide and ideally there should be a main path wide enough to comfortably accommodate a wheelbarrow.

Such a layout of permanent beds and paths is the ideal basis for gardening by the no-dig or deep bed systems. Apart from suiting the lazy gardener, the no-dig system is thought by many (and especially by organic gardeners) to be more beneficial to the soil; the soil is not compacted and therefore the bacteria and earthworms are not disturbed.

The no-dig gardener has to earn his or her right to a seat in the sun by thorough deep digging at the start, adding plenty of manure or compost. Thereafter a generous annual top-up with organic mulch is distributed through the soil by worms.

There is no evidence that one method works better than another. It is a matter of personal choice. Once you have made your choice, you will get into an annual routine. There is no difference between vegetables and other plants

except that you can eat vegetables and, with a few exceptions, you will find them easy to grow, if you follow the techniques for cultivation and propagation described in Parts 1 and 2.

Crop rotation

As well as 'to dig or not to dig' there is the question of 'to rotate or not to rotate'. The theory of rotation is that you never grow the same crop on the same plot two years running. Botanically related plants with the same cultural requirements are grouped together and grown on a different plot each year. During three or four years, each type of crop moves to a new plot until it has come full circle.

Most gardeners use a three-year rotation on four plots:

- Plot 1, perennial plants (rhubarb, asparagus, artichokes, fruit and herbs). These require permanent positions, so this plot is not rotated.
- Plot 2, legumes (peas and beans). Add organic matter (manure or compost) during autumn or winter before spring sowing or planting. Short-term crops, including salads, onions and leeks, are not part of the rotation but can be grown here anyway.
- Plot 3, brassicas (broccoli, cabbage, cauliflower, sprouts). Add lime the autumn before planting.
- Plot 4, roots (potatoes, carrots, beetroots, parsnips). Add organic matter during autumn or winter (optional). In a four-year rotation potatoes would have their own separate plot.

The rotation is partly designed to reduce risk of pests and disease. Ailments like club root in brassicas are specific to that family and build up in the soil. Giving the soil a rest from that crop for two or three years prevents the build-up by starving the pest of its host. It also makes nutritional sense for the plants. The legumes enjoy organic material, so their plot has manure or compost added. Legumes add nitrogen to the

Above Perennial crops such as rhubarb, asparagus and artichokes (shown here) are not part of the rotation system and are given a bed of their own.

Far left Plot 2 in the rotation system is given over to legumes, such as runner beans (shown here) and peas.

Left Lettuces are not part of the crop rotation and can be grown wherever there is space.

Above Plot 3 is given over to brassicas, including cabbages, sprouts, kale and broccoli.

soil, which is important for the brassicas. Then come the potatoes and roots, then the merry-go-round begins again.

It is not practical to have a strict rotation of crops in a small vegetable plot, but the general principle of not growing the same crop in the same spot two years running is a sound one.

Best use of space

In small gardens there is sometimes nowhere to go except upwards. Take advantage of vertical space, which is so often neglected, to grow raspberries, climbing French beans, runner beans and peas. They can be trained against a boundary fence, a bamboo wigwam or a narrow cylinder of wire netting anchored with canes, and are decorative enough to clothe an arch or pergola, either alone or as companions to roses, honeysuckle and other climbers. Trailing marrows can also be trained upwards, but need a sturdy support to carry the weight of the fruit.

Peas can be planted to form low barriers to divide plots. They cast little shade: the tallest varieties will not reach any higher than about 1.2m (4ft).

Even if you only have a balcony or window ledge you can grow vegetables in pots. A sunny, sheltered city terrace or roof is a better environment than the open garden for tender vegetables such as peppers and aubergines. Dwarf French beans and lettuces are worthwhile crops for window boxes.

Fruit trees can be trained against walls and fences as horizontal espaliers, as fans and as angled cordons.

Intercropping

For maximum productivity, plant quick-growing crops like lettuces and radishes in between slower plants like cabbages. By the time the cabbages have grown to fill their allotted space you will have harvested the salad crop.

Right Plot 4: root vegetables. Carrots need a fertile, friable soil, manured in the previous autumn. Fresh manure will cause roots to fork.

Choosing vegetables

In order to grow a wide variety of vegetables in great enough quantity to feed the average family you would need to be (or to employ) a full-time gardener. My policy is only to grow vegetables which have a definite advantage over those bought from a good greengrocer. I honestly cannot tell the difference between a home-reared and a bought cabbage, except that the home-grown one is more likely to have caterpillars in it. The same goes for most of the brassica family with the possible exception of purple sprouting broccoli.

Every gardener has his or her favourites among vegetables. In our household we grow the following: the varieties listed here are well-flavoured and fairly trouble-free. An asterisk (*) denotes exceptionally good flavour.

To pick when very young

BROAD BEAN *'Aquadulce Claudia' (sow in autumn), *'Exhibition Longpod', 'Express', 'Relon', 'Windsor Green'. Neutral/slightly acid soil. Open site for spring and summer sowings, shelter and good drainage for winter sowing. Pests: black bean aphids; when you see them on the tops of the plants, pinch out the top shoot.

FRENCH BEAN 'Aramis', 'Delinel', *'Pros', 'Purple Queen'. Climbers: 'Blue Lake', 'Climbing Purple'. Light, neutral to slightly acid soil, open but sheltered site.

CARROT 'Early Nantes', 'Nantes Express', *'Rondo', 'Sytan'. Light, well-drained soil, from slightly acid to slightly alkaline. Warm, sheltered site for early sowings, open site for later. Pest: carrot fly; this pest is low flying, so surround crop with a barrier of horticultural fleece, clear polythene 60cm (2ft) high or cover with a fine mesh tunnel. Alternate rows of carrots with rows of onions, or mix annual flower seed with carrot seed and sow together.

COURGETTE 'Supremo', 'Ambassador', 'Early Gem'. Squashes and marrows have similar requirements to courgettes. Eat the flowers as well as the fruit. Rich, moisture-retentive soil, slightly acid to neutral. Add organic matter, water in dry spells.

PEA 'Bikini', 'Kelvedon Wonder', *'Little Marvel', 'Onward', *'Senator'. Rich, moisture-retentive soil. Open but sheltered site. Avoid sun-baked sites. Wait till soil has warmed up before sowing. Pests: mice eat the seeds (set traps). Birds attack seedlings (protect with nets). After flowers appear, water in dry spells. Mulch to conserve moisture and keep roots cool.

Left If you don't have a greenhouse, grow the tomato 'Gardener's Delight' in a sunny, sheltered place outside.

Better flavour when taken straight from garden to pot or salad bowl

ASPARAGUS 'Connover's Colossal', 'Lucullus'. A permanent crop with a bed of its own. Plant plenty: you can never have enough. Any well-drained soil including clay and sand. Slightly alkaline (pH 6.3 to 7.5) so add lime if needed. Add manure or compost. Pests: slugs; asparagus beetle (black and yellow beetles, grey-green larvae). Spray with pirimiphos-methyl or Derris.

MID-SEASON POTATO *'Pink Fir Apple', *'Ratte'. Best on acid (pH 5 to 6) but any well-drained soil will do. Open site. Add manure or compost. Pests: cutworm, eelworm, slugs, wireworm. Diseases: several, but only potato blight is really serious, seen as brown patches on leaves. Lift crop early, before disease appears. Cut off and burn diseased stems.

NEW POTATO 'Duke of York', 'Vanessa'.

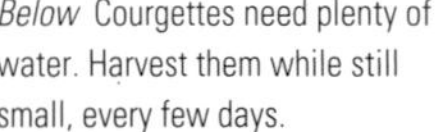

Below Courgettes need plenty of water. Harvest them while still small, every few days.

Above Ruby chard looks good in the flower border.

CELERIAC 'Marble Ball', 'Monarch', 'Snow White'. Moisture-retentive soil. Damp areas, light shade. Add organic matter, keep soil moist. Pests: slugs.

TOMATO *'Gardener's Delight', *'Sungold'. The cherry tomato 'Gardener's Delight' can be grown outdoors on a sunny, sheltered site in moisture-retentive neutral to alkaline soil. But Gro-bags in a cold greenhouse are more reliable. Feed plants with high-potash tomato (or rose) food. Pests and diseases: as potatoes.

CARROT, PEA See above.

Below Peppers thrive in containers. They will ripen outdoors in a good summer, but in Britain they more often need the warmth of a greenhouse or conservatory.

Worth freezing

BROAD BEAN, PEA See above.

Not easily available in shops

SORREL A hardy perennial with sharp, lemony leaves; good in salads or soups or mixed with spinach. Almost any soil. Sun or light shade. Remove flower heads and keep picking leaves for a constantly replenished supply. Grow from seed, renewing plants every few years.

SALAD ROCKET *Eruca vesicaria* ssp. *sativa*, Mediterranean rocket, Italian cress (not to be confused with *Hesperis matronalis*, sweet rocket). Annual grown from seed. Hardy in all but the most severe winters, therefore useful in winter salads. Any soil, sun or light shade.

Ornamental

CLIMBING FRENCH BEAN 'Hunter' (white flowers), 'Purple Podded' (purple flowers).

RUNNER BEAN 'Desirée' (white flowers), 'Streamline' (red flowers).

BEETROOT 'Bull's Blood' (deep red leaves). Light soil from slightly acid to alkaline. Open, sunny site.

ENDIVE 'Ruffec Green', 'Wallonne'. Curly leaved, attractive foliage plants for edging or planting in groups and to provide salad well into the winter. Any reasonable soil with a pH near neutral. Sun or light shade. Pests: slugs.

GLOBE ARTICHOKE 'Vert de Laon' is the hardiest. Magnificent perennial thistles with huge silvery leaves and edible flower buds. Height and spread at least 90cm (3ft). If the flowers are left to develop they dry well. Rich, well-drained soil. Add manure or compost. Shelter from wind.

KALE Ornamental forms of curly kale come in shades from cream to magenta pink. Use them for winter effect in pots or borders. Well-drained soil, preferably slightly acid. Sun.

LETTUCE 'Lollo Rosso', 'Salad Bowl', 'Red Salad Bowl'. Some of the prettier lettuces are good edging and foliage plants. Good, moisture-retentive but light soil, slightly acid to slightly alkaline. Water in dry weather. Pests: aphids, cutworms, leatherjackets, slugs, snails. Diseases: botrytis, lettuce mosaic virus.

RED CABBAGE 'Ruby Ball'. The dusky colouring goes well with red roses and with purple-leaved shrubs. Moisture-retentive soil, preferably slightly acid. Sun. Add nitrogenous fertilizer. Pests: numerous. Disease: clubroot – soil-borne, so observe strict crop rotation and cultivate soil thoroughly.

RUBY CHARD A relation of spinach with spectacular scarlet-crimson fleshy stems. Rich, moisture-retentive soil, neutral to slightly alkaline. Sun or light shade. Add manure or compost. Nitrogenous top dressing. Pests: birds. Disease: downy mildew.

Suitable for containers

AUBERGINE A bushy tropical plant, height and spread about 60cm (2ft). Sow seeds in general-purpose compost in a heated greenhouse or conservatory, or buy young plants. Put them in a sunny, sheltered place outdoors when risk of frost is past. Water regularly, feed with tomato food. Pests: aphids, red spider mite, whitefly.

PEPPER Sweet and chilli peppers with their intriguingly shaped and colourful fruits are a little less hardy than tomatoes, but can be grown outdoors in very mild areas. Safer, however, in greenhouse or conservatory. Slightly acid moisture-retentive soil or compost, sun and warmth. Pests: aphids, red spider mite and whitefly when grown indoors.

CARROT, CHARD, COURGETTE, FRENCH BEAN, LETTUCE, PEA, RUNNER BEAN, TOMATO See above.

Choosing fruit

The list of pests and diseases may look daunting, but in practice it is seldom necessary to take precautions against them, except for protecting fruit from marauding birds. It is, however, important when buying young fruit plants to make sure you are getting virus-free stock. The nursery's list or the label on a garden centre plant should give this information. If in doubt, ask. The varieties recommended in the following table are reliable and disease resistant. Again, an asterisk (*) denotes exceptional flavour.

BLACKBERRY 'Loch Ness' (thornless), ripe late summer to early autumn; 'Oregon Thornless', early autumn.

BLACKCURRANT *'Ben Lomond' late summer, 'Ben Sarek' late summer. Sun or light shade. Avoid exposed positions and frost pockets. Any moisture-retentive soil including clay. Add manure or compost when planting and mulch in spring. 1.2-1.5m (4-5ft) apart. Prune in winter removing the oldest stems (one-in-three) from the base. Pests: birds eat buds and fruit; blackcurrant gall mites cause 'big bud' and spread viruses; aphids. Diseases: mildew, honey fungus.

GOOSEBERRY 'Invicta': green, mildew-resistant cooking variety midsummer; Whinham's Industry: reddish, can be eaten raw mid- to late summer; *'Keepsake': cooking variety midsummer; Leveller: yellow, also eaten raw mid- to late summer; Captivator: nearly thornless midsummer. Easy to grow. Sun or light shade. Ordinary to heavy soil. Add manure and compost. Mulch in spring. Plant 1.2-1.5m (4-5ft) apart. Prune in winter removing oldest stems (one-in-three) from the base. Standards with round heads on 1.2m (4ft) stems are pretty but less robust than bushes. Pests: birds (specially bullfinches) eat buds in winter; gooseberry sawfly larvae eat leaves. Diseases: mildew, rust, grey mould, honey fungus.

LOGANBERRY (near relation of blackberry): 'L654' (thornless) late summer.

RASPBERRY Good varieties: 'Glen Moy' midsummer, 'Glen Prosen' midsummer, *'Malling Jewel' midsummer, 'Autumn Bliss' late summer to autumn. Sun or semi-shade, any well-drained soil except thin, chalky. Add manure or compost when planting and as a mulch each spring. Plant in autumn. Make a support with posts 3m (10ft) apart with wires stretched horizontally 45cm (18in) apart. Tie the new canes to the wires as they develop. After harvesting, cut fruited canes to ground level and tie the new canes to the wires.

Left Loganberry: a hybrid berry between a species of blackberry *(Rubus ursinus)* and a raspberry.

TIP

Rhubarb plants over two years old can be 'forced' to provide early, pale and sweet stems by covering them with a traditional rhubarb pot in winter (December or January). A bucket or plastic dustbin does the job as well if less elegantly. Plants should not be forced two years running as it weakens them.

Above Cultivated blackberries include several thornless varieties.

Left If space is limited, raspberries can be trained against a fence or on cane wigwams.

Right Blackcurrants are easy to grow. They are a rich source of vitamin C.

Above and right White and red currants are extremely decorative. Use the fruit with raspberries in summer puddings and tarts, or alone in sorbets.

DESIGN TIPS

- Red, white and black currants look pretty trained as fans against a low fence or railing. Raspberries, currants and gooseberries can be grown successfully in pots.
- Grow strawberries as an edging to beds and borders, mulched with polythene to prevent the fruits getting muddy.

Pests: raspberry beetle, maggots, aphids. Diseases: grey mould, honey fungus, raspberry viruses, cane blight.

RED CURRANT, WHITE CURRANT 'Laxtons No. 1' (red) midsummer, *'Red Lake' midsummer, *'White Grape' midsummer, 'White Versailles' mid- to late summer. Decorative as standards or fan-trained on a low fence. They are also grown as bushes. Easy to grow. Sun or light shade. Any fairly well-drained soil. 1.2-1.5m (4-5ft) apart. Net to protect from birds. In winter prune 5-7cm (2-3in) off tips of main shoots. Cut side shoots back to one bud from parent shoot. Pests: leaf blister, aphids. Diseases: coral spot, honey fungus.

RHUBARB 'Cawood Delight', 'Hawke's Champagne', 'Victoria'. Height 60cm (2ft), spread up to 1.8m (6ft). Herbaceous plant, grown for succulent stems, which are treated as fruit. It is a handsome ornamental plant with its huge leaves and pinkish stems. Sun or light shade. Rich, well-drained soil. Plant between autumn and spring. 90cm (3ft) apart or solo in the flower border. 2.5cm (1in) soil above the bud on light soil, buds above ground on heavy soil. Every spring mulch with manure or compost plus fertilizer. Increase by dividing. Pests: eelworm. Diseases: honey fungus.

WARNING Rhubarb leaves are poisonous.

STRAWBERRY *'Cambridge Late Pine', 'Cambridge Vigour', 'Providence', *'Royal Sovereign', *'Silver Jubilee'. Sun. Any soil. Plant late summer to early autumn. Add manure, compost or NPK fertilizer. Rows or blocks 45cm (18in) apart. Plant in early autumn through slits in polythene mulch or mulch with straw or polythene after flowers appear. Net to protect from birds. The best crop is from young plants. Use runners from established plants to make a new row each year and grub up the oldest row. Pests: eelworms, birds, slugs. Diseases: grey mould, strawberry virus (buy plants certified virus-free).

TAYBERRY Mid- to late summer. Sun or light shade, any soil, preferably slightly acid. Add manure or compost. Plant 3-4m (10-12ft) apart. Train along fences or wires or allow the plants to form arching shrubs. If trained, prune after fruiting by cutting out the old canes at the base. Train the new season's canes to the support. They will bear fruit the following year. Pests: raspberry beetle maggots. Diseases: grey mould, rust.

WORCESTERBERRY Like gooseberry bushes but larger, with heavy crops of gooseberry-type fruit. Easy to grow. Mid- to late summer.

Fruit trees

The beautiful blossom of fruit trees makes them versatile garden plants, decorative as well as productive. Many varieties are available grafted onto robust rootstocks, ensuring healthy plants. By using different rootstocks, the size of the tree can be controlled: dwarf rootstocks produce small trees suitable for small gardens or for gardeners who don't want to get up a ladder to harvest the crop.

Apples, pears, plums and greengages can be trained as free-standing espaliers with a few evenly spaced horizontal branches coming from a central stem. Grown in this way they make attractive dividers between different parts of the garden, and take up less space than a hedge. Trained over arches, fruit trees can be used to form arbours and tunnels. Against walls or fences they can be trained as cordons (single stems trained at an angle), espaliers or fans. 'Step-over' fruit bushes are trained horizontally just above ground level; they make an unusual edging to raised beds.

All fruit trees will grow faster and be more healthy if competition from grass and weeds is eliminated. If you grow fruit trees in an orchard or on the lawn, keep an area 1m (3ft) round the stem mulched and free of turf and weeds.

To get bigger, better fruit, thin out the clusters if they are overcrowded. This is important with plums as the weight of the fruit may break the branches.

Some fruit trees are self-fertile; others will not produce any fruit if planted alone because they need to be pollinated by a different variety. They need a compatible variety nearby. The list that follows suggests compatible varieties where necessary, but your nursery should be able to advise you.

APPLE Sun or light shade. Any soil except shallow or chalky. Plant from autumn to spring. Pests: birds, codling moth and apple sawfly larvae, aphids, capsid bugs, numerous caterpillars. Diseases: canker, mildew, scab, honey fungus. Rootstocks: M27 (1.2-1.8m/4-6ft height and spread); M9 (1.8-3m/6-10ft); MM106 (3.6-4.8m/12-16ft); MM111 (4.5-6m/15-20ft, traditional orchard tree). These eating apple varieties will pollinate each other: 'Discovery' (late summer) + 'Fiesta' (autumn to late winter) + 'Greensleeves' (autumn) + 'James Grieve' (early autumn) + 'Sunset' (autumn to winter). Still the best cooker, 'Bramley' (late autumn to late winter) needs two pollinators from eaters listed above.

CHERRY Sun. Any soil except shallow. Plant from autumn to spring. Rootstocks: cherries are large trees, and 'Colt' (4.2-4.8m/14-16ft) is the only manageable size. Net to protect from birds (easiest if fan-trained against a wall). In summer, thin or shorten branches of trees if needed. On fan-trained plants in summer, remove some old wood to thin out if needed, tie in new shoots and shorten if needed. Pests: birds eat buds and fruit; aphids. Diseases: canker, honey fungus, silver leaf. 'Stella' (self-fertile) is a sweet cherry. 'Morello' (self-fertile) is a cooker which will grow against a north wall. Excellent for jam.

Above 'Bramley's Seedling', an old variety, but still the best all-purpose cooking apple.

Left Morello cherry: a good fruit to train on a high and wide north-facing wall.

TIP

Most apple varieties can be pollinated by ornamental crab apples.

DESIGN TIP

For tubs or large pots choose fruit trees grafted onto M27 dwarf rooting stock. The restriction of its roots in the container will help to keep it a manageable size.

FIG Shelter, sun, any well-drained soil, including poor and stony. In harsh climates, grow figs in large pots and move into the greenhouse in winter. In good soil restrict the roots by growing in a pot, minimum 30cm (1ft) diameter, or planting in a pit, 60cm (2ft) square and 30cm (1ft) deep. Line the pit with paving slabs or breeze-blocks, leaving the bottom open for drainage. Grow figs against a sunny wall at least 2.2m (7ft) high and 3m (10ft) wide or plant 6-8m (20-25ft) apart. In spring cut back any damaged shoots. If the bush is dense, remove some branches to let light in to the centre. Cut back young shoots to one bud. In autumn remove larger fruits that have not ripened. Leave those that are the size of a pea: they will come through the winter to provide fruit next summer. Pests: birds eat the fruit. Diseases: coral spot, grey mould. 'Brown Turkey' is the hardiest.

PEAR Shelter, sun and good soil. Avoid shallow soil and chalk. Rootstocks: Quince A or Quince C (2.4-3.6m/8-12ft). Grow as standards, cordons, espaliers, fans. Compatible pollinators: 'Beth' (late summer) + 'Concorde' (autumn) + 'Conference' (autumn).

PLUM Shelter, sun, any well-drained soil except shallow or chalk. Rootstocks: St. Julien A (growth 3.6-4.8m/12-16ft); Pixy (2.4-3m/8-10ft). Grow plums as standards, cordons, espaliers, fans. Pruning: in late spring or early summer remove some older branches to let light in, and shape and tie in wall-trained plants. Pests: birds eat buds, wasps, plum sawfly. Diseases: canker, honey fungus, silver leaf. 'Marjories Seedling' (self-fertile) late summer to early autumn; 'Oullins Gage' (self-fertile) late summer; 'Victoria' (self-fertile) late summer.

APRICOT, NECTARINE, PEACH All need trouble taken and a measure of skill. The blossom is lovely, but don't expect much fruit. Choose a variety suitable for outside cultivation and, except in very mild areas, plant it against a sunny, south-facing wall. Peaches flower early, and so need protection from frost. Because there are few insects around to pollinate the flowers at that time of year, you should pollinate by hand to be sure of fruit. Feed in late winter with fertilizer high in nitrogen and potash, and again with potash after flowering. Mulch to conserve moisture round the roots. Apricots are slightly easier but apt to suffer from dieback of the branches. Pests: red spider mite, aphids, birds and wasps eat fruit. Diseases: peach leaf curl, serious on nectarines and peaches, canker, honey fungus, silver leaf. The best bets outdoors are: apricot – 'Hemskerke', 'Moorpark' (self-fertile); nectarine – 'Lord Napier' (self-fertile); peach – 'Peregrine' and 'Rochester' (both self-fertile).

OTHER FRUIT Medlars, mulberries and quinces are traditional fruits seldom used in the kitchen nowadays, but they are all fine ornamental trees. Medlars and quinces both have beautiful blossom as well as edible fruit.

WARNING *Don't plant a mulberry where you will sit or where it will overhang gravel or paving: the fruit stains indelibly.*

Protecting fruit

Inevitably the birds will get to your fruit the day before it is ripe enough for you to pick it. With tree fruits and with raspberries and blackcurrants, if you grow a few more plants than you think you need there will be enough fruit for your family and the birds. But cherries, strawberries and red currants need to be protected with nets.

Pruning fruit trees and bushes

See above list; also Chapter 8, Planting and Transplanting, and Chapter 10, Pruning.

Below left Pears can be grown as full-sized orchard trees or on dwarfing rootstocks. They can also be trained on walls or as espaliers.

Below centre Apricots and peaches flower very early, so it is wise to protect the flowers from frost with fine-mesh netting.

Below right Peach 'Peregrine' is a good variety for the English climate, but needs the warmth and shelter of a south-facing wall. Spray against peach leaf curl.

Greenhouses

Addicted gardeners like to be able to garden come rain, come shine or come frost, and a greenhouse enables them to do just that. From Christmas onwards there are seeds for the next season's edible and ornamental crops to be sown, cuttings to be tended and house plants to be potted up or potted on. Unless you are a very methodical gardener there is nearly always some tidying to do in the greenhouse. At any time of year except a hot summer day, the warmth and shelter of the greenhouse make it a pleasant place to be. It is also an ideal place to go for a sulk.

On the other hand, there is no point in having a greenhouse unless you have the time to spend in it and the money to spend on it: greenhouse gardening needs regular attention and unless you are content with an unheated house which will not be frost-proof in a bad winter, your heating bill will increase. However, the cost of heating may be cancelled out by the saving made by raising your own plants instead of buying them from a garden centre or a greengrocer.

Above This conservatory is a compromise between extra living space and a working greenhouse.

Left A heated conservatory increases your living area and allows you to grow a wider range of plants, including tropical and sub-tropical species. The brick floor shown in this example will withstand water splashes and can be damped down in hot weather.

Above Greenhouses don't have to be rectangular. Choose a shape to suit the available space.

Heating is a fairly obvious expense. But there are other hidden costs involved in installing a greenhouse: the empty structure will need some staging (shelves and workbench) and blinds or some other form of shading. And you may be tempted by such gadgets as automatic ventilation and irrigation.

A conservatory is a possible alternative to a heated greenhouse. It is, of course, many times more expensive but will give you the benefit of an extra living room. However, if plants rather than increased living space are your primary concern, check before buying a conservatory that you will be able to shade and ventilate it adequately.

Choosing a site

To help you position your greenhouse check the following list:

- Greenhouses should be in a sunny position in the open.
- Ideally the longest side of the greenhouse should run from east to west.
- Lean-to houses should be against an east- or west-facing wall. A wall facing north gets too little sun, a south wall too much.
- A brick wall provides good insulation as brick absorbs heat from the sun.
- A lean-to against a house wall will benefit from the indoor heating.
- Shelter from the wind is important (our greenhouse blew away during the 1987 storm).
- A position sheltered from the north and east will reduce the risk of frost in an unheated greenhouse, and the fuel bills in a heated one.
- If the greenhouse is near the house and easily accessible in wet and windy weather it will be used more often.
- To prevent arguments about pocket money to replace broken panes, avoid siting it near where children play football or practice cricket.
- Check that electricity and water can be laid on from an existing supply in the house or garage. Electricity is needed for lighting and perhaps for heating, and one or two power points to plug in heated propagators are useful. The water supply should be near, if not in, the greenhouse.

WARNING *Overhanging trees reduce light available and cause problems with falling leaves. There is also a risk of falling branches smashing the glass.*

DESIGN TIP

The greenhouse may become your pride and joy, but it is unlikely to be a building of architectural distinction, so you may want to position it where it cannot be seen from the house.

Choosing a greenhouse

Ready-to-assemble greenhouses come in many shapes and sizes, and if none of them are what you want, you can (at greater cost) have one custom built to your requirements.

Materials

Greenhouses are made in various materials, glass being the one that all have in common. Glass has several advantages over plastic: it allows good transmission of light; it does not discolour; it retains more heat; it is less easily scratched; and it is cheaper.

Greenhouse frameworks are made of wood, steel or aluminium:

CEDAR is the traditional material and has the advantage over other timber that it does not rot or warp and weathers to a pleasing silver-grey colour. Manufacturers claim heat loss is less.

SOFTWOOD frames are less expensive than cedar but they need repainting every few years to prevent deterioration.

STEEL is the cheapest material, but also needs repainting and treating against rust.

ALUMINIUM is very light, an advantage for the DIY assembler, and is virtually maintenance-free, but is more expensive than steel.

Design

Greenhouses are available in a number of different shapes:

TRADITIONAL SPAN Rectangular with a pitched roof. Well lit, economical of space for general garden use.

THREE-QUARTER SPAN A lean-to with one side against a wall.

HEXAGON, OCTAGON Fancy shapes may look appealing but they make less efficient use of the available space.

DOME Worth considering if the greenhouse has to be on a site exposed to the wind: the shape offers little wind resistance and admits plenty of light. Headroom is restricted.

Size

The minimum practical size for a rectangular greenhouse is 1.8x2.5m (6x8ft). This provides space for 60cm (2ft) wide staging on each side with a 60cm (2ft) path between.

If you plan to plant in borders within the greenhouse rather that in pots and Gro-bags, or if you want access for a wheelbarrow or a wheelchair, 2.5m (8ft) is the width to go for.

Check the height of the structure before you buy. It is irritating, tiring and bad for the back to have to stoop all the time. If you are tall and cannot find a suitable greenhouse, a standard model can be erected on a base of two or three courses of bricks.

Lean-to mini-greenhouses are available and might be the answer if you are not sure how keen you are going to become. A mini-greenhouse should be sited against a west- or east-facing wall to avoid overheating. For good insulation it should be glass rather than plastic or polythene and should be efficiently ventilated.

Using the greenhouse

Propagation

Unless you use the greenhouse for plants with specific requirements, its main function will be to provide the right environment for seeds and cuttings. See Chapter 15, Increase and Multiply.

TIP

If you choose a greenhouse constructed in standard modules, when you outgrow it, you can add to the length.

Left Some greenhouses are made in modular units that can be adapted to fit awkward sites, in this case the corner of a walled garden.

Below left A traditional timber-framed greenhouse.

Right The modern aluminium greenhouse is light, strong, fairly simple to assemble and virtually maintenance-free.

Below The dome is structurally strong, offers less wind resistance and gives good light transmission. There is less headroom, however, and staging is hard to place.

Food crops

A greenhouse also provides extra warmth and shelter for tender plants like tomatoes, peppers and cucumbers. Hardy vegetables, salads and fruits such as strawberries can be ripened earlier to extend their season.

Ornamental plants

Chrysanthemums, fuchsias and geraniums can all be grown in the greenhouse and then brought into the house or planted out in the garden during the summer.

Garden plants

Shrubs and perennials of doubtful hardiness can be brought into the greenhouse for the winter.

Equipment

Staging (shelving)

Staging will help you make maximum use of the available space. Greenhouse suppliers also make either wooden or aluminium staging in ready-to-assemble form, with solid or slatted surfaces.

The main shelf should be on a level base at comfortable working height for the individual gardener. If you are tall, the height of standard equipment can be raised by propping it on bricks. Short gardeners can saw down the legs of wooden staging to the required height.

The ideal greenhouse staging has a lower shelf for shade-loving plants and sections that can be removed to accommodate tall plants standing on the ground. Make sure shelving is robust enough to carry the weight of pots full of wet compost.

Slatted shelves allow the air to circulate freely, minimizing the spread of fungal diseases.

If your budget does not run to purpose-made greenhouse furniture, you can improvise with junk furniture bought at auction (old kitchen tables with drawers are suitable) or use a wall-paper-hanger's trestle table, although this won't bear much weight.

Heating

This is necessary if the greenhouse is to remain frost-free during the average British winter.

PARAFFIN HEATERS Cheap, but they can be dangerous, and topping them up with paraffin is a nuisance. They also produce a lot of water.

ELECTRIC FAN HEATERS Designed specially for use in the greenhouse, these are clean and efficient. Most are fitted with a thermostat. A 2000W heater should keep a 1.8x2.4m (6x8ft) greenhouse at a temperature of 5°C (40°F) in an average winter, and a 3000W heater will do the same for a greenhouse of 2.4x3m (8x10ft).

Ventilation

In summer the greenhouse can become so hot that plants are put under stress and may die as a result. To prevent this there should be at least one vent in the side as well as a roof vent to get a draught running through.

TIPS

- Insulate the greenhouse with bubble polythene during the winter months. It helps keep the frost out if you don't have heating and saves on fuel bills if you do.
- In hot weather, keeping the air moist and damping down the floor helps to cool the greenhouse, so be vigilant about watering.

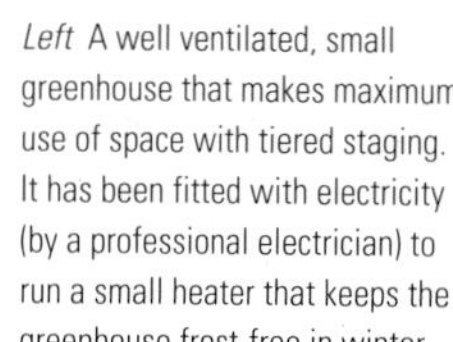

Left A well ventilated, small greenhouse that makes maximum use of space with tiered staging. It has been fitted with electricity (by a professional electrician) to run a small heater that keeps the greenhouse frost-free in winter.

Right A modern aluminium greenhouse with good all-round light and purpose-built staging that makes very efficient use of space.

Below A greenhouse with traditional slatted wooden staging.

Shading

To keep the greenhouse cool in summer, shading is advisable. This can be of woven fabric or special whitewash which is painted on for a season and brushed or dusted off when no longer needed.

Irrigation

The available types vary from a hosepipe attached to the kitchen or garage tap to an ultra-sophisticated computer-operated system. One advantage of the latter is that it will take care of the watering when you are away from home.

PERMANENT WATER SUPPLY Even if the gadgetry has to come later, it is probably worth the expense of running a permanent water supply to a tap inside the greenhouse at the start.

AUTOMATIC MIST SPRAYER Rigged up over a propagating area, this saves time hand-spraying cuttings and seedlings.

CAPILLARY MATTING Feeds water from below to plants in small pots. It is labour-saving and reduces the risk of over-watering.

WATERING CAN WITH A FINE ROSE For watering by hand – never completely eliminated.

HAND SPRAYERS Keep three permanently in the greenhouse, one for pesticide, one for fungicide and one for foliar feed.

Electric propagator

The combination of cables to heat the soil with an overhead mister provides the optimum conditions for propagating many plants, and is a good investment for the enthusiast. The equipment needed for sowing seeds and taking cuttings is described in Chapter 15, Increase and Multiply.

Water Gardening

The natural landscape is made up of three elements – stone, plants and water – and a garden without water is, in a sense, incomplete. The sight and sound of even the smallest water feature give pleasure out of all proportion to the cost of a basin, pool or pond for your garden.

The sparkling movement of water in a fast-flowing stream, waterfall or fountain is light-hearted and energetic. It provides ever-changing patterns of light and sound.

The style of water feature will be dictated partly by the site and partly by your own taste. On a level site with a formal layout, a rectangle, circle or oval with brick or stone edging is appropriate. Naturalistic gardens, on the other hand, need naturalistic ponds or streams.

Making a water feature

If water flows naturally in your garden in a stream or from a spring, you can either leave it in its natural course or divert it into a more elaborate scheme. If there is no natural source, water can be circulated with a simple electric pump to form a series of pools linked by channels.

On a sloping site, a series of formal pools can be connected by falls of different heights and widths, so that the water looks and sounds different at each change of level. In informal gardens a stream flowing through rocks of different shapes and sizes has the same effect, so that the water babbles, splashes and gurgles.

Even the smallest courtyard garden can accommodate water dribbling or spouting from a wall-mounted mask into a basin below. For a tiny water garden, a half-barrel or other container can be filled with water to grow a few aquatic plants.

In gardens where there are small children, safety is the first consideration. A wall-mounted spout or free-standing 'bubble' fountain that spills onto an area of pebbles or cobbles with the pump concealed below them is the safest arrangement. The water should barely cover the pebbles.

Left *Ranunculus aquatilis* (water crowfoot) will grow in running water 15-30cm (6-12in) deep and flowers from spring to mid-summer. Thin it out in spring or autumn to prevent it taking over.

Above An informal pool with a naturalistic waterfall.

There is scope for originality in the creation of concrete water-chutes based on the Indian *chadar*. Using patterns of concrete or clay pipes or inverted ridge tiles, channels can be constructed to break the vertical or sloping fall of water. In Japanese gardens streams are carried along giant bamboo canes split lengthwise. Or water can be designed to flow from a mysterious mossy grotto lined with shells. The gardener's ingenuity is the only limit to the different effects that can be created.

WHERE? A naturalistic pond should either be sited at the lowest point of the garden or in a natural depression. A pond perched halfway up a slope never looks right unless you create an illusion by careful mounding and planting. If there is already a water-logged area in the garden, take advantage of it by siting your pond there; if the soil is clay it may hold water without the additional insurance of a liner. However, pools should be sited where overflowing after heavy rain will not cause problems.

- A fairly open site, as most water plants need sun to thrive. One-third of the water surface should be in sunlight.

Right Pontederia cordata (N. American pickerel weed), *Ranunculus lingua* (great spearmint) and *Sagittaria sagittifolia* (arrowhead) are marginal plants which thrive in shallow water. *Sagittaria* is too invasive for small ponds.

- Clear of overhanging trees, to let light in and spare you the chore of fishing out the gunge produced by decaying leaves every autumn.
- If an open site is not available, an attractive water garden can be made in the shade using ferns, mosses and other shade-tolerant plants.
- Check what you will see reflected in the water when you are sitting in the garden or looking out from the house windows.
- Fountains and cascades should be positioned so that the prevailing winds will not blow spray on to an area where you like to sit or stand.

WHEN? Any time of year when conditions are right for digging; wet soil is more difficult to shift than dry, but frost need not deter you.

- The time to put in aquatic plants is late spring and early summer, so timing should be planned to have everything ready by then.

Tools and materials

- Mechanical digger and a skilled operator: worthwhile if you are planning a sizeable pond and/or a long stream.
- Mini-digger: if your site has restricted access, machines that can go through a 1.2m (4ft) gap are available for hire and are not difficult for amateurs to operate.
- Spade, wheelbarrow and a lot of muscle power: all you need to dig out a small pond.
- Hosepipe: to mark out the serpentine outline of an informal pool, to fill the pool initially and to top up the level as required.
- String line, pegs and right-angled T-square, if you are making a rectangular pool.
- Black Butyl for the waterproof lining, 7mm (1/4in) thick. Black lining is best: it reduces the growth of algae, which can become a problem, and provides the best background for reflections. This can be bought from specialist suppliers (try the Yellow Pages under 'Aquarium' or 'Water Garden Services'). Butyl will last for forty to fifty years. PVC is cheaper but may only last from five to ten years. For circular or irregular pools, draw an imaginary rectangle around the widest parts; use these dimensions to calculate the size of the liner. It should be the maximum width of the pool plus twice its depth, times the length plus twice the depth. Allow at least an extra 15cm (6in) of width and length.
- Plank and spirit level.
- Sand or fibreglass blanket (insulating material) to make a smooth surface on which to lay the liner. Old carpet or underlay will be adequate and cheap.
- Heavy duty scissors or a Stanley knife to cut the liner.
- Stones, bricks or turf to hold the perimeter of the liner in position and to hide it.

Below Lemna minor (common duckweed) can become a menace. If it appears in your pond, pull it out.

Right Nuphar lutea (brandy bottle, yellow water lily) has small yellow flowers and decorative seed heads. It grows to 1.5m (5ft) diameter and will tolerate light shade.

DESIGN TIPS

- If two or more pools are linked it looks best if the lower pool is bigger than the upper.
- In a small garden an expanse of water reflecting the sky will bring light into the garden and give an illusion of space.

Making a pond

HOW? Mark out the perimeter with string and pegs or, for an informal pool, lay a hose or rope on the ground and move it around until the shape is right.

- To test visually how the pool will fit into the garden, spread a sheet of light-coloured polythene to fill the marked area or cover it with a thin layer of white sand. Look at it from every angle and make adjustments until you are satisfied. For a rectangular pool a length that is double the width makes a pleasing proportion.
- Dig out the pool to a depth of at least 60cm (2ft). This is a good depth for water lilies. In shallower pools the water warms up too quickly in summer and causes algae to develop. Even in large pools the maximum depth need be no more than 3ft (90cm).
- Make the sides slope inwards at an angle of 20° to prevent frost damage. Make a shelf around all or part of the pool 23cm (9in) wide and deep, for marginal plants.
- The bottom of the pool should slope slightly towards the narrowest point; this makes it easier to empty if you ever need to. If the pool is on a slope, use the excavated soil to build up the downhill bank.
- If you are using a pump, dig a trench to lay an electric cable from the nearest supply point. Fit a safety cut-out device.
- Using a plank wide enough to lay across the pool and a spirit level, check that the rim is level all round.
- Remove stones or roots that might puncture the lining and ensure the surface of the sides and bottom is smooth. Lay the sand and/or fibreglass blanket smoothly over the surface of the hole.
- Stretch the liner across the pool and lower it in. This is a job for two or more people. Keeping it slightly stretched, weight it down around the edge with bricks or stones. Don't worry about the pleats that will form in the liner.
- Start filling the pool with a hose. The weight of the water will stretch the liner and mould it to the contours of the pool. As the pool fills, move the weights around the edge as necessary and adjust the pleats as evenly as you can.
- When the pool is full, cut off surplus liner, leaving 15cm (6in) overlapping the rim.
- If you are edging the pool with paving slabs, bed them in mortar on top of the liner overlap. The slabs should overhang the pool rim by an inch or two to conceal the liner. The same applies to rocks around informal pools. Where stone edging is not being used, leave some pockets of soil for waterside plants and lay turf round the rest of the rim so that it hangs down a few inches below the water surface.

MAKING A POND

1 Mark the perimeter of the pool using a rope or hosepipe.

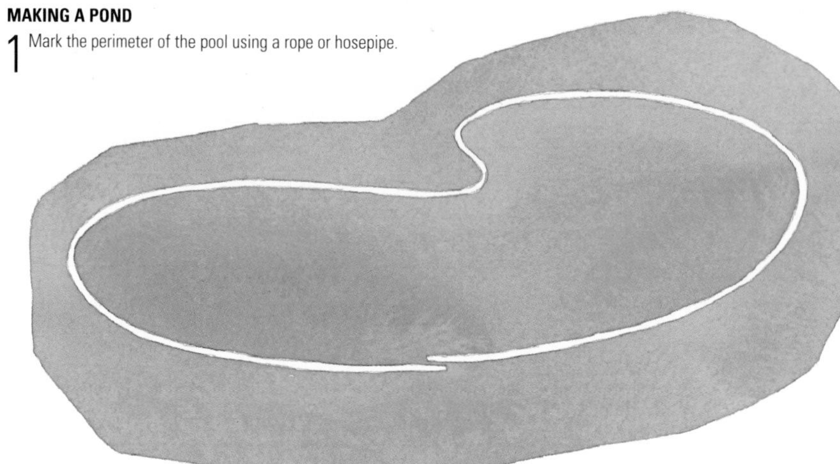

2 Remove the turf and topsoil. Insert a wooden peg at the margin, its top level with the rim of the pond. Using this as the datum point, insert pegs at 90cm (3ft) intervals around the perimeter, using a straight edge and spirit level to make sure they are level with the datum peg. It is important to get the pond rim level.

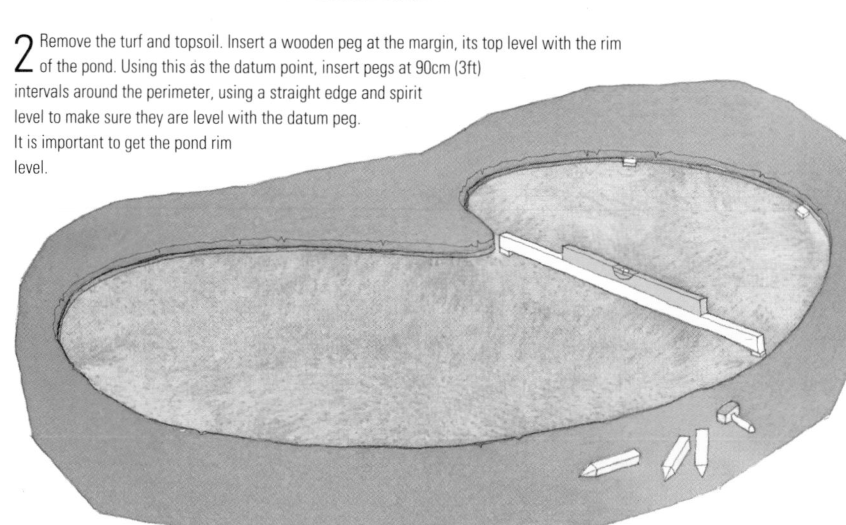

Left Careful planting conceals the edge of an informal pond.

DESIGN TIPS

- A simple shape looks better than a restlessly serpentine one and is easier to construct.
- It looks more natural if some rocks are placed partly in the water on the marginal shelf and others half-buried in the bank above them. As far as rocks are concerned, big is always beautiful: one whopper has more impact than half a dozen small pieces.

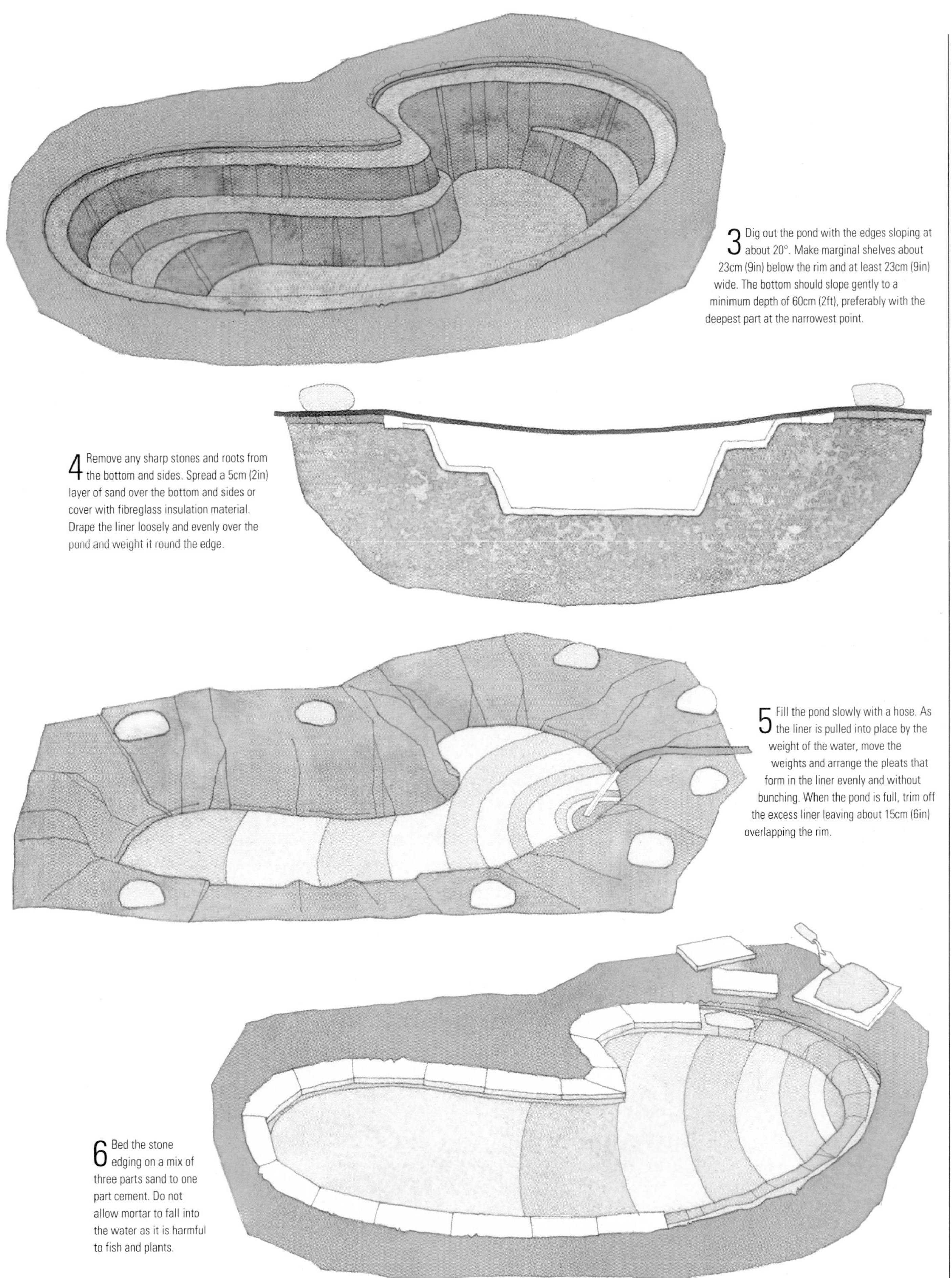

3 Dig out the pond with the edges sloping at about 20°. Make marginal shelves about 23cm (9in) below the rim and at least 23cm (9in) wide. The bottom should slope gently to a minimum depth of 60cm (2ft), preferably with the deepest part at the narrowest point.

4 Remove any sharp stones and roots from the bottom and sides. Spread a 5cm (2in) layer of sand over the bottom and sides or cover with fibreglass insulation material. Drape the liner loosely and evenly over the pond and weight it round the edge.

5 Fill the pond slowly with a hose. As the liner is pulled into place by the weight of the water, move the weights and arrange the pleats that form in the liner evenly and without bunching. When the pond is full, trim off the excess liner leaving about 15cm (6in) overlapping the rim.

6 Bed the stone edging on a mix of three parts sand to one part cement. Do not allow mortar to fall into the water as it is harmful to fish and plants.

Making a stream

HOW? • Dig the channel out in a series of level steps, not as a continuous slope. Even if the site only slopes gently, make a series of long, shallow steps.

• Lay the liner as described above. It can be laid in several overlapping pieces.

• Add stones and pebbles of different sizes to hide the liner and make a varied watercourse. The aim is to achieve a natural look.

MAKING A STREAM

1 Mark the line of the stream with pegs and string. Starting at the bottom, dig a series of steps. Make them slightly deeper immediately beneath the fall. At the top dig out a header pool at least 60cm (2ft) wide by 40cm (16in) deep.

2 Remove any sharp stones and compact the stream bed with a spade. Line with a layer of polyester matting and the flexible liner. This should overlap the edges of the stream by at least 30cm (1ft). Smooth and tuck the liner in place. Trim off excess liner.

3 Starting at the bottom, arrange rocks to form the lip of the falls, then the sides of the stream. Bring the liner up around the rocks and pack soil behind it to hold it in place above the final water level. Secure the rocks with waterproof cement or self-expanding polyurethane. Lay a flexible hose for the circulating pump in a trench 25cm (10in) deep, alongside the stream.

4 Plant the edges of the stream to soften the outline. Edges and liner can be disguised with a layer of rounded pebbles.

Above Rocks, the larger the better, are carefully placed to give the water course a natural appearance.

Above right Where space is limited a wall-mounted fountain can provide the lively sound and sight of running water.

Water circulation

Your retailer will advise you on a suitable pump. The size of the pump will depend on not only the volume of water to be moved but also the height of the overall fall. For smaller ponds a submersible pump is easiest.

To pump water through a fountain or to move it from a low pool to a higher one:

- Put the pump in place below the fountain or in the lowest pool.
- Conceal it with rocks.
- Bury the pipe that carries water from the pump to the top level.
- Bury the cable connecting the pump to the electricity supply.

WATER CIRCULATION
Electrical fittings must have approved waterproof connections and be protected with armoured sleeving. They should have a residual current device. Place the pump on bricks to keep it clear of sediment on the pond bottom. Disguise it with rocks or a stone slab. Attach a flexible hose with a non-return valve to the pump and run it alongside the water course to the header pool, burying it in a trench 25cm (10in) deep.

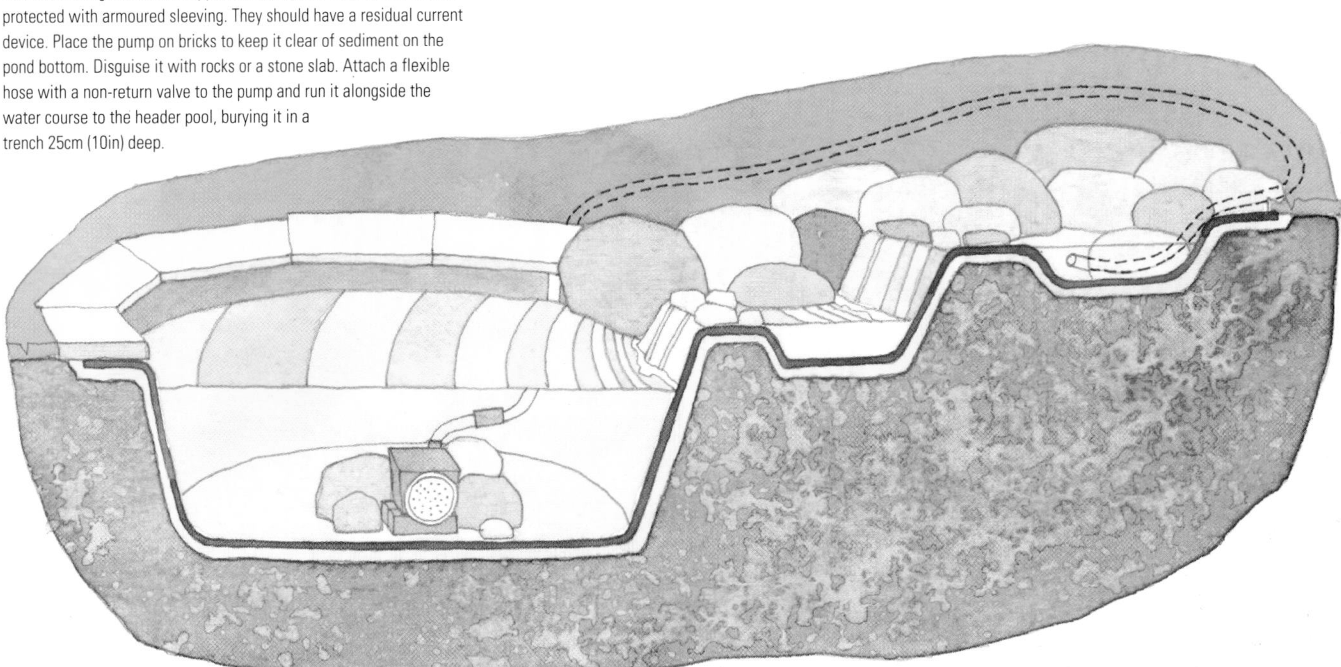

Choosing and planting

Tools and equipment

- Containers: plastic mesh baskets are obtainable in different sizes from garden centres and specialist suppliers. Anything smaller than 25cm (10in) square will stunt the growth of even small marginal plants. Larger plants obviously need larger containers.
- In deep water, plants can be raised to the correct level by planting them in plastic dustbins filled with rubble: either sit the mesh basket on top of the dustbin or fill the top 30cm (1ft) of the bin with soil and plant directly into it.
- Hessian or plastic fabric to line containers.
- Heavy duty scissors to cut hessian.
- Soil to fill the containers: ordinary garden soil on the heavy side.
- Chopped turf to add if soil is light and sandy.
- Enough gravel or pebbles to cover surfaces of containers.
- Spade.
- Trowel.
- Watering can.
- Waders or shorts and bare feet or flipflops, or for lakes and large ponds a small boat.

WARNING *Avoid manure, fertilizers and proprietary composts (unless the latter are specifically designed for aquatic plants); they encourage algae. And avoid peat; it floats to the surface.*

Plant types

Water garden plants fall into four categories: **BOTTOM PLANTS** grow on the floor of the pond (different plants need different depths).

Above Nymphaea alba needs 60-120cm (2-4ft) depth of water and spreads to 3m (9ft), so is only suitable for a very large pond.

Far left Carex pseudocyperus, a graceful but invasive reed-grass, only for large ponds.

Left Typha latifolia (greater reed-mace): not strictly a bullrush but tall and dense enough to hide a Moses basket. Too invasive for even the largest lakes.

Opposite Hottonia palustris, one of the prettiest floating plants.

TIP

Most water plants, including water lilies, do not thrive in moving water, so a still pool is the best place to grow them.

Right and below Oxygenating plants: submerged but, not having a proper root system, they often float to the surface. Use a few *Callitriche verna* (water starwort, *right*) in deeper water. *Myriophyllum proserpinacoïdes (M. aquaticum,* parrot's feather, *below)* is not reliably hardy, so keep some in water indoors through the winter.

MARGINAL PLANTS live in shallow water along the banks.

SURFACE PLANTS float, drawing their nutrients directly from the water.

OXYGENATING PLANTS are mainly submerged at different depths.

Oxygenating plants

Before planting, the water must settle for at least a week. Don't worry if it becomes murky and green. This is caused by algae, minute green plants which colonize the water as it warms up. The water must go through this stage and will clear when the right balance between oxygen (given off by plants and absorbed by fish), and carbon dioxide (given off by fish) is established.

Moving the water around through fountains and waterfalls helps increase the oxygen but it is still important to include oxygenating plants for clean, healthy water. They are submerged and have no proper root system.

Myriophyllum proserpinacoïdes (M. aquaticum), Fontinalis antipyretica, Callitriche verna (water starwort) and *Ceratophyllum demersum* (hornwort) are excellent oxygenating plants. Breeding newts wrap their eggs in the leaves of the last two plants.

- Buy some of each species from a specialist supplier.
- They must be kept wet at all times, so take them straight home in a sealed polythene bag.
- Put them into the pool without delay. Either drop them into the water in bunches with lead weights attached to carry them to the bottom, or tuck them into the same containers as water lilies and other bottom plants.

WARNING *Avoid Canadian pondweed* (Elodea canadensis) *and Australian swamp stonecrop* (Crassula helmsii *or* Tillaea recurva)*; they are invasive.*

Surface plants

Initially, floating plants help to discourage the growth of algae by excluding sunlight. Later, when permanent plants such as water lilies are providing good cover, some or all of them can be removed.

Hottonia palustris (water violet). Spreads indefinitely but controllably. Ferny light green leaves are submerged and spikes of delicately pretty, pale lilac flowers break the surface in early to midsummer. Outstanding.

Hydrocharis morsus-ranae (frogbit). Spread 10cm (4in). Rosettes of miniature water-lily leaves increase by runners making new plantlets, which remain attached to the parent, forming a group up to 90cm (3ft) wide. Small, three-petalled white flowers appear from mid- to late summer.

Stratiotes aloïdes (water soldier). Semi-evergreen rosettes of spiky olive-green leaves produce small white or pink-tinged flowers in midsummer. A spreader needing control.

WARNING *Avoid aggressive colonizers like duckweed* (Lemna *species*) *and* Azolla caroliniana *(water fern).*

Plant these floaters by dropping them onto the surface at random. No need for artistry in positioning them as they will not stay where you place them; the wind will move them hither and thither.

Bottom and marginal plants

The depth of planting is important for success. Unfortunately the depth of the water will fluctuate: water is lost through evaporation in dry spells and gained at times of heavy rainfall. Take the average between high water and low water as the norm.

The floor of your pond is probably more or less the same level all over but you can vary the planting depths by varying the height of the plant containers: either buy containers of different heights or raise them to the required height on bricks or breezeblocks.

In the plant list that follows the recommended depth is that of the soil surface in the container. All are hardy and like a sunny position unless stated otherwise.

SHALLOW WATER AND MUD AT THE MARGIN

Caltha palustris 'Plena' (the double kingcup) 25x25cm (10x10in). Long-lasting yellow flowers sometimes bloom twice in a season.

Cardamine pratensis 'Flore Pleno' or the double form of cuckoo flower (lady's smock) 45x30cm (18x12in). Dense sprays of double pale lilac-pink flowers in spring.

Myosotis scorpioïdes (*M. palustris*) (the native, water forget-me-not) 15x30cm (6x12in). The variety 'Mermaid' bears small blue flowers all summer. It spreads but is easy to yank out where not wanted.

DEPTH 5-15CM (2-6IN)

Acorus gramineus 'Variegatus' 25x15cm (10x6in). A foliage plant with stiff grass-like leaves, dark green striped with cream.

Calla palustris (bog arum) 25x30cm (10x12in). Handsome heart-shaped leaves and white arum, flowers mid- to late summer.

Iris laevigata 45-60cm (18-24in) high. Plant 25-45cm (10-18in) apart. A beardless Japanese iris with brilliant blue flowers in midsummer. 'Variegata' has silver-white and green leaves and soft blue flowers, 25cm (10in) tall.

Nymphaea 'Pygmaea Alba' *(N. tetragona)* The water lily to grow if your water garden is in a sink or shallow bowl. A miniature, it flowers from mid- to late summer, spreads to 30cm (1ft) and has fragile-looking star-shaped single white flowers.

Nymphaea x *helvola* 45cm (18in) spread. Soft yellow semi-double flowers and olive-green leaves mottled with purplish brown.

DEPTH 15-30CM (6-12IN)

Menyanthes trifoliata (bog bean) 23x30cm (9x12in). Triple, rather bergenia-like leaves on which the elephant hawk moth's larvae feed. In late spring upright sprays of small, star-shaped white flowers with fine-fringed petals.

Orontium aquaticum (golden club) 60cm (2ft) spread. Clumps of waxy blue-green leaves float on the surface. In late spring white and yellow club-like spikes appear like arum flowers without the petal spathe.

Pontederia cordata (pickerel weed) 75x45cm (30x18in). One of the few blue-flowered water plants. Hyacinth-like flower spikes appear in late summer from clumps of broad, spear-shaped, dark green, shiny leaves.

Zantedeschia aethiopica (arum lily) 60-75cm (24-30in) tall. The lovely white arum lily is hardy once established, and hardier with its feet in water than in the border. 'Crowborough' 45x45cm (18x18in) is the trustiest variety.

OVER 30CM (1FT) DEEP

Aponogeton distachyos (water hawthorn) 1.2m (4ft) spread. Clusters of forked, deeply lobed, sweet-scented white flowers are carried intermittently all summer and into autumn just above flat, floating paddle-shaped leaves.

Butomus umbellatus 90x45cm (36x18in). The flowering rush is an elegant plant with slender twisted leaves and umbels of delicate pink, three-petalled flowers in midsummer.

TIPS

- One-third of the pool should be covered with plants in order to keep algae at bay.
- Water lilies are best started in shallow water with their leaves just floating on the surface and moved to their correct depth when they are growing strongly. Either start them on the marginal shelf or prop the container on bricks that can be removed later.

Below Orontium aquaticum (golden club), for water 15-30cm (6-12in) deep.

Invasive Plants

Avoid the following invasive plants:

MARGINALS *Alisma plantago-aquatica, Caltha polypetala* (giant kingcup for large ponds only), *Carex pseudocyperus* (only for large ponds), *Carex riparia, Cyperus longus* (only for large ponds), *Glyceria aquatica variegata, Glyceria maxima, Juncus effusus, Mentha aquatica* (water mint), *Schoenoplectus lacustris* (bullrush), *Sparganium erectum* (bur-reed), *Spartina pectinata variegata* (only for large ponds), *Typha angustifolia* and *T. latifolia* (lesser and greater reedmace).

BOTTOM PLANTS The following water lilies are only suitable for large lakes. *Nymphaea alba, N.* 'Attraction', 'Marliacea Carnea', 'Marliacea Rosea' and 'Gladstoneiana', a huge white lily splendid in very deep water.

OTHER INVASIVE PLANTS *Nymphoïdes peltata*, the native buck bean, is worth growing only if it can be isolated in a small pool of its own. *Polygonum amphibium* (a weed). *Sagittaria sagittifolia*, the native arrowhead has beautiful leaves and flowers but needs isolation or lots of space. The double form is more manageable.

Above *Pontederia cordata* makes a big clump, easily divided to increase stocks.

Above right *Nymphaea* 'Escarboucle', a water lily for a large pool, spreading to 3m (10ft).

Right *Caltha palustris* (kingcup, marsh marigold): a colourful, easy to grow native plant for the mud at the water margin.

Far right *Nymphaea* 'Marliacea Albida', a water lily with scented flowers.

Below *Iris laevigata* 'Variegata', one of the most beautiful of all plants for the water's edge.

WATER LILIES

Nymphaea 'Laydekeri Fulgens' 90cm (3ft) spread. Plentiful crimson flowers and tidy leaves. Plant 23-60cm (9-24in) deep.

Nymphaea 'Laydekeri Lilacea' 90cm (3ft) spread. Light mauve-pink, free-flowering. Plant 23-60cm (9-24in) deep.

Nymphaea 'Marliacea Chromatella'. Spread up to 1.8m (6ft). Large, semi-double soft yellow flowers and marbled leaves. Tolerant of partial shade. Plant 30-90cm (1-3ft) deep.

Nymphaea 'Marliacea Albida' Similar with scented white flowers; 'Carnea' is soft pink.

Nymphaea 'Escarboucle' Spread up to 3m (10ft). Magnificent if you have the space. Deep crimson flowers with yellow centres and dark green leaves. Plant 60-120cm (2-4ft) deep.

Planting bottom and marginal plants

WHEN? In late spring or early summer, you should buy plants which have already started into growth.

If you cannot plant them immediately, keep the plants in their containers wet: stand them in a bath, tank or tray of water, although the bath and the kitchen sink will not be very practical locations.

HOW? Choose a container the right size for the plant. Line the container with hessian (sacking) or alternatively an open-weave plastic fabric to keep the soil in. Trim off surplus hessian with scissors.

Fill up the container with soil and water thoroughly.

Put the plant in and press the soil really firmly round and above the root system, so that the plant will not float out when submerged. Cover the soil surface with gravel to stop the soil floating out.

Carefully lower the container into position in the water.

Making a bog garden

HOW? The easiest way to grow bog plants along a stream or beside a pool is to make separate artificial bog areas.

- Dig out soil to a depth of 20cm (8in), with a slight downhill slope.
- Lay polythene on the base. Any polythene will do: bin liners or the bags that compost or fertilizer comes in. Its purpose is to delay drainage rather than prevent it.
- Puncture the polythene here and there with a garden fork.
- Replace the soil mixed with at least one-third of peat.

Plants for bog areas

Most bog plants like partial shade, so an area adjacent to the pond or stream that is overshadowed by trees or shrubs is ideal. If there is no shade it can be created with strategically placed groups of shrubs or small trees or even tall herbaceous plants.

There is an enormous number of bog-lovers to choose from and the list below gives just a few of the best and easiest. Some need acid soil and where this is the case I have mentioned it.

Ajuga reptans 'Atropurpurea' 15x90cm (6x36in). The purple-leaved bugle is excellent ground cover, spreading its leaf rosettes under taller plants by means of runners. The spikes of blue flowers appear in spring. Sun or shade.

Arum italicum 'Pictum' 20x25cm (8x10in). Beautiful dark green, arrow-head leaves veined and netted with white or cream. Pale green-white arum flowers in spring are followed by red berries. The leaves remain all winter.

Astilbe Fine, ferny leaves often coloured bronze-red in spring. The flowers are feathery plumes held from mid- to late summer. 'Bressingham Beauty' 75cm (30in), rich pink. 'Bridal Veil' 75cm (30in), green in bud, then white fading to cream. 'Fanal' 45cm (18in), dark crimson, 'Federsee' 60cm (2ft), rose red, 'Irrlicht' 60cm (2ft), one of the best whites. Sun or shade.

Aruncus dioicus (*A. sylvester*) 2x1.2m (6x4ft). A stately plant with clumps of large multiple leaves and tall, loosely branching plumes of tiny cream flowers in midsummer. For small gardens *A. d.* 'Kneiffii' reaches 90x50cm (36x20in). Sun or shade.

Filipendula ulmaria 'Aurea' 30x30cm (1x1ft). A form of meadowsweet grown for its pretty yellow-green divided leaves. They become creamy yellow as they mature. Insignificant flowers. Light shade.

Above Gunnera manicata, the king of marginal and bog plants. It needs a protective covering of bracken or conifer branches in winter until established.

Fritillaria meleagris Snake's head fritillary.

Gunnera manicata 1.8x2.4m (6x8ft) It is hard to resist this great brute, though few gardens have the space for it. The leaf buds are like gnarled and hairy giant's fists and unfurl into huge umbrellas. For hardiness *Gunnera* can't quite be trusted and needs a sheltered spot and a

Above Plants for natural or artificial bog areas: *(left to right) Matteuccia struthiopteris* (shuttlecock fern), *Arum italicum* 'Pictum', *Lysichiton camtschatcensis, Primula japonica* (candelabra primula).

MAKING A BOG GARDEN

A simple bog garden can be made by lining a hollow with perforated polythene and filling it with a mixture of soil and peat. A more sophisticated version allows you to water the bog garden in dry periods.

Dig a hollow about 25cm (10in) deep, sloping slightly towards one end. Line it with polythene and make small perforations, one per sq m/sq yd. Tuck the edges under the surrounding turf.

Lay a perforated polythene pipe on a layer of gravel in the bottom of the hollow, and close the submerged end of the pipe with a bung. Leave the other end above soil level so that you can attach a hosepipe to it.

Cover with a further layer of gravel. Backfill with soil.

mulch over the crowns in winter. For the faint-hearted *Gunnera tinctoria* (*G. chilensis*) is only 1.5x1.5m (5x5ft).

Hemerocallis Day lilies are so called because each flower lasts a day. But they keep on coming over a long period. One of the earliest is *H. lilioasphodelus* (*H. flava*) 60x60cm (2x2ft) with pale yellow, sweetly scented trumpets. Other good yellow varieties include 'Marion Vaughn', 'Golden Chimes' and 'Stella de'Oro'. 'Golden Orchid' and 'Lochinvar' are soft shades of orange and 'Alan' and 'Bess Vestale' are maroon-red. Easy in sun or light shade.

Hosta Among the best of foliage plants, hostas thrive in damp, shady conditions, though they will tolerate sun. The flowers are either pale mauve or white, like loosely arranged hyacinth bells. *H. fortunei* var. 'Albo-picta' 75x60cm (30x24in) has butter-yellow ribbed leaves with green margins. 'Honeybells' 90x60cm (3x2ft) has scented, pale lilac flowers above wavy-edged light green leaves. The most spectacular is *H. sieboldiana* var. 'Elegans' 75x60cm (30x24in) with huge, deeply ribbed leaves of quite startling blue-grey. Slugs love hostas.

Iris ensata (*I. kaempferi*) 60-90cm (2-3ft). Plant 30-45cm (12-18in) apart. A beardless Japanese iris with ribbed leaves and large, velvety purple, red-purple, lilac or white flowers. They need sun and rich lime-free soil.

Iris sibirica 90x45cm (36x18in). These easy irises will grow anywhere but look as if they belong near water. 'Emperor' is rich purple blue, 'Perry's Blue' sky blue, 'Snow Queen' white and only 60cm (2ft) and 'Tropic Night' dark violet. Sun or semi-shade.

Leucojum aestivum and *Leucojum vernum*, 45cm (18in) and 15cm (6in) tall respectively, are the summer and spring snowflake, two bulbs which resemble large snowdrops and love a moist site. Sun or shade.

Lysichiton camtschatcensis 75x60cm (30x24in) Not such a thug as its yellow-flowered relation the skunk cabbage. Flower spikes surrounded by elegant white spathes emerge in spring followed by large, smooth, bright green leaves. Sun.

Lysimachia nummularia 'Aurea' 2.5cm (1in), indefinite spread. Creeping ground cover for shade or sun. The rounded leaves are buttery yellow in sun, more limey in shade. Lots of yellow buttercup flowers bloom in summer.

Matteuccia struthiopteris 90x60cm (3x2ft). The ostrich plume or shuttlecock fern has fronds springing out symmetrically around its crown. Light shade.

Osmunda regalis 2x1m (6x3ft). Another handsome fern with smooth, divided bright green fronds. Light shade.

Primula japonica 30-60x30cm (1-2x1ft). Candelabra primulas make a wonderful contribution to the water garden in early summer. When suited they will self-seed generously. The flowers are arranged in whorls up the stems, hence the name. 'Miller's Crimson' and 'Postford White' are reliable varieties. Light shade.

Primula pulverulenta 60x30cm (2x1ft). Another candelabra flowering a little later, dramatic magenta crimson on floury white stems. Keep this and *P. japonica* separated from *P. bulleyana* and *P. florindae*, which are orange and yellow respectively. Light shade.

Rodgersia aesculifolia 120x60cm (4x2ft). Fine leaves, bronze and shaped like those of a horse-chestnut tree. Flower stems uncurl to form plumes of creamy pink in midsummer. For large gardens there are other species of *Rodgersia*, all handsome. Sun or light shade.

Saxifraga fortunei 'Rubrifolia' 30x30cm (1x1ft). A good ground-cover plant for damp shade with red-green leaves and, in autumn, tiny, starry white flowers on dark red stems.

Schizostylis coccinea 60x25cm (24x10in). The kaffir lily is a moisture lover rather than a bog plant, flowering in autumn when there is little competition. Grassy leaves and flowers like miniature gladioli. 'Grandiflora' is bright crimson and 'Mrs Hegarty' pale pink. Sun.

Trollius europaeus 60x45cm (24x18in). The globe-flower has rounded lemon yellow flowers in spring, and glossy, deeply divided leaves. Sun or shade.

Trollius ledebourii (*chinensis*) 'Golden Queen' 90x45cm (36x18in) Taller, orange flowers.

Containers and Hanging Baskets

Gardeners without gardens can fulfill their creative urge by growing and tending plants in pots, tubs, troughs, window boxes and hanging baskets, both indoors and out.

Choosing a style

On balconies and in small town gardens an assortment of pots of different sizes and shapes provides architectural embellishment as well as leaf and flower texture, colour and scent.

Where space is very limited, not only the more usual bedding plants but also permanent shrubs and climbers can be grown in tubs to clothe the walls of town houses or cascade from roofs and balconies. A large container holding a tree or shrub will also have space for bedding plants to add summer colour.

In grander gardens pots or urns can be used to dress an empty stone terrace, to mark the end of a flight of steps and to punctuate a vista.

Terracotta, stoneware and even concrete pots can be beautiful objects in their own right, and serve the same focal purpose in the garden as a sculpture or sundial, probably for a considerably smaller investment. In large gardens a handsome pot can draw the eye along a vista or define the spot where paths cross.

By growing plants in containers you can give them the conditions they require: azaleas and camellias in tubs of ericaceous compost can decorate the terrace of a chalk or limestone garden; tender plants in pots can be brought inside during the winter months for protection from frost. Containers can be kept moist or dry according to the plants' preferences, and slug victims like hostas can be raised up out of harm's way.

The half-hardy annuals that were once fashionable for formal bedding schemes are now more often grown in hanging baskets and other containers, giving spectacular flower colour from early summer until autumn.

Growing plants in containers also provides an opportunity to experiment with different combinations of plant shapes, leaf textures and flower colour before you commit yourself to a permanent planting; the pots can be moved around to try out different groupings and combinations.

WHERE? Before you decide on the site for a container or group of containers, check that there is a water supply nearby; you don't want to carry heavy cans of water from one end of the garden to the other.

Balcony, roof or window ledge. For container gardening on a small scale all that is needed is a balcony or window ledge. If even these are lacking, shelves at different levels, resting on brackets attached to an outside wall, can provide space for boxes or pots.

Above Sansevierias in plain terracotta flower pots make a strong impact marching up a flight of steps. Winter them indoors at a minimum temperature of 7°C (45°F), keeping them dry.

Above A well-planted hanging basket should be so full that the container is invisible.

Far left Chimney pots are real eye-catchers, and form a striking addition to paths and borders.

Left Large pots are beautiful objects in their own right, and can be used to dress terraces or punctuate a vista.

DESIGN TIPS

- For maximum impact it is sometimes wise to let a really beautiful pot stand on its own without the distraction of plants spilling from it.
- It is a mistake to scatter pots around the garden with too much abandon. A single well-composed group makes more impact than a lot of individual pots dotted about.
- Think about the background when you are placing containers. Pots of colourful flowers show to best advantage against sober green-leaved shrubs or an ivy-covered wall or yew hedge.

WARNING Make sure that the roof or balcony will support the weight of a pot full of wet compost, and that water draining from pots will not cause damage to buildings or to other plants growing below. If necessary sit the pots in a wide, deep saucer or tray.

Right A topiary hen broods on a nest of busy lizzies in a wall-mounted metal basket.

Below A lemon tree in a pot can be moved on to the terrace to provide garnish for summer gins and tonics and over-wintered in a frost-free greenhouse, conservatory or shed.

Below right Trailing ivies in a Versailles tub provide the basis of a winter display.

- In small gardens. The best design for a small town garden is often a combination of raised beds and paving at different levels, with pots grouped on the paving to focus views from the house. It is also surprisingly labour-saving: no mowing and not much weeding, just regular watering and feeding, and the gardener can take care of that by installing automatic irrigation.
- To fill gaps in planting schemes. Even the most carefully thought out planting scheme occsionally goes through seasonal doldrums when the garden looks tired. Ornamental pots of annuals or biennials can be positioned strategically to provide the missing colour, or pots of lilies and other choice flowers can be sunk into borders: the great gardener Gertrude Jekyll did this as a regular routine to extend the season of her herbaceous borders.
- For elderly or disabled gardeners. Containers can be arranged on tables or shelves so that the gardener can work in a sitting position.
- As eye-catchers. When siting containers, look at your garden with a critical eye. Identify dull corners, paths that seem to lead nowhere and no-go areas where the ground cannot be cultivated. Any of these places might benefit from a pot or a group of pots to form a focal point.
- By the front door. A group of pots at the entrance to the house is welcoming and helps visitors to identify the way in.
- Outside windows. Pots can focus the view into the garden.
- Flanking a flight of steps.
- Symmetrically, on or below a retaining wall.

WARNING Avoid windy positions and positions where gutters or trees will drip onto the containers. Even in heavy pots, tall plants are easily blown down.

Choosing containers

There is a very wide choice available: baskets, bowls, growing bags, pots, tanks, troughs, tubs, vases, urns. Or the keen recycler can choose from baths, cisterns, lavatories, sinks, chimneys and car tyres. The whimsical may choose wheel-barrows or hollowed-out logs. The important thing is that they must have a drainage hole.

The materials from which containers are made are also numerous: stone, terracotta (Italian for 'cooked earth') and lead are the traditional types; concrete, timber, fibreglass and plastic are more modern alternatives.

Your choice will be dictated by the style of your garden and house, the plants you intend to grow, and your wallet. The latter is probably the overriding consideration, but it is worth remembering that containers made of natural materials like stone and clay will mellow with age like good wine whereas a plastic imitation of terracotta will always remain a plastic imitation. So go for the genuine article if you can afford it.

Don't be put off by the bright orange colour of new clay pots; mineral salts and algae will weather them to a softer shade in a couple of seasons.

An honest, modern plastic container is not to be despised if it comes in a simple shape and an unobtrusive colour such as grey, sludge green or a soft shade of flowerpot red. It is fakery that strikes a false note in the garden.

However, well-crafted imitations of antique stone urns, made of a mixture of ground stone and cement, are often successful. They attract algae and lichens in the same way as the genuine article and after about five years it is hard to tell the difference. Impatient gardeners can help the process by sloshing diluted manure, sour milk or yoghurt over them or by leaving them in a damp shady place for a season.

Unpainted timber also weathers well, fading to a silvery grey-buff, but to prevent rot it needs painting with wood preservative every few years. Protective coats of paint also need renewing every third year.

The design of the containers should reflect the style of the garden and the house in which it is to be placed. An eighteenth-century stone urn (or copy of one) would look right in the garden of a Georgian rectory but out of place in a cottage garden. In large gardens with an architectural structure of paved terraces and steps, materials can be mixed harmoniously: stone, brick, terracotta and lead (or its fibreglass replica) blending and contrasting. But in small, informal gardens it is usually better to stick with one material: red terracotta pots for buildings made from brick and stone troughs for Cotswold stone cottages, for instance. Modern houses are best suited by unornamented containers with clean, simple lines: a well-designed concrete or plastic pot is probably more appropriate than a genuine or reproduction antique.

When in doubt, chose simple designs; the purpose of the pot is to show off the plants. Hand-made pots have a natural look that suits plants, and it can be a pleasure when travelling to seek out local craftsmen for something to add to your collection.

Your choice of container will also be influenced by what you intend to grow in it. Small trees, climbing plants and large shrubs can be grown in containers, provided the container is large enough. It should also have a wide and stable base, as top-heavy plants catch the wind and topple over rather easily.

The traditional square, wooden container known as a Versailles tub is very stable, but the plants in it will have to be disturbed every few years for the wood to be repainted. I wish Versailles tubs and other containers needing occasional maintenance were supplied with inner linings of rigid plastic that could be lifted out. The next best thing is to line it yourself with strong black polythene, with plenty of drainage holes in the base. This will make it easier to remove the plant when you need to without damaging the rootball.

Above Productive and decorative: a diminutive peach tree under-planted with white geraniums.

Below A group of stone troughs planted with choice alpine plants.

Above Fuchsias and trailing lobelias fill a planter fixed to a wooden balcony.

Timber, lead, plastic and most stone pots are frost-proof. Some terracotta pots are more weather-resistant than others, but even the strongest may crack in a very severe frost. It is safer to bring them inside in winter. The cracking is caused by moisture in the pot freezing and expanding; those most at risk are pots with narrow necks or incurving tops which leave the compost nowhere to expand to when it freezes.

Oak half-barrels with metal hoops are enduring containers for large plants, and terracotta orange pots (extra-large flower-pot shapes) are handsome, specially as matching pairs on either side of an entrance or terrace. They are designed for orange and lemon trees, which look splendid in them, and can grace your terrace if you have a frost-free place in which to overwinter them.

Large pots and tubs are also useful for making mixed displays of bedding plants with something tall and dramatic at the centre: a standard fuchsia, perhaps, or a canna lily or *Phormium*.

Medium-sized containers look best with just two kinds of plant in harmonizing or contrasting colours or foliage: white geraniums with light blue lobelias or violet petunias with lime-grey *Helichrysum*, for example.

When pots are grouped together, it is easier to make a pleasing arrangement if they are all of the same material but different sizes and shapes. It helps to vary the height of the pots as well as the plants. If each pot is planted with a single type of flower or foliage plant there is scope for arranging them in many different combinations.

The most decorative pots can be arranged in the front of a group to conceal workaday plastic at the back. If all your pots are workaday plastic, the front rank can be planted with large-leaved plants or trailing ivies to completely hide the pots. Gertrude Jekyll always grouped pots of hostas or bergenias in front of her displays of lilies or hydrangeas to hide the flower pots and to make a firm foundation of foliage as background to the flowers.

Terracotta pots are porous and lose water through evaporation, so that they need watering more frequently than plastic pots. You can get round this either by lining terracotta pots with black polythene or by using plastic pots inside them if the shape and size makes this possible.

Drainage is vitally important. Good-sized drainage holes in the base of the container help, and in wooden or plastic tubs they can be enlarged, or additional holes can be made by burning through the material with a red hot poker. Obviously this is dangerous and should not be done when children or animals are around. Wear thick gloves and keep a bucket of water by you to douse the poker and the pot in case of fire.

Planting

WHEN? • Any time for a permanent display of hardy plants.
• Autumn. Biennials for winter and early spring display: pansies, polyanthus, wallflowers and forget-me-nots. Bulbs for spring display.
• Early summer. When there is little risk of further frost, the spring plants come out and the summer plants go in: geraniums, petunias and many more.
• The best time of day to plant is in the late afternoon or evening so that plants can recover overnight.

TOOLS
- Trowel.
- Compost.
- Drainage material (stones or broken crocks).
- Slow-release fertilizer granules (optional).
- Wheelbarrow.
- Canes to support climbers (if needed).
- Twiggy sticks to support floppy plants (if needed).
- String.
- Secateurs.
- Small fork for weeding.
- Watering can.

Planting containers

It is best to fill and plant containers *in situ* rather than lug them into place after planting, hence the need for a wheelbarrow to transport drainage stones and compost.

For seasonal planting, use a proprietary multi-purpose compost. If you are uneasy about encouraging the extraction of peat from the diminishing area of wetlands, there are peat-free brands available.

If you are planting permanent trees, shrubs or climbers, a loam-based compost will provide nutrients over a longer period.

The best formula is John Innes No. 3 which can be bought from garden centres: look for the JIMA (John Innes Manufacturers' Association) seal of approval. If using other loamless media, you will need to incorporate some slow-release fertilizer. For the small amount you will need, it is hardly worth the trouble of making up your own.

HOW? • If the compost has dried out in its bag, water it thoroughly the day before you use it.
• Water the plants that you are going to put in an hour or so before you start.
• Put canes or other supports, if needed, into the pot and wedge them in place with stones.
• Cover the base of the container with a good layer of stones or crocks. How deep the layer can be depends on the size of the container.
• If the container is deep enough, add a layer of chopped turf, well-rotted manure or garden compost on top of the drainage material.
• Fill to within 1.25cm (1/2in) of the top with multi-purpose or John Innes No.3 compost. A slow-release fertilizer in granular form can be added at the recommended rate at this stage. It will save having to feed your plants for the best part of a season.
• If the compost is still rather dry, water it and wait an hour or two before planting.
• Plant as described in Chapter 8, Planting and Transplanting. If you are planting a group of plants in the same container, start in the middle and work outwards.
• Tie plants to supports if needed.
• Water thoroughly.

Planting up hanging baskets

HOW? The larger the basket the better.
• Sit the wire basket on a bucket or large flower pot for stability.
• Line it with 3cm (1 1/4in) sphagnum moss or thatch raked from the lawn, pushing it well down.
• Optional: add an inner lining of black polythene with holes cut in it large enough to plant small plants into.
• Add compost mixed with vermiculite and a granular, slow-release fertilizer to about 5cm (2in) deep.
• Tuck the roots of trailing plants in through the sides of the basket and through the holes in the polythene (if used). A roll of paper can be used to minimize damage to fragile roots.
• Add more compost and more plants.
• In the top layer, plant tallest plants centrally.
• Fill with compost and firm around the plants.
• Water thoroughly and leave to drain before hanging.

AFTERCARE If you included slow-release fertilizer all you need do is water the basket daily (twice a day in hot, dry weather). This is easiest using a 1-litre (2-pint) plastic bottle.

Looking after container plants

WATERING The compost must always be kept moist. Pots standing in the sun may need watering twice a day. If peat-based composts dry out, they are very difficult to re-wet. Permanent plants in containers should never be allowed to dry out completely, but in winter the compost should be just moist and never wet. Wet compost freezes and can damage the plant's roots and break the pot as the ice expands.

TIPS

- Don't forget to leave enough space between the soil surface and rim of pot to allow adequate watering.
- A watering can with a narrow spout can reach under the foliage of the plants to ensure that the water reaches the compost and does not run off the leaves.

Below A wall-hung container of pansies makes use of vertical space in a tiny garden.

PLANTING UP A HANGING BASKET

1 Water plants thoroughly and allow to drain. Stand the basket on a bucket or large pot. Line the bottom of the basket with 3cm (1¼in) of sphagnum moss. Or use a proprietary basket liner, or a sheet of thin black polythene, punctured for planting and drainage.

2 Cover the sphagnum with a 5cm (2in) layer of lightweight, general purpose compost. For best results, add slow-release fertilizer granules.

3 Insert plants through the side of the mesh, without disturbing the roots, so that the rootballs lie on top of the compost. Spread a layer of compost over them and, working upwards in layers, repeat until the sides of the basket are evenly planted.

4 If the roots are too large to fit easily through the mesh, wrap them in a cone of paper and push the pointed end of the cone through the mesh. Once in place, the cone can be torn away. This method protects the roots and the delicate neck of the plant.

5 When the sides are completed, fill the rest of the basket with compost and plant the top, with the tallest plants in the centre. Water thoroughly and leave overnight in a sheltered place to drain.

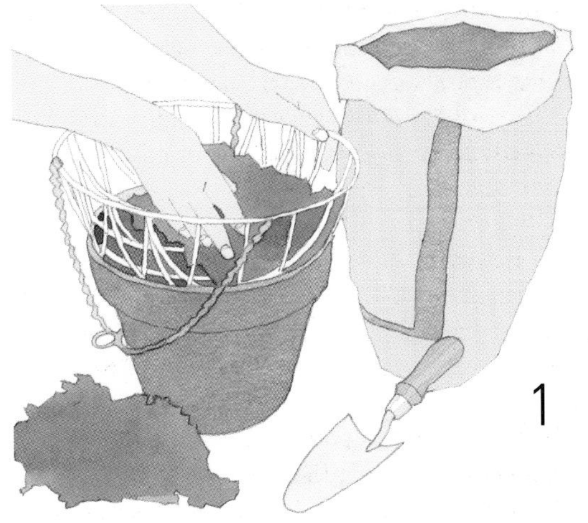

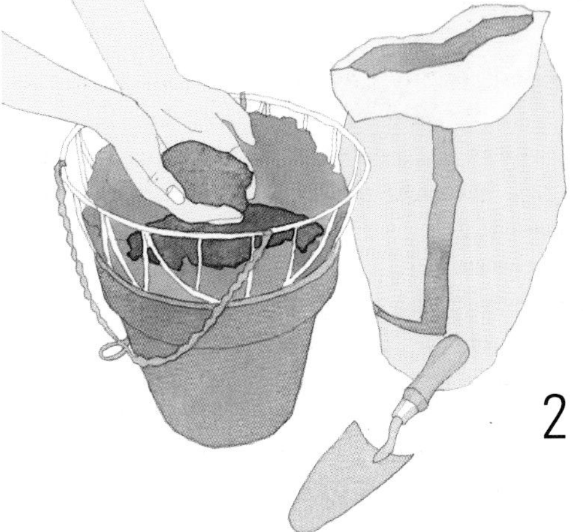

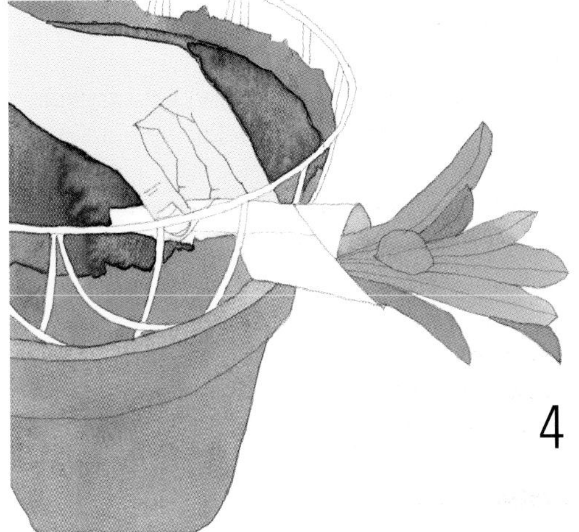

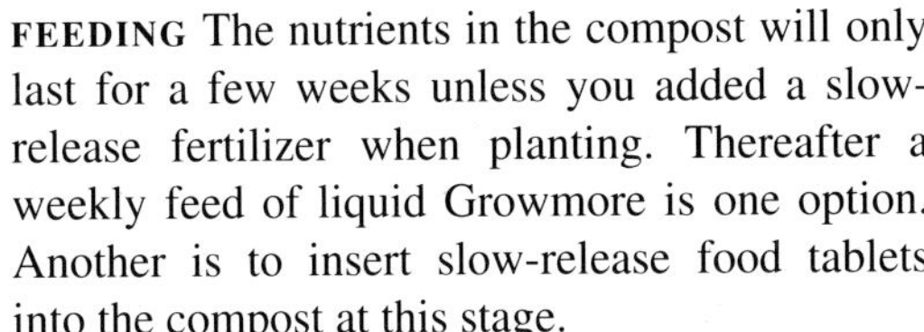

FEEDING The nutrients in the compost will only last for a few weeks unless you added a slow-release fertilizer when planting. Thereafter a weekly feed of liquid Growmore is one option. Another is to insert slow-release food tablets into the compost at this stage.

WEEDING If you have planted as densely as you should, weeds will not be a problem, but watch for them in the early stages before the leaves of the plants shade them out. Pull or fork them out.

Buying container plants

Many garden centres only sell bedding plants in mixed colours, so if you are working to a colour scheme (and your display will look much better if you do), you must buy individually potted plants when they are already in flower, and pick the colours you want. This is more expensive than buying in trays. The cheapest way to have plants of the right colours is to grow them from seed (see Chapter 15, Increase and Multiply).

Many garden centres and mail order suppliers now sell bedding material as plantlets, or plugs, which are cheaper. These are seedlings rooted into a wedge-shaped plug of compost. They should be temporarily planted in small pots or trays and grown on in a greenhouse or in a light window until they are big enough and the weather is right to put them out.

Unless you have greenhouse space, postpone buying until you are ready to plant. A late frost could carry off all your plants, so in Britain it is safest to wait until the end of May or until the danger of a last frost is passed.

Check the quality of the plants before you buy. You are looking for dense, bushy plants with several strong flowering stems, in bud rather than in full flower.

Container plants

Trees

The container restricts the roots, and the tree's top growth is correspondingly restricted so that it will not outgrow the garden. A tree in a container will not live as long as one in the open ground but it will give many years of pleasure and provide the vertical element that so many gardens cry out for.

Besides the potted bay tree that often marks the centre of a classic herb garden, there are plenty of trees that do well in containers.

Trees need a lot of water regularly, so make sure that there is easy access to water and that the water reaches to the base of the container.

POT SIZE Minimum 50cm (20in) wide and deep.

Acer negundo 'Variegatum' Quick-growing with a spreading head of bright green leaves margined in white with a touch of pink. Sun.

Crataegus laevigata (*C. oxyacantha*, hawthorn) Dense, spreading heads, attractive in their natural form but they can also be clipped into lollipop or mushroom shapes. Scented white flowers in late spring and early summer, crimson haws in autumn. 'Paul's Scarlet' is smothered in pinky-red double flowers. Very hardy. Sun or light shade.

Eucalyptus gunnii A very fast-growing evergreen with bright blue-grey rounded leaves and attractive peeling bark. Prune hard every spring to maintain foliage in its juvenile state. Sun, shelter.

Ilex aquifolium (holly) In containers, hollies are more shrub-like than tree-like. There are many pretty, variegated forms and they are good topiary plants. Very hardy. Sun or shade.

Laurus nobilis (sweet bay) Bay trees make elegant topiary specimens, as round-headed standards, pyramids or cones. Sun, shelter.

Malus (edible and crab apples) Apple trees grown for their fruit are as ornamental as the crab apples grown for their blossom and ornamental but less edible fruits. If you want fruit, you need two varieties to pollinate each other (see Chapter 16, The Kitchen Garden). Fruit trees on dwarfing M27 rootstock are ideal for containers. Suitable crab apples include 'Evereste' with deep pink and white flowers and orange-red apples; 'Red Jade', pink and white flowers, small red apples, pendulous branches; x *robusta* 'Yellow Siberian', pink and white flowers, yellow apples. All are very hardy. Sun or semi-shade.

Olea europaea (olive) Only hardy in very sheltered gardens, but a nice reminder of the Mediterranean, Tuscan or Greek landscape. Sun, shelter. Move indoors for winter.

Left and right Small trees such as crab apples *(left)* and hawthorn *(Crataegus laevigata, right)* can be grown in large containers. The restricted root system will keep the top growth under control.

Prunus (flowering cherries, etc.) Crab apples give better value than most *Prunus* but the pink almond blossom of *Prunus amygdalus* is a delight at the start of the year. Of the cherries *P.* x *yedoensis* arches gracefully with scented blush white flowers in early spring. Sun.

Sorbus aucuparia Some varieties of mountain ash give triple value: flowers, berries and autumn leaves. 'Asplenifolia' has bright red berries for the birds and ferny leaves red in autumn, 'Xanthocarpa' has yellow berries not much liked by birds. Sun or light shade.

Sorbus cashmiriana and *Sorbus vilmorinii* Both are graceful trees with fine, ferny leaves and long-lasting pink berries. Sun or light shade.

Evergreen shrubs

Evergreen shrubs provide a restful background to colourful groups of flowering plants in summer, and in winter are appreciated for their own sake. Many also have beautiful flowers in their seasons.

Grey-leaved shrubs do particularly well in pots as they are not demanding as far as food and water are concerned, and can even stand some neglect. Containers provide the opportunity to give lime-hating azaleas and camellias the soil they prefer, and they are among the most rewarding pot plants. Plant them in ericaceous (lime-free) compost.

There are many other shrubs which will grow happily in containers, including herbs (see Chapter 21, Growing Herbs). Below a select few are described.

POT SIZE Varies according to the size of the plant's rootball and top growth. A pot that is too small will cramp the roots and will be unstable

Below *Camellia* x *williamsii* 'Donation' is one of the most floriferous varieties. If your garden soil is too alkaline for camellias and azaleas, grow them in containers of lime-free compost.

in a windy situation. Start with a pot the right size for your young plant: the same or slightly larger than the pot it comes in when you buy it. 'Pot on' into the next size up as the plant develops. Minimum recommended sizes for plants approaching maturity are given after the name of the plant. The rule of thumb is that the pot should be a quarter to a third as tall and wide as the shrub in it.

Arundinaria (bamboo) Pot 50cm (20in). The botanists are always changing the names of bamboos, which makes it difficult to get what you want unless you see it in a nursery or plant centre. They are elegant plants for modern, uncluttered gardens. The suckers, which can be a nuisance in the open garden, are restrained when they are grown in containers. In time bamboos provide a free supply of canes. All are fairly shade tolerant, specially *A. nitida* (*Sinarundinaria nitida*, now called *Fargesia nitida*). It has gracefully arching purple canes up to 3m (10ft) tall. If you want something smaller, *A. viridistriata* (*Pleioblastus auricomus*) is 1.5m (5ft) high with purplish stems and soft yellow leaves with green stripes. Don't allow the compost to dry out.

Azalea, *Rhododendron* Pot 50cm (20in) for large varieties, down to 23cm (9in) for dwarf azaleas. Just to confuse us, the botanical name for azalea is *Rhododendron.* Both azaleas and 'true' rhododendrons make excellent pot plants because they have dense, compact root systems and will not outgrow their pots for many years. They vary in size from 12m (40ft) trees to prostrate shrubs less than 30cm (1ft) high and come in colours from white and palest yellow, through orange, flame, scarlet, crimson, magenta and all shades of pink and mauve, to so-called blue, which is really a blue-mauve. Flowering times vary from March to June, but May is the spectacular month in rhododendron gardens. Azaleas and rhododendrons are woodland plants, so a sheltered position in dappled shade suits them best. They hate lime, so water with rainwater, not tap water.

WARNING *Azaleas sold as house plants are not hardy. To keep them going from year to year, sink the pots in the garden in light shade after risk of frost is past and bring them in again in autumn, repotting if necessary in ericaceous compost.*

Buxus sempervirens Pot 50cm (20in) for large specimens. Box, large-leaved, small-leaved or variegated, clipped into architectural or fantasy shapes, does well in containers. It is fairly slow-growing, so if you want instant topiary, use ivy instead, trained over a wire frame.

Camellia japonica and *Camellia* x *williamsii* Pot 50cm (20in). Camellias do wonderfully well in the shelter of small town gardens and are happy against a north-facing wall but need protecting from north and east winds. Avoid an east aspect as early morning sun after frost damages the flowers. Camellias should be planted in containers that are only slightly larger than the rootball and watered regularly. An occasional overhead spray refreshes them. If the bushes need shaping, prune them lightly after flowering. Replace the top 1cm (½in) of compost at the same time.

The dense bushes of glossy rich green leaves make camellias wonderful background plants when not in flower. The beautiful flowers appear between February and May and can be single, semi-double or double, from deep to light crimson and from shocking to palest pink, or white. 'Lady Vansittart' and 'Contessa Lavinia Maggi' are pink-and-white striped. Camellias are slow growing. The following are faster than most and among the easiest to grow: 'Anticipation' deep rose pink double; 'Donation' peach-pink semi-double; 'J.C. Willams' soft pink single; 'Alba Plena' white and double; 'Adolphe Audusson' blood red semi-double.

Convolvulus cneorum 60x80cm (24x30in). Pot 20cm (8in). A very remote and rather aristocratic relation of bindweed, it has nothing in common except the pinkish-white funnel-shaped flowers. It is a compact, bushy shrub with leaves covered in silver silky hairs, irresistible to touch. By growing it in a pot you can see and touch it without stooping. It is not entirely hardy and should be brought inside if severe frost is forecast. However, it usually survives a bad winter as long as it is kept dry at the roots. Must have sun and shelter. Likes really poor soil.

Euonymus fortunei Pot 30cm (1ft). Indispensable variegated shrubs grown for the leaves not the insignificant flowers, good in mixed tubs to set off flowering plants. 'Silver Queen' 40x100cm (16x36in) has the prettiest cream-white variegation, tinged with pink in winter, and sometimes has pink berries. If planted against a wall, it will climb slowly. Sun or shade.

Fatsia japonica 1.5x1.5m (5x5ft) or more. Pot 50cm (20in). The huge, glossy, fingered leaves on stout branches make it look like a jungle plant, but it will do in a dank, sunless basement area. Globular clusters of white flowers appear on stiff stems in autumn. It has been crossed with ivy to produce a less gross (or less dramatic) shrub, x *Fatshedera lizei.* Both plants are great survivors provided they have a sheltered position. Sun or shade.

Phormium Pot 50cm (20in) for the biggest varieties. These tropical-looking New Zealanders will come through all but the hardest winters, but, if in doubt, wrap them loosely in sacking or bubble plastic or bring them inside for the coldest months. Phormiums have dramatic, sword-like leaves, in some varieties strikingly striped. Names like 'Cream Delight', 'Tricolor', 'Bronze Baby' and 'Maori Sunrise' tell it all. *Phormium tenax* 'Purpureum' at 1.5m (5ft) is twice as tall as most of the stripys, with dusky red-bronze leaves. Sun. Moist compost.

Vinca minor 5-10x60-90cm (2-4x24-36in). Pot 15cm (6in). The lesser periwinkle is denser and less sprawly than the greater (*V. major*). At the perimeter of a mixed group its leafy stems will arch downwards to soften the rim of a pot or tub. In borders vincas root down to form ground cover. *V. minor* 'Variegata' has cream-white leaf margins and pale mauve flowers, 'Atropurpurea' has deep plum-purple flowers, 'Bowles' Variety' is pale blue and 'Gertrude Jekyll' white. The flowers bloom in spring and early summer with a few later. Easy-going in sun or shade.

Yucca Pot 50cm (20in). Architectural plants which gardeners seem to love or hate, yuccas carry rosettes of long spiky leaves. *Y. gloriosa*, 1-2m (3-6ft) tall and wide, does not flower for its first five years, then produces a huge spire of drooping, bell-shaped, cream flowers tinged with red. *Y. filamentosa* is smaller, 75x90cm (30x36in), and has cream-white flowers after two or three years. Yuccas must have sun, will grow in the poorest soil and will survive if you forget to water them occasionally.

Deciduous shrubs

When space is limited, plants must sing for their supper. To be worth growing in containers shrubs should either have an exceptionally long flowering period or more than one asset: autumn colour, perhaps, a particularly graceful shape or beautiful leaves or fruit as well as flowers. Any shrub is worth trying in a pot if you long for it and have nowhere else to grow it.

Above Potentilla fruticosa 'Tangerine'. Potentillas are very good value for containers as well as in the border. Rounded domes are covered in flowers all summer.

Acer palmatum Pot 50cm (20in). *A. p.* var. *dissectum* and *A. p.* 'Bloodgood' are just two varieties of Japanese maple. They all have beautiful shape and foliage, and most have spectacular autumn colour. Slow-growing, but they can be bought in large sizes, at a price. Semi-shade, shelter from wind, and plentiful water supply.

Hydrangea macrophylla 1.5x1.5m (5x5ft). Pot 50cm (20in). The hortensia or mop-head hydrangeas have the appearance of florists' plants and look more at home in pots on a terrace than in a mixed border or shrubbery. They are in flower from mid- to late summer into autumn. If you want blue hydrangeas to stay blue, plant them in lime-free compost; they turn dirty pink in alkaline soil. Reliable varieties are 'Madame E. Mouillère', white with a hint of pink; 'Alpen Glow', strong red (not easy to place with other plants); and 'Hamburg', which starts deep pink or blue according to the soil and in autumn turns to glowing red. Another worthwhile hydrangea is *H. arborescens* 'Annabelle'. It is rather a floppy plant but has huge round heads of small green-tinged white flowers. Semi-shade, moist compost, shelter from wind and early morning sun. Leave dead heads on until early spring to protect the new buds from frost.

Potentilla fruticosa 60x90cm (2x3ft) average. Pot 30cm (1ft). Their tidy habit of growth and long flowering season make potentillas exceptional plants in any garden. Dense low bushes with small, neat leaves can be pruned to keep them at the size you want. The flowers are like small wild roses in shape and cover the plants in great profusion. Among the best are 'Abbotswood', white and the earliest to flower; 'Primrose Beauty'; 'Goldfinger' with large gold-yellow flowers; and 'Daydawn', apricot pink. They prefer sun or light shade; cutting back by one-third with shears in spring will encourage flowering and keep the bushes dense and shapely.

Right and below Phormium cookianum 'Tricolor' *(right)* and *Yucca filamentosa (below)*, shown here growing in the border, make an equally strong statement when grown in pots on a terrace or balcony. Both need sun.

Roses

Even if all your gardening has to be done in containers, you can still grow roses. The bigger the container, the wider your choice of roses. The minimum size for the average shrub rose is 45x45cm (18x18in). Roses grown as standards or half standards are particularly pretty in pots and can be underplanted with low-growing bedding plants. Those listed here are either continuous or repeat flowering and form fairly dense bushes. All are scented. Grown in pots, they may not reach their full size. Best in sun. See Chapter 19, Growing Roses, for the most suitable varieties. Others include:

'Chinatown' 150x90cm (5x3ft). Cluster-flowered (floribunda). Clear unfading yellow.

'Everest Double Fragrance' 120x90cm (4x3ft). Cluster-flowered (floribunda). Double, pale apricot-pink.

'Iceberg' 1.5x1m (5x3ft) Cluster-flowered. The most floriferous of all white roses. Good as a standard.

'James Mason' 1.5x1.2m (5x4ft). Modern shrub. Semi-double dark crimson, old-fashioned style.

'Lady Hillingdon' 90x60cm (3x2ft). Large-flowered (hybrid tea). Semi-double apricot-yellow. Wonderful scent. Sheltered position.

'Mary Rose' 1.2x1.2m (4x4ft). English. Very double, old-fashioned, rose pink.

'Mousseline' 90x60cm (3x2ft). Moss. Semi-double creamy pink.

'Nathalie Nypels' 60x60cm (2x2ft). Polyantha. Double rose-pink.

'Rose de Rescht' 90x60cm (3x2ft). Very double, small crimson pompoms.

Climbing plants
Provided the pot is big enough, minimum 50cm (20in), climbing roses, clematis, vines and other climbers can be grown successfully. The pot can be placed against a wall or fence, or a support of trellis or bamboo canes can be 'planted' in the container. But – as ever – you must be prepared to water regularly.

Seasonal bedding plants
These plants provide non-stop colour from early summer until the first frosts. As soon as the danger of a late frost has passed, it is out with all the bulbs and wallflowers and in with the geraniums, petunias, lobelias, busy lizzies and *Nicotiana*. For a truly spectacular display, you should:

- Be generous with plants: cram them in so that when they have reached their full size they are spilling out in all directions.
- Include foliage plants as well as flowers.
- Feed them once a week.
- Be vigilant about watering: always keep the compost moist.

Summer bedding plants for foliage
Decorative foliage gives a firm foundation to mixed or single flower colours.

Ferns: Pot 23cm (9in). For pots in full shade, for example in a basement area, ferns and ivies combine well. Shade; moist soil.

Hedera helix (ivy) Pot 30cm (1ft). Invaluable for its trailing tendrils, to drape elegantly from an urn or to hide a plastic pot or Gro-bag. Many leaf shapes, plain or variegated. Sun or shade. Pots, hanging baskets.

Helichrysum petiolare Up to 30x60cm (1x2ft). Pot 20cm (8in). Elegant trailing stems of silvery woolly leaves. 'Limelight' has soft lime-yellow leaves which contrast beautifully with violet, purple and red flowers. It is best in semi-shade as the leaves scorch in strong sun. *H. microphyllum* has small leaves. Sun or semi-shade. Pots, hanging baskets.

Senecio maritima (*Cineraria maritimus* now called, confusingly, *Senecio cineraria*) 30x30cm (1x1ft). Pot 15cm (6in). Sub-shrub usually treated as an annual. 'Silver Filigree' has finely cut silver-white leaves. Sun. Pots.

Cabbage and kale: Pot 15cm (6in). More curious than beautiful, ornamental cabbages and kales have leaves shading from cream to magenta pink and purple. Several in a large pot provide colour from late summer well into the winter.

Summer flowering plants
The plants listed below are reliable for less experienced gardeners, but there are endless possibilities and scope for the gardener's individual creativity.

Above As soon as spring bedding plants like tulips and wallflowers fade, take them out and plant up containers with summer flowers: *(top) Impatiens* or busy lizzie; *(above) Lobelia* 'Emperor William'.

Argyranthemum frutescens (*Chrysanthemum frutescens*) Tender perennials 60x60cm (2x2ft). Pot 18cm (7in). Sometimes called marguerites, the pretty daisy flowers bloom above finely cut leaves from early to late summer. *A. foeniculaceum* (white) and its pink form bear masses of flowers over blue-grey leaves. *A. gracile* 'Chelsea Girl' has very fine grey-blue leaves and white flowers; *A.* 'Jamaica Primrose' pale yellow flowers, sea-green leaves. Overwinter in a cold greenhouse or cool, light room and take cuttings of basal shoots in early spring. Sun. Pots.

Bidens aurea Tender perennial. 45x45cm (18x18in). Pot 18cm (7in). A sprawler with finely cut leaves and golden yellow, star-shaped, single flowers which keep going into mild winters. Sun. Pots, hanging baskets. Can be grown from seed.

Brachyscome iberidifolia (Swan River daisy) 30x30cm (1x1ft). Annual. Pot 12cm (5in). Masses of small, many-petalled daisy flowers all summer and autumn, deeply cut bright

Above A terracotta pot of pelargoniums is evocative of the Mediterranean.

green leaves. Colours available are blue, violet and white. Sun. Pots, hanging baskets. Seed.

Felicia amelloïdes Tender perennial. Up to 45x45cm (18x18in). Pot 15cm (6in). Delicate azure daisies with yellow centres. Sun. Pots. Comes through mild winters in sheltered positions. Softwood cuttings can be taken in summer.

Fuchsia Perennial. Pot 30cm (1ft) for bushes and standards. Numerous varieties, some hardy, some not, in shades of white, pink, red and purple; as bushes, standards or trailers. In flower from mid-summer until the first hard frost. Sun or semi-shade. Pots, hanging baskets. Increase by tip cuttings in early spring.

Heliotropium arborescens (heliotrope or cherry pie) Tender perennial treated as annual. 45x45cm (18x18in). Pot 15cm (6in). Heliotrope only does well in a warm summer, but is worth risking for its big clusters of scented violet-purple flowers which attract butterflies. Sun. Dwarf cultivars are especially good for pots: *H.* 'Princess Marina'; 'Regal Dwarf'. Seed.

Impatiens (busy lizzie) Tender perennial treated as annual. Average 25x25cm (10x10in). Pot 10cm (4in). Colours are bright, hot oranges, scarlets and magentas or soft shades of pink and mauve. Also white. Accent Series F1 and Super Elfin Series F1 are reliable. Sun or part shade. Moist compost. Pots, hanging baskets. Seed.

Lobelia Tender perennial treated as annual. Average height 10-15cm (4-6in). Bushy or trailing plants smothered in diminutive white, blue, mauve, violet or crimson flowers all summer and into autumn. Reliable bush varieties include 'Cambridge Blue', pale blue, white eye; 'Crystal Palace', dark blue, bronze leaves; 'Emperor William', sky blue. Those in the Fountain and Cascade series are trailing plants. Sun or semi-shade. Pots, hanging baskets. Grow from seed.

Nasturtium (*Tropaeolum majus*) Hardy annual. Height 20-38cm (8-15in). Bushy or trailing. Nasturtiums flower best in poor soil in a hot spot; on a rich diet they are too leafy. The flowers are cream, yellow, apricot, orange, mahogany. Some have creamy variegations on the leaves. Sun. Pots, hanging baskets. Seed.

Nicotiana (tobacco plant) Annual, various heights from 30cm (1ft) to 1.5m (5ft). Pot 23cm (9in) for the largest kinds. The best varieties for scent and flowers are Domino Series F1 (30cm/1ft), with white, lime or pink flowers. *N. sylvestris* is a stately plant (up to 1.5m/5ft) with a head of sweet-scented, long tubular white flowers. Sun or light shade. Pots. Seed.

Pelargonium (geraniums) Perennial. Pot 18cm (7in). Every conceivable shade of red and pink. Also white. Many have decorative leaves as well. Century Series, Multibloom Series and Orbit Series are all reliable. Choose plants in flower or from a catalogue. Sun. Pots, hanging baskets. Overwinter under glass. Some varieties can be grown from seed.

Petunia Annual. Average height 30cm (1ft). Pot 15cm (6in). Habit varies from compact to semi-trailing. The wide trumpet-shaped flowers can be plain, striped, margined or ruffled, in shades of red, pink, magenta, lavender, violet-purple, blue and white. There are doubles as well as singles. Petunias can be ruined by wet weather, but Carpet Series are a reliable compact variety. Super Cascade are good for baskets. Sun, shelter. Pots, hanging basket. Seed.

Bulbs and spring bedding

In early autumn all containers except those permanently planted should be emptied, cleaned and refilled with drainage material and fresh compost. They can then be planted with bulbs and winter and spring bedding plants.

The choice of bulbs is so much a matter of personal taste and there are so many to choose from that I will not recommend particular varieties. It does not matter how close you plant bulbs in containers, they can touch each other if necessary. By planting bulbs in layers you can have flowers from late winter until it is time to make room for the summer display. Start with a layer of tulips 15-20cm (6-8in) below the surface. These should be alternate early and late flowering varieties. Just cover them with a layer of compost and plant a layer of *kaufmanniana* or other March-flowering tulips. In the top layer plant alternate winter- and spring-flowering crocuses.

Tulips also look good growing up through forget-me-nots or with cream, tawny or blood red wallflowers.

Right Senecio cineraria: foliage plants provide a good foil to colourful flowers.

Growing Roses

A rose is a rose is. . . just another shrub. Yet there is hardly a garden in Britain without at least one rose growing in it, and traditionally a special area is set aside for these shrubs alone: the rose garden.

If you get hooked on roses you will discover that their history as garden plants goes back as far as the history of gardens, and that there is a rose for almost every site in the garden: there are climbing roses to cover the highest wall or swarm up trees; shrub roses to make dense, prickly hedges keeping out livestock and the most determined vandal; gracefully arching shrub roses to stand alone; ground-cover roses and compact little rose bushes to edge borders.

Rose flowers, many of them scented, range from opulent, many-petalled cabbage roses to fragile single flowers or neat little pompons. For colour you can choose from white, palest blush, yellow, buff, apricot, many shades of pink, dusky purple, scarlet and crimson. And as if all that were not enough, some rose bushes are in flower from early summer until the first frosts. Those that have one glorious burst of flowering in midsummer or a little later are described as once-flowering. Many varieties flower at midsummer then take a rest and flower again at the end of the summer or in early autumn. They are called repeat-flowering, or remontant. A few are genuinely continuous flowering but this term is often used to describe repeat-flowering roses which manage to produce the odd bloom in-between their two bursts of flowering.

Above 'Ballerina' growing as a shrub; the same rose as a standard is shown below-left.

Choosing a site

Shelter roses from strong winds, specially from the north and east, or create shelter with a hedge or fence. A fence, besides providing shelter, will give support to climbing roses. However, roses like a fairly open situation; air circulating around them helps prevent diseases taking hold.

Far left The shrub rose 'Ballerina', grafted as a standard, gives height to a formal border of 'Nypel's Perfection', a polyantha rose.

Left *Rosa moyesii* x 'Highdownensis', a tall (10ft) species rose with crimson single flowers followed by a spectacular autumn display of orange hips.

Right 'Mme Grégoire Staechelin', a wonderfully prolific climbing rose suitable for a north wall.

Above The continous flowering climber 'Zéphirine Drouhin' with *Clematis* 'Niobe'.

Above 'La Sevillana', a strong and healthy shrub rose.

Above 'Empress Josephine', one of the most reliable gallica roses.

Above *Rosa banksiae lutea*, a beautiful early-flowering climber.

There are a few roses which are better off out of full sunlight as the colour of the flowers is bleached out, but most prefer a sunny position. Some will flower well on a north-facing wall or in partial shade, but will not thrive under dripping trees. In general the alba roses are the best bet for shade.

Roses prefer soil on the acid side of neutral, and if there is clay, so much the better. But do not be deterred if your soil is not ideal. On chalk or sand the best remedy is to dig a large planting hole for each rose and use generous amounts of farmyard manure or compost. In very poor soil the albas and rugosas will usually perform well.

WARNING Do not plant new roses in soil where roses have been growing before. The soil may be rose sick. If you are replacing roses in a derelict rose garden you must remove the soil to a depth of 25cm (10in) and replace it with soil from elsewhere in the garden. The only alternative is to have the soil sterilized by a qualified contractor.

Climbers

If you become fond of climbing and rambler roses you will soon run out of walls and fences to support them. Bear in mind that they can also be trained up trees, over arches, on pergolas, arbours, free-standing pillars, posts or tripods, and on catenary ropes.

Standards and weeping standards

- Grow them formally marching down each side of a path or as centrepieces in knot garden beds or vegetable plots. Used informally they give height in mixed borders.
- Small standards are excellent pot plants.

In pots and tubs

If your garden is a small patio, roof or balcony, there are many roses that will grow happily in pots; the larger the container can be, the better they will do. Look for patio roses, or miniature floribundas. See also Chapter 18, Containers and Hanging Baskets.

Making Separate Rose Beds

If you are making separate rose beds, keep the design simple.

- Two wide beds, straight or curved, with a grass or paved path between them look better than an elaborate geometric layout.
- Large-flowered and cluster-flowered varieties are best grown in separate beds, but shrub roses associate happily with other plants in mixed borders and even in the wild or woodland garden.

Types of rose

Roses divide roughly into three groups, with subdivisions in each group. It helps when you are looking at nursery catalogues or books about roses to have an understanding of the groups and their different qualities.

Species roses

These roses grow wild in different parts of the northern hemisphere. Some, like *Rosa mulliganii* and *R. wichuraiana,* grow to heights of 7.5m (25ft) and carry great clusters of small flowers. They are the ancestors of the garden ramblers and, where there is space, are magnificent cascading out of a tree. Species include the European dog rose (*R. canina*) and the sweet briar (*R. eglanteria*, syn. *R. rubiginosa*). Others are shrubs of various sizes and some are prostrate. Many have attractive, ferny leaves and a graceful, arching shape. Most species have relatively small, single flowers and flower once only in early or midsummer, but many have a fine autumn display of hips. The scent of many species is incomparable.

SCOTTISH (BURNET) ROSES *R. pimpinellifolia* (formerly *R. spinosissima*). Low-growing, prickly, suckering shrub, very hardy and good on sandy soil. The species has profuse small single white flowers in early summer. There are varieties with yellow and double flowers. Closely related species are often listed with them, for example, *R. filipes* 'Kiftsgate' and *R.* 'Geranium'.

Old roses

Also sometimes referred to as old-fashioned roses, heritage roses or historic roses, they are mostly taller than the more formal hybrid tea and floribunda bush roses. They were cultivated in gardens in ancient Greece and Rome, and in India, Persia and Europe from medieval times. They fall into several categories.

Above You don't need a rose garden to grow roses. In this small garden the damask rose 'Comte de Chambord' grows in a mixed border.

There is really no need for gardeners to be able to distinguish between these categories, but if you become interested in rose history you will soon learn to. Most of the old-fashioned roses flower once in midsummer and do not repeat, but they are worth growing in all but the smallest gardens for their wonderful scent and for some of the forms and colours which are rare among modern roses.

GALLICA ROSES Probably the oldest of garden roses, gallicas were grown by the Greeks and Romans and cultivated in Persia, whence they are said to have been brought to Europe by the Crusaders. From the seventeenth century onwards Dutch and French breeders developed new varieties. The characteristics of gallicas are strong and delicious fragrance, one prolific flowering at midsummer, usually with flat, many-petalled flowers in rich shades of crimson, purple or dusky pinks fading to

Left 'Charles de Mills', one of the most robust gallica roses.

mauve. The shrubs are short and bushy. Average height and spread 120x90cm (4x3ft).

DAMASK ROSES Another ancient group, probably of Middle Eastern origin. Mostly once flowering except for *Rosa* x *damascena bifera*, or Quatre Saisons, the autumn damask, which is the oldest known repeat-flowering rose. Fragrant pink or white flowers, often symmetrically quartered and sometimes with a small green 'eye'. The bushes are fairly open and the branches sometimes flop with the weight of the flowers unless the plants are pruned quite hard. Average 1.5x1.2m (5x4ft).

ALBA ROSES One of the healthiest, most trouble-free groups, good in difficult conditions and poor soils. Grown in European gardens since the Middle Ages, albas range in colour from clear pink through blush to white. Their fragrant semi-double or double flowers have a look of delicacy. The stems are strong and the leaves greyish. Once flowering slightly earlier in midsummer than most other old roses. Average 1.8x1.2m (6x4ft).

PORTLAND ROSES Bred in the mid-nineteenth century from a China damask hybrid, they combine the qualities of damask roses with the ability to produce a second crop of flowers in late summer/early autumn.

CENTIFOLIA ROSES The rose seen in many Dutch flower paintings. Highly perfumed many-petalled flowers, often large, ranging from white to rich violet-crimson. Mostly lax and floppy if left unpruned and unsupported, except for some neat miniature roses, 'De Meaux' and 'Petite de Hollande'. Large leaves and many-thorned stems. Once flowering. Average 1.5x1.4m (5x4ft).

MOSS ROSES Centifolia or damask roses which have developed moss-like growth on the sepals of the flowers. The amount of moss varies. Most are highly scented. Average 1.5x1.2m (5x4ft).

CHINA ROSES What they lack in scent they make up for by flowering almost continuously from summer till the first severe winter frosts. This ability has been an important component in the breeding of modern roses. Single or double, small- to medium-sized flowers on twiggy branches, stronger than they look. Average 120x90cm (4x3ft).

BOURBON ROSES Not called after French kings but after the Island of Bourbon (Réunion) where the first Bourbon rose was found. Most Bourbon roses date from the second half of the nineteenth century. They combine the scent of the damasks with the continuity of China roses. Opulent white, pink or striped flowers on tall, slender plants. Average 1.8x1.2m (6x4ft).

HYBRID PERPETUAL ROSES These crosses between Portland, Bourbon and China roses were popular with Victorian and Edwardian gardeners. The best of them remain in cultivation, combining strong growth with large, fragrant flowers, including some good reds and crimsons which do best in light shade. Average 120x90cm (4x3ft).

POLYANTHA ROSES Small, tidy bushes with small flowers carried in large clusters continuously. White, apricot and pink, a few are scented. Robust constitution. Average 75x60cm (30x24in).

HYBRID MUSK ROSES Strong shrubs with clusters of mostly highly scented flowers in all colours, but the white, buff apricots and pinks are outstanding. After flowering in mid-summer they take a rest before an even more spectacular burst of flower in early autumn. Bred early in the twentieth century by the Rev. Joseph Pemberton in Britain. Average 1.5x1.5m (5x5ft).

RUGOSA ROSES Distinctive shrubs, bred from a Japanese species different in shape, foliage and flower from other roses. Rugosas have luxuriant, bright green, rough textured leaves, large or very large flowers in white, pink or magenta crimson, and on some varieties spectacular big red hips. The best rugosas are tough and healthy, good for difficult sites. Repeat flowering. Average 1.8x1.5m (6x5ft).

Below Rugosa roses have distinctive rough-textured, ridged leaves and prickly stems. Some have showy hips and many are dense enough for ground cover. *(Left to right)* The hips of 'Fru Dagmar Hastrup'; 'Blanche Double de Coubert'; *Rosa rugosa*.

Modern roses

ENGLISH ROSES This 'group' bred by David Austin in the 1970s, '80s and '90s bridge the gap (not chronologically but stylistically) between old roses and modern roses. At their best they combine the best qualities of both old and modern, taking scent and flower shape from old roses and blending these with continuity of flower, robust constitution and a colour range of yellows and soft apricots from modern varieties. Average 1.2x1.2m (4x4ft).

LARGE-FLOWERED (HYBRID TEA) AND CLUSTER-FLOWERED (FLORIBUNDA) ROSES These are the roses usually grown in formal rose beds. In 1979 the World Federation of Rose Societies decided to change the names of the two main classes from hybrid tea to large-flowered bush and from floribunda to cluster-flowered bush. Certainly the new names are more descriptive, but old habits die hard and many nurseries as well as gardeners have stuck to the old familiar categories. Both categories are more upright and stiff in their growth than old-fashioned and modern shrub roses. Patio roses are dwarf versions of floribundas.

Large-flowered bush roses (hybrid tea) have been the most popular roses for the greater part of the twentieth century, when roses were usually grown in rose beds away from other plants, and valued as cut flowers. The large, conical flowers are beautiful in bud but sometimes blowsy when fully open. Most hybrid teas bloom repeatedly throughout summer and autumn with an occasional rest. They are grown mainly for the sake of the individual blooms; the plant as a whole lacks grace. In the past breeders concentrated on producing shapely flowers in strong, sometimes startling, and even harsh colours at the expense of scent, but more recently scent and subtler colours have reappeared. Average 90cm (3ft) tall. Plant 45cm (18in) apart. Prune hard.

Above 'Alec's Red', a highly scented rose with typical, long hybrid tea buds.

Left 'Pink Bells', one of the modern class of ground cover roses: low growing with a wide spread, dense habit of growth and small, tidy leaves and flowers.

Above 'Mme Grégoire Staechelin', a wonderfully prolific climbing rose of hybrid tea origin, suitable for a north wall.

- Cluster-flowered bush roses (floribunda) are more continuous and more colourful, bearing trusses of smaller flowers. Uniform, bushy growth makes them ideal for mass planting. Average 75x60cm (30x24in).

MODERN SHRUB ROSES Most are informal in style and associate well with both old and modern roses. Many are robust and disease resistant and some flower continuously or repeat. Choose from single and double flowers in all colours and sizes. Many are fragrant and some have good hips. Sizes vary from 2.7x2.5m (9x8ft) ('Cerise Bouquet') to 60x75cm (24x30in) ('Little White Pet').

GROUND-COVER ROSES A recent development of roses with dense, spreading habit which smother weeds, provided they are planted in weed-free ground. This group includes the gamebird series (Grouse, Pheasant) and the County series (Surrey, Hampshire).

Climbers, ramblers and standards

Apart from the species roses, climbing roses, invaluable in small gardens, divide into two main groups of different form and habit.

Climbers

Climbers have a similar habit of growth to large-flowered bush roses and cluster-flowered roses, with stout, branching stems, but are much, much taller. They flower on lateral stems produced from a permanent framework of branches built up over the years. Some are climbing versions of modern bush varieties and many others have flowers of similar size and shape to hybrid teas and floribundas and are repeat or continuous flowering. Older varieties include:

- Climbing bourbons, mostly repeat flowering.
- Climbing tea roses, a group developed from roses brought from China in the early nineteenth century. Fragrant and repeat flowering, they need a warm south-facing wall.
- Noisette roses, climbers of old rose style, were bred in America and introduced by Philippe Noisette in 1817. Fragrant, and repeat flowering, they also need a warm, sheltered site.

Ramblers

Ramblers differ from climbers in their flowers, which are smaller but very numerous and carried in clusters on stems produced in the previous season. Their habit of growth is different from that of climbers: long, flexible stems are produced each year, often springing from the base of the plants. They are ideal for bending over arches and pergolas. The very tall varieties are spectacular grown up trees or over a shed. Most are once-flowering and many are scented.

Standards and weeping standards

Buds are grafted on to a single stem to form a miniature tree. Standard ramblers weep with a graceful, trailing habit.

Right 'Frühlingsgold', a modern shrub rose bred from the Scots briar, is smothered in large single flowers in early summer.

Choosing roses

In each group there are dozens, and in some groups literally hundreds, of varieties of roses, and choosing which ones to buy and cultivate can be confusing.

If you are making a separate rose garden, or growing roses in separate beds, resist the temptation to grow one of each of your favourites. The overall effect will be more pleasing if you work to a restricted colour scheme. This applies particularly to large-flowered and cluster-flowered bush roses.

Your choice of shrub roses and old roses to grow with other plants in mixed borders will be influenced by the colours, shapes and sizes of their neighbours.

When choosing climbing roses, make sure the height of the rose is right for the purpose: a rose that will surround your bedroom window with fragrance will be nothing but trouble on a 1.8m (6ft) arch. Consider the background the rose will be seen against. Magenta and blue-ish pinks do not show to advantage up against red brick walls, and white flowers are lost against a white background.

Not all roses are easy to grow: some are slightly tender, some are more prone to diseases than others, and some have a weak constitution. If you stick to the reliable roses from the tables that follow, you should not be disappointed. I have listed the roses in the categories used by most rose growers in their catalogues. With the exception of one or two, they are all scented.

MODERN SHRUB ROSES
Top 'Nevada', modern shrub.
Above 'Gipsy Boy' ('Zigeunerknabe').

LARGE-FLOWERED BUSH AND CLUSTER-FLOWERED ROSES
Below 'Just Joey', large-flowered.
Below centre 'Troika', large-flowered.
Bottom 'Korresia', cluster-flowered.

Large-flowered Bush (Hybrid Tea) and Cluster-flowered (Floribunda) Roses

The selection listed below are all scented. Highly bred roses like these are often prone to disease. Some varieties flourish healthily for generations and then become sickly for no apparent reason. At the time of writing those listed are comparatively resistant to blackspot, mildew and rust. For best results they should be grown in full sun in the open and pruned quite hard.

Codes: Lf = large-flowered bush; Cf = cluster-flowered bush; S = tolerates light shade; P = suitable for pots.

Plant Name	Codes	Height	Comments
White			
Dove (La Paloma)	Cf	60cm (2ft)	Almost pure white.
Lady Rachel	Cf	60cm (2ft)	Cream.
Polar Star	Lf	1m (40in)	Ivory tinged with green.
Pristine	Lf	60cm (2ft)	White tinged with pink.
Yellow			
'Arthur Bell'	Cf	90cm (3ft)	Warm yellow fading to cream.
Dutch Gold	Lf	90cm (3ft)	Deep golden yellow.
'Korresia'	Cf	75cm (30in)	Bright yellow.
Mountbatten	Cf S P	1.2m (4ft)	Mimosa.
Peaudouce	Lf	90cm (3ft)	Pale primrose.
Apricot/Orange			
Amber Queen	Cf	75cm (30in)	Golden amber.
Fragrant Delight	Cf	80cm (30in)	Light coppery salmon.
Just Joey	Lf	90cm (3ft)	Soft copper-orange.
'Southampton'	Cf	1m (40in)	Orange apricot.
Troika	Lf	90cm (3ft)	Copper orange.
Pink			
Anna Livia	Cf	75cm (30in)	Salmon pink.
'English Miss'	Cf	75cm (30in)	Delicate light pink.
Escapade	Cf S P	1.2m (4ft)	Mauve-pink single flowers.
Pink Peace	Lf	1m (42in)	Strong pink.
Silver Jubilee	Lf	75cm (30in)	Peach pink.
Red			
Alec's Red	Lf	90cm (3ft)	Cherry red.
'Deep Secret'	Lf	90cm (3ft)	Very dark crimson.
Royal William	Lf	90cm (3ft)	Deep crimson.
The Times Rose	Cf	75cm (30in)	Crimson red.
Velvet Fragrance	Lf	90cm (3ft)	Deep crimson.

Species Roses, Old Roses and Modern Shrub Roses

Old roses and modern shrub roses are often listed together and can be treated in the same way as other shrubs in mixed borders, or grown in informal rose beds. Many need little or no pruning. Some form graceful arching bushes.

Codes: C = continuous flowering; R = repeat flowering; H = good hips; S = tolerates light shade; P = suitable for pots.

Plant Name	Type	Codes	Height x Spread	Comments
White				
'Alba Semi-Plena'	Alba	H S	1.8x1.5m (6x5ft)	White, greyish leaves. Scent. A great survivor.
'Blanche Double de Coubert'	Rugosa	R S P	1.8x1.5m (6x5ft)	In flower almost continuously from early summer to late, leaves colour in autumn.
'Madame Hardy'	Damask	S	1.5x1.5m (5x5ft)	White flowers have green eye. Scent.
'Nevada'	Modern shrub	R	2.5x2m (8x7ft)	Large single cream flowers all along the branches.
'Penelope'	Hybrid musk	H S P	1.5x1.2m (5x4ft)	Profuse pale, creamy pink flowers, small coral hips. Scent.
'Prosperity'	Hybrid musk	R S	1.5x1.2m (5x4ft)	Arching with large clusters of cream-white flowers. Scent.
Rosa rugosa 'Alba'	Rugosa	R H S	2x1.8m (7x6ft)	Large single white flowers, big red hips. Very robust.
'White Pet'	Modern shrub	C S P	60x60cm (2x2ft)	Small white pompon flowers in big clusters.
'Yvonne Rabier'	Polyantha	C S P	90x60cm (3x2ft)	Blush white, almost thornless.
Yellow				
'Cantabrigiensis'	Species	H S	2.5x2.5m (8x8ft)	Masses of pale yellow flowers, late May and early June, elegant ferny foliage. Easier than 'Canary Bird'.
'Frühlingsgold'	Modern shrub	S	2x1.5m (7x5ft)	Large, strongly scented, single yellow flowers in early summer all along the arching branches. 'Frühlingsmorgen' has smaller, rose-pink flowers.
Graham Thomas	English rose	C	1.2x1.2m (4x4ft)	Apricot yellow. Scent.
Rosa xanthina hugonis	Species	S	2x1.8m (7x6ft)	Creamy single flowers, early. Ferny leaves on arched stems.
Apricot				
'Buff Beauty'	Hybrid musk	C S	1.5x1.5m (5x5ft)	Warm apricot-yellow double. Scent.
Charles Austin	English rose	R	1.5x1.2m (5x4ft)	Yellow apricot.
'Cornelia'	Hybrid musk	C S	1.5x1.5m (5x5ft)	Apricot-pink double. Scent.
'Fritz Nobis'	Modern shrub	H S	1.8x1.5m (6x5ft)	A strong rose covered with clove-scented light salmon-pink flowers in early summer.
'Nymphenberg'	Modern shrub	C	2x1.5m (7x5ft)	Large, double salmon-pink apple-scented flowers borne continuously on strong arching branches.
Pink				
'Ballerina'	Modern shrub	C S P	1.2x1m (4x3ft)	Smothered in dense, compact clusters of small apple-blossom-like flowers.
'Bloomfield Abundance'	Modern shrub	C	1.8x1.5m (6x5ft)	Very distinctive elegant miniature tea roses, flesh pink, from perfect little pointed buds held in open sprays.
'Fantin-Latour'	Centifolia		1.5x1.2m (5x4ft)	Blush pink. Scent.
'Felicia'	Hybrid musk	C P	1.2x1.2m (4x4ft)	Silver-pink double. Scent.
'Fru Dagmar Hastrup'	Rugosa	C H S P	1.5x1.5m (5x5ft)	Clear pink single flowers, large crimson hips, good autumn colour.
'Madame Knorr' ('Comte de Chambord')	Portland	C	1x0.6m (3x2ft)	Warm pink, grey-green leaves. Strong scent.
'Marguerite Hilling'	Modern shrub	R	2.5x2m (8x7ft)	Large single pink, sister to Nevada.
'Mary Rose'	English rose		1.2x1.2m (4x4ft)	Robust, branching shrub, old-fashioned warm pink flowers. Scent.
'Queen of Denmark' ('Königin von Dänemark')	Alba	S	1.5x1.2m (5x4ft)	Soft glowing pink. Full-petalled flowers, rich scent.
Red				
'Cerise Bouquet'	Modern shrub	S	3x3m (10x10ft)	Magenta pink, small greyish leaves. Sometimes repeats.
'Charles de Mills'	Gallica		1.5x1.2m (5x4ft)	Deep velvety crimson. beautifully quartered double flowers.
'Gipsy Boy' ('Zigeunerknabe')	Bourbon	S	1.5x1.2m (5x4ft)	Dark crimson-purple old-fashioned flowers in early summer, strong, prickly shrub. Scent.
Rosa moyesii 'Geranium'	Species	H S	2.5x1.5m (8x5ft)	Single scarlet flowers, large hips.
'Roseraie de l'Hay'	Rugosa	R S	2x2m (7x7ft)	Dense shrub, apple-green leaves yellow in autumn, magenta-crimson double flowers, strong scent.
'Scarlet Fire' ('Scharlachglut')	Modern shrub	H S	2.5x2m (8x7ft)	Glowing scarlet single flowers on arching branches, large red hips.
'Tuscany Superb'	Gallica	P	120x90cm (4x3ft)	Dark crimson purple. Scent.

Climbers

Best displayed against walls, fences, trelliswork or pillars.

Codes: C= continuous flowering; R=repeat flowering; N=suitable for north wall; O=once flowering.

Plant Name	Codes	Height	Comments
White			
'Madame Alfred Carrière'	C N	6m (20ft)	Palest blush. Scent.
'Mrs Herbert Stevens, Climbing'	R N	6m (20ft)	White. Scent.
'White Cockade'	C	3m (10ft)	White.
Yellow			
'Alister Stella Gray'	R	4.5m (15ft)	Soft yellow. Scent.
Golden Showers	C N	3m (10ft)	Golden yellow.
Highfield	C	3m (10ft)	Primrose yellow.
Apricot			
Breath of Life	C	3m (10ft)	Apricot pink. Scent.
'Compassion'	R	3m (10ft)	Salmon apricot. Scent.
'Maigold'	N O	3.5m (12ft)	Apricot yellow. Scent.
'Lady Hillingdon, Climbing'	R	4.5m (15ft)	Apricot yellow. Scent
Pink			
'Madame Grégoire Staechelin'	R N	6m (20ft)	Clear pink, hips. Scent.
'New Dawn'	C N	4.5m (15ft)	Pale pink. Scent.
'Aloha'	C	3m (10ft)	Rich pink. Scent.
Red			
'Copenhagen'	C	2.5m (8ft)	Deep scarlet.
'Etoile de Hollande, Climbing'	O	5m (16ft)	Deep crimson. Scent.
Dublin Bay	C	2m (7ft)	Blood red.

CLIMBERS
Below left 'Golden Showers', a reliable and very continuous short climber, tolerant of poor soil.
Bottom left 'Maigold', very prolific and one of the earliest to flower.
Below 'Madame Alfred Carrière', her legs hidden by a large-flowered clematis.

RAMBLERS
Top 'Crimson Showers'.
Above 'Sanders' White Rambler'.

Ramblers

Their flexible shoots make ramblers ideal for training on arches, pergolas and ropes. Mostly highly scented.

Codes: C= continuous flowering; R=repeat flowering; N= suitable for north wall.

Plant Name	Codes	Height	Comments
White			
'Wedding Day'	N	9m (30ft)	Cream white single. Scent.
'Albéric Barbier'	N	6m (20ft)	Lemon cream, almost evergreen. Scent.
'Seagull'	N	4.5m (15ft)	Pure white single. Scent.
'The Garland'	N	4.5m (15ft)	Pink-tinged, white, daisy-like. Scent.
'Sanders' White Rambler'		5.5m (18ft)	Pure white double. Scent.
Yellow			
'Emily Gray'	N	4.5m (15ft)	Soft, pale yellow. Scent.
'Goldfinch'	N	3m (10ft)	Yolk yellow fading to white. Scent.
Apricot			
'Paul Transon'	R	4.5m (15ft)	Copper salmon. Scent.
'Phyllis Bide'	C N	3m (10ft)	Pink and gold. Few thorns. Slight scent.
Pink			
'Paul's Himalayan Musk'	N	9m (30ft)	Pale lilac pink. Scent.
'François Juranville'	N	6m (20ft)	Coral pink. Few thorns (like the well-known 'Albertine' but better). Scent.
'May Queen'	N	6m (20ft)	Lilac pink. Scent.
'Debutante'		4.5m (15ft)	Clear rose pink. Scent.
'Veilchenblau'	N	3.6m (12ft)	Purple fading to lilac. Best colour in shade. Scent.
Red			
'Crimson Shower'		4.5m (15ft)	Bright crimson. Slight scent.

Ground-Cover Roses

Codes: C = continuous; R = repeat flowering; S = tolerates light shade; H = good hips.

Plant Name	Codes	Height x Spread	Comments
Bonica	C H	75x120cm (3x4ft)	A tidy bush with clusters of small, soft pink flowers, continuous.
Grouse	R S	60cmx3m (2x10ft)	Vigorous prostrate branches covered with small glossy leaves and, in July and August, small single pale pink flowers. Partridge, white single flowers and Pheasant, double pink, are similar. Good weed-smotherers.
Pink Bells, Red Bells and White Bells	C	60x120cm (2x4ft)	Neat, glossy leaves and clusters of small, pompom flowers.
'County' series, including Kent (white), Northamptonshire (flesh pink)	C	Various: 30-60cm (1-2ft)x 60-100cm (2-3ft)	

GROUND COVER
Right 'Pink Bells', one of the modern class of ground-cover roses: low-growing with a wide spread, dense habit of growth and small, tidy leaves and flowers. 'Red Bells' and 'White Bells' are similar except in colour.

Buying roses

Until fairly recently you could only buy roses with bare roots. You ordered them from a grower's catalogue during the summer and they were delivered at any time from late autumn till early spring. You could also buy them during the planting season packaged from stores and village shops, or lifted from peat beds in a garden centre at the time of purchase.

Today you can still buy in these ways but garden centres are also stocking an ever-increasing range of roses in containers all the year round. You pay more for containerized plants, but you can choose them when in flower and you can plug gaps in the garden as soon as you spot them.

You will not find all the roses listed above in a garden centre, and probably not all in one rose grower's catalogue. The best way to make your selection is to visit the display gardens of a grower or those of the Royal National Rose Society at St Albans in Hertfordshire during the summer. If you note the names of the roses that

Above 'Bonica', one of the most reliable ground cover roses for prolific and continuous flowers.

Left 'American Pillar', a favourite rambler in the Edwardian era and the 1920s for pergolas and arches.

Far right, above 'Royal William', large-flowered (hybrid tea), unfading velvet red flowers on strong stems.

Far right, below 'Marie Louise', a strongly scented damask rose, compact and bushy.

appeal to you, you can check them later against the above list or in a supplier's catalogue.

The best catalogues are honest about which roses are disease prone or susceptible to weather damage. If in doubt, look for the words 'healthy' and 'vigorous' in the descriptions. Beware of 'best in a warm position' and 'repays careful cultivation'.

Container-grown

- Look for at least two strong shoots (about as thick as a pencil) growing from the base.
- Avoid those with spindly shoots.
- Reject plants with signs of disease on the leaves or stems.
- Give the plant a gentle tug to make sure it is established in its container; newly potted roses are difficult to grow on successfully.
- Avoid those with matted roots coming out of the base of the pot.

Below The large-flowered (hybrid tea) rose 'Pink Peace' in a bold colour partnership with *Lilium* 'Golden Melody'.

Bottom right *Rosa filipes* 'Kiftsgate', a huge plant that will reach the top of a tall tree.

Bare-rooted

- Look for strong shoots and smooth and flexible stems, not dry and wrinkled.
- Look for branching root system with some fibrous roots, moist and without twisted and tangled main roots.
- Nurseries deal with orders in rotation, so you cannot specify a delivery date.
- Order as soon as you receive your catalogue to be sure of getting the plants in November rather than February.
- If your roses arrive at an inconvenient time or during unsuitable weather for planting, 'heel them in'. This means planting them temporarily in a trench, and firming the soil with your heel. If the ground is frozen or waterlogged, lay the roses in a box or plastic bag and cover their roots with damp peat or soil. Keep them in a shed or garage until the weather improves.

If weak or unhealthy plants are delivered, always send them back immediately.

Planting

WHEN? As with other bare-rooted shrubs, late autumn is the best time, ensuring that the plants are well established by the time growth starts the following spring. But any time while the plants are dormant is satisfactory.

Container-grown roses can be planted at any time provided they are always kept watered during dry weather.

HOW? • Prepare the soil well in advance of planting, digging in lots of manure and compost (roses are greedy feeders).

• Planting distances for shrub roses should allow for their mature spread. Large-flowered and cluster-flowered roses can be planted from 45cm (18in) to 60cm (2ft) apart.

WARNING Climbers often suffer from drought because they are planted too close to a wall. Plant them with the centre of the plant at least 30cm (1ft) and preferably 45cm (18in) out from the wall.

• Follow the instructions for planting shrubs in Chapter 8, Planting and Transplanting.

• Add a spadeful of compost and a handful of bone meal and mix it into the base of the planting hole.

• Plant roses deeper than most other shrubs: the final soil level should be 2.5cm (1in) above the union of the shoots with the roots or rootstock.

• Nurseries send out roses which are already pruned. Nevertheless, after planting, tidy up any ragged or broken shoots, cutting above a bud. Cut long shoots back to 15cm (6in) on shrub roses, 8cm (3in) on large- and cluster-flowered bushes. This may make you nervous but it will pay dividends by ensuring that new growth starts near the base, thus building up a shapely plant in time.

Climbers and ramblers

SUPPORTS Where space is limited, house walls, fences, pillars and trellises offer opportunities to grow roses vertically.

On walls a proper framework of wires or trellis work is better-looking and easier to manage than a random system of nails banged in as and when needed. This makes tying in much easier and allows air to circulate between the roses and the wall, substantially reducing the likelihood of disease.

Attach wires to long vine eyes. The frame should project out from the wall by 8-10cm (3-4in). Use wires that are stretched vertically as well as horizontally to form a mesh 25-30cm (9-12in) square.

Alternatively, panels from a roll of pig wire can be cut to fit the space, or you can fix wooden battens to the wall and trellis panels to the battens.

TYING IN CLIMBERS Tie them in during the summer as new growth develops or alternatively when you prune.

Use rubber ties to attach stout rose branches to climbing frames and stakes, and jute string for slender shoots. The string will break and need replacing every two or three years, but this is not a problem as you will want to rearrange the plants' framework from time to time.

WARNING Wire ties tend to throttle the branches as they expand.

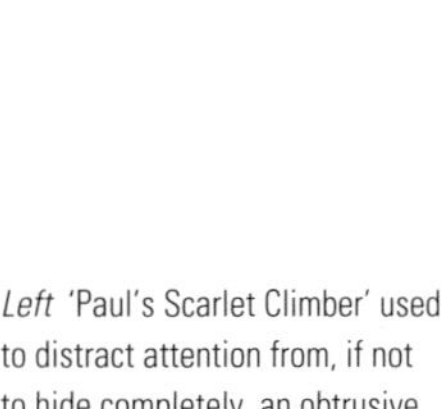

Left 'Paul's Scarlet Climber' used to distract attention from, if not to hide completely, an obtrusive drainpipe.

Below The popular rambler 'American Pillar' with long, flexible stems which have been trained horizontally to cover an informal boundary fence.

Above The rambler 'Mrs F.W. Flight' trained tightly to an arch. Strict pruning and tying in after flowering ensures a spectacular display the following summer.

Above right Roses trained horizontally flower more prolifically than those with vertical stems. 'Leuchstern' (rambler).

HOW? If necessary, untie and untangle branches that need rearranging.

Aim at getting the branches into positions as near to horizontal as possible; this stimulates the plant to produce many more flowers.

Tie shoots to the front of the frame, resisting the temptation to weave them in and out. If you do this, the rose's expanding branches will weaken the frame.

Tie firmly but not too tightly, doubling the string for stouter branches. Use a reef knot. It is easier to untie than a granny knot.

Make several ties along each branch to hold it firmly: loose branches can be damaged by wind and, if they are near a doorway, may damage you with their thorns.

Training roses up trees

Roses growing up trees or rambling through shrubs use their thorns to grapple their way upwards but they need a little help.

HOW? When you plant, lean a long cane from the planting hole against the tree and secure it. Tie the rose's shoots to the cane.

As the shoots grow, tie them to the tree.

When the shoots are out of reach, use a long forked stick to guide them in the right direction.

Right The rambler 'Apple Blossom'. If they are carefully trained and tied in firmly, ramblers will flower their hearts out for their short season.

Looking after roses

Weeding, feeding, watering

Routine care of roses differs little from that for other plants.

EARLY SPRING

- Weed.
- Feed with a top dressing of granular fertilizer (use a brand prepared specially for roses) or mulch with manure.
- After a good spell of rain mulch to conserve moisture and suppress weeds.

MIDSUMMER

- Top-dress with fertilizer again. It helps the plants fight off disease and encourages a second flush of flowers from those varieties that repeat.

Diseases and pests

See Chapter 14, Diseases and Pests.

Greenfly (aphids) and other insects will not kill roses but they may disfigure them. The best remedy is a systemic insecticide which does not harm ladybirds.

Three debilitating and disfiguring diseases attack roses: blackspot, powdery mildew and rust. When visible signs appear it is too late to treat these diseases, so prevention should be the aim.

To prevent diseases spreading, watch plants for signs of disease on leaves and stems. Cut them off and burn them.

- Pick up and burn dead leaves on the ground.
- Remove and burn any dead wood on the plant and any branches wounded by being rubbed against each other, not just at pruning time but as soon as you notice them.
- To be completely sure that you have done all you can, spray your roses with a systemic fungicide every two weeks from the time the leaves open in spring. Choose a product that deals with blackspot, mildew and rust.
- Roses need a certain amount of extra care and attention, but the rewards are out of all proportion to the effort.

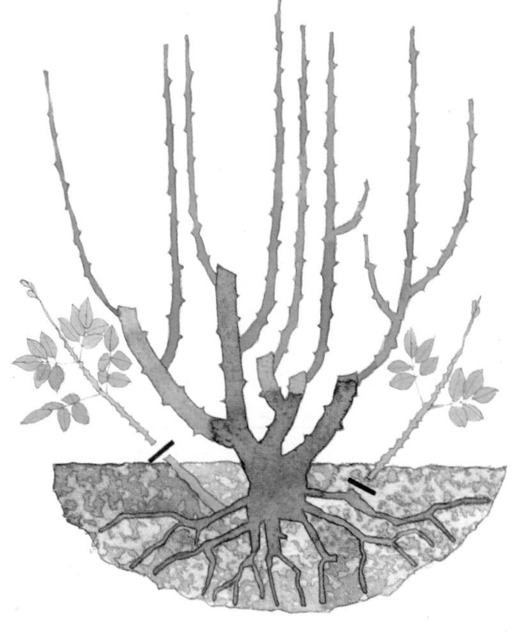

REMOVING SUCKERS
Trace the sucker stems back to their source at the root, gently removing soil to do so. If they are slender, a sharp pull and twist should remove them. Stouter suckers should be cut with a sharp knife or secateurs as close as possible to the root from which they spring. Do not cut them off at soil level, this just encourages them to produce more growth.

Dealing with suckers

A sucker is a shoot thrown up by the rootstock on which the rose is grafted. Suckers are more vigorous than the grafted shoots and if left will take possession of the whole plant.

Suckers are not recognized by the number of leaflets to each leaf, as we used to be told: there is no such easy formula. Look out for a rogue shoot that is different from the rest; it may be a different colour or have thorns of a different shape or spaced wider or closer on the stem. The leaves may have more leaflets, they may be of a different colour or texture. Often suckers are thicker and more vigorous than 'genuine' stems. If in doubt, remove some soil to check whether the supposed sucker comes from below the rootstock joint. If it does, remove it.

Suckers should be removed as close to the root they spring from as possible. The usual advice is to pull them off. Easier said than done, but if you catch the sucker early enough a sharp tug with a twist of the wrist may do the trick. Or, scrabble in the soil till you find the base of the sucker and cut it off with knife or secateurs.

Below The diseases that trouble roses are mildew *(left)* and blackspot *(right)*. Both can usually be controlled by spraying with a systemic fungicide at fortnightly intervals from the time the leaves appear in spring. Don't wait till the disease appears. In bad cases cut back affected branches after the first flowering. The new shoots that appear should be disease-free and can be sprayed to keep them so.

Pruning

This is no longer the thorny problem it may once have seemed. The gaff has been blown on the mystique of rose pruning by recent experiments at the Royal National Rose Society's gardens. Trials were held comparing three methods of pruning beds of large-flowered bush and cluster-flowered roses: conventional hard pruning, lighter pruning and clipping over the rose beds with a powered hedge trimmer. The skilled experts were surprised and ham-fisted amateur rose lovers delighted to find that the third method resulted in more and finer blooms.

This method is fine for massed roses grown for a display of summer colour. It is less satisfactory if you grow roses in mixed borders with other plants and wish them to form shapely shrubs at all seasons. In those circumstances normal pruning principles should be applied.

How severely you prune climbing roses and shrub roses is a matter of personal taste and style. Disciplined pruning results in elegance in the French style and a policy of *laissez faire* produces a typically relaxed English-looking tangle of bloom.

WHEN? In autumn, shorten the stems of tall shrub, hybrid tea and floribunda roses by one-third if they are exposed to strong winds. This will prevent the wind catching the plant and loosening the hold of roots in the ground.

The traditional time to carry out the final, thorough pruning is early spring. This is certainly the best time to prune repeat-flowering roses, but many experts tend to prefer pruning once-flowering shrub roses immediately after they flower. In other words, to treat them in the same way as other flowering shrubs.

The best time to prune roses will vary from year to year depending on how severe the winter is and how early spring comes. The job should be done earlier in southern gardens than in the north. If you prune too early the new growth may be nipped by frost and you will have to prune again, cutting back to undamaged wood.

For spring pruning there are various traditions about the exact date that is best. Some gardeners swear by 1 April, and others say the job must be completed by St Patrick's Day (17 March).

A good rule of thumb is to prune when buds half way up the stem begin to swell.

HOW? **ONCE-FLOWERING SHRUB ROSES**

Leave them to grow naturally or prune them by the one-in-three system like any other flowering shrub.

- After flowering, remove weak or diseased stems and crossing branches.
- Tidy the bush by removing the flowered stems and shortening others if wished. On shrubs of lax and floppy growth, cut back the stems by one-third. Always cut just above an outward-facing bud (see Chapter 10, Pruning).
- If the plant has become dense and bushy, thin the centre to let light and air in, removing the oldest branches.

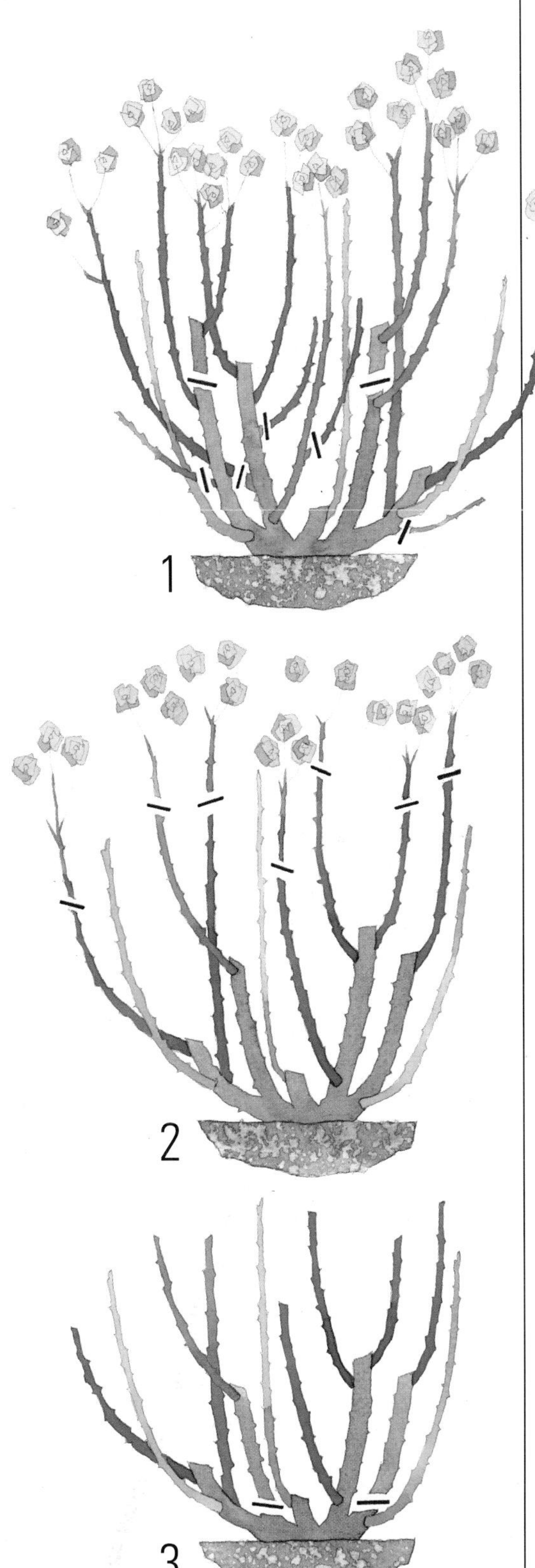

ONCE-FLOWERING SHRUB ROSES

1 After flowering, remove weak and diseased stems, and crossing or badly placed branches. The shrub roses generally have a graceful habit and naturally rounded outline. If you prune too ruthlessly you will spoil this effect.

2 Remove the flowered stems, and if you wish, shorten the stems by up to one-third, cutting back to a promising, outward-facing bud.

3 If the plant is dense and congested, remove the oldest branches to let light and air in to the centre. This reduces risk of disease and allows new growth from the base to develop.

REPEAT-FLOWERING SHRUB ROSES Prune as for once-flowering shrub roses but leave them until early spring.

LARGE-FLOWERED BUSH AND CLUSTER-FLOWERED ROSES In the past pruning them has been fraught with rules and old wives' tales. Now, the experiment described above at the Royal National Rose Society's trial grounds implies that only those gardeners whose roses are destined for the show bench need fret about how best to prune them.

The experiment shows that shearing over rose beds with an electric hedge-cutter is as good a pruning method as any. Moreover this rough pruning produced stronger growth. It remains to be seen whether in the long term these methods will weaken the plants.

If you prefer to stick to traditional methods, prune annually in spring.

- Remove dead and weak branches.
- Cut back the rest to about 30cm (1ft) long, always pruning to an outward-facing bud.
- The harder you prune, the fewer – but larger – the blooms.

GROUND-COVER ROSES No pruning needed, but they can be clipped over lightly with shears in spring to keep them tidy and dense.

CLIMBERS should be pruned in early spring to maintain a good framework covering wall, trellis or other support. Once the framework is established, shorten new side shoots to within two or three buds of the parent branch. Only remove main stems when they are tired and unproductive.

RAMBLERS These flower mainly on the previous year's growth, the best shoots growing up from ground level. After flowering, cut out at ground

TIPS

- Species roses look best if allowed to grow naturally. Remove dead or overcrowded stems every few years. Cut them out as close to the base as you can get. The branches can be shortened if necessary but this destroys the graceful, arching shape of these plants.
- Postpone pruning roses with ornamental hips until late winter or early spring.

PRUNING CLIMBERS

1 Climbers should not be pruned when planting except to remove dead or very weak stems. If pruned they may develop a bush rather than a climbing habit. As the stems grow, tie them in. There may be a few flowers there the first summer. After flowering, or in midsummer, trim back sideshoots by half.

2 In subsequent years, cut back all sideshoots by about two-thirds, or back to two or three strong buds, in early spring. Do not prune the main stems. Cut back flowered sideshoots by half after flowering, to improve the quality of the second flush of bloom. Only remove main stems when they become unproductive. Cut out dead or diseased wood in late autumn or winter.

level the stems that have flowered and tie in the new growth to the support. If taking out flowered stems leaves you with too few new growths, apply the one-in-three rule (see Chapter 10, Pruning).

Renovating old rose bushes

If you take over a neglected garden, there are likely to be neglected rose bushes in it. Spindly bushes with all the leaf and flower at the top and climbers which only flower at gutter level need drastic treatment.

HOW? During the dormant season (late autumn to early spring) cut the whole plant down to 60cm (2ft) high.

- Remove all weak, dead or diseased shoots at the base.
- In spring, apply general fertilizer around the root area and mulch. Water if necessary.
- Early in the following spring, if new shoots have appeared, remove the weakest and retain the best.
- Continue to feed, weed and water.
- If the plant is making a good recovery, follow a normal pruning regime.

This is a matter of 'kill or cure' and you will lose a season's flowers. Success is a bonus, so do not blame yourself (or me) if the plant dies after all.

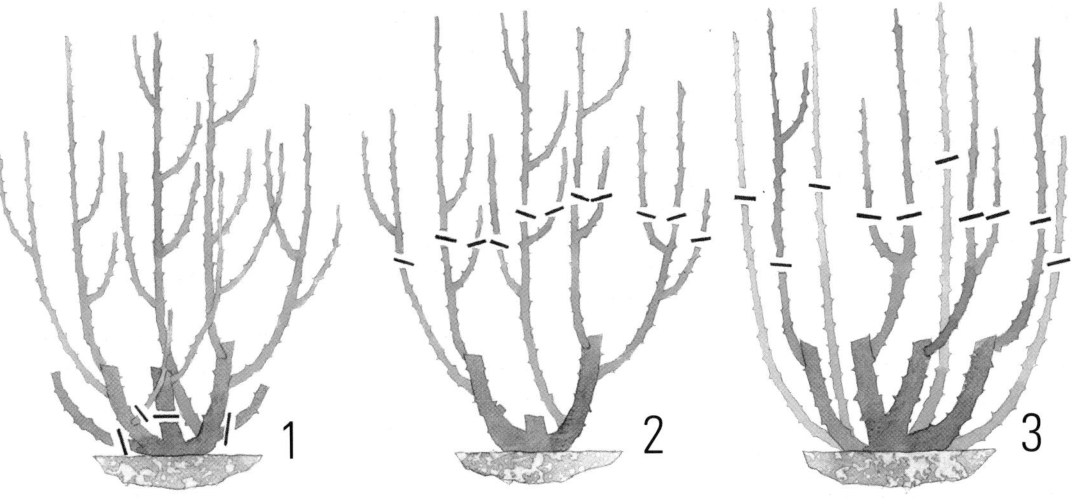

LARGE-FLOWERED BUSH AND CLUSTER-FLOWERED ROSES

1 In early spring, remove dead, weak and crossing branches.

2 For hybrid teas and hybrid perpetuals, cut back strong stems to about 30cm (1ft), or about six buds, always cutting to an outward facing bud. Cut back weaker stems to four buds to encourage stronger growth. If you cut back harder than this, you will get fewer, but larger blooms.

3 Hard annual pruning will eventually weaken floribundas. After removing dead, weak and crossing branches, cut back last season's basal shoots by just one-third. They are lighter in colour and more flexible. Cut back older wood to 30cm (1ft), as for hybrid teas. This ensures a succession of replacement growth.

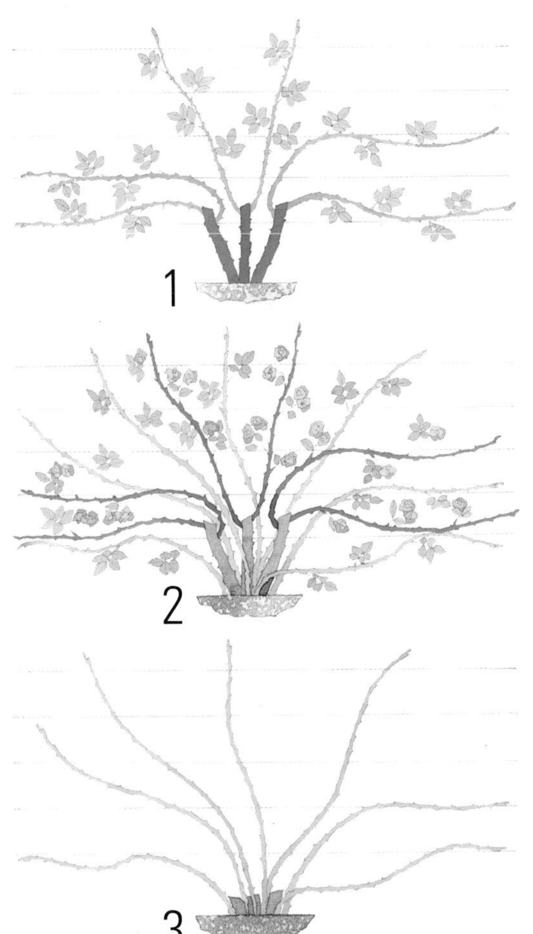

PRUNING RAMBLERS

1 On planting in autumn, cut back ramblers to three or four strong shoots. During spring and summer, long, flexible growths will be produced. As the shoots develop, tie them in to wires. There will be no flowers this season.

2 In the summer of the second year, last year's shoots will flower on sideshoots, and new shoots will emerge from the base of the plant.

3 After flowering cut out at the base the shoots that have flowered. Tie in the lengthening new shoots. These will bear next year's flowers. If only a few new shoots have emerged, retain some of the older shoots to fill in the space, and cut back their side shoots to two or three buds.

Dead-heading

Since most roses are not so obliging as to shed their faded petals after flowering, dead-heading with secateurs or sharp scissors is essential for the sake of appearance. Dead-heading also keeps the flowers coming, prolonging the flowering season.

'Dead-heading' is a rather misleading term; it is best to remove not just the flower head but also part of the stem bearing it, cutting back to just above the second leaf joint below the flower. Take the opportunity to cut back stems that spoil the shape of the bush. Towards the end of the summer leave the dead heads on those varieties which produce hips.

DEAD-HEADING LARGE-FLOWERED BUSH ROSES

1 Roses that produce a single flower on each flowering stem, such as hybrid teas, should be cut back to just above the second true leaf joint below the flower. The bud in this leaf axil will produce a second crop of flowers later in the season.

DEAD-HEADING CLUSTER-FLOWERED ROSES

2 Floribundas, which produce clusters of smaller flowers on each flowering stem, should also be cut back to just above the second true leaf joint below the flowerhead.

Growing Alpines

These brave little plants are (fairly obviously) known as alpines because many of them grow in the Alps. The term has been extended to embrace plants from high altitudes in all parts of the world and is also used loosely by gardeners for any low-growing plants that do well in rock gardens. Alpine plants include evergreen and deciduous shrubs, herbaceous perennials and bulbs.

The conditions in which true alpines grow are harsh. Above the tree line in mountain ranges like the Alps or the Himalayas they are subjected to strong winds and extremes of temperature. They often lie resting in darkness under an insulating layer of several feet of snow during the winter months. In spring, which comes late, and during the short summer, they are in brilliant light, hot sun and pure, dry air, usually with an abundant supply of clean, fresh meltwater that drains so quickly that it never gets a chance to become stagnant – quite a contrast to winter conditions in most gardens.

Alpines have responded to their native climate in various ways.

- Shrubs and perennials: low, creeping habit of growth, forming mats and cushions of foliage.
- Bulbous plants remain underground until the snows melt and the sun's warmth draws them out.
- Alpines tend to have deep roots, for anchorage and to penetrate cool nooks and crannies in search of moisture and nutrients.
- Many have fleshy, hairy or leathery leaves to protect them from water loss in sun and wind.
- Because they have to get all their flowering done during a short season many alpines flower very freely.
- The flower colours are often of a jewel-like brightness not found in other plants: the blue of gentians, for example. This helps attract insects quickly and reliably to ensure pollination and the setting of seed during the short summer.

Why grow alpines? Some people collect French Impressionists, some collect vintage cars, some collect beer mats and some collect alpine plants. They seem to be addictive for some gardeners.

Besides the beauty of the plants anything miniature has an undeniable fascination. Add the ability of alpines to thrive in a hostile environment, the possibility of building up a good collection in a relatively small space and the challenge of growing some of the more 'difficult' species, and you have a recipe for addiction.

Left Old lichen-covered flagstones colonized by *Campanula cochleariifolia* in the foreground and red valerian *(Centranthus ruber)* beyond.

Below *Helianthemum* (rock rose) seeds itself in paving cracks with gay abandon.

Left *Dianthus*, thymes and other alpines encroach prettily onto a path, softening its hard edge.

The first epidemic of alpine addiction spread when Victorian hikers botanized the Alps whilst in pursuit of sublime mountain views. The little treasures that came home in their sponge bags had to have a suitable home, and quarries did good business heaving outcrops of rock into suburban gardens to create mini-Alps.

Choosing a site

There are many suitable sites for alpines in today's small gardens besides the random heap of pieces of rough stone that all too often passes as a rock garden:

- An open situation where the air can circulate freely around them.
- A south or south-west aspect. Most alpines need sun for a good part of the day. Those that prefer a shady site can be planted on the shaded side of taller plants.
- Dappled shade. Alpines will not grow under dripping trees but some are happy in dappled shade cast by more distant trees.
- A north-facing slope. There are alpines adapted to north-facing slopes and sparse woodland, so if your only available site is north-facing you will still be able to grow a limited range of plants.
- A cool root run. Most alpines like to get their roots under stones or into the shade of other plants.
- Grown in raised beds or containers, troughs or pots, alpines give a great deal of pleasure to elderly or disabled gardeners.

Below The paving has almost disappeared under a carpet of alpine flowers.

Soil

On the mountains many alpines grow in next to no soil or very poor, stony soil. Some alpines need an acid or an alkaline soil, but many others are not fussy.

A recommended mix for raised beds and troughs is two parts of ordinary garden soil to one part of peat and one part of coarse sand or grit. If your garden soil is not 'ordinary' (medium loam), modify the recipe by reducing the amount of grit for light soil and increasing it for heavy soil.

If you are planting alpines straight into garden beds and borders, prepare the ground by digging in peat and grit, half and half.

Drainage

Good drainage is the paramount requirement for growing alpines: wet roots in winter mean death for many of them. If you are preparing raised beds or troughs, put in a good layer of stones or broken crocks at the bottom.

Landscaping

A raised bed or trough can never look like an Alp, but a few rocks strategically placed and a mulch of grit or stone chippings can make it look the sort of place alpine plants like to grow.

- Arrange rocks off-centre in the bed or trough.
- Make sure the bedding planes, if visible, all run in the same direction.
- Bury half to two-thirds of each rock.
- Don't overdo it. A group of three with perhaps one outlying rock is enough.

Rock garden

If your garden has a natural outcrop of stone or a bank of shale, you have the ideal environment for alpines. If such conditions do not occur naturally, it is possible to import them. A well-designed rock garden with really large pieces of stone deeply embedded in a slope according to their natural bedding planes is a thing of beauty. Douglas Knight's annual exhibit on the rock bank at Chelsea Flower Show is a fine example. But few gardens have the space and few gardeners or contractors the skill to create such a garden.

Raised beds

These make an excellent environment for alpine plants, bringing them closer to eye level so that they can be enjoyed in close-up.

If you are making a raised bed, decide whether you want to work at it standing, sitting or kneeling, and build it higher or lower accordingly. Tailor the bed to the space available and to the time you intend to spend working at it, making sure the back of the bed is within reach, if it is against a wall, and the centre, if it is free-standing. Be sure to build in drainage holes at the base of the wall.

Raised beds can be built of very nearly any material. Choose something that is in keeping with your house and the rest of your garden. If you use brick, consider topping it with a stone coping so that your colour range of plants is not restricted by the colour of the brick.

- Dry-stone retaining walls are ideal: grow plants in the vertical face of the wall as well as at the top.
- Breeze blocks can be scrubbed with diluted mud to tone them down; or plant small-leaved ivies at the base to climb up and disguise them.
- Peat blocks (sold by some alpine nurseries) can be used for low walls where acid-loving plants are to be grown.
- Turfs are the cheapest and most easily available material with which to construct a raised bed. Weedkill the grass and build with the grass side down, staggering joints as you would with a brick wall.

Paving and the ground

Ideal conditions are often found in a paved area.

- Crazy paving usually has suitable crevices to tuck plants into. If you are laying flagstones, position them in a random pattern leaving small gaps here and there and do not mortar the joints.

Above A whimsical container made from hypertufa.

Left Phlox subulata softens a flight of stone steps.

Grey or buff stone makes the most pleasing background for plants. Avoid paving tinted green or pink at all costs.

- Brick colours clash with some of the hot pinks, reds and magentas of alpine flowers, but the small scale of brick paving makes it ideal in other respects. In existing brick paving random bricks can be lifted to accommodate a plant.
- Gravel, either laid specifically for alpines, or on a seating area or path, suits alpines well. It provides good drainage and protects the plants from mud splashes. Plant informally around the perimeter leaving space at the centre to walk down the path or reach the seat.
- Troughs, old sinks, shallow pots and terracotta pans all make good homes for alpines, provided that you have easy access to water. A range of different shapes and sizes look attractive together and some or all can be raised to different heights on bricks or blocks. Stone troughs are expensive to buy but DIYers can make acceptable substitutes out of 'hypertufa' (see panel below).

Beds and borders

If you have very free-draining soil none of these special environments is necessary: plant your alpines at the front of borders.

DESIGN TIP

Young plants from the garden centre or nursery are tiny and it is tempting to plant them too close initially. Resist the temptation or the effect will be spoiled when they begin to crowd each other. Fill the gaps with dwarf bulbs and plants like small violas, thymes and camomile which can have an afterlife elsewhere.

Making a Hypertufa Trough

- Either make a rectangular timber mould to the size required or use two stout cardboard boxes, a smaller inside a larger.
- Put pieces of potato at the bottom of the mould or of the large box. They are to make drainage holes and will be removed after the hypertufa has been poured and set.
- For reinforcement, line the mould or the space between the boxes with chicken wire.
- Mix the hypertufa: one part sand, one cement and two sphagnum peat mixed with water.
- Pour it into the mould.
- When the hypertufa has set, dismantle the mould and remove the potatoes to leave drainage holes.

TIPS

- You need to be able to reach the back of the bed to plant, weed and generally titivate your plants.
- Building a dry-stone wall may look easy but it is really not a job for the average DIY practitioner. The craft has been revived in recent years, and it is worth getting a skilled waller to do the job.

Greenhouse

If you become a collector, you will acquire some alpine treasures that need special protection. Grow them in pots and keep them in a well-ventilated cold greenhouse. In an ordinary greenhouse, you will probably have to introduce additional side vents.

Buying, planting and maintaining

Buying alpines

When choosing alpines in garden centres or nurseries:

- Look for plants with dense, healthy foliage growing in weed-free moist compost.
- Avoid plants with yellowing, brown or withered leaves, leggy growth and those with roots coming out of the base of the pot.

GARDEN CENTRES are a good source for a starter collection, but although the range of alpine plants in the average garden centre is impressive, it only scratches the surface.

SPECIALIST NURSERIES cultivate a vast range of alpines. If you buy from them you have the added advantage of expert advice on cultivation.

Planting alpines

WHEN? Plant alpines in early autumn or in spring.

HOW?
- Water the plants thoroughly an hour before planting.
- Remove the top 0.5-1.25cm (1/4-1/2in) of soil from around the plant in its pot, carefully, taking any moss or weeds off with it.
- With a trowel make a hole 8cm (3in) wider than the plant's root ball.
- Put the plant in the hole to the same depth as it was in the pot.
- Firm soil around it.
- Top dress with grit, heaping a little around the neck of the plant.
- Water during dry spells.

Looking after alpines

HOW?
- Water when necessary in summer, taking care not to overdo it.
- Hand weed vigilantly: young alpines are small and fragile and one aggressive dandelion or thistle can do a lot of damage.
- Dead head flowering plants, using nail scissors for the tiniest.
- In spring and again after flowering, trim over straggly plants like helianthemums to keep them dense and bushy.
- In wet winters, cover the more fragile plants with open-ended cloches to keep the rain out.
- Every autumn, top dress with grit.
- Every third year add a little bonemeal to the top dressing.
- Never overfeed alpines, they will become lush, straggly and out of character – they thrive on a lean diet.

Below It may be stretching a point to describe the lobelias growing in this wall as alpines, but many alpine plants would enjoy the same conditions, and it would be an unusual way to display them.

Choosing alpines

The plants listed below are not difficult to grow and a choice made from them will prove a good introduction to alpines. They include some plants that are not recognized as particularly good rock garden plants but mix well with the genuine article.

Decide whether, with your choice of alpines, you want to make a big impact for a short season or have something interesting to see all the year round, and customize your shopping list accordingly. Decide too whether you want to work to a definite colour scheme or make a Joseph's Coat of plants. Many alpines are slow growing and will take several years to reach their mature size.

Almost any grouping of plants benefits from vertical accents, and this particularly applies in the case of alpines which tend to form low cushions and hummocks, producing a monotonous effect if unrelieved by a contrasting shape. The indiscriminate use of dwarf conifers produces a spotty effect, but a few used with discretion give the vertical accent that is needed. A group of three slender *Juniperus communis* 'Compressa' or a single broad pyramid of *Chamaecyparis obtusa* 'Nana Gracilis' rising behind or opposite the group of rocks will do the trick.

Left Saxifraga oppositifolia, a ground-hugging evergreen needing shade at midday.

Left Saxifraga 'Peter Pan', a compact mossy saxifrage, just one of many varieties to choose from.

Left Aubrieta, one of the easiest and most popular alpine plants.

Left Phlox douglasii 'Crackerjack'. Alpine phloxes are a mass of colour in early summer.

Spring flowering

Aethionema 'Warley Rose' 15x38cm (6x15in). A mat-forming evergreen with grey-green leaves and dark pink flowers in late spring.

Androsace sempervivoïdes 5x25cm (2x10in). Flat rosettes of bright green leaves, clusters of bright pink flowers in late spring and early summer.

Arabis ferdinandi-coburgi 'Variegata' 8x15cm (3x6in). Evergreen mat of small, cream-splashed light green leaves with small white flowers in clusters.

Aubrieta 10x20cm (4x8in). Sometimes invasive but always easy and very reliable. Good hanging from walls. Choose when in flower to obtain the unusual shades of blue, violet and red-purple.

Erysimum 15x30cm (6x12in). Perennial wallflowers, mat-forming. 'Jubilee Gold' is bright yellow, 'Moonlight' soft, pale yellow and 'Rufus' rusty red. 'Sprite' makes a primrose yellow carpet 7cm (3in) high. Poor, well-drained soil in full sun.

Phlox douglasii 'Crackerjack' 5x20cm (2x8in). A compact cushion of evergreen linear leaves smothered in magenta crimson, single flowers from late spring to early summer. Cut back after flowering.

Phlox subulata 'G.F. Wilson' 8x20cm (3x8in). Neat leaves are invisible beneath the mass of mauve-blue flowers in mid- to late spring. Other good varieties: 'Oakington Blue Eyes', 'White Delight'. Cut back after flowering.

Primula marginata 10x20cm (4x15in). Mauve-blue flowers in clusters above a rosette of silver-edged green leaves dusted with white. Likes alkaline soil.

Saxifraga x *apiculata* 10x20cm (4x15in). Tight cushions of evergreen leaves, clusters of pale

TIP

Plant small bulbs in raised beds or crevices at the top of a wall where their delicate flowers can be seen in close-up. They take up very little space in the garden and are the earliest plants in flower.

yellow flowers from early to mid-spring. Needs semi-shade.

Saxifraga x *elisabethiae* 2.5x10cm (1x4in). Tight evergreen cushion, bright yellow flowers. Needs semi-shade.

Saxifraga 'Jenkinsiae' 8x15cm (3x6in). Large, open, cup-shaped, pale pink flowers are borne on tight grey-green cushions. Grows best in semi-shade.

Saxifraga oppositifolia 2.5-5x15cm (1-2x6in). Prostrate evergreen with flowers varying from dark purple to pink. Protect from midday sun.

Saxifraga 'Peter Pan' 8x20cm (3x8in). A dwarf, dark green, mossy saxifrage (the dense, cut and curled leaves look like moss) with crimson flowers fading to pink. Best in light shade and alkaline soil. There are many more saxifrages to choose from, mostly flowering late spring. Make your choice when they are in flower from a supplier who can advise on cultivation.

Right Tulipa praestans 'Fusilier', one of many small tulips suitable for rock and alpine gardens.

Right Crocus chrysanthus 'E.A.Bowles' *(right)* and *Crocus tommasinianus (below right)* are in flower before winter ends. Plant them to grow up through later-flowering alpines.

Spring bulbs to grow with alpines

There is a wide choice of crocuses: the delicate looks of winter-flowering species and their hybrids associate better with alpines than the fat Dutch hybrids.

Crocus chrysanthus 'E.A. Bowles' 8cm (3in). Yellow, bronzed at base, scented, very early.

Crocus chrysanthus 'Snow Bunting' 8cm (3in). White with narrow purple stripes, scented, very early.

Crocus tommasinianus 8cm (3in). Violet purple, very early.

Ipheion uniflorum 'Wisley Blue' 15cm (6in). Mauve-blue, upward-facing, star-shaped flowers in mid- to late spring.

Iris danfordiae 8cm (3in). Yellow, flowers very early. Plant bulbs deep for success.

Iris reticulata 15cm (6in). Grass-like leaves and delicate, violet-purple, iris flowers with yellow ridges on the falls. Very early. Pale blue, dark blue and red-purple varieties are available.

Narcissus bulbocodium 10cm (4in). Golden yellow, very early. The hoop-petticoat daffodil has a bell-shaped trumpet and small, narrow outer petals. Ssp. *bulbocodium* var. 'Citrinus' has pale lemon flowers.

Narcissus cyclamineus 15cm (6in). Golden yellow flowers with outer petals swept back like those of a cyclamen. Very early.

Narcissus canaliculatus 23cm (9in). Several flowers on each stem, back-swept white petals with short yellow trumpet, scented. Mid-spring.

Narcissus triandrus (Angel's Tears) 12cm (5in). The trumpet is like a tear drop and the narrow petals are back-swept.

Puschkinia var. *libanotica* 15cm (6in). Dense spikes of star-shaped flowers, very pale blue with narrow dark blue stripes on each petal. Strap-shaped leaves.

Tulipa praestans 'Fusilier' 30cm (12in). Several scarlet flowers are held on each stem above grey-green leaves. Early.

Tulipa tarda 15cm (6in). Several glistening, white-tipped, yellow flowers on each stem.

Early summer flowering

Alchemilla alpina 15x30cm (6x12in). Miniature lady's mantle with milky green, rounded leaves and sprays of tiny yellow-green flowers. Plants offered as this are often *Alchemilla conjuncta*, which are very similar in effect.

Antennaria dioica 2.5x40cm (1x16in). A mat of tiny, greyish, woolly leaves with fluffy white flowerheads. 'Nyewoods Variety' is compact with deep rose-pink flowers.

Aquilegia alpina 'Hensol Harebell' 20-30cm (8-12in). A deep mauve-blue columbine with soft blue-green, fine-cut leaves.

Aquilegia bertolonii 10-15cm (4-6in). Miniature in everything except the flowers, which are 5cm (2in) long and a rich purple blue. The rounded leaves are grey-green.

Aquilegia flabellata var. *nana* 15cm (6in). The flowers are soft light blue and white over grey-green, deeply dissected leaves.

Aquilegia fragrans 15-40cm (6-16in). The pale cream flowers are scented. Needs shade.

Campanula cochleariifolia (*C. pusilla*) 8cm (3in) high and indefinite spread. Creeping mats of tiny round leaves produce rounded, pale blue or lavender, bell flowers whimsically known as fairy thimbles.

Dianthus alpinus 'Joan's Blood' 6x15cm (2½x6in). Glowing, blood red flowers on a cushion of bronze-tinged leaves.

Dianthus deltoïdes 'Brilliant' 15x15cm (6x6in). An evergreen mat with lots of small, flat, brilliant crimson flowers.

Dianthus gratianopolitanus 15x30cm (6x12in). The native Cheddar pink has evergreen greyish leaves and scented, single pale pink flowers.

Dianthus 'Nyewoods Cream' 8x15cm (3x6in). Cream flowers on dense blue-grey cushions.

Dianthus 'Pikes Pink' 10x15cm (4x6in). Of the many delightful pinks for the rock garden this is one of the best. The scented double flowers are borne all summer over a cushion of spiky grey-green leaves.

Dryas octopetala 6cm (2½in) high, spread indefinite. An evergreen mat of leathery, dark green leaves with creamy anemone-like flowers followed by attractive seed heads.

Gypsophila cerastioïdes 2x10cm (¾x4in). Not at all like the gypsophila of the herbaceous border. This one has small mats of rounded velvety leaves and white saucer-shaped flowers with fine purple veins radiating from the centre.

Helianthemum 20x30cm (8x12in). Rock roses spread quickly to form a mat and are well suited to walls, paving and the fronts of borders. Give them space so that they don't smother smaller plants. They are shrubby plants with plentiful small leaves varying in colour from dark green to grey. The flowers are shaped like small wild roses with petals like thin, crumpled silk. Colours range from crimson to orange, yellow and white. Among the best are 'Alice Howarth': semi-double, mulberry crimson flowers, green leaves;

Above Campanula cochleariifolia, a prostrate campanula, spreading indefinitely but never invasive.

Below Lithodora diffusa (Lithospermum diffusum) 'Heavenly Blue', as good as its name, but not for alkaline soil.

Above Helianthemum nummularium 'The Bride', just one of many colourful rock roses.

Below Thymus 'Doone Valley'. Thymes are invaluable carpeting plants, though fairly short-lived.

Bottom Gypsophila cerastioïdes, pretty and very prostrate, best seen creeping over a rock.

'Rose of Leeswood': double pink, grey green leaves; 'Henfield Brilliant': deep flame-orange flowers and grey leaves; 'Amy Baring': apricot yellow, green leaves, compact growth; 'Wisley Primrose': primrose yellow with grey leaves; 'The Bride': white flowers, silver-grey leaves. Clip over the plants with shears after flowering to encourage dense, tidy growth.

Lithodora diffusa (*Lithospermum diffusum*) 'Heavenly Blue'. Evergreen sub-shrub with tidy little hairy leaves and masses of small, true blue flowers. Cut back hard after flowering. Hates lime.

Mazus reptans 5x30cm (2x12in) or more. Forms a spreading mat of toothed green leaves. The strangely shaped, light purple flowers have red and yellow spotted lips. 'Albus' is a white form.

Saxifraga paniculata (*S. aïzoön*) var. 'Baldensis' 4x8cm (1 1/2x3in). Hard little cushions of silver rosettes, small white flowers.

Saxifraga 'Rosea' 15x15cm (6x6in). Rosettes of grey-green leaves and sprays of pink flowers.

Sedum spathulifolium 'Cape Blanco' 5cm (2in) high, indefinite spread. Evergreen with flat rosettes of fleshy silver grey sometimes flushed with purple. Clusters of tiny yellow flowers.

Sedum spurium 'Fuldaglut' 10cm (4in) high, spread indefinite. Deep purple fleshy leaves, bright pink flowers. Good to drape over the edge of a wall or trough.

Sempervivum arachnoïdeum ssp. *tomentosum* ('Laggeri') 8x10cm (3x4in). One of the most intriguing of the house leeks, a family more curious than beautiful, but gardeners do get hooked on them. They sometimes colonize the tiled roofs of old houses, hence the name. This one forms a mat of fleshy-leaved rosettes rather like globe artichokes. The red leaf tips are covered with a web of white hairs. Other recommended sempervivums are *S. giuseppii, S. grandiflorum* and 'Commander Hay'.

Thymus 'Doone Valley' 12x20cm (5x8in). Evergreen mat of dark green, gold-flecked leaves. Mauve flowers. All thymes should be clipped over after flowering to prevent them becoming straggly.

The following thymes are prostrate and good carpeters for paving or gravel or as a background to other plants. Mix them at random for a tapestry effect:

Thymus pseudolanuginosus 5x20cm (2x8in). Minute furry grey leaves, pale pink flowers.

Thymus serpyllum albus 5x20cm (2x8in). Fresh bright green leaves, pure white flowers; *coccineus* 5x20cm (2x8in), dark crimson flowers; 'Pink Chintz' 5x20cm (2x8in), greyish leaves, lilac-pink flowers.

Veronica prostrata 'Kapitan' up to 30cm (1ft) high, indefinite spread. Vibrant true blue flowers on erect spikes on a mat-forming plant. *V. p.* 'Trehane' 15cm (6in), indefinite spread, has similar flowers but yellow-green leaves.

Mid- to late summer

Campanula garganica 5x30cm (2x12in). Blue, star-shaped bell flowers are borne along stems with small ivy-shaped leaves. Good in or on walls.

Campanula 'Birch Hybrid' 10x30cm (4x12in). A vigorous, free-flowering plant with violet bell-shaped flowers all summer above a mat of small evergreen leaves.

Dianthus 'Little Jock' 10x10cm (4x4in). One of the best dwarf pinks, with strongly scented, pale pink flowers with crimson eyes.

Diascia 'Ruby Field' 8x15cm (3x6in). Pretty, pale green leaves set off the soft salmon pink, (not ruby) tubular flowers. Like other diascias, it flowers on and on all summer. It may not be entirely hardy.

Gentiana septemfida 20x30cm (8x12in). Gentians are not the easiest plants to grow but don't let anyone tell you that other blue-flowered plants will do instead. There is no colour in the plant world like gentian blue. This one is the easiest. Needs humus-rich soil, acid or alkaline.

Gentiana sino-ornata 5x30cm (2x12in). The best of the autumn-flowering gentians (from August to October). The trumpet flowers are that rich blue which has both brilliance and depth. Needs moist soil, hates lime.

Geranium cinereum 'Ballerina' 10x30cm (4x12in). The soft greyish leaves are round and deeply divided. The mauve-pink cup-shaped flowers have deep purple veins and centres. In flower all summer and good in any sunny position.

Geranium cinereum var. *subcaulescens* 10x30cm (4x12in). Similar to 'Ballerina' but with startlingly brilliant magenta flowers with black veins and centres.

Geranium dalmaticum 10x20cm (4x8in). Evergreen, dark green divided leaves and shell pink flowers. Sun or light shade.

Hypericum olympicum 'Citrinum' 15-30x15-30cm (6-12x6-12in). A mound of blue-green leaves, covered in wide open, pale lemon-yellow flowers all summer long.

Nierembergia repens 5x20cm (2x8in). Large white, open bell-shaped flowers, which last all summer, on a mat of small light green leaves.

Papaver alpinum 10cm (4in). Fragile-looking miniature poppies in white, pink, yellow and orange above tufts of grey leaves. They are short-lived perennials but will seed themselves. Sun and good drainage essential.

Potentilla x *tonguei* 5x25cm (2x10in). Rounded, lobed leaves and orange-yellow flowers with red centres on prostrate branches throughout the summer.

Above *Anthemis punctata* ssp. *cupaniana* rapidly forms a dense mat of finely cut silvery leaves and is covered with daisy flowers throughout the summer.

Left *Acaena microphylla*, one of a family of close-carpeting foliage plants from New Zealand.

Viola Good value as they flower over a long period, many violas need a cool, moist site and some shade, so are not well suited to raised beds or troughs. The following are happy in the sunny, well-drained conditions that most alpines enjoy:
'Bowles' Black' 10x8cm (4x3in). Darkest violet-black, velvet, miniature pansy flowering non-stop from spring to autumn. It is short-lived so it is not your fault if it vanishes after the first year. Raise more from seed or hope that it will seed itself.
'Haslemere' 10x15cm (4x6in). Delicate pinkish-mauve flowers. Needs moisture.
'Huntercombe Purple' 10x20cm (4x8in). Ever-widening clumps of rich violet flowers from spring to late summer. Can be increased by division.

Foliage

Many of the plants listed above have attractive, weed-suppressing foliage. A few others which are outstanding in this respect are:

Acaena microphylla 5x45cm (2x18in). An evergreen carpet of small bronze-greeny leaves is enlivened in autumn by spiky crimson burrs. *Acaena* 'Blue Haze' spreads wider and has steel-blue toothed leaves and dark red burrs.

Anthemis punctata ssp. *cupaniana* 30x45cm (12x18in). A mat of dense, finely cut, silver filigree, evergreen leaves with white daisy flowers as a bonus. Don't let it smother smaller plants.

Hedera helix ssp. *helix* 'Congesta' 45x60cm (18x24in). An interesting ivy that does not climb. Small, slightly twisted leaves are held on erect stems. Use it for vertical effect instead of dwarf conifers.

Hedera helix ssp. *helix* 'Little Diamond'. A grey and white variegated ivy with small diamond-shaped leaves. Graceful, slow ground cover.

There are many more compact, small-leaved ivies, including the tiny 'Spetchley', which would suit the smallest trough or pot. Others make good ground cover in raised beds, soften the stonework in rock gardens and drape over the sides of walls and troughs. Visit a specialist supplier to choose.

Top right Gentiana septemfida, everyone's idea of a classic alpine plant.

Centre right Geranium dalmaticum, a prostrate hardy geranium, evergreen in all but the coldest winters.

Right Nierembergia repens, not 100 per cent hardy, so protect with a cloche or pane of glass in winter.

Writing about alpines makes me long to see them growing in the wild again. There are few thrills to beat the first sighting of a gentian at the snow line, and then the discovery of more, and more and more. The alpine area of the garden is a reminder of such moments.

Growing Herbs

The Concise Oxford Dictionary defines herb as a 'plant of which leaves etc. are used for food, medicine, scent, flavour, etc.'. The latter 'et cetera' includes cosmetics, drinks, dyes, cleansers, insect repellents, preservatives, disinfectants and decorations.

Today, herbs are more likely to be found in the kitchen than in the bathroom or the medicine chest, and out of the great number that can be grown in the garden, most cooks will only use perhaps half-a-dozen. They will probably have been bought from the grocer or supermarket, dried, in jars or packets. There is a world of difference between the flavour of dried herbs and that of herbs freshly picked in the garden and added immediately to salad or saucepan.

Some culinary herbs are three-star decorative garden plants as well as essential ingredients in certain dishes. There are other highly valued ornamental plants which rate as herbs because of their scented flowers or foliage: lavender, cotton lavender (santolina) and artemisia fall into this category. Even if you don't get round to making lavender bags, or infusing lavender flowers to make a cure for acne, flatulence or halitosis, you will want a few plants in your garden to set off the roses and attract bees and butterflies.

Herbs and their history can be a fascinating subject. Did you know, for example, that southernwood (*Artemisia abrotanum*) planted near hen houses will deter lice, or that an infusion of oregano can prevent seasickness and relieve gall bladder disorders?

Layout and design

A seat in an enclosed herb garden on a sunny day is almost guaranteed to induce a mood of tranquil contentment. There is something soothing about herbs.

Most herbal plants have attractive foliage and modest flowers with gentle colouring. If the herb garden is well planned, your feet will release the scent of thyme and camomile, and from your seat you will be able to reach out and crush the aromatic leaves of cotton lavender, myrtle or sweetbrier. The soothing buzzing of bees working the flowers of hyssop, monarda and catmint induces meditation, and you will be mesmerized by the fluttering of butterflies on calamint and marjoram.

Part of the pleasure of a herb garden lies in the close intimacy that one can develop with the plants, and it is easier to achieve this in a small area than a large one.

Traditional herb gardens have geometric layouts, varying from a simple square divided by crossing paths to elaborate interwoven knot patterns outlined in clipped box, santolina or teucrium. Vertical interest is often provided by

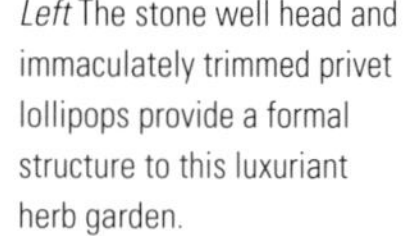

Left The stone well head and immaculately trimmed privet lollipops provide a formal structure to this luxuriant herb garden.

TIP

Seeds of annual and biennial herbs like chervil, coriander, dill, parsley and summer savory can be sown in pots in late summer to grow indoors for a winter supply. Provided the herbs have plenty of light they will grow on to give a cut-and-come-again supply for many weeks.

Above Many herbs have beautiful foliage, green, golden or silver. They are also a source of nectar for bees.

Far right In this informal herb garden the apparently random mixture of brick, stone and plants is in fact the result of careful planning to achieve balance between the different elements.

box topiary or by a bay tree neatly clipped to form a lollipop or pyramid. But an informal herb garden with paths winding to conceal and then reveal plant groups can be just as effective.

Essential requirements

SHELTER Enclose the herb garden with walls, hedges or trellises. If that is not possible, try and protect the herbs by a wall or hedge on the north and east sides. Even a low hedge of lavender or rosemary will give shelter to low-growing and medium-sized herbs. In mixed borders small groups of herbs can be planted on the south side of evergreen shrubs.

SUN A southerly aspect is the ideal.

GOOD DRAINAGE To improve drainage on clay soils dig plenty of grit and organic material like mushroom compost into the bed before planting.

Choosing a site

Herbs need not be set apart in a garden of their own. Most shrubby and herbaceous herbs associate well with other plants in mixed borders and are particularly compatible with shrub roses.

Make use of their decorative qualities when you are planning a mixed planting scheme. If you become addicted to herbs, they are liable to take over, and other plants will start to play a secondary role.

THE VEGETABLE GARDEN Keen cooks may prefer to grow some of their herbs lined out in rows in the vegetable garden to make harvesting that bit easier.

NEAR THE KITCHEN Culinary herbs used most regularly are best positioned within easy reach of the kitchen in order to avoid a trek through mud and rain every time your recipe demands a bouquet garni. The ones most frequently used in cooking are mint, bay, rosemary, sage, thyme, tarragon, parsley, chives and savoury.

SHADE There are a few herbs that are happy in shade: even in a north-facing town garden you can grow chives, mint and parsley.

Using Herbs in the Ornamental Garden

Plants to grow with herbs

Fruit trees, roses, honeysuckle, traditional cottage garden plants, small bulbs to provide interest early in the year.

Herbs to grow in mixed borders

Statuesque herbs for the back row: fennel (feathery foliage) and angelica (striking, lime-yellow, umbrella flowers).

Edging herbs for formal beds or as informal front-row groups: chives, parsley, wild strawberries and hyssop.

Herbs for paving and gravel

Thyme (low, creeping varieties), camomile. Both will survive being walked over occasionally and have a softening effect on paved surfaces.

CONTAINERS Many herbs can successfully be grown in containers: a window box on a sunny kitchen windowsill can provide the cook with fresh herbs within arm's length of the stove. Patios, balconies and roof gardens often provide the right sun-baked conditions for herbs and, grouped in terracotta pots of different shapes and sizes, they make a pleasant sight.

Planting

WHEN? Winter is the best time to lay paths and paving, and prepare the soil, if you are planning a herb garden from scratch, while spring is usually the best time for planting herbs. However, herbs in containers can be bought and transplanted to garden, window box or pot at any time from spring to autumn.

For herbs grown from seed, see the list below for individual planting times.

The demand for herbs in the kitchen is not reduced during winter, but the supply from the garden is. To get over this problem, essential herbs can be cut back, dug up, potted into compost and brought indoors in autumn. Chives, mint and marjoram respond to this treatment.

HOW? Each herb plant falls into one of the normal categories of shrub, herbaceous perennial, biennial, annual or bulb, and the methods of cultivation and propagation are described in Parts 1 and 2. Any special treatment needed is noted in the list of herbs that follows.

Choosing herbs

The list below includes the most useful culinary herbs and others which merit a place in any garden for their decorative qualities, scent or ability to attract bees, butterflies and other pollinating insects.

Shrubs

Bay *Laurus nobilis* Bay will grow into a handsome evergreen tree 7m (23ft) high in mild districts. It is often seen trained and clipped into a lollipop or pyramid, and makes a fine pot plant. Sun, shelter, rich soil. Propagate from cuttings or layers taken in late summer.
Uses: a single bay leaf makes all the difference to meat and fish dishes. Classic component of bouquet garni. Infuse in milk for custards and puddings. Bay topiary can be decorated as an alternative to Christmas trees.

Curry plant *Helichrysum italicum (angustifolium)* A pretty, evergreen grey-leaved shrub, but not reliably hardy. The downy silver leaves are soft to the touch and needle-thin. When crushed they smell of curry. Clip over in spring to make a tidy edging or knot garden plant. As an insurance against loss in hard winters, take cuttings in summer. Sheltered position in full sun and well-drained soil.
Uses: mainly decorative, but the leaves can be used to flavour soups and stews.

Hyssop *Hyssopus officinalis* Another tidy evergreen which can be clipped to edge borders or to form knot-garden patterns. Set out 25-30cm (10-12in) apart. Prune hard in spring. Rich blue flowers on spikes from midsummer on are often covered with bees and butterflies. There are also pink- and white-flowered forms. Sun, alkaline soil.
Uses: the bitter-flavoured leaves can be used in game dishes. If grown near cabbages, hyssop may distract cabbage-white butterflies from their primary target.

Lavender *Lavandula angustifolia* Lavender has a long history of cultivation for the perfume industry. Bushy spikes of narrow grey or grey-green leaves. Flower heads in various shades of blue and mauve (also pink and white in some varieties) at the top of slender bare stalks. Sun, alkaline soil and good drainage. Annual pruning with shears in late autumn or early spring is essential to prevent the plants becoming leggy. Remove only the current year's growth, avoid cutting into old wood.
Uses: the flower stems can be cut, dried and stripped to fill muslin sachets to scent drawers and cupboards and keep away clothes moths. Important ingredient in potpourri. Lavender tea has a calming effect.

Marjoram *Origanum* Dense cushions of rounded leaves. Clusters of small white, pink or purple-pink flowers in mid- and late summer on branching, wiry stems. Marjorams are easily propagated by pulling off rooted stems in spring or autumn and potting them up or replanting them straight into their new site. All marjorams are attractive in flower and loved by bees and butterflies. *O. vulgare* 'Aureum' is a low-growing (25-30 / 9-12in), yellow-leaved form for the front of a border, the top of a wall or between paving stones. The leaves may scorch if not shaded from the midday sun. Sun, alkaline soil and good drainage.
Uses: the leaves are good in fish and meat dishes (add during last minutes of cooking) and can be chewed to relieve toothache.

Rosemary *Rosmarinus officinalis* Dark, grey-green aromatic leaves, spikes of mauve-blue flowers in early spring and sporadically until autumn. Rosemary reaches 2m (7ft), more if grown against a wall, and a width of 1.8m (6ft). The best variety for a hedge is 'Miss Jessopp's Upright'. Straggly bushes or those which have outgrown their space can have all branches shortened by half in spring. Sun, good drainage. Alkaline soil increases its fragrance.
Uses: Tuck a sprig under a joint of lamb or inside a chicken before roasting, or burn branches on a barbecue. Traditional component of wedding bouquets.

Rue *Ruta graveolens* Nowadays rue is not much used as a kitchen herb but grown for its ornamental foliage. The leaves are soft and

Above Golden sage (*Salvia officinalis* 'Icterina') is an invaluable evergreen shrub, forming low mounds of soft yellow and grey-green foliage.

Above *Santolina pinnata* ssp. *neapolitana* 'Edward Bowles'. A refined variety of the ever-grey cotton lavender, with pale primrose button flowers.

Left Hyssop *(Hyssopus officinalis)* carries spires of true-blue flowers from mid- to late summer.

Above Lavandula angustifolia 'Rosea', a pink form of lavender, one of the most familiar herbs.

rounded, of a unique blue-green shade. The bluest is 'Jackman's Blue'. Keep the plants bushy at a height of about 45cm (18in) by clipping over them every year in late spring. The yellow flowers are not particularly desirable and can be removed.

TIPS

- Bay is susceptible to frost when young. Grow it in a pot and bring inside during severe weather.
- There is a tradition that rosemary, the herb of remembrance, should be grown from a cutting given by a friend, and this is not difficult to observe since cuttings root easily. If taken in early autumn or late spring, they can be pushed straight into their permanent site.

WARNING *Handling rue leaves may cause a serious skin rash.*

Sage *Salvia officinalis* There are three good forms, each with a different leaf colour or variegation, all worth growing at the front of a border or billowing out onto paths and paving. The leaves of the common sage are a soft, greyish green. 'Purpurascens Variegata' is grey flushed with purple, and 'Icterina' has creamy gold variegation on green. Up to 60cm (24in) high by 80cm (30in) wide, needs firm pruning every autumn (spring in cold areas) to keep it bushy. Plants need replacing after four or five years. Sun, light, even poor soil. Easy from summer cuttings, they often layer themselves without any help.
Uses: sage and onion stuffing is a classic with pork, goose or duck. Fry whole leaves crisp to serve with liver.

Santolina (cotton lavender) *Santolina chamaecyparissus* is one of the lightest and brightest silver-leaved plants. It forms a low mound 45cm (18in) high by 80cm (30in) wide. Use the dwarf var. 'Nana' for knots and edgings. Its tight, serrated, woolly spikes form a dense little bush 30x45cm (12x18in). *S. pinnata* ssp. *neapolitana* is graceful with looser, feathery foliage. Cut off the untidy stems of mustard-yellow button flowers, unless you can find 'Sulphurea' which has flowers of a delicate primrose shade.
Uses: add the aromatic leaves to potpourri. Branches in cupboards deter clothes moths.

Thyme *Thymus* Dense creeping branches form mats of tiny leaves in various colours, flowers in shades from purplish crimson to white. Plant a Shakespearean 'bank where the wild thyme blows', a thyme-covered seat or a carpet, using the shorter varieties with the colours of leaves and flowers mixed at random. Sun, well-drained, preferably alkaline soil. Clip with shears or lightly mow two or three times during the summer to keep them dense.
Uses: A good bee plant. In the kitchen it is a component of bouquet garni and associates well with poultry, shellfish and mushrooms.

Right Thymes grow happily in the well-drained conditions on a gravel path. Behind them, pot marigolds and an edging of *Santolina chamaecyparissus* 'Nana'.

Perennials

Camomile *Chamaemelum nobile* An evergreen with aromatic, bright green, fine, feathery leaves, camomile creeps along the ground rooting as it goes. The scent is delicious – kneeling on a camomile lawn to weed it is a heady experience. It is one of the most therapeutic of all garden scents. The variety 'Treneague' does not flower and is low and compact, therefore best for lawns or growing in cracks between paving or making a camomile seat. The species has small white daisy flowers and *C. n.* 'Flore Pleno' has very pretty cream double flowers. Buy and plant small rooted pieces in spring 15cm (6in) apart. A camomile carpet needs weeding carefully until the plants knit together, then becomes fairly trouble-free. Mow or clip over once or twice a year. To increase, pull the roots apart and replant each piece. Sun, well-drained soil. Uses: the flowers can be steeped in boiling water to make a rinse for blonde hair, a sedative nightcap or a lotion to relieve the pain of sunburn.

Catmint *Nepeta* x *faassenii* Mounds of soft grey foliage and lavender flower spikes carried throughout the summer months make catmint invaluable in any sunny or slightly shaded part of the garden. *N.* x *faassenii*, 30-45cm (12-18in) high, and the larger variety 'Six Hills Giant' are good edging plants. Lovely with old roses and against brick paving. The pale-yellow-flowered *N. govaniana* is seldom seen and well worth growing. Cut down the stems when the first lot of flowers fade; a fresh crop will soon develop and keep going well into autumn. Sun or light shade, well-drained soil.
Uses: nectar plant for bees and insects. Infusions of the leaves are a source of vitamin C.

Fennel *Foeniculum vulgare* The soft plumes of thread-like leaves make fennel one of the most decorative tall herbs for the border, particularly in its bronze-leaved form. The broad, yellow, upturned umbrella flowers reach 2.1m (7ft). Grow from seed sown in spring or propagate by dividing the roots, planting the pieces 30-45cm (12-15in) apart. Sun or partial shade. Uses: the leaves and seeds have an affinity with fish. The Romans ate fennel as a slimming aid.

Lovage *Levisticum officinale* Another stately umbellifer, to 2m (7ft), leaves similar to celery but dark green. Yellow-green flowers in dense clusters. Once you have a plant it will self-seed. Sun or partial shade.

TIP

In autumn, cut down fennel stems, bunch them and hang them to dry in an airy place. Laid on a grill or a barbecue they impart a wonderful flavour to fish cooked over them.

Left Variegated apple mint (*Mentha rotundifolia* 'Variegata') can, like other mints, be invasive unless its roots are confined in a pot or sink.

Far left Double-flowered camomile (*Chamaemelum nobile* 'Flore Pleno') forms a pretty, fragrant cushion. For a lawn choose the compact non-flowering variety 'Treneague'.

Left Lovage *(Levisticum officinale)* is a tall plant with handsome leaves.

DESIGN TIP

If space permits, take advantage of the wide range of height, colour and leaf textures among mints by allowing them a border to themselves where they cannot encroach on other plants.

Above Sweet cecily *(Myrrhis odorata)* is pretty in leaf and flower, but it can be an aggressive colonizer.

Below Catmint (*Nepeta* 'Six Hills Giant') is not a culinary mint, but a decorative, fast-growing herbaceous plant with fragrant grey-green leaves and long-lasting spikes of mauve-blue flowers attractive to bees and butterflies.

Uses: the leaves have a strong flavour and can be used sparingly in salads and stews. The stems can be added to soups and stews.

Mint *Mentha* (several species) A Mafia plant, mint creates an underground network of roots and rubs out any plants that stand in its way. It needs to be restrained in a straightjacket: plant it in a bucket with the bottom knocked out or a large plastic flowerpot with a layer of pebbles for drainage, and sink the container in the border. It will provide ground cover under trees provided the soil is moist. Sun or shade. Tolerates clay soil. The best mints for culinary use are apple mint (*Mentha suaveolens* syn. *M. rotundifolia*) and spearmint (*Mentha spicata*). Apple mint is the prettier of the two. It has soft, hairy apple-green leaves with rounded tips and grows to 60cm (2ft). *M. suaveolens* 'Variegata' has cream-margined leaves and is a good foliage plant in any garden. Spearmint, or common mint, is the same height with mid-green veined leaves. Corsican mint (*Mentha requienii*) is a prostrate creeper with tiny bright green leaves smelling of peppermint. It is an excellent plant to soften paving in semi-shade. To increase mint, detach rooted shoots between autumn and spring. Pot and bring indoors for a winter supply.
Uses: infuse in vinegar for English mint sauce to serve with lamb – a practice much despised by gourmets of other nations. Mint is absolutely necessary to bring out the full flavour of new potatoes and peas; finely chopped and stirred into plain yoghurt it makes a refreshing and palate-cleansing dish; mint tea is also refreshing.

Sweet cecily *Myrrhis odorata* A refined version of cow parsley, fresh green ferny leaves and flat umbels of tiny white flowers in late spring. 1m (3ft). Self-seeding can be tiresome as the thick taproots are difficult to get out, so deal with unwanted seedlings early. Ordinary soil, in light shade or full soil.
Uses: cooked with fruit such as rhubarb and gooseberries, the leaves reduce its acidity. The seeds, gathered while still green, are sweet and nutty and can be added to fruit salads or ice creams.

Tarragon *Artemisia dracunculus* A bushy plant 60-90cm (2-3ft) high with narrow greyish green leaves. The flavour of the leaves deteriorates after a few years, so dig up the plant in spring and cut off rhizomes from the outer part. Plant them 5-8cm (2-3in) deep in pots or outdoors. It is a wise precaution to do this yearly as tarragon is not reliably hardy and can be killed by hard frosts. Sun, shelter, light well-drained soil.
Uses: tarragon chicken is one of the great classic dishes. Also used in sauce Béarnaise and Tartare sauce. The root is said to cure toothache.

WARNING Make sure you buy French tarragon. The kind sold as Russian tarragon has less flavour.

Bulbs

Chives *Allium schoenoprasum* Clumps of grass-like tubular leaves 15-25cm (6-10in) high. Mauve-pink flowers in globular heads are borne in midsummer. Sow seeds outdoors in March or plant bulbs in autumn or spring 15cm (6in) apart. For winter use dig up a clump, cut the leaves down to 1cm (½in) and transfer to a pot in late summer. Every four years, divide into clumps of about six shoots and replant 30cm (1ft) apart. Sun or light shade.

Uses: snip the leaves on to salads, stews and soups, especially vichyssoise. Chives have a mild, sweet onion flavour. Said to deter aphids and mildew if planted among roses.

Hardy annuals

Borage *Borago officinalis* Loose clusters of hairy buds open to star-shaped flowers of a beautiful true blue on 30-75cm (12-30in) stems above a clump of rather coarse, hairy leaves. Borage will seed itself on light soil to the point where it becomes a weed. If you don't want the seedlings, pick off the flowerheads before the seed ripens.

Uses: borage is best known for its flowers, used to garnish the drink Pimm's No. 1 and in salads; young leaves have a cool cucumber flavour and can also be added to drinks.

A good bee plant, said to encourage strong growth in strawberries if planted near them.

Chervil *Anthriscus cerefolium* A delicate version of cow parsley; light green fern leaves and clusters of tiny white flowers. Grows to 25-40cm (10-16in) tall. Light shade under deciduous trees or shrubs. Sow in the intended site at monthly intervals from March to August. Thereafter the plants will self-seed.

Uses: the fresher the leaves, the better the parsley-like flavour. They can be chopped into salads, soups and fish dishes. They enhance the flavour of other herbs and are one of the classic *fines herbes* of French cuisine. A source of vitamin C. An infusion from the leaves can be used cosmetically to discourage wrinkles.

Coriander *Coriandrum sativum* Height 60cm (2ft). The flower heads are umbrella-like, with small white flowers followed by green seeds on slender spokes radiating from the centre. The lower leaves are like broad-leaved parsley and those on the flower stalks are fine-cut and feathery. The seeds can be sown in the final position in early spring or in pots indoors in late summer for a winter supply.

Uses: the lower leaves are the best. They and the seeds have different, distinctive spicy flavours and are valued in Middle Eastern and Indian cookery. The fresh leaves go well with fish dishes, mushrooms, parsnips and carrots.

Below left Dill *(Anethum graveolens).* A culinary herb good with fish or potato salad and pretty enough for the flower garden.

Below Borage *(Borago officinalis).* A useful, self-seeding plant for the herbaceous or mixed border, in flower for a long time. The flowers are an essential garnish for Pimm's No. 1.

Right Parsley *(Petroselinum crispum)*. An indispensable kitchen herb, parsley also makes a neat edging. Planted under roses it is said to keep them disease-free.

Dill *Anethum graveolens* A pretty plant with feathery, thread-like, blue-green leaves and minute yellow flowers in flat clusters on nearly bare stems. Grows to 60cm to 1.5m (2-5ft). Sow seeds in full sun directly into required site at monthly intervals from spring to midsummer. Cut the young leaves but let some plants flower for garden decoration and to provide seeds. Dill self-seeds readily. Uses: the leaves have a mild aniseed flavour good with fish dishes and potato salad. Gravadlax is salmon pickled with dill and served with dill sauce. The seeds are added to cabbage, apple pie and bread. Dill is rich in mineral salts; dillwater is given to babies to relieve colic.

Pot marigold *Calendula officinalis* The cheerful, clear, orange daisy flowers appear non-stop from late spring until autumn frosts if the plants are dead-headed. Like so many herbs it self-seeds freely and is also easy to grow from seed sown in spring *in situ* or in pots. It reaches a height of 30-50cm (12-20in), revels in sun and will grow in any old rubble. Uses: the petals, if used generously, will flavour and colour sweet and savoury dishes. An ointment made from the flowers is said to be good for varicose veins.

Tender annuals

Basil *Ocimum basilicum* The spicy warmth of a crushed basil leaf is redolent of the Mediterranean. Bushy upright stems of broad green leaves to 30-45cm (12-18in). There is a purple-leaved form which is decorative but less strongly flavoured. Grow from seed sown in spring at a temperature of 13°C (55°F). The seedlings can be grown on in pots on the kitchen windowsill or planted outdoors in a warm, sheltered spot 30cm (1ft) apart when all

Below Basil *(Ocimum basilicum)*. The essential herb in the cookery of the Mediterranean, basil needs shelter and lots of sun to succeed outdoors. It does well in a greenhouse or on a sunny windowsill.

risk of frost is past. Pinch out flower buds to encourage more leaves. The commonest causes of failure are over-watering seedlings and sowing too early.

Uses: Keats' heroine Isabella buried her dead lover's head in a pot of basil. Outside poetry, basil pounded with garlic and pine nuts makes the classic Italian pesto sauce. The leaves torn and scattered on tomato salad make all the difference, and they enhance the flavour of cooked tomatoes too.

Hardy biennial

Parsley *Petroselinum crispum* Small parsley plants can be bought in pots. Although plants will self-seed, germination from sown seed can be slow and erratic; it helps to soak the seed overnight in warm water before sowing. Parsley can be grown in pots indoors. Sow in early spring and again in midsummer to provide a supply lasting into the winter. Being a biennial, parsley does not flower till its second year but will produce plenty of leaves to cut in the first season if sown in early spring. The familiar tightly curled parsley is the most decorative and makes a neat edging plant, but flat-leaved parsley, also known as French or Italian parsley, has a stronger flavour. Good soil, sun or light shade.

Uses: rich in vitamins, minerals and chlorophyll. Used in bouquets garnis, parsley sauce, and as a garnish. Parsley makes an excellent soup with potato to thicken it. Chewing raw parsley helps to freshen garlicky breath.

Growing Wild Flowers

Many native plants have the same garden-worthy qualities as exotics from distant countries, yet we seldom thought of using them in the garden until comparatively recently. Familiarity bred, if not contempt, at least neglect.

A decade or so ago even the most familiar meadow and roadside flowers were at risk of extinction through intensive farming methods and local authority policies. The conservation movement and tighter public expenditure budgets have both been influential in bringing about a change. Wild-flowering plants are now returning to the country landscape.

Nevertheless, just as childhood will not come again, neither will the rich variety of plants that could once be enjoyed in the course of a short country walk. If you want to be sure of finding campions, cornflowers, cranesbills, foxgloves, meadowsweet, ox-eye daisies, poppies, ragged robin, scabious and toadflax, you had better grow them in your garden.

One of the rewards that growing wild flowers brings is the abundance of wildlife that feed and breed on them. The sight of butterflies, the sound of bees and the presence of birds are among the pleasures of gardening. Wild flowers will also attract beneficial insects, which will help pest control.

Wild flowers are a great standby for the lazy gardener. The soil and climate of your garden is likely to echo that of the landscape beyond it; plants that are native to the area will thrive in your garden with minimum care. In fact, as the garden soil has almost certainly been cultivated and improved at some time, native plants will probably grow bigger and better for you than they do outside.

For the city dweller, the way to assuage any nostalgia for the countryside is by bringing it into the garden.

Woodland flowers

To grow woodlanders like foxgloves, bluebells and windflowers you do not need a wood. The right conditions can sometimes be found under a

Above Cow parsley *(Anthriscus sylvestris)* and wood cranesbill *(Geranium sylvaticum)*, thrive in semi-shade in hedgerows or woodland margins.

Below Daisies *(Bellis perennis)*, bird's-foot trefoil *(Lotus corniculatus)* and germander speedwell *(Veronica chamaedrys)* have colonized a grassy bank.

single tree, between groups of shrubs or in a north-facing border. The requirements of woodland plants are sunshine during winter and spring when the trees are leafless, and dappled shade during the summer months. In woods leafmould is present naturally. In the garden it helps woodland plants if you supply it.

Meadow flowers

If you have room for a lawn, you have room for a wild flower meadow, but for a natural effect, space is necessary. A few square yards of grass in a city back garden is not really a suitable site. The ideal is a lawn with extensive verges around it treated as meadow in contrast to the close-mown sward.

It is more difficult to create a flowery meadow than many people assume, but can be very rewarding.

An English Flower Garden

As a compromise between a completely natural effect and a more conventional garden style I have planted an 'English Garden' using native plants arranged in large separate drifts of each kind. I lifted turf from an area of rough grass to make each drift. Three years after planting, they are well established and some of the wild flowers have colonized the grassland which is mown just twice a year with close-cut paths winding through it. The result is as colourful through a long season as more conventional planting schemes.

Native shrubs

Elder, hazel, guelder rose, hawthorn and other hedgerow trees and shrubs are seldom considered as possible garden plants. If they were rare and difficult to grow, we might appreciate their qualities more.

Plant them to mingle with garden shrubs, particularly at the garden's boundaries to mark the transition from garden to natural landscape.

Herbaceous perennials, biennials and annuals

Plant these to grow in meadows and at the base of hedges as they do in the wild, or group them in borders with other plants. Annuals should be sown where they are to flower, but biennials and herbaceous perennials can be raised in seed beds, boxes or pots and planted out in autumn.

WHEN? SHRUBS AND PERENNIALS Plant any time between autumn and spring.

MEADOW Late summer or early autumn so that the seeds can germinate and establish before winter sets in.

ANNUALS, BIENNIALS AND PERENNIALS Seeds are best sown at the time when the flowers would naturally be shedding their ripened seeds: late summer or early autumn in most cases. The alternative is early spring when seeds would naturally wake from winter dormancy. Sowing times are given in the lists that follow later in this chapter.

HOW? Whatever style of wild flower garden you decide on, it is important to give the plants the conditions they are used to in their natural habitat.

Wild plants grow in unimproved soils with competition from other plants, so well-cultivated garden soils are often too rich for them. Some wild plants will relish the luxurious conditions of the garden, growing taller and producing more and larger flowers than in the wild, but others will sicken on an over-rich diet.

If they are flowers of the chalk downs, like the clustered bellflower, meadow clary or viper's bugloss, do not plant them in rich clay or feed them buckets of manure. Their natural habitat is thin topsoil over free-draining chalk, so they prefer an austere regime.

If you long for wild plants that are not suited to local conditions you can create special areas for them, just as you would if you wanted to grow azaleas in a limestone district. The plant lists below tell you what conditions each prefers.

Wild flower seeds are available from many retailers and, with a few exceptions noted in the lists, they are easy to grow.

WARNING Never dig up plants from the wild to introduce them to your garden. It is now illegal even to pick them.

Follow the methods of planting, maintenance and propagation described earlier in Part 1 and Part 2 for shrubs, herbaceous plants, annuals and biennials. Plants can be bought from specialist nurseries and occasionally from garden centres, or raised by sowing seeds, dividing plants or taking cuttings.

TIPS

- Plant bulbs for naturalizing before you sow meadow seeds.
- Observe your local wild flower population for clues as to what will thrive in your garden.

Right A meadow in Missouri, USA. The flowers include *Monarda didyma*, alliums and clovers.

Making a flowery meadow

Don't imagine that it can be done by scattering seeds on the lawn or in the field and waiting for them to bloom. It is difficult for seeds to find a root-hold in densely matted turf and even if a few brave seeds succeed, the competition from coarse, lush grasses will soon knock them out.

The chances of success are greatly enhanced if you concentrate on plants which flower *either* in spring *or* after midsummer. Many early-flowering species are adapted to pasture land that is grazed from early summer onwards. They coincide conveniently with naturalized spring bulbs but will not stand being shaded out by grass that is allowed to grow long for the sake of later-flowering plants.

What flowers you can introduce successfully and what seeds will naturally colonize your meadow depends on the soil and climate of your garden, but also to a great extent on the mowing regime you adopt. If you prefer to keep the garden relatively tidy, you will want to start mowing as soon as the spring flowers have seeded themselves, and keep the grass short for the rest of the summer. If you want mid- to late-summer-flowering plants to thrive, you must accept long grass which may look unkempt when flattened by summer storms.

To get the best of both worlds you could opt for a spring meadow and grow later-flowering wild plants in borders, either amongst compatible garden plants or in an area that has been specially designated.

Introducing wild flowers in existing turf

The two methods described below will only succeed on a site where coarse, aggressive grasses, including rye grass, are not present:

- Experiment with different mowing regimes on your lawn, keeping some of it close mown, cutting part of it at midsummer (hay-making time in the agricultural world) and leaving part of it until late summer or early autumn. If you stick to this system for a few years, you may be surprised by how many species appear of their own accord. You may need to spot-weed aggressive plants like thistles, docks and nettles. This method works best on poor, well-drained soils which provide the low fertility that many wild plants enjoy most.
- Reduce the fertility during the season by removing all the grass clippings when you mow. Don't add fertilizer or water in dry spells. The conditions will then be much more favourable for introducing wild flowers as plugs somewhere between a seedling and a young plant. Plugs are obtainable from specialist suppliers but it is much cheaper, and much more satisfying, to grow your own. If you start with a few plants they will increase by seeding themselves if conditions are right. Take out plugs of turf with a trowel or bulb planter, and plant bought or home-grown plugs or wild flower plants.

Above A summer meadow of cow parsley, cranesbill and buttercups.

Left The sweet briar *(Rosa eglanteria*, syn. *R. rubiginosa)* has fragrant leaves, specially after rain. Grow it in a mixed hedgerow, train it over an arch, or clip it into a formal hedge.

Starting from scratch

Extensive areas of meadow are best grown from seed. Buy a seed mix to suit your soil. Specialist suppliers sell mixes designed for alkaline, acid, clay and sandy soils and for hedgerow and woodland sites. If you are in any doubt at all, consult the supplier.

Meadow seed mixes are expensive. You will be buying a mix of 80 per cent fine grass and 20 per cent wild flower seed, and it is the wild flower seed that bumps up the cost. For a relatively small area you may get better results with a higher proportion of flowers to grasses. Your supplier may be able to make up a special mix for you or you could buy extra flower seed separately and add it to the standard mix.

Prepare the ground in much the same way as you would for a new lawn. The main difference is that the meadow needs poor, thin soil with low fertility.

HOW? • In spring or early summer, remove existing vegetation. In an area of manageable size this can be done by lifting the turf and using it elsewhere in the garden, composting it or stacking it to make loam. Weeds like docks, nettles and thistles should be dug out. With the turf some of the topsoil will be removed, too, which will help reduce the fertility. Larger areas are best cleared by spraying or watering with a non-residual glyphosate weedkiller. If you prefer a non-chemical solution, a mulch of old carpet or black polythene left in place for six months will eliminate most vegetation.

- Cultivate the ground either with a rotavator or by hand.
- Firm the ground by rolling or treading.
- Rake it, removing stones and other debris.
- Allow a crop of weeds to grow, and hoe or rake them off. Remove the weed seedlings so they do not rot down and feed the soil.
- On rich soils, spread a 1.25cm (½in) layer of sand before sowing.
- In late summer or early autumn, mix the seeds with dry sand to aid even distribution, one-tenth seed to nine-tenths sand.
- Sow the seed as you would for a lawn (see Chapter 9, Lawns) but more thinly.
- Rake the surface gently.
- Firm by rolling or treading.
- Water with a fine sprinkler, and if it doesn't rain, water regularly.
- For the first season hand-weed or weedkill perennial weeds. You can ignore annuals like chickweed and groundsel.
- Mow when the sward has reached 10cm (4in) with the cutters set at 5cm (2in) and the grass box on to remove the cuttings. Repeat every time the grass reaches 10cm for the first season.

Looking after your meadow

HOW? • Cut two or three times a year, keeping the height at 8cm (3in). Always remove the grass cuttings to prevent increasing fertility. If your mower is not designed to collect long grass, rake the cuttings up by hand.

- Time the cuts to allow flowers to seed as much as possible. If you want your meadow to flower in summer, the first two cuts can be made in spring, leaving out areas where bulbs are planted, and the third in autumn, when the summer-flowering plants have seeded.
- For spring flowering, take the first cut at midsummer. A few late-flowering species will appear before the final autumn cut. It is important to finish the season with a fairly short cut so that spring bulbs and flowers are given the best possible chance.

Right Our Lady's milk thistle *(Silybum marianum)*, Bermuda buttercup *(Oxalis pes-caprae)*, spurge *(Euphorbia)* and borage *(Borago officinalis)*.

Choosing wild flowers

The list that follows concentrates on some of the more decorative, garden-worthy and easy-to-grow, British, flowering plants. If you become a wild-flower enthusiast, you will want to add many more.

Shrubs

Mix them to create a hedgerow, if you have the space. It will provide shelter and food for nesting birds, pollinating insects and butterflies and a hospitable site at its base for hedgerow flowers. Native shrubs can also be planted as part of a mixed border or in groups of three or more in the wilder parts of the garden.

Blackthorn (sloe) *Prunus spinosa* Height and spread 3-4.5m (10-15ft). In early spring the bare branches are smothered in white blossom before the leaves come. The grape-sized bloomy fruits are blue-black. Use them to make sloe gin, a cockle-warming (and intoxicating) beverage to carry in a flask on winter walks. Dense, twiggy growth and numerous sharp thorns make it a stock-proof and vandal-proof hedging plant. Very hardy and wind-resistant. Any well-drained soil.

Broom *Cytisus scoparius* 1.8x1.5m (6x5ft). The emblem of the Plantagenet dynasty until the Wars of the Roses divided them. The slender, upright green stems are covered in small, bright yellow pea-flowers in early summer. Later the seed pods explode with an audible pop. Many hybrids with flowers from cream to crimson have been bred but the native species is still a star in its own right. An excellent shrub for sandy soils, it will also perform on clay. Avoid very alkaline sites.

Dyer's Greenweed *Genista tinctoria* 80x120cm (30x48in). A later-flowering golden yellow broom, low growing. Good on poor soil but must have sun and good drainage.

Elder *Sambucus nigra* 4x4m (14x14ft). The large shrub that transforms hedgerows in early summer with a foam of cream-white flowers. Tiny flowers in large flat clusters, juicy black berries from which a passable country wine is made. Leaves turn in autumn sometimes to pinky yellow, sometimes to purple. Fast growing, provides food and shelter for birds. The reason we don't love it and plant it more is that it self-seeds wickedly and quickly establishes very obdurate roots. Any soil, sun or shade.

Goat willow (pussy willow) *Salix caprea* 3x2.5m (10x8ft) or more. The catkins on whippy bare stems are an early sign of spring. On the female plant they are covered in silver-grey silky fur. Male catkins have creamy yellow anthers. The leaves are silver on the underside. If left unpruned, this willow develops into a small tree, but to get the best

Left Dyer's greenweed *(Genista tinctoria)*, a good shrub for poor, well drained soil in sun.

Left Goat willow *(Salix caprea)* has 'pussy-willow' catkins in early spring.

Below The guelder rose, *Viburnum opulus*, seen here in the cultivated form *V. o.* 'Compactum', has creamy lace-cap flowers, red berries and colourful autumn leaves.

Above Hawthorn *(Crataegus monogyna)* is one of the best and hardiest plants for hedges, and is charming grown as a specimen tree. It tolerates a wide range of problem soils.

Below *Daphne mezereum*, a small shrub to plant where you can enjoy its fragrant winter flowers.

Right The wayfaring tree *(Viburnum lantana)* is a familiar component of hedgerows and woodland margins in chalk and limestone districts.

Below The spindle bush *(Euonymus europaeus)* has surprising pink and orange berries and colours well in autumn.

display, cut it hard back after flowering. Sun or shade, any soil. Food for birds and bees.

Guelder rose *Viburnum opulus* 3x2.5m (10x8ft). Handsome by any standards, this native *Viburnum* is listed in many catalogues of garden plants. An upright branching shrub with maple-like leaves which turn orange and red in autumn. Flat heads of scented, cream-white, lace-cap flowers in early summer are followed by bunches of translucent red berries enjoyed by birds. Cultivated forms include 'Compactum', a smaller, free-berrying bush, and 'Xanthocarpum' with yellow berries. For the best display of berries plant three or more shrubs together. Very hardy. Sun or shade, moist soil.

Hawthorn *Crataegus monogyna* 4.5x3m (15x10ft). Hawthorn, quickthorn or may. Quickly develops a dense, thorny framework making it an invaluable component of hedges and hedgerows. Profuse clusters of single white flowers in May. Heady scent. Crimson berries or haws. Double-flowered and pink and red forms are excellent small garden trees. Ultra-hardy, any soil, tolerates drought or waterlogging. Sun or light shade.

Hazel *Corylus avellana* 3x2m (10x7ft) or more. The long, yellow, lambs' tail catkins are the first signal that winter is ending. They appear on bare branches in February and sometimes earlier, with the snowdrops. In late summer clusters of hazelnuts are decorative as well as edible (if you get to them before the squirrels). Hazel bushes produce a lot of suckers which should be removed in March to restrict the plant to a few main stems. In time it makes a picturesque tree. Ordinary soil, sun or partial shade. Reliable for cold, exposed sites and for clay and sandy soils; resists air pollution and will grow in reclaimed, consolidated ground.

Mezereon *Daphne mezereum* 150x90cm (5x3ft). Winter-flowering shrub now seldom found in the wild. Sweetly scented flowers cluster along the ends of leafless stems, violet-red to pale lavender pink. This small shrub blends unobtrusively into the border for the rest of the year. Sun or partial shade, chalk, limestone, any well-drained soil.

Roses:

Burnet rose, Scotch brier *Rosa pimpinellifolia* 90x90cm (3x3ft). This brave little rose colonizes almost any soil with its suckers. Remove them to restrict its spread. In the wild it grows on sand dunes, cliffs and heaths, and will tolerate partial shade. Prolific single flowers in late spring, creamy white with yellow stamens; round, black-purple hips. Stems are protected by a dense covering of fine prickles, small and fern-like leaves. Splendid ground cover in difficult places.

Dog rose *Rosa canina* Up to 3x1.8m (10x6ft). The 'English, unofficial rose' provided rose hip syrup, a source of vitamin C for a generation of British children. Scented, blush pink, single flowers on arching stems here today and gone tomorrow, but abundant hips make a fine autumn display. Grows almost anywhere in sun or partial shade.

Sweet briar, eglantine *Rosa eglanteria, (rubiginosa)* 3.5x2.5m (12x8ft) with support, 1.8x1.8m (6x6ft) as a shrub. The sweet briar is distinguished from the dog rose by apple-scented leaves, specially strong after rain and from the young growth. To encourage it, clip in spring. Sweet briar treated this way makes a delicious hedge. Not fussy about soil or a little shade, grows on chalk in the wild.

Spindle *Euonymus europaeus* 3x2m (10x7ft). Inconspicuous green flowers, but the fruit is spectacular. Bunches of shocking pink, lobed capsules split open to reveal bright orange seeds. Chalk or ordinary soil, sun or partial shade. Good autumn colour.

Wayfaring tree *Viburnum lantana* 3x2.5m (10x8ft) or more. A shrub rather than a tree in spite of its name. The oval leaves are matt and wrinkled. Creamy white flowers in tight, fluffy clusters are followed by translucent oval berries changing from red to black as they ripen. Native on chalk or limestone but grows on other soils. Useful for damp and swampy ground and exposed sites.

Climbers

Hop *Humulus lupulus* 4m (14ft) and more. The wild hop is better known in its golden-leaved form *H. l.* 'Aureus', a spectacular twining plant. The plain version is handsome in a quieter way with vine-like leaves and clusters of flowers with papery, pale, pinkish-green, overlapping scales. Herbaceous, dying down in the winter and shooting again in spring. Cut down the branches when the leaves have died. Dried flowering branches are decorative. Well-drained soil, sun or partial shade.

Far left The wild hop *(Humulus lupulus)*, seen here in its cultivated golden form, is a herbaceous climber. It will clamber over shrubs or fences, or form ground cover.

Left Old man's beard, also known as traveller's joy *(Clematis vitalba)*.

Honeysuckle, woodbine *Lonicera periclymenum* Up to 9m (30ft). The leaves are soft-textured and the clusters of pink-flushed, pale yellow trumpet flowers are honey-scented. They are followed by shiny red berries in tight clusters. Tough and dense enough to hide ugly fences and buildings, and beautiful enough for a prime position on a pergola or arch. Honeysuckle attracts butterflies and moths. The scent is strongest in the evening, so plant it by the door or where you sit. Tolerates a wide range of conditions but prefers light shade and soil with some leaf mould added.

Ivy *Hedera helix* There are plenty of ornamental ivies but the native ivy is hard to beat for quickly covering eyesores in shady places, and for ground cover in dense shade. Allow ivy in a mixed hedge or on a wall or fence to reach its adult, flowering and fruiting phase as it is one of the best plants for wildlife.

Old man's beard (traveller's joy) *Clematis vitalba* The wild clematis that festoons woodland trees and hedges with cotton wool seed-heads in autumn has less noticeable green-white flowers. Too rampant for small gardens, but lovely rambling through a high hedge. Limy soil suits it best.

Above Bloody cranesbill *(Geranium sanguinem)* makes excellent ground cover for any sunny site.

Perennials

Campion:

Bladder campion *Silene vulgaris* 45cm (18in). Has soft green leaves and white single flowers with rounded petals growing from inflated, bladder-like calices. In flower early to late summer. Border, meadow or hedgerow. Butterflies.

Above Cuckoo flower or lady's smock *(Cardamine pratensis)* does best in a damp position.

Red campion *Silene dioica* 60cm (2ft) or more. Deep rose-pink single flowers held erect on a slender plant from late spring for a long period. Any soil, sun or partial shade. Border, meadow, hedgerow, woodland.

Sea campion *Silene uniflora (maritima)* 20cm (8in). Broad-petalled white single flowers borne singly throughout the summer on a sprawling plant with narrow greyish leaves. Rock gardens or on a drystone wall.

Chicory *Cichorium intybus* 90cm (3ft). The daisy-like flowers are an unusual bright but soft blue, said to be the eyes of a girl weeping for her drowned sailor lover. They close after five hours each day. Sun, alkaline soil. Border, meadow.

Meadow clary *Salvia pratensis* 80cm (30in). A plant of chalk downs now rare in the wild. Spikes of violet blue, tubular lipped flowers in midsummer on almost leafless stalks above a clump of wrinkled sage-like leaves. Sun, neutral to alkaline soil.

Clustered bellflower *Campanula glomerata* Up to 45cm (18in). Clusters of violet-blue bells on stout stems, early to late summer. Too invasive for the border but will colonize wild areas. Sun or light shade. Any soil.

Cowslip *Primula veris* 25cm (10in). Rosettes of broad, wrinkled leaves and nodding heads of scented yellow flowers. Part of our spring-time heritage. Sun, any well-drained soil, specially limestone. Meadow, border.

Cranesbill:

Bloody cranesbill *Geranium sanguinem* 25x30cm (10x12in) or more. Although rare in the wild, widely available as a garden plant. Dense hummocks of rounded, deeply divided, dark green leaves, good ground cover. Magenta-pink shallowly cupped flowers throughout summer. Sun, ordinary or stony soil. Borders, rock gardens.

Meadow cranesbill *Geranium pratense* 60x60cm (2x2ft). Wide clumps of handsome deeply cut leaves colouring in autumn. Wide saucer flowers of intense purplish blue on long stalks. Sun, ordinary soil. Border, meadow, hedgerow, ground cover.

Mourning widow, dusky cranesbill *Geranium phaeum* 75x45cm (30x18in). The intriguing early summer flowers are dark maroon purple, almost black. The leaves are soft green. Good ground cover for shade.

Cuckoo flower (lady's smock) *Cardamine pratensis* 30cm (1ft) or more. Revels in damp conditions. Pale mauve-pink, four-petalled flowers in loose clusters on slender stems above leafy rosettes spring to midsummer. Orange Tip butterflies feed on it. Sun. Stream and pond margins, watermeadows.

Flax *Linum perenne* 30-45cm (12-18in). A short-lived perennial, but easily raised from seed. Single, satiny flowers of ravishing sky blue all summer on slender stems. The grassy leaves are grey-green. Sun, well-drained soil, specially chalk or limestone. Border, rock garden.

Harebell, Scottish bluebell *Campanula rotundifolia* 30cm (1ft). Rounded bells of pure pale blue hang nodding from slender stems in mid- to late summer. Evergreen rosettes of rounded leaves. Dry grassland, borders, drystone walls. Sun or light shade. Poor, dry soil, acid or alkaline.

Right Perennial blue flax (*Linum perenne*), now rare in the wild, likes a sunny position on alkaline soil.

Kingcup, marsh marigold, mollyblobs *Caltha palustris* Up to 60cm (2ft). Doesn't mind its feet being in the water, but can also be planted in any moist ground. Giant buttercups with the same glittery sheen, set off by dark green, broad rounded leaves. Sun or shade. Stream and pond margins, bogs, moist fertile soil.

Knapweed, greater and common *Centaurea scabiosa, C. nigra* 90cm (3ft), 60cm (2ft). Both plants provide nectar for butterflies and bees. Purple-red flowers appear in midsummer with narrow, ragged petals radiating from a central knob or knap. Sun. Well-drained neutral to alkaline soil. Meadow, border.

Meadowsweet, queen of the meadow *Filipendula ulmaria* Up to 90cm (3ft). Loose, fluffy plumes of small cream flowers have a strong honey scent. Mid- to late summer in watermeadows, ditches and damp hedgerows. Sun or part shade, moist soil.

Musk mallow *Malva moschata* Up to 75cm (30in). Easy to grow and generous with its seedlings. The five-petalled, funnel-shaped flowers are a soft rosy pink (there is also a white form) with delicate darker veining. They flower all summer and, if the spent flower stems are cut down, into autumn. Well-drained soil, even the poorest, sun or light shade.

Ox-eye daisy, dog daisy, moon daisy *Leucanthemum vulgare* Up to 60cm (2ft). This is often the only plant that succeeds in attempted wild flower meadows apart from a few buttercups and dandelions. In the border it is a nuisance, pushing out other plants with its colonizing roots. Sun. Any ordinary soil. Meadow.

Pasque flower *Pulsatilla vulgaris* 30x30cm (1x1ft). This plant is beautiful in all its parts and rare in the wild so it deserves a place in every garden. The leaves are finely cut. The flower buds are veiled in fine, silky hairs and open into light blue-purple cups with yellow stamens. The seedheads are surrounded by silky fluff. As the name implies they usually bloom at Easter. Sun, soil rich in humus, which can be added in the form of leaf mould or compost. Front of border, rock garden.

Primrose *Primula vulgaris* 20cm (8in). Although they self-seed freely, primroses are not easy to grow from seed in trays and pots. They do divide easily, and if you buy a few plants, you can soon multiply them. Grow primroses on shady banks, along a stream, between the roots of trees or at the base of a hedge. Also under roses, in window boxes and in small pots to bring indoors and have by you on your work table or desk. Any fairly moist soil, part shade.

Purple loosestrife *Lythrum salicaria* 1.2m (4ft). The flowers are strong magenta pink in the second half of summer when many plants have already given of their best. Thrives in fertile soil, sun or shade. Pond and stream margins, bogs, borders. Dead-head to prevent self-seeding.

Above The white form of the musk mallow *(Malva moschata alba)* seeds itself with abandon, so use it where it will not smother more delicate plants.

Below left Great knapweed *(Centaurea scabiosa)* flowers from mid- to late summer and is visited by bees and butterflies.

Below Pasque flower *(Pulsatilla vulgaris)* deserves a prime position where you can enjoy it in close-up.

margins. Branching heads of white flowers appear in early summer. Sun, well-drained soil, neutral to alkaline. Drought-resistant. Border or vegetable garden.

Toadflax, purple *Linaria purpurea* 90x45cm (36x18in). Narrow grey-green leaves and slender spikes of tiny, mauve snapdragon flowers all summer. Self-seeding. Sun, any free-draining soil.

Toadflax, yellow *Linaria vulgaris* Up to 60cm (2ft). Spikes of pale yellow snapdragon flowers with an orange-yellow lip. Self-seeds too freely in the border, but its long flowering season and value as a bee and butterfly plant make it worth growing in grass or grouped alone. Sun, any ordinary soil, not acid.

Violet, sweet *Viola odorata* Up to 15cm (6in). A few plants will soon colonize several square feet of ground with runners and by seed. Flowering in early spring, it is a useful nectar plant and the caterpillars of some butterflies feed on it. Light shade, well-drained soil, not too acid. Front of border, under hedges and shrubs and at the base of trees.

Wild strawberry *Fragaria vesca* 15cm (6in). The wild strawberry's three-lobed, serrated leaves are a fresh, bright green, the little white flowers are delicately pretty and continue from spring until the frost, and the succulent red fruits are edible. It can be invasive, spreading rapidly by over-ground runners. Ordinary soil, sun or shade. Ground cover under shrubs and trees, edging.

Above Purple loosestrife *(Lythrum salicaria)* likes to get its roots into water on river banks, ditches or marshes. Here it is grown in a formal pond.

Right The ox-eye daisy *(Leucanthemum vulgare)* is a staunchly reliable plant to bring sparkle to a meadow.

Ragged robin *Lychnis flos-cuculi* 60cm (2ft). Flowers like those of red campion but ragged petals give them a slightly manic look. Sun, moist soil. Meadow, water margin, border. Attracts butterflies and moths.

Scabious *Knautia arvensis* (field scabious) 75cm (30in). One of the easiest meadow flowers to establish. Evergreen rosettes of matt grey-green leaves throw up long bare stalks with flat pin cushions of tiny lavender blue flowers. Scabious attracts butterflies and bees. Sun, well-drained soil, not too acid. Meadow, hedgerow, border.

Sea holly *Eryngium maritimum* 50cm (20in). Too decorative to be left in its shingly beach habitat. The spiked and serrated silver-green leaves are thistle-like and the flowers which appear in late summer are steel-blue cones with spiked silvery ruffs. Sun, well-drained soil, neutral to alkaline. Border.

Sea kale *Crambe maritima* 60x60cm (2x2ft). Another seaside plant, cultivated as a vegetable for its succulent stems. Gertrude Jekyll loved its dramatic blue-grey leaves with frilled

Bulbs and rhizomes

Bluebell *Hyacinthoïdes non-scripta* 30cm (1ft). Woods can still be seen carpeted with a blue haze in spring. Individual plants are beautiful, with their shiny, dark green, strap-shaped leaves and juicy spikes of hanging hyacinth bells. Although in the mass the flowers seem to be a soft but intense true blue, in close-up they have a touch of mauve. Bluebells become a nuisance in borders. Plant them in generous drifts under trees or along hedges, setting the bulbs 10-15cm (4-6in) deep. They can be raised from seed but will not reach flowering size for about five years. Sun or shade. Any well-drained acid, neutral or alkaline soil.

Flag iris *Iris pseudacorus* 90cm (3ft) (taller in water, shorter in borders). A dramatic and indispensable component of waterside planting, the native iris's sword-shaped, blue-green leaves are also valuable for vertical emphasis in the planting design of borders. The large yellow flowers appear in the first half of summer and are followed by bulging green seed capsules. Sun or light shade, moist or wet soil from slightly acid to alkaline. In ponds or streams (plant 45cm/18in deep), beside water, in ditches, bog areas, borders.

Snake's-head fritillary *Fritillaria meleagris* 30-45cm (12-18in). Seen as a colony growing in grass or as individual plants, this fritillary is one of the most beautiful of all bulbs. The tulip-shaped flowers hang their heads from slender stems. The pale petals are overlaid with an intricate chequerboard pattern of maroon-purple, which gives them the appearance of snakeskin. In a naturalized colony there will be all-white flowers here and there. The leaves are greyish green and grassy. Fritillaries must have moist ground to thrive: in two dry summers I lost all but a few of a large colony. A damp meadow is ideal, but make space in a border or raised bed for a few plants so that you can see them in close-up. Sun, moist ordinary soil.

Solomon's seal *Polygonatum multiflorum* 60cm (2ft). A plant for shade, associating well with ferns and hostas. The dark green, ribbed leaves are poised along arching stems, and clusters of green-white bell flowers appear in late spring. Partial or full shade, any soil. Leaves may be stripped by sawfly caterpillars but this will not usually kill the plant. Woodland, shady borders.

Wood anemone, windflower *Anemone nemorosa* 15cm (6in). Perhaps the loveliest woodland flower of all, the fragile starry white flowers are brave in the face of chill March winds. The soft green, divided leaves are beautiful too. The wood anemone is far more robust than it looks and colonizes wide areas with underground creeping rhizomes. In some woods there are sheets of anemones overlapping in their flowering with the bluebells. Shade, alkaline soil or any that is not too acid.

Below Wood anemone *(Anemone nemorosa)* flowers in early spring and is more robust than its fragile flowers suggest.

Above Snake's-head fritillaries *(Fritillaria meleagris)* will grow in grass provided the soil is moist.

Above right Solomon's seal *(Polygonatum multiflorum)* is an invaluable plant for shade. Here it forms a background in early summer to forget-me-nots, hostas, tulips and wallflowers.

Below Wild foxgloves *(Digitalis purpurea)* are so handsome that they are grown as often in beds and borders as they are in the wild garden.

In woodland, under deciduous trees, along hedges, underplanting in shrub beds.

Biennial

Foxglove *Digitalis purpurea* Up to 1.5m (5ft). A stately plant with tall stems covered in bell-shaped flowers that fit neatly over one's fingers. They vary in colour from darkish purple pink to white and are intriguingly spotted on the inside. The flower spikes appear in the second season from a rosette of handsome, broad grey-green leaves which are good weed suppressors. Foxgloves are plants of woodland glades and margins on acid soil but are tolerant of some lime provided the soil is kept moist. Sun or light shade. Borders (especially with old-fashioned roses), under deciduous trees, woodland edge and hedgerow. White-flowered seed strains are available.

Annuals

Although the field poppy holds its own, other former weeds of the cornfield are seldom seen today: cornflowers, corn cockle, corn marigold and corn camomile can be added to the seed mix when sowing a flower meadow to give a colourful display in the first year. They are unlikely to reappear, however, once grasses and other plants have established themselves.

These flowers can also be used as an easy and quick disguise for waste areas awaiting development. In thin, poor soil poppies, cornflowers and the other cornfield species can be helped to seed themselves by roughly cultivating the ground after cutting any crop down in late summer. Cornfield mix can be used as a feature in its own right, although it needs annual turning over and perhaps reseeding.

USEFUL ADDRESSES

The Alpine Garden Society
AGS Centre
Avon Bank
Pershore
Hereford & Worcester WR10 3JP
Tel (01386) 554790

Arboricultural Association
Ampfield House
Romsey
Hampshire SO51 9PA
Tel (01794) 368717

The Cottage Garden Society
5 Nixon Close
Thornhill
Dewsbury
West Yorkshire WF12 0JA
Tel (01924) 468469

The Garden History Society
5 The Knoll
Hereford
Hereford & Worcester HR1 1RU

Gardens for the Disabled Trust
Church Cottage
Headcorn
Kent TN27 9NP

The Hardy Plant Society
Little Orchard
Great Comberton
Pershore
Hereford & Worcester WR10 3DP
Tel (01386) 710317

Henry Doubleday Research Association
National Centre for Organic Gardening
Ryton-on-Dunsmore
Coventry
West Midlands CV8 3LG
Tel (01203) 303517

The Herb Society
134 Buckingham Palace Road
London SW1W 9SA
Tel (0171) 823 5583

Historic Houses Association
2 Chester Street
London SW1X 7BB
Tel (0171) 259 5688

Horticultural Therapy
Goulds Ground
Vallis Way
Frome
Somerset BA11 3DW
Tel (01373) 464782

The National Association of Flower Arrangement Societies
21 Denbigh Street
London SW1V 2HF
Tel (0171) 828 5145

National Council for the Conservation of Plants and Gardens
The Pines
Wisley Garden
Woking
Surrey GU23 6QB
Tel (01483) 211465

The National Gardens Scheme (publishers of the Yellow Book)
Hatchlands Park
East Clandon
Guildford
Surrey GU4 7RT
Tel (01483) 211535

National Society of Allotment and Leisure Gardeners
O'Dell House
Hunters Road
Corby
Northamptonshire NN17 5JE
Tel (01536) 266576

National Trust
36 Queen Anne's Gate
London SW1H 9AS
Tel (0171) 222 9251

National Trust for Scotland
5 Charlotte Square
Edinburgh EH2 4DU
Tel (0131) 226 5922

National Vegetable Society
56 Waun-y-Groes Avenue
Rhiwbina
Cardiff
South Glamorgan CF4 4SZ
Tel (01222) 627994

Natural Pest Control Ltd
Yapton Road
Barnham
Bognor Regis
West Sussex PO22 0BQ
Tel (01243) 553250

Northern Horticultural Society
Harlow Carr Botanical Gardens
Crag Lane
Harrogate
North Yorkshire HG3 1QB
Tel (01423) 565418

The Royal Caledonian Horticultural Society
28 Silvernose
Southway
Edinburgh EH4 5PX
Tel (0131) 336 5488

The Royal Horticultural Society
80 Vincent Square
London SW1P 2PE
Tel (0171) 834 4333

Royal National Rose Society
The Gardens of the Rose
Chiswell Green
St Albans
Hertfordshire AL2 3NR
Tel (01727) 850461

Scotland's Garden Scheme
31 Castle Terrace
Edinburgh EH1 2EL
Tel (0131) 229 1870

The Scottish Allotments and Gardens Society
14/1 Hoseasons Gardens
Edinburgh
Lothian EH4 7HQ

Scottish Rock Garden Club
1 Hillcrest Road
Bearsden
Glasgow G61 2EB

The Wild Flower Society
68 Outwoods Road
Loughborough
Leicestershire LE11 3LY

PLANT INDEX

SUBJECT INDEX

PICTURE CREDITS

The author and publishers would like to thank the following for their invaluable help in allowing us to reproduce the pictures used in this book:

Andrew Lawson Photography
Gothic House
Church Street
Charlbury
Oxford OX7 3PP

A-Z Botanical Collection
Bedwell Lodge
Cucumber Lane
Essendon
Hatfield
Hertfordshire AL9 6JB

The Garden Picture Library
Unit 15, Ransome's Dock
35 Parkgate Road
London SW11 4NP

Harry Smith Horticultural Photographic Collection
Hyde Hall
Rettendon
Chelmsford
Essex CM3 8ET

The author and publishers would also like to thank the following for use of additional pictures:

Biofotos, Highways, 6 Vicarage Hill, Farnham, Surrey GU9 8HJ; Clive Boursnell; Holt Studios International, The Courtyard, 24 High Street, Hungerford, Berkshire, RG17 0NF; Marston & Langinger Conservatories, 192 Ebury Street, London SW1W 8UP; and Clay Perry.

Picture researcher: Toby Chapman-Dawe